IMPERIAL ECONOMIC POLICY 1917–1939
Studies in Expansion and Protection

IMPERIAL ECONOMIC POLICY 1917–1939

Studies in Expansion and Protection

by

IAN M. DRUMMOND

Professor of Economics
University of Toronto

London . George Allen & Unwin Ltd

Ruskin House . Museum Street

First Published in 1974

ISBN 0 04 330243 2 Hardback
ISBN 0 04 330244 0 Paperback

Printed in Great Britain by
Alden & Mowbray Ltd
at the Alden Press, Oxford

PREFACE

I have written this book because I am convinced that we can understand the impact of the Imperial phenomenon on world economic history only if we scrutinise the actual behaviour of the Imperial powers. Except in the final section I have refrained from polemic. If I had commented on the views of others I should have prolonged the book excessively. Some readers may conclude that the entire text is in fact polemical, at least implicitly. I do not think this is so. But I should not be sorry if the evidence is offensive to those it is most likely to offend.

The present text draws upon research materials which have been accumulated with the aid of grants from the University of Toronto and from the Canada Council. This assistance is gratefully acknowledged. An early draft of Chapter 2 was read to a seminar in the Research School of Social Sciences, Australian National University. Material from Chapter 7 was presented in a seminar at the University of Sussex. Chapter 5 formed the basis for a seminar at Cambridge University. A preliminary and much shorter version of Chapters 1 and 9 was read to a meeting of the Canadian Economics Association. I should like to thank the participants in these seminars and meetings, whose questions and comments have helped me a great deal. I must also thank Malcolm Knight, Donald Moggridge, Donald Patterson, L. S. Pressnell, and Robert L. Patterson for informal discussion and argument which have helped to refine the contents. From my research students at the University of Toronto, and especially from Paul Davenport, I have learned much. Finally, the work would have been impossible without the help and co-operation of librarians and archivists, especially at the Public Record Office, the Universities of

Cambridge, Birmingham, Sheffield, New Brunswick, and Newcastle upon Tyne, the Public Archives of Canada, the Australian National Library, and the Commonwealth Archives Office, Canberra.

Ian M. Drummond
Toronto and London, 1972

CONTENTS

DRAMATIS PERSONAE

United Kingdom Prime Ministers are in general omitted

ADDISON, Dr Christopher, first Viscount (1945). 1869–1951. First Liberal, then Labour. Physician. Educated St Bartholomew's. MP (Liberal) 1910–22; MP (Labour) 1929–31 and 1934–45. Minister of Munitions 1916–17, of Reconstruction 1917. President of Local Government Board 1919. First Minister of Health 1919–21. Minister without Portfolio 1921. Parliamentary Secretary, Ministry of Agriculture and Fisheries 1929–30. Minister of Agriculture and Fisheries 1930–31. Secretary of State for Commonwealth Relations 1945–47. Paymaster General 1948–49. Lord Privy Seal 1947–51.

AMERY, Leopold Stennett. 1873–1955. Politician, author, publicist, visionary. Unionist-Conservative. Born in India. Educated Harrow and Oxford. Barrister, Inner Temple, 1902. *The Times* editorial staff 1899–1909. MP 1911–45. Assistant Secretary to War Cabinet and Imperial War Cabinet 1917. Parliamentary Under-Secretary of State for the Colonies 1919–21. Parliamentary and Financial Secretary to the Admiralty 1921–22. First Lord of Admiralty 1922–24. Secretary of State for the Colonies 1924–29, and for Dominion Affairs 1925–29. Secretary of State for India and Burma 1940–45.

AMERY, William Bankes. 1883–1951. Public servant. Educated Christ's Hospital. Entered government service 1916. Representative of United Kingdom in Australia under Empire Settlement Act 1925–28. Assistant Secretary, Dominions Office 1937. Head of UK Food Mission to Australia 1942–45. UK Member, Board of British Phosphate Commissioners, after 1946.

BATTERBEE, Sir Henry Fagg. b. 1880. Public servant. Educated Oxford. Entered Colonial Office 1905. Assistant Secretary, Dominions Office, 1925–30. Assistant Under-Secretary of State, Dominions Office, 1930–38. High Commissioner for UK in New Zealand 1939–45.

BELL, Sir Francis. 1851–1936. New Zealand barrister and politician. Educated New Zealand and Cambridge. MLC 1912. Minister for Internal Affairs and Immigration, followed by other portfolios, 1912 and thereafter. Prime Minister, 14 to 20 May 1925. Delegate to League 1922 and 1928. Attended Imperial Conference 1926.

BENNETT, Richard Bedford, first Viscount (1941). 1870–1947. Canadian barrister, businessman, Conservative politician. Born New Brunswick. Moved to Calgary, Alberta. MLA territorial legislatures and Alberta legislature 1898–1905, 1909–11. MP, Federal Parliament, 1911–17. Minister of Justice in Meighen Governments of 1921 and 1926. Returned to Parliament 1925–38. Chosen leader of Conservative Party 1927. Prime Minister, Minister of Finance, Minister for External Affairs, 1930–35. Leader of opposition 1935–38. Retired to England 1938.

BORDEN, Sir Robert Laird. 1854–1937. Canadian Conservative politician and barrister. Born Nova Scotia. MP 1896–1905, 1908–21. Leader of Conservative Party 1901–20. Prime Minister 1911–1920. Attended Imperial War Conferences and Imperial War Cabinets in 1917 and 1918. After resigning leadership, an elder statesman in Canadian Conservative Party.

BRUCE, Stanley Melbourne, first Viscount Bruce of Melbourne (1947). 1884–1967. Australian importer, politician (first Nationalist, then United Australia), diplomat. Born Melbourne. Educated Cambridge and Middle Temple. MP, 1918–19 and 1931–33. Commonwealth Treasurer 1921–23. Prime Minister 1923–29. Australian Minister resident in London 1932–33. Australian High Commissioner in London 1933–45. Represented Australia at Imperial and Economic Conferences of 1923, 1926, and 1932, and at World Economic Conference 1933. In later life, resided in the UK.

CAHAN, Charles Hazlitt. 1861–1944. Canadian barrister and Conservative politician. Born Nova Scotia. Practised law in Nova Scotia, Mexico, and Montreal. Nova Scotia MLA 1890–94. Federal MP 1925–40. Secretary of State in Bennett Government 1930–35.

CHAMBERLAIN, Arthur Neville. 1869–1940. Conservative politician. Educated Rugby and Birmingham. Lord Mayor of Birmingham 1915–16. Director of National Service 1916–17. MP 1918–40. Postmaster General 1922–23. Paymaster General 1923. Minister of Health 1923, 1924–29, 1931. Chancellor of Exchequer 1923–24 and 1931–37. Chairman of Conservative Party 1930–31. Prime Minister 1937–40.

CLARK, Sir William. 1876–1952. Public servant and diplomat. Educated Eton and Cambridge. Entered service of Board of Trade 1899. Member for Commerce and Industry of council of Viceroy of India 1910–16. Comptroller General, Commercial Intelligence Department, Board of Trade, 1916–17. Comptroller General, Department of Overseas Trade, 1917–28. First UK High Commissioner in Canada 1928–34. High Commissioner in South Africa 1934–39. Retired 1940.

CLARK, William Clifford. 1889–1952. Canadian economist and public servant. Born in Canada. Educated Queen's at Kingston and Harvard. Professor of economics, Queen's, 1915–23. Investment banker, Chicago and New York, 1923–31. Professor of commerce and director of courses in commerce and administration, Queen's, 1931–32. Financial adviser, Imperial Economic Conference 1932 and World Economic Conference 1933. Deputy Minister of Finance, Ottawa, from 1932 till his death.

COATES, Joseph Gordon. 1878–1943. New Zealand politician (Reform). Born New Zealand. Joined Massey Government 1919. Held various ministerial offices 1919–28. Prime Minister 1925–38. In Coalition Ministry (1931–35), was Minister of Public Works, Transport, Unemployment, Roads 1931–33 and Minister of Finance, Customs and Transport 1933–35. Represented New Zealand at Ottawa Conference and at later London negotiations in 1935. Member of New Zealand War Cabinet 1940–42.

CUNLIFFE-LISTER, Sir Philip *see* Swinton, 1st Earl.

DALTON, Sir Robert William. 1882–1958. Commercial diplomat. Educated Leeds Grammar School. Entered Board of Trade 1900. UK Trade Commissioner in New Zealand 1916–22. UK Senior Trade Commissioner in Canada 1923–24. UK Senior Trade Commissioner in Australia 1924–48. Attended Ottawa Conference 1932.

DUNNING, Charles Avery. 1885–1958. Canadian farmer and Liberal politician. Born Leicester. Arrived Canada 1902. Farmhand and homesteader in Saskatchewan. MLA 1912, Minister of Agriculture in provincial government 1919, provincial premier 1922. In 1926, resigned to become Minister of Railways and Canals in federal government. Minister of

Finance in King Government, 1929–30 and 1935–39. Came to London for negotiations on renewal and revision of Ottawa Agreements in 1936.

ELLIOT, Walter. 1888–1958. Scottish physician and politician (Unionist). Educated Glasgow University. MP 1918–23, 1924–45, 1946–58. Minor government offices 1923—26, 1926–29. Financial Secretary to Treasury 1931–32. Minister of Agriculture and Fisheries 1932–36. Secretary of State for Scotland 1936–38. Minister of Health 1938–40.

FERGUSON, George Howard. 1870–1946. Canadian barrister and Conservative politician. MLA, Ontario, 1905–30. Minister of provincial governments. Premier of Ontario 1923–30. Resigned to become Canadian High Commissioner in London 1930–35.

FIELD, Frederick William. 1884–1960. Anglo-Canadian journalist and diplomat. Editor, *Monetary Times of Toronto,* 1906–17. UK Trade Commissioner at Toronto 1918–24. UK Senior Trade Commissioner in Canada 1924–48.

FORBES, George William. 1869–1947. New Zealand farmer and politician. In father's mercantile firm 1886–93. Thereafter farming his own homestead. MHR (Liberal) 1908. Leader of Nationalist Party following retirement of Wilford. Leader of United Party 1928. Various portfolios 1928–31. Prime Minister in United ministry 1930–31, then in Reform-United Coalition ministry 1931–35. Attended Imperial Conference 1930 and Ottawa Conference 1932.

GARDINER, James. 1883–1962. Canadian Liberal politician. Minister of Agriculture in King and St Laurent governments 1935–57. Came to London in 1936 with Dunning and Euler to negotiate revision of Ottawa Agreement. Premier of Saskatchewan 1926, 1929, 1934–35.

GILMOUR, Sir John. 1876–1940. Scottish Unionist politician. MP 1910–40. Junior Treasury Lord 1921–22. Secretary of State for Scotland 1924–29. Minister of Agriculture and Fisheries 1931–32. Secretary of State for Home Department 1932–35. Minister of Shipping 1939–40.

GULLETT, Sir Henry Somer. 1878–1940. Australian farmer, journalist, historian, politician (first Nationalist, then United Australia). Born in Australia. Director of Immigration 1920. Minister for Trade and Customs 1928–29 and 1932–33.

Minister for Trade Treaties 1934–37. Minister for External Affairs and Information 1939–40. MHR, Commonwealth Parliament, 1925.

HANKEY, Sir Maurice Pascal Alers, first Baron (1939). 1877–1963. Naval officer, author, public servant. Educated Rugby. Naval Marines 1895, naval intelligence 1902–6. Assistant Secretary, Committee of Imperial Defence, 1908–12. Secretary, Committee of Imperial Defence, 1912–38. Secretary, War Cabinet and Cabinet, 1916–38. Secretary general of Imperial Conferences 1921, 1923, 1926, 1930, 1937. Minister Without Portfolio in War Cabinet 1939–40. Chancellor of Duchy of Lancaster 1940–41. Paymaster General 1941–42.

HANKINSON, Sir Walter Crossfield. b. 1894. Public servant and diplomat. Educated Oxford. Entered Colonial Office 1920, Dominions Office 1925. Acting Representative of HMG in UK in Australia 1931–32 and 1935–36. Principal private secretary to successive Dominions Secretaries 1937–39. Excessive middle-level career in Commonwealth diplomacy thereafter, until 1955.

HARDING, Sir Edward. 1880–1954. Public servant. Educated Oxford. Entered Colonial Office 1904. Called to bar 1912. Secretary, Dominions Royal Commission, 1912–17; visited all the Dominions. Assistant Secretary, Colonial Office, 1921–25. Assistant Under-Secretary of State, Dominions Office, 1925–30. Permanent Under-Secretary, Dominions Office, 1930–40. High Commissioner in South Africa 1940–41. Retired 1941.

HAVENGA, Nicolaas Christiaan. 1882–1957. South African attorney and politician (Nationalist, then Afrikaner, then Nationalist again). MP since 1915. Minister of Finance in Hertzog government 1924–39, and in Malan governments 1948–53. Leader of Afrikaner Party 1939–48; when it rejoined the Nationalists in 1948 he became Minister of Finance again.

HENDERSON, Sir Hubert. 1890–1952. Economist. Educated Rugby and Cambridge. Fellow of Clare College 1919–23. Editor, *Nation and Athaneum*, 1923–30. Joint Secretary of Economic Advisory Council 1930–34. Member of West Indies Royal Commission 1938–39. Economic Adviser, Treasury, 1939–44. Professor of Political Economy, Oxford, 1945–51.

HERTZOG, Dr General James Barry Munnik. 1866–1942. South African military leader, advocate, politician. Cabinet minister under General Botha 1910–12; resigned from Cabinet and established National Party. Prime Minister 30 June 1924 to

6 September 1939. Gold Standard crisis of late 1932 led to *rapprochement* with Smuts; jointly they established United South African National Party. Retired to his farm after his parliamentary defeat, 6 September 1939.

HEWINS, William Albert Samuel. 1865–1931. Economist, administrator, publicist, and politician. Educated Oxford. First Director of London School of Economics and Political Science 1895–1903. Joined Joseph Chamberlain's Tariff Reform Campaign, MP (Unionist) 1912–18. Under-Secretary of State for the Colonies 1916–19. Secretary of the unofficial Tariff Commission 1903–17.

HUGHES, William Morris. 1864–1952. Australian politician (Labour, then Nationalist, then United Australia). Born in Wales. Arrived Australia 1884. MP from 1901. Held office in Labour governments 1904–15. Prime Minister 1915–23. Attended Imperial War Cabinet 1918 and Imperial Conference 1921. Member of UK War Cabinet. Held ministerial offices in United Australia and Liberal Governments 1934–41.

INSKIP, Sir Thomas, first Viscount Caldecote (1939). 1876–1947. Barrister and politician (Conservative). Educated Cambridge. MP 1918–29, 1931–39. Various offices 1928–29, 1932–40. Dominions Secretary 1939, 1940.

JORDAN, Sir William Joseph. d. 1959. Emigrated to New Zealand 1904. Labour Party functionary. New Zealand High Commissioner in London 1936–51. MP 1922–36.

KEYNES, John Maynard, first Baron (1942). 1883–1946. Economist, author, public servant, publicist. Educated Eton and Cambridge. India Office 1906–8. Treasury 1915–19. Fellow and Bursar of King's College. Editor of *Economic Journal*, 1911–44. Author of, *inter alia*, *General Theory of Employment, Interest and Money* (1936). Member of Committee of Economic Information of Economic Advisory Council in the 1930s. Treasury adviser and economic diplomat in and immediately after Second World War.

KING, William Lyon Mackenzie. 1874–1950. Canadian economist and politician (Liberal). Born Ontario. Educated University of Toronto and Harvard (Ph.D. 1909). Deputy Minister of Labour, Canada, 1900–8. MP 1908–11, 1921–49. Minister of Labour 1909–11. Leader of Liberal Party 1919–48. Prime Minister 1921–26, 1926–30, 1935–48. Represented Canada at Imperial Conferences 1923, 1926, 1937.

LARKIN, Peter Charles. 1856–1930. Canadian tea magnate and diplomat. Born Montreal. Invented the sealed lead-lined tea package. High Commissioner in London 1922–30 (i.e. till his death). Friend and confidant of Mackenzie King, whom he subsidised.

LEITH-ROSS, Sir Frederick William. 1887–1968. Public servant, economic diplomat, banker. Educated Merchant Taylors School and Oxford (1st class Mods. and Lit. Hum.). Entered Treasury 1909. Chief economic adviser to HMG in the UK 1932–46. Principal British Financial Expert at Hague Conferences 1929 and 1930. *Ad hoc* member of Committee of Economic Information of Economic Advisory Council. Financial diplomat during the 1930s. Governor, National Bank of Egypt, 1946–51. As of 1965, Deputy-Chairman, National Provincial Bank; Vice-Chairman, Standard Bank; Director, National Discount Company Ltd.

LLOYD-GREAME, Sir Philip *see* Swinton, 1st Earl

LONG, Walter Hume, first Viscount (1921). 1854–1924. Unionist politician. MP 1880–1921. Miscellaneous offices 1886–1905, 1915–16. Secretary of State for the Colonies 1916–18. First Lord of the Admiralty 1919–21.

LYONS, Joseph Aloysius. 1879–1939. Australian politician (Labour, then United Australia). Born in Tasmania. Trained as elementary school teacher. Successfully won Labour seat in Tasmania House 1909. Tasmanian Treasurer 1914–16. Premier 1923–38. Member Commonwealth Parliament 1929–39. Postmaster-General etc. in Scullin Government. Resigned January 1931 and aligned himself with the Nationalist opposition to form United Australia Party. Prime Minister November 1931–April 1939. Died in office.

MACHTIG, Sir Eric Gustav. b. 1884. Public servant. Educated Cambridge (1st class 2nd division Classical Tripos). Entered Colonial Office 1911. Transferred to Dominions Office 1930. Assistant Under-Secretary of State for the Dominions 1936; Deputy Under-Secretary 1939; Permanent Under-Secretary 1940. Retired from service 1949.

MACDONALD, Malcolm. b. 1901. Politician (Labour and National Labour) and diplomat. Educated Oxford. MP 1929–45. Parliamentary under-secretary, Dominions Office, 1931–35. Secretary of State for Dominion Affairs 1935–38 and 1938–39. Secretary of State for the Colonies 1935 and 1938–40.

Minister of Health 1940–41. UK High Commissioner in Canada 1941–46. Governor General of Malaya 1946–48. Commissioner General for UK in South-East Asia 1948–55. High Commissioner for UK in India 1955–60. Governor and Commander in Chief, Kenya, 1963.

MACNAGHTEN, Terence Charles. 1872–1944. Public servant. Educated Charterhouse and Oxford. Vice-Chairman, Overseas Settlement Committee, 1918 *et seq.* Assistant Secretary, Dominions Office. Administrator of St Kitts-Nevis, 1929–31.

MASSEY, Vincent. 1887–1969. Canadian political figure, businessman, diplomat, author. Born Toronto. Educated Toronto University and Balliol. Lecturer in History, Toronto, 1913–15. President, Massey-Harris Company, 1921–25. Minister without Portfolio, 1925. Canadian Minister to the USA 1926–30. High Commissioner for Canada in the UK 1935–46. Governor General of Canada 1952–59.

MASSEY, William Ferguson. 1856–1925. New Zealand politician. Prime Minister, Reform Government, 1912–15; Prime Minister, National Government, 1915–19; Prime Minister, Reform Government, 1919–25. Died in office. Represented New Zealand at Imperial War Cabinet and Conference 1917 and 1918; Imperial Conference and Economic Conference 1921 and 1923.

MEIGHEN, Arthur. 1874–1960. Canadian teacher, barrister, politician (Conservative), businessman. Born Ontario. Educated University of Toronto. Barrister 1903. MP (Liberal-Conservative) 1908–32. Solicitor-General 1913. Secretary of State 1915–17. Minister of the Interior 1917–20. Prime Minister 1920–21, 1926. Senator 1932–41. Left political life 1941. Represented Canada at Imperial Conference, 1921.

MENZIES, Sir Robert Gordon. b. 1894. Australian barrister and politician (United Australia, then Liberal). Born Australia. Educated Melbourne University. State MP 1928–34. Held offices in Victorian Governments 1932–34. Attorney General of Australia 1934–39. Treasurer 1939–40. Prime Minister of Australia 1939–41, 1949–61. Leader of opposition 1943–49. Member of Australian delegation to the meat talks 1935 and 1936.

MILNER, Sir Alfred, Baron (1901) and first Viscount (1902). 1854–1925. Civil servant, proconsul, publicist, cabinet minister. Educated King's College London and Balliol. Fellow of

New College Oxford. Barrister, Inner Temple, 1881. Journalist 1882–85. Private Secretary to Chancellor of Exchequer 1887–89. Under-Secretary for finance in Egypt 1892–97. Chairman, Board of Inland Revenue, 1892–97. Governor of the Cape of Good Hope 1897–1901, of Transvaal and Orange River Colony 1901–5. High Commissioner for South Africa 1897–1905. Founder of Round Table. Member of War Cabinet (without portfolio) 1916–18. Secretary of State for War 1918–19. Secretary of State for the Colonies 1919–21.

MORRISON, William Shepherd, first Viscount Dunrossil (1959). 1893–1961. Politician (Conservative). Educated Edinburgh University, Inner Temple. MP 1929–59. Minor offices 1931–36. Minister of Agriculture and Food 1936–39. Chancellor of Duchy of Lancaster 1939–40. Minister of Food 1939–40. Postmaster General 1940–43. Minister of Town and Country Planning 1943–45. Speaker of House of Commons 1951–59. Governor General of Australia 1959–61.

NASH, Sir Walter. 1882–1968. New Zealand politician (Labour). Born Kidderminster. Arrived New Zealand 1909. Secretary, New Zealand Labour Party, 1922–32. Minister of Finance, 1935–49. Prime Minister 1957–60.

PAGE, Sir Earle Christmas Grafton. 1880–1962. Australian physician and politician (Country Party). Born Sydney. Educated Sydney. MHR since 1919. Leader, Australian Country Party, 1919–39. Commonwealth Treasurer 1923–29. Acting Prime Minister August 1923–March 1924, September 1926–January 1927, February to August 1935, and April to July 1937. Minister of Commerce and Deputy Prime Minister 1934–39. Prime Minister April 1939. Various ministerial posts thereafter.

PASSFIELD, first Baron (1929) (Sidney Webb). 1849–1947. Publicist, founder Fabian Society, barrister, public servant. In public employment 1878–91. President of the Board of Trade 1924. Secretary of State for Dominion Affairs 1929–30. Secretary of State for the Colonies 1929–31.

RUNCIMAN, Walter, first Viscount (1937). 1870–1939. Politician (Liberal and National Liberal). Educated Cambridge. MP 1899–1902, 1902–18, 1924–37. Parliamentary Secretary to Local Government Board 1905–7. Financial Secretary to the Treasury 1907–8. President, Board of Education 1908–11. President, Board of Agriculture, 1911–14. President, Board of

Trade, 1914–16, 1931–37. Lord President of the Council 1938–39.

RYCKMAN, Edward Baird. 1866–1934. Canadian barrister and politician (Conservative). Born Huntington, Quebec. Practised in Toronto. MP 1921–34. Minister of Public Works 1926. Minister of National Revenue 1930–33.

SCULLIN, James Henry. 1876–1953. Australian politician (Labour). Born Ballarat. Joined Labour Party 1903. MHR 1910–13. Journalist 1913–22. MHR 1922 *et seq.* Leader of Federal Labour Party 1928–35. Prime Minister 1929–31.

SKELTON, Oscar Douglas. 1878–1941. Canadian economist/historian and public servant. Born Orangeville, Ontario. Educated Queen's at Kingston, Chicago (Ph.D. 1908). Taught at Queen's 1908–25. Adviser at Imperial Economic Conference 1923. Under-Secretary of State for External Affairs 1925–41.

SMUTS, Jan Christian. 1870–1950. South African advocate, general, politician. Minister of Finance and Defence, South Africa, 1910–19. Attended Imperial War Conference and Cabinet 1917 and 1918. Member of War Cabinet, United Kingdom. Prime Minister of South Africa 1919–24, 1939–48. Deputy Prime Minister 1932–39. Attended Imperial Conference and Imperial Economic Conference 1921 and 1923.

STAMP, Josiah Charles, first Baron (1935). 1880–1941. Economist, civil servant, businessman. Educated London University. Entered civil service 1896 – Inland Revenue, Board of Trade. Resigned 1919. Secretary and Director, Nobel Industries Ltd, 1919–26. Director, Imperial Chemical Industries, 1927–28. Member, Committee for Economic Information of Economic Advisory Council after 1931.

STANLEY, Oliver Frederick George. 1896–1950. Politician (Conservative). Educated Eton. MP 1924–50. Parliamentary Under-Secretary, Home Office, 1931–33. Minister of Transport 1933–34, of Labour 1934–35. President of Board of Education 1935–37, of Board of Trade 1937–40. Secretary of State for War 1940, for Colonies 1942–45.

STEVENS, Henry Herbert. 1878–1973. Canadian accountant, broker and politician (Conservative, then Reconstruction). Born Bristol, went to Canada 1887. MP 1911–40. Minister of Customs and Excise 1926. Minister of Trade and Commerce

1921 and 1930–34. Resigned from Government to form party and contest election of 1935. Leader of Reconstruction Party 1934–38.

SWINTON, 1st Earl. 1884–1972. (Philip Lloyd-Graeme, assumes name Cunliffe-Lister 1924, Viscount Swinton 1935) Politician (Conservative). MP 1918–35. Minor offices 1920–22. President of Board of Trade 1922–23, 1924–29, 1931. Secretary of State for the Colonies 1931–35. Secretary of State for Air 1935–38. Other offices held 1942–45, 1951–52. Secretary of State for Commonwealth Affairs 1952–55.

TE WATER, Charles Theodore. 1887–1964. South African barrister, politician, diplomat. MP 1924–29. South African High Commissioner in London 1929–39. President of Assembly of League of Nations 1933.

THOMAS, James Henry. 1874–1949. Union leader and politician (Labour then National Labour). General secretary, National Union of Railwaymen, 1918–24 and 1925–31. MP 1910–36. Secretary of State for Colonies 1924 and 1931, 1935–36. Lord Privy Seal and Minister for Employment 1929–30. Secretary of State for the Dominions 1930–35.

WARD, Sir Joseph George. 1856–1930. New Zealand politician. Associated with W. F. Massey in National Government 1915–19. Attended Imperial War Conferences and Cabinets 1917 and 1918. Prime Minister 1928–30.

WILFORD, Sir Thomas Mason. 1870–1939. New Zealand barrister and politician (Liberal). MP 1896, 1900, 1903–30. Leader of Liberal Party 1919–25. Minister of Justice and Defence 1928–29. High Commissioner for New Zealand in London 1930–34. Attended Imperial Economic Conference 1932. London director, National Bank of New Zealand, 1934–37.

WILSON, Sir Horace. b. 1882. Public servant. Educated London School of Economics and Political Science. Entered civil service 1900. Permanent Secretary, Ministry of Labour, 1921–30. Chief Industrial Adviser to UK Government 1930–39. Seconded to Treasury for service with Prime Minister 1935. Permanent Secretary of Treasury and official Head of Civil Service 1939–42. Independent Chairman, National Joint Council for Local Authorities' Administrative, Professional, Technical, and Clerical Services,1944–51. Attended Imperial Economic Conference, Ottawa, 1932, as adviser to UK delegation and co-ordinator of officials' negotiations and of staff work.

Chapter 1

INTRODUCTION: THE EMPIRE IN BRITISH ECONOMIC POLICY 1917–1939

I. THE SCENE AND THE CHRONOLOGY

Long ago Sir Keith Hancock wrote two volumes on Commonwealth economic policy.[1] They are still essential reading. To some extent this book is merely a gloss on Sir Keith's work. But it is now possible to test his opinions against primary documentation which he could not have used in the 1930s. Further, his point of view now seems an odd one. He was writing about problems of economic policy in the interwar Commonwealth as if the Commonwealth was an entity which could be said to have an economic policy. In fact, there was no sense in which it did – or could. Therefore, I have organised my thoughts rather differently. I have asked, instead, where did 'imperial' economic questions fit into the fabric of *British* economic policy-making? In this fabric, how important were they? What ends were British Government pursuing when they made economic decisions *vis-à-vis* the Empire? How were these decisions actually reached?

Today we are almost bound to assume that Britain somehow 'exploited' her Empire. We might imagine this to occur through price manipulations, capital transfers, or the artificial creation of vent for over-priced British products. I originally chose to work on Imperial economic policy because I wanted to learn how well such exploitation assumptions fitted the interwar facts. In the last chapter of this book, I present some tentative conclusions about exploitation. However, in the course of my work I discovered that though in the interwar period British economic controversy was obsessed with the Empire, the terms were unfamiliar to me. Hence the second section of the present chapter summarises my findings with respect to these much more traditional and less fashionable topics – Imperial preference and Empire settlement. As I studied them, and the related matter of commodity management, I came to believe that there were certain unifying themes in British economic policy *vis-à-vis* the Empire. In the final chapter of the book, I suggest what these were. In the balance of the present section I summarise the chronology of Imperial economic policy-making. The body of the book offers detailed accounts of three phenomena: Empire settlement, the Ottawa negotiations and Agreements, and the aftermath of Ottawa. I have had to make these three chapters extremely circumstantial. To those who dislike the minutiae of economic diplomacy, I offer my regrets. Unfortunately, I think it is impossible to understand the events of these years unless one works through the details. Generalisations will be superficial, misleading, or both, unless supported by such information. As a partial recompense, I have tried in this first chapter and in the last to paint with a much broader brush.

There is now almost too much primary material for the historian of the interwar Empire. Five years ago, the United Kingdom Government changed the rules for access to public records; with few exceptions, British Government documents are now open to scholars after no more than thirty years have elapsed. The relevant materials are found in the records of several departments: the Board of Trade, the Foreign Office, the Treasury, the India Office, and especially the Colonial Office, the Dominions Office, and the Cabinet Office. Since 1916, the UK Cabinet has kept minutes of its day-to-day decisions. These minutes record, in greater or lesser detail, the discussions within Cabinet and the bases on which decisions were taken. They become steadily fuller and more informative as the years pass. The Cabinet minutes also list the documents which had been circulated to the several ministers in advance of each meeting. These documents, too, can be examined, and often can be traced back into the personal and departmental drafting processes from which they emerged. Thus the researcher can reconstruct the process of decision-making, working backwards from the

Cabinet and forwards from the government departments. Further, the departmental records can reveal a good deal about processes of decision and inter-departmental discussion which never reached Cabinet. They are especially revealing with respect to the pressures on the governmental machine. These were many and varied – a request from a Dominion or a colony, a suggestion from a pressure group, the bright idea of an official, a ministerial obsession, even a Question in the House. Admittedly, the process of 'weeding' has destroyed some documentation. But the registration and filing systems are sufficiently good to show what has been weeded. Further, the papers which one department has discarded can sometimes be found in another office. Finally, at Cabinet level absolutely nothing has been thrown away.

Unfortunately, by itself this governmental documentation is not quite enough. One must supplement it with memoirs, and with the private papers of politicians. Happily, memoirs are fairly numerous, and private papers are rapidly becoming available. The papers of L. S. Amery and Neville Chamberlain are still 'closed'. This is a pity, as these two men were so intimately involved with our topic. Nor can one yet use the papers of S. M. Bruce, the Australian Prime Minister who led the Commonwealth delegation to Ottawa, and who served as Australian High Commissioner in London throughout the 1930s. But Mackenzie King's papers are open for the whole interwar period. And so are the papers of Baldwin, Hewins, and Runciman.

In the chronology of Imperial economic policy-making, there are no surprises. The chronology on page 41 summarises the main events. The balance of this section is, in effect, a narrative comment on this chronology.[2] There is a sense in which the history of these interwar policy initiatives stretches back to 1846, to the era of the Navigation Acts and even to the sixteenth century, with its staple legislation and its 'political Lent'. We begin, however, in the middle of the First World War – at the Imperial War Cabinet and Conference of 1917.

In 1917, at the Imperial War Cabinet, the UK committed herself to encourage Empire settlement and to introduce preferential tariffs. The initiative came from the Prime Minister of New Zealand, who was almost certainly responding to the manipulations of W. A. S. Hewins. But Lloyd George committed himself in fear and trembling. Both he and Bonar Law remembered the prewar disputes; neither was prepared to impose new tariffs for the sake of preferential concessions; both feared the revenue impact of a preferential system. But Austen Chamberlain was 'an unrepentant advocate of food taxes'. And Lord Milner was a strong advocate of a preferential system. When he became Colonial Secretary in 1918, he insisted that Leo Amery join him as Under-Secretary – replacing Hewins, who had just lost his seat after beginning the elaboration of preferential tariffs for the Cabinet. Amery worked hard both for preferences and for the subsidisation of emigration. The 1919 Budget and the 1922 Empire Settlement Act represent considerable triumphs for him. So do the preferential arrangements in the Safeguarding of Industries Act. But these triumphs were won over very considerable internal opposition. Lloyd George himself was long opposed to any emigration measure; Churchill and others believed the UK should retain her manpower, not export it; many ministers thought unemployment would quickly pass; Chancellors and Treasury knights insisted that the country could not afford to grant preferential tariff-cuts, or to spend 3 million per year on emigration subsidy. Indeed, Amery himself was widely distrusted; Niemeyer later described him as a 'mad Mullah Minister'.

These distrusts and reservations affected the final arrangements of 1919–22. Amery got only £3 million per year, not £5 million, to spend on Empire settlement. The settlement bill was delayed for more than two years, and was eventually brought forward largely in response to continuous pressure from Australia. The preferences of 1919 were less generous than Hewins' proposals of 1918; instead of a one-third reduction on almost all duties, they granted only a one-sixth reduction on 'normal' duties. The exchequer could not afford a larger concession. Only on the McKenna duties did Amery extract a one-third cut – largely, he tells us, because there was no revenue involved. Indeed, he reports, the Chancellor may not have known that Canada had any motor industry at all.

Similar perplexities and confusions surround the events of 1922–23 – the Imperial Economic Conference and its aftermath. Late in 1922, Sir Philip Lloyd-Greame, the eminent tariff reformer at the Board of Trade, was pressing hard for a generous scheme of aid to Empire development. Amery was elaborating a similar idea – a £50 million Empire Development Loan. When Bonar Law invited the Dominions to an economic conference these ideas were already circulating, though nothing had been done about them. In the months between November 1922 and October 1923, when the conference assembled, they occasioned a major intra-governmental row.

Baldwin was first Chancellor and then Prime Minister. In the former capacity he read and transmitted the hostile Treasury brief: such subsidy and borrowing would congest the new issue market, raise interest rates, divert savings from more productive investments, and encourage Empire over-borrowing – especially by such profligates as Australia. In the latter capacity, Baldwin listened once to Hewins, received a memorandum from the eminent Tariff Reformer,[3] installed a sick man as Chancellor, and resisted the efforts of the Overseas Settlement Office to give emigration a prominent place at the coming conference. Meanwhile, Amery was urging the Dominions to ask for new preferential tariffs. And cabled ultimatums arrived from Australia: Britain must grant more preferences, or risk the loss of her privileged position in the Australian market. Baldwin replied that Bonar Law's pledge prevented his government from imposing extensive new duties. But his government put its officials to work on the question, and resolved to make concessions on luxury fruits and dried fruits – the products of most concern to Australia.

Baldwin's government does not seem to have had any clear strategy for the conference. It produced an emasculated version of the Amery-Lloyd-Greame proposals, offered its paltry list of tariff cuts, and announced its willingness to consider all Dominions requests. Canada modestly said she was interested in anything and everything – wheat, meat, timber, metals, and many manufactures. With vigour Australia pursued wine, spirits, and fruits. In the course of the conference, by a process which remains obscure, Baldwin became convinced that Britain should impose more duties, for the sake of home protection and Empire development. He called Lord Milner out of retirement to devise a protective and preferential tariff for the UK. But in the course of the campaign he promised to impose no duties on basic foodstuffs – the only products of real interest to Canada, Australia, New Zealand, South Africa – or, for that matter, Britain's own farmers. And his government lost the election of 1923 – apparently on the issue of protection and food taxes. At least, so many Conservatives soon came to believe.

The first MacDonald Government was as confused and divided as Baldwin's or Lloyd George's. Snowden would not tolerate tariffs if he could help doing so; on grounds of principle he repealed the McKenna duties, and the preferences which went with them. The pleas of Canada's High Commissioner were of no avail. He was inclined to resist developmental spending, especially on Imperial projects. But the Labour cabinet was as interested in emigration as the Coalition and Conservative cabinets had been. And some Labour ministers shared Amery's romantic interest in agrarian settlement. Hence William Lunn welcomed Australian proposals for an umbrella agreement by which Britain would share the interest cost of Australian Government borrowings for development, in exchange for an Australian commitment to absorb specified numbers of British emigrants. And the Cabinet approved the Baldwin Government's proposals for co-operation in financial assistance to economic development. Embodied in the Trade Facilities Act of 1924, these were in effect – though not effective – until 1927.

When the second Baldwin Government took office late in 1924, its members were bound by their internal disagreements, and by Baldwin's own election pledges, to eschew food taxes. Baldwin does not seem to have noticed that Churchill, his Chancellor of the Exchequer, would fight the protectionist, preferential, and developmental plans of Amery and Sir Philip Cunliffe-Lister (who had changed his name from Lloyd-Greame earlier in the year). In the event, he acquiesced in five years of free-trade orthodoxy – no new duties, and preferences only on existing duties. In the end, Churchill even abolished the tea duty, and with it the tea preferences – one of the few significant preferential concessions which Britain had extended to her Empire in 1919 or thereafter.

The Baldwin Government quickly enacted the preferential tariff-cuts which they had promised in 1923, and they granted free entry to Dominion goods whenever new safeguarding duties were imposed. But they imposed no new food duties. With enormous difficulty Amery and his allies extracted a few hundred thousand pounds per year to fund an Empire Marketing Board. By spending on research and on advertising, the Board was to create a 'non-tariff preference' for Empire goods in the British market. It lumbered on until after the Ottawa Conference. But Churchill never allowed it to receive the full £1 million it was in theory supposed to draw each year. Denied any prospect of movement on the preference front, Baldwin's tariff reformers were obliged to concentrate upon Empire settlement.

Building on staff work which Baldwin's ministry had put in hand, in 1929 the MacDonald Government quickly introduced a Colonial Development Bill. For the first time there would be regular grants to help colonial development. In the same year, J. H. Thomas went to Canada with mass-migration in mind. And in 1931 we find George Lansbury urging the Labour cabinet to plant thousands of British coal miners on Western Australia's wheat fields. Of course nothing was done.

Thomas's adventures of 1929 are the last manifestations of the expansionary theme in Imperial economic policy before 1940. In the thirties the theme is not expansion but protectiveness – a solicitous care for the welfare of producers in Britain and overseas.

Even before the Ottawa Conference, Chamberlain and some other British ministers had hoped to give British agriculture some measure of protection. However, they had no plans to take to the 1932 meeting. They had already dealt with home wheat, under the special legislation of

1932 which introduced deficiency payments. Meat, butter, and other temperate foodstuffs continued to perplex them before, during, and after August 1932. But thereafter, one product after another became 'sensitive'; hence, in part, the immensely extended and tangled intra-Imperial trade negotiations of the later thirties whose course is traced in our sixth chapter. Faced with Dominion recalcitrance, and Argentine intransigence, the British government was eventually obliged to give more deficiency payments. Thus this characteristic feature of British agricultural protectionism has its roots partly in the intra-Imperial trading pattern, partly in the Ottawa Agreements themselves, and partly in the unemployment problem, which made British ministers extremely unwilling to put their export trade at risk for the sake of their home agriculture.

When Canada's R. B. Bennett put monetary questions on the Ottawa agenda, his instinct was sound. But Chamberlain and the Treasury were terrified of two things: premature stabilisation of sterling *vis-à-vis* the dollar, and pressure for a commitment to an excessively inflationary monetary policy. Hence Chamberlain was evasive at the conference's monetary committee, and never made any helpful proposal. The obvious solution to the imperial problem would have been a devaluation of Empire currencies *vis-à-vis* sterling, and a reduction in intra-Imperial tariff rates, combined with stable tariffs *vis-à-vis* foreign countries. So far as the documents show, no such idea was ever considered.

It is easy to explain Chamberlain's imperceptiveness. Like every British politician he was hypnotised by the 'tariff question'. As he once confessed to Baldwin, he never had a firm grasp of financial affairs. At Ottawa, he can be seen slavishly reproducing the extremely cautious and unimaginative Treasury memoranda. And after all, Empire free trade, food duties, and the preferential system were part of his family inheritance. Hence it is not surprising that neither he nor any other British politician seems to have seen the Ottawa Conference in terms other than tariff bargaining and preferential concessions. In the confused period between the 1931 election and the passage of the Import Duties Act, preferences agitated the British cabinet almost as constantly as protection did. Which foreign foods could safely be taxed? Could *any* Empire food safely be taxed? What would the Dominions give? And what would they ask? In the fifth chapter we trace out these gyrations.

The Ottawa Conference, in fact, was a muddle, and its Agreements were the result of *ad hoc* concessions and desperate last-minute bargaining. Nothing could have been less contrived or calculated – less 'Imperial'. Indeed, if anything, it was Australia's S. B. Bruce and Canada's R. B. Bennett who were manipulating a confused and divided British delegation – not the reverse. Many observers saw the conference as an evil plot by perfidious Albion. They could not have been more wrong. The conference should not be seen as a protectionist triumph – or even a Tory one. Consider the agreements themselves. Observe the behaviour of the British delegation. The British government itself had only the most remote responsibility for the project, or for its outcome. The National Government had not called the conference; it had inherited the whole scheme from the Imperial Conference of 1930, which was itself the result of a Canadian initiative during 1929.

Whether we assess it as protectionism or as trade diversion the Ottawa Conference was not very helpful for Britain. The new tariffs and preferences did not arrest the decline in Britain's share of the Empire's import trade; they complicated her dealings with other countries, as Runciman had foreseen, and with her own farmers, as no one had foreseen; they irritated other nations, especially the USA; they involved the UK in an endless chain of intra-Imperial negotiations, especially on food policy but also on 'domestic competition', and even on Britain's own trade with the USSR. Many of these troubles arose because certain clauses had been badly or vaguely drafted. Others arose simply from the importunities of Britain's farmers and of the Dominions both at Ottawa and thereafter. Still others reflected the fact that at Ottawa the UK made certain commitments with respect to the food trades. In our seventh and eighth chapters we follow this 'Ottawa Aftermath' up to the outbreak of war.

The Ottawa commitments were increasingly embarrassing as British ministers became ever more eager to protect their own home livestock industry. Hence in 1934–37 British ministers tried to modify the Ottawa Agreements. They wanted to impose duties on Empire meat and butter; they wanted Australia and New Zealand to control production and exports of both products. For the sake of Britain's own agriculture, they asked these dominions, in effect, to delay or restrict their own recovery. In 1936 they were obliged to make the same requests of Canada and South Africa. Until the very beginning of the war, they were trying to reconcile their commitments to the Dominions, to foreign allies and trading partners, and to their own farmers. In comparison with this 'meat problem', the Anglo-American trade negotiations, interlocked though they were with the preferential trading system, were simple, straightforward, and unambiguous.

II. UNEMPLOYMENT, DEVELOPMENT STRATEGY, AND THE WHITE DOMINIONS

To understand the protective measures of the 1930s we need no special intellectual equipment. But to understand the 1920s, and especially the Empire settlement programme of this decade, we must remind ourselves of the development strategy which informed British initiatives between 1917 and 1930. In another place I have labelled this strategy 'the Imperial vision'.[4] In the final chapter of this book I trace relations between the vision and the exploitation of the dependent Empire, especially its African parts. In this section, as an introduction to the next two chapters, I sketch the vision in its relation to the 'white Dominions' – Canada, Australia, New Zealand, and South Africa.

The developmental measures of the 1920s have a certain coherence because they reflect certain common ideas. L. S. Amery articulated these ideas but did not invent them; he borrowed them from W. A. S. Hewins, from Lord Milner, and from a sort of common imperialist consciousness. All the visionaries were tariff reformers – Hewins, Milner,

tariffs were supposed to raise rates of return within the Empire, relative to rates on foreign projects. So more capital goods would be added to the Empire's stock, and fewer to foreign capital stocks. This investment process, in turn, would have short-run effects on Empire output because the plant and equipment would tend to be Empire-made. Further, in the longer run the development process would certainly raise the value of the Empire's natural resources. Similarly, if migrants remain within the Empire their total output is Empire output. Also, their presence is likely to develop Empire natural resources. Rents will then accrue to owners, and total gross output will be higher because Empire resources are being used up. But if migrants leave the Empire, they contribute to Empire potential only in so far as they remit foreign exchange to the UK. Also, of course, they are lost to the defence effort. From the short-run viewpoint, any emigration, regardless of destination, has the same direct impact on British unemployment. But from the long-run viewpoint it would be much better to settle the migrants within the Empire, and to provide them with the capital goods they need so that they can ultimately add to Empire output. In the process, of course, total demand will increase, and the British economy will be more active because demand has risen.

So Amery and his friends argued. In effect, they wanted to continue economic growth on the prewar model, but to accelerate it by means of preferential tariffs, state-aided Empire settlement, and subsidised capital-export not only via the Colonial Stocks Acts but also by more direct encouragement, especially for the finance of emigration and for African projects. Both Conservatives and Liberals disagreed about preferences and tariffs; no Chancellor was eager to disgorge funds for Empire projects. Yet between and within the major parties there was a large measure of agreement on the proper shape of Empire economic development – and on Britain's role in shaping that development.

On the other hand, the initiatives of 1917–29 were not a gradual working-out of a great coherent plan. They were ideologically coherent, because they all came from the same rather meagre stock of ideas, but each was a response to particular pressures. British governments, like governments elsewhere, were really stumbling along from expedient to expedient. Indeed, they were largely passive, responding partly to pressures from the Dominions and partly to domestic crises and troubles. In explaining their imperial economic policy these continuous concerns are at least as important as the common ideology.

Nor should one think that the visionaries were sensible merely because they were reasonably consistent. Amery himself was capable of extravagant nonsense with respect to particular development projects. He and others consistently talked nonsense with respect to the allocative effects of a protective tariff system. On monetary matters he was sometimes perspicacious but often confused. And in the 1920s he and others certainly overestimated the effect of the symbolic steps towards a preferential tariff system which were all that free-trade orthodoxy would permit.

Recall that in 1919 Britain still had few tariffs. She taxed a few tropical foodstuffs, wine and spirits, tea, coffee, sugar, and the 'luxury' consumer goods on which McKenna had imposed duties in 1915. Preferences here could be useful only as a gesture, not as a help, except to India and the West Indies. The Dominions produced few of the taxed commodities; they exported little of them to Britain, who, in turn, drew few of her supplies from the white Empire. If preferences were to be given on the 'old duties' the main gainers would be India and the West Indies. Perhaps such a concession might extract a preferential duty from the Indians, but it would do little to stimulate the sort of Empire development for which many in Britain hoped. Preferential tariffs made sense only if they were granted on a wider range of duties; that is, new duties would be needed to effect Imperial development. The UK could not tax raw material; to do so would be to hurt her export industries *vis-à-vis* foreign competitors. So manufactures and foods must be taxed – the former for the sake of tariff bargaining and trade-diversion, the latter for the sake of preferential concessions and Empire development.

None of this was news to anyone. The Dominion premiers had been saying it since the turn of the century, and Joseph Chamberlain had long since made it a political issue. And everyone knew the immediate effects. The controversy was still mired in the swamp where it had been left before the First World War. Tariff reform would mean higher prices for food in the UK, but might mean higher employment – especially when sterling was overvalued. In the 1920s the free traders of all parties had not advanced beyond these simple articles of faith: higher food prices are evil. And the tariff reformers had not really faced and dealt with this objection. They continued to talk about something else – the employment pay-off from the preferential system. But since tariff reform was only briefly a possibility, during the 1920s they concentrated upon other aspects of their programme. Empire settlement and empire investment had not been very important in the prewar tariff controversies. In the 1920s, Parliament and the Dominions heard much more of them.

Within each Dominion the visionaries hoped for development along the lines I have sketched in Figure 2 (page 38). This Figure is little more than a generalisation of the development paths which all Dominions had followed before 1914. But already by 1920 the model was a poor fit to their actual economies, largely because their electorates and leaders were no longer satisfied by it. New Zealand wanted to control immigration, and she appeared to have few undeveloped resources; her hydro-electricity did not fit into the Imperial development scheme, as it could not be exported. Canada had developed a large and very carefully protected manufacturing sector. Australia showed signs of doing so. South Africa would shortly do likewise. Indeed, the model did not fit the youngest Dominion, which welcomed neither settlers nor Imperial arrangements. This fact is ironic. Joseph Chamberlain himself was visiting Cape Colony when he saw the vision. Amery, Milner, and others had formed their visionary consensus while working in South Africa. And the more visionary aspects of the settlement proposals recall Rhodes's dreams for Central Africa.

Figure 2 *Sociogram of Dominions' development*

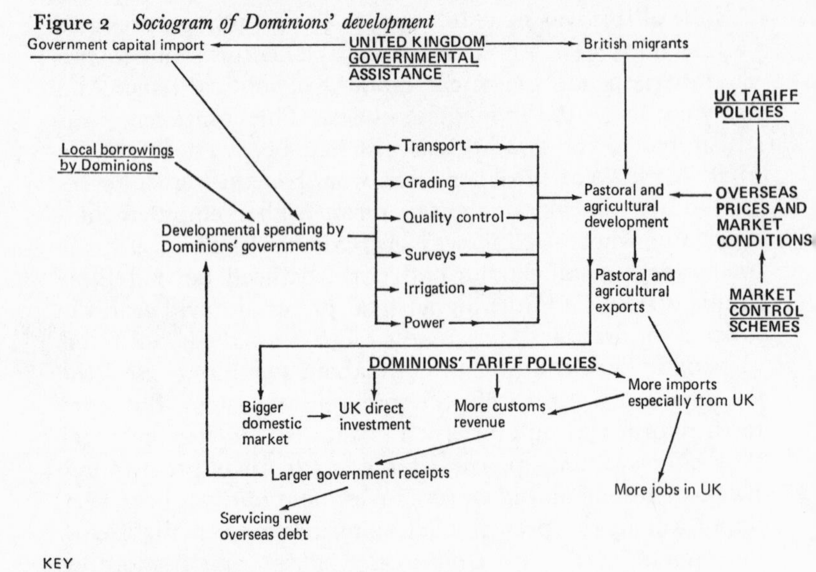

KEY

BOLD FACE TYPE, UNDERLINED: basic policy decisions of governments

Lower-case type, underlined: external events which are in part determined by events or circumstances in the Dominion or colony

Lower case type without underlining: items within the economy which the development programme affects

Arrows: show direction of pressure, influence, or causation

Simplifying a little, we can say that the Imperial vision sprang from South Africa but did not apply there.

Nevertheless, during the twenties, Empire politicians found it convenient to adopt the Imperial rhetoric when dealing with London in matters of economic policy. Indeed, one might say that the Dominions had invented the visionary strategy in the first place. Certainly they invented the modern preferential tariff, which they had begun to adopt without pressure or encouragement from Britain, and, indeed, for twenty-two years without reciprocal concessions. All of them wanted capital funds from abroad. All but South Africa wanted immigrants. Naturally they welcomed anything which offered them the tariff-assistance they had long desired, and subsidised resource-flows as well.

In the event, therefore, the Dominions' lobbying was one of the main weapons in the visionaries' armoury. Australian pressure helped put the British tariff on the agenda for the

1923 Imperial Economic Conference. Canadian representatives pressed in private for concessions, while in public the Canadian prime minister disclaimed any desire to influence the British fiscal system. South African politicians stood a little aloof, but pressed consistently for British tariff reform. Australia was aggressively eager for a British preferential tariff, while New Zealand's eagerness was almost pathetic. It had been New Zealand's prime minister who had introduced a preferential resolution at the Imperial War Cabinet of 1917.

Thus the vision was popular with governments, though not with Labour oppositions, in the more British of the white Dominions, and especially in Australia. Unfortunately, the Dominion governments wanted some other things, especially local industrialisation, which were inconsistent with the vision at least in its simpler forms. In Canada, South Africa, and Australia governments wanted to develop *everything* – not just primary production. And to this end they protected their own manufacturing industries, small scale and high cost though these often were. Such Dominion tariffs reduced the feedback from the subsidised British exports of capital and labour: more Dominion aggregate demand would be retained at home, and less would generate a demand for British export goods. The tariffs also hindered the development of the primary producing industries in which Britain was chiefly interested. As new jobs were created in protected manufacturing, in agriculture labour became scarcer and more expensive. And as the tariffs raised the domestic prices of manufactures, they raised costs and reduced real returns in the primary producing sectors, which exported most or much of their outputs. In New Zealand, this link was recognised, and the recognition kept tariffs low throughout the 1920s. In Australia too it was recognised, but the result was 'protection for everybody' through an increasingly elaborate system of market-control which aimed to raise farm incomes. In South Africa, where leaders feared the exhaustion of the gold mines and observed the drift of poor whites to the cities, manufacturing was protected to create new 'civilised' jobs for the white labour force. Thus in the three southern Dominions one can see reasonably clear-cut strategies for development: pastoral development in New Zealand, agriculture plus import replacement in Australia, and import replacement on the foundation of gold and diamonds in South Africa. In Canada, economic policy during the 1920s was incoherent. The Liberal Government, wishing to encourage both industrialisation and agricultural growth, but committed in principle to *laissez-faire* and to low tariffs, tacked and changed course in response to electoral pressures and to whims of ministerial fancy. Further, this Government distrusted Britain's Conservative administrations. Prime Minister King believed that Amery conspired with the Canadian Conservative party to propose migration schemes merely to embarrass the Liberal government in Canada. O. D. Skelton, King's chief adviser, smelt the dreadful odour of imperial federation in every proposal for co-operation. The visionaries in London would need imperialists in the Dominions if they were to achieve their ends. In Canada, they found only the politically powerless. In South Africa the politicians saw inconvenient visions of their own. Only in Australasia were there powerful politicians who saw things more or less the right way.

A Chronology

1917 Imperial War Cabinet and Conference endorse the principle of tariff-preference, and urge measures to induce British stock to settle under British flag.
1918 Imperial War Cabinet and Conference re-endorse the decisions of 1917.
1919 Finance Bill introduces imperial preferences in UK. India acquires *de facto* fiscal autonomy.
1920 In December, UK resolves on large-scale state-aided emigration.
1921 In February, conference of Dominion representatives endorses proposals for state-aided Empire settlement. In June, Imperial Conference endorses these also.
1922 Empire Settlement Act passed. UK begins to sign emigration agreements with Dominions.
1923 Imperial Economic Conference. UK proposes new food duties, wider preferential margins, co-operation for financial aid in development programmes.
1924 First MacDonald Government rejects tariff proposals of 1923 Conference and repeals McKenna duties but continues financial co-operation plan.
1925 Second Baldwin Government introduces some of the preferential proposals of 1923 and, in lieu of the others, proposes to spend up to £1 million per annum on Empire marketing propaganda and research. Constitutes Imperial Economic Committee, recommended in 1923, to investigate marketing problems in Empire produce. Signs £34 million agreement with Australia. Arranges special financing for transport development in East Africa. Temporary control of overseas issues as UK returns to the gold standard.
1926 Imperial Conference devotes little time to economic questions.
1929 Canadian Government proposes an economic conference

for 1930. J. H. Thomas visits Canada. Colonial Development Act passed.

1930 In October, Imperial Conference deadlocks on question of tariffs and preferences, also confuses itself over a 'wheat quota' plan. An end *de facto* to assisted emigration.

1931 In September Britain leaves the gold standard, and is followed by Australia and New Zealand but not by South Africa or Canada. India is required neither to float the rupee nor to devalue it *vis-à-vis* sterling. Abnormal Importations Act imposes many new duties. Financial crises in Australia and New Zealand. Wheat crisis in Canada.

1932 UK imposes general protective tariffs, with preferences to Empire suppliers, in February. Ottawa Conference (21 July to 20 August) stabilises and somewhat increases these preferences, while committing UK to control imports of foreign meat. Continuing financial crisis in Antipodes. In December, South Africa devalues and joins the visibly forming sterling area.

1933 World economic conference endorses principle of supply-restriction to raise prices. UK signs trade agreements with Argentina, Denmark, other Baltic countries.

1934 Price-problems in meat and dairy products lead UK to consider further import-restrictions.

1935 Complex negotiations with Australia, New Zealand, and Argentina on the question of livestock products.

1936 Further negotiations on meat, and on revision of Anglo-Canadian trade agreement. From New Zealand, Walter Nash arrives to propose a bilateral-balancing plan for Anglo-New Zealand trade and payments.

1937 In February, new Anglo-Canadian trade agreement signed. Nash fails to secure bilateral balancing. At Imperial Conference, Dominions are asked to co-operate with UK to make Anglo-American trade talks a success. Empire Settlement Act renewed, but with smaller maximum annual appropriation.

1938 New Anglo-Canadian and Anglo-American trade agreements. Australia and UK agree to ignore Australia's commitments with respect to 'domestic competition'. UK presses New Zealand not to discriminate against UK in licensing schemes under exchange control.

1939 New Anglo-Indian trade agreement signed, replacing Ottawa arrangements. West Indies Royal Commission reports.

1940 Colonial Development and Welfare Act passed.

Chapter 2

THE BIRTH OF EMPIRE SETTLEMENT, 1916–1922

This chapter traces the development of British official thinking and government policy with respect to Empire settlement, between 1916 and 1922. In the latter year, Parliament passed the Empire Settlement Act – a measure which, for the first time in many years, committed the UK Government to spend on emigration. Admittedly, the poor law authorities and the charitable associations had long been helping British subjects to emigrate. But for many decades the central government had remained aloof. Indeed, to find the faintest parallels for the Act, one must look in the first half of the nineteenth century. Thus the Act did represent a major revolution of policy. Further, its effects are still with us. The 1922 Act was to expire in 1937. But it was renewed, in modified form. And even today, the UK contributes to the subsidised passages of emigrants who are leaving for Canada and the Antipodes. The devices – passage assistance and special emigrants' fares – originate in the 1920s, in the first eight years of operation under the Empire Settlement Act, when the UK authorities were actively encouraging emigration. What caused this revolution of policy? In small part, the rhetorics of Imperial development and Empire solidarity. In much larger part, Britain's unemployment problem. But we cannot properly understand the evolution of policy, or its precise content, if we remain at this level of high generalisation. The Empire Settlement Bill did not spring full-blown from the mind of Leo Amery, who introduced it with such strong advocacy and who brooded lovingly over the subsequent operations under the Act. The Bill did not enact the recommendations of the Dominions Royal Commission, or of Lord Tennyson's committee on ex-service migration, though both reports were significant in the early stages of the process which began in 1916 and which eventually produced a statute in 1922. We can hope to understand this process only if we follow it, in some detail, through these six years. As we do so, we shall see how government policy evolved along with the administrative devices which were meant to effect that policy. We shall also observe how long-term commitments were made on the basis of short-term pressures – most of which came from Australia.

I. WARTIME DEVELOPMENTS AND THE EMIGRATION BILL, 1917–1918

During the First World War the British Government did not develop an emigration policy for the postwar period, and did not really try to do so. The Colonial Office had acquiesced in the efforts of Sir Rider Haggard and the Royal Colonial Institute, but in 1916–18 the officials were unable to decide definitely whether they wished to encourage or discourage the emigration of ex-servicemen after the war. They knew that before the war the country had a surplus of women, and that the war had increased this surplus, while biting heavily into the male population. They worried about the supply of labour to the postwar British economy, especially though not exclusively in agriculture.[1] Some wondered whether the UK could finance assisted-migration schemes.[2] Some of them thought that prewar emigration had been overdone, and that the blandishments of passage agents and steamship companies were partly to blame. These ones soon learnt that the agents would so propagandise the ex-servicemen as to generate a new unwarranted emigration.[3] But they recognised the possibility that the British economy might have difficulty in absorbing the demobilised, especially as there had been no emigration during the war itself. They knew that Professor Chapman had forecast a two-million-man 'surplus of labour'.[4] But, the officials reminded one another, no one knew what the postwar demand for labour might be. Naturally they thought that emigrants, however few or many they might be, should be kept within the Empire.[5] Here their thinking was military not developmental; there is no sign of concern with the market impact of Empire settlement, the theme which Leo Amery was later to develop so strongly. W. A. S. Hewins made some slight effort to feed this theme into the system, but his ideas on the subject, which were extremely general in form and expression, did not become part of the Colonial Office attitude.

The Office's uncertainties were reflected in the attitudes of the Colonial Secretary, Walter Long. Prime Ministers Borden and Massey were doubtless right in thinking that Long was more eager to restrain than to encourage postwar emigration. This was certainly the Office's view of *probable* postwar policy. But Long himself did not then have a policy, and was not urging one on the War Cabinet. Rather wistfully he hoped that the Central Emigration Authority, which he worked so hard to create, would solve the problem for him, and for the Government, by determining the right course. Indeed, in drafting the Emigration Bill of 1918, he and his advisers deliberately provided that the Authority would have the power to create whatever emigration policy it thought best – and they deliberately refrained from any statements, in the Bill or in the House, about the proper nature of such a policy.

In all this there are certain remarkable omissions with respect to the evidence. The Office was unwilling to ask servicemen whether they wanted to emigrate. It feared that such questions would appear to be propaganda for emigration, and it did not know whether such emigration would be desirable. Also, the Government as yet had no policy for settling soldiers on the land within the UK. Hence the Office recognised that the soldiers could not make a rational choice between emigration and land settlement at home. There is a modicum of common sense in these Office reservations, but there is no sense whatever in its failure to elaborate more fully the demographic basis of the postwar situation. The number of troops, their age distribution, and their occupational backgrounds could surely have been made known to the Office. So could the Census returns from 1911, and such information as was available on the size and composition of the wartime civil labour force. Hewins, with his intense though uninformed interest in physical planning, might have been expected to thrust such data on the Office. There is no evidence that he did so. Thus the Office and the politicians remained dependent upon the Tennyson Committee and the Dominions Royal Commission. Both bodies had been prolific, but their findings were non-numerate, and were not focused upon the question of postwar emigration policy.

Further, the Office and the politicians were inclined to confuse things. They did not distinguish clearly between two questions. How many people would want to emigrate after the war? Should the Government encourage or discourage such emigration? And they were not clear whether a policy should be short-term or long-term.

When discussing whether postwar emigration was desirable, they tended to focus on the immediate postwar period. In this connection, they worried about the demobilisation problem, the availability of shipping,[6] and the *short-term* absorptive capacity of the Dominions, especially in land-settlement schemes. Presumably they intended the Central Emigration Authority to formulate a general policy which would be very short-run indeed – changeable from month to month rather than from year to year. They did not face the administrative and statistical problems which would face the Authority if it should try to do this. The Dominion representatives could hardly be in close touch with current events overseas, if only because it took six weeks for mail to reach London from Australasia. And nobody envisaged an adequate staff. When Long constituted the Overseas Settlement Committee, he asked the Treasury for one principal clerk, two more junior clerks, and a female typist. Presumably no one had thought that the full-blown Authority should have more.

The genesis of the postwar settlement schemes is to be found in the wartime concern with soldier settlement, which was linked with the desire to retain bloodstock as a safeguard for the future. Late in 1915 the Royal Colonial

Institute had begun to lobby vigorously for the retention of ex-servicemen: they should be kept within the Empire, either at home or overseas. Finding little encouragement in the Colonial Office or at the hands of Bonar Law, the Colonial Secretary, the Institute dispatched Rider Haggard on a private expedition to the Dominions. The Colonial Office took some pains to ensure that the colonies did not think Haggard an official emissary; there was risk of confusion because the Dominions Royal Commission, on which Haggard had served, had not yet reported, and was, indeed, proposing further sittings. When Haggard set off, the Colonial Office believed that he would get nowhere; the Australian climate was thought to be unpropitious because there were Labour governments both in the Commonwealth and in several States. There was a certain glee in the mandarins' response to Haggard's lack of success in New South Wales and South Australia. However, they were obliged to admit that on the whole his initiative had been successful: the Dominions did seem interested in accepting some UK ex-servicemen – if the terms were right.[7]

Haggard's success in effect forced Whitehall's hand. Meanwhile, pressure was coming from another quarter. On 29 February 1916, Lord Selborne suggested to Bonar Law that there should be a conference between the UK and the Dominions to plan for the future settlement of ex-servicemen on the land.[8] The Colonial Office was far from enthusiastic, believing that there was neither need nor point in such an exercise. But the Board of Agriculture continued to press its suggestion. Its reason only gradually became clear: it feared that if there was no common planning the Dominions would outbid the UK in the struggle for agricultural labour, and the shortage in the postwar UK, which it already feared, would be worsened. The Reconstruction Committee of the Cabinet was painfully asking for advice. Should the government encourage postwar emigration, or discourage it, and how might it effect the preferred policy?[9] Well might it ask; at this time a Colonial Office official was writing that though he knew Bonar Law did not want to encourage postwar emigration: 'I am not at all clear what our policy in this

Office is towards emigration, and I have no notion what the policy of HMG is likely to be.'[10]

In fact the policy was one of watchful waiting. On 25 July, Bonar Law told the Earl of Crawford, Selborne's successor at the Board of Agriculture, that though a conference was certainly desirable it would be better to wait until there was full word about Haggard's mission.[11] He also wanted word about the Australian Premiers' Conference, which had met at Adelaide, with Haggard in attendance, during May.

Haggard had first visited Southern Africa, where some persons had promised help, and Rhodesia, on whose behalf the British South Africa Company had offered half a million acres. He was to go on to New Zealand and Canada. While in Australia he personally canvassed the State premiers, and attended their Adelaide conference in May 1916. The premiers uniformly responded warmly, though not in identical terms. Thanking them, Haggard spoke of the need for organisation in soldier settlement, saying, 'I venture to submit . . . that so large an affair seems to pass beyond the reach of mere private enterprise.'[12] The conference resolved to treat British soldiers 'in a manner similar to' Australian.[13]

Haggard believed that after the war there would be a spontaneous and large emigration which, unless channelled, would flow to the areas which the war had spared – primarily North and South America. In the discussion of his requests it became clear[14] that several State premiers neither favoured nor sought immigration, fearing the advent of the townbred and the further growth of Australia's cities. At this point they were prepared to accept migrants but not to encourage immigration actively.

Haggard also enjoyed some success in New Zealand and Canada, which he visited after Australia. Thus the result of his mission was sufficiently encouraging to force action from a Colonial Office which the Board of Agriculture was still chivvying. In August the Office began to prepare a proposal for the Dominions: a central authority for ex-servicemen's emigration. This body would 'formulate plans and co-ordinate efforts'.[15] The Dominions would be represented on it. Meanwhile, they were asked to report on their plans for ex-servicemen's settlement, and to name representatives to the central authority.

The results were discouraging. New Zealand reported that it preferred to leave the whole question for the New Zealand Prime Minister to discuss on his next visit to London.[16] Australia deferred comment. South Australia responded in highly pessimistic terms.[17] Only Western Australia expressed eagerness to accept large numbers . . . though it emphasised that money would be needed.[18]

Hence the Colonial Office, though originally unenthusiastic about the whole idea, tried to prod the Dominions into some sort of response. On 19 December a cable reminded all the Dominions that the matter was urgent, and asked rather querulously, 'when may I expect further reply?'[19] The Canadian Government, after noting that the matter was complicated, told Whitehall that a provincial premiers' conference would discuss it on 10 January.[20] In Australia a premiers' conference was in fact discussing it when the Whitehall cable arrived. But it was necessary to adjourn the conference and reconvene in January 1917 before a final statement could emerge. At the January session, Prime Minister Hughes bullied his premiers shamelessly, pointing out:

'our chances of getting money largely depend upon the extent of the facilities we will offer British soldiers to take up land in Australia. Sir Rider Haggard in his report stresses this point very much . . . the amount of money necessary to settle British soldiers will, of course, be added to that which we estimate will be necessary for our own men, so that it is not a question of money so far as the British soldiers are concerned, but merely of offering facilities.'[21]

This did not mean that Britain would *give* Australia the money, but that she would allow Australia to borrow it. Because the Australian states were already worrying about the financing of settlement for their own soldiers, Hughes had constructed a cunning argument: no UK soldiers, no money for settling our own. In the end he extracted a specific commitment about the status of British soldier-migrants, and about the conditions on which they could take up land in each state.[22]

Canada finally produced a response of a sort. So did the other Dominions. But the 'central authority' seems to have excited neither hostility nor admiration. Though no such body was ever set up for soldier settlement, or indeed for any purpose, as a proposal it appeared in a new guise when the Emigration Bill was before the House of Commons in 1918.

Meanwhile, the Colonial Office proceeded to set up a consultative committee which would brood about ex-servicemen and postwar migration. Lord Tennyson presided over this intra-Imperial body, which began in February 1917 with twenty-five members, and which eventually reached thirty-three. The Dominions, the Australian States, and the Whitehall ministries were all represented. Caucussing separately before the Committee had begun to meet, the UK representatives agreed that in the postwar period, land settlement within the British Isles would be more important than emigration.[23]

In its report, Lord Tennyson's Empire Settlement Committee was obliged to admit that it did not know whether or not Britain would have trouble absorbing its own ex-servicemen after the war. Hence it was unable to say whether or not postwar emigration should be actively assisted. However, it did recommend free passage to Empire destinations for ex-servicemen who wished to proceed directly on demobilisation. It was also prepared to see the UK finance overseas land-settlement schemes.[24] And it wanted a central body to plan and administer emigration schemes for ex-servicemen. On this body the Dominions were to be represented.

At the same time, the Dominions Royal Commission issued its final report.[25] The Commission, which had been at work for many years, was remarkably vague about migration policy, to which it devoted several pages. Like the Tennyson Committee, it did not know what postwar policy should be. But it did know that there had been abuses before the war. Agents had boomed passages to places in which the migrant could not hope for a good life. Hence it recommended a central emigration authority, which would have power to regulate passage brokers, agents and propaganda.

Not surprisingly, the Colonial Office decided to splice these two recommendations. By 16 July 1917, the decision had been taken.[26] Additional steam was provided by the Imperial War Cabinet and Conference of 1917. The conference had seen the Dominions Royal Commission report, and certainly knew what the Tennyson Committee was doing. On 26 April 1917, with almost no debate, the Imperial War Cabinet had recorded its support for 'arrangements by which intending emigrants from the United Kingdom may be induced to settle under the British flag.'[27]

When a UK Cabinet Committee was set up to implement this and other IWC resolutions, it decided not to treat emigration, as the Tennyson Committee and the Dominions Royal Commission had already dealt with the matter. Thus these two reports became the basis for further development. And they were hardly concerned with *policy* – only with *machinery*.

By mid-July 1917, the Colonial Office had begun to draft an Emigration Bill which would establish a Central Emigration Authority with power to censor migration propaganda, license passage brokers, agents, and regulate conditions on migrant ships, as the Dominions Royal Commission had recommended.[28] In the Office's own view, the Bill was needed for four reasons. The prewar situation had left the Dominions free to recruit the men the UK could least afford to lose. The sex disproportion in the UK was such that migration planning was essential. Otherwise, too many men would go, and too many women would stay. There was need to arrange for the postwar migration of ex-servicemen and others. And it was necessary to act on the recommendations of the Tennyson Committee and the Dominions Royal Commission. The proposed Central Migration Authority was to have very wide powers: it was to be able to advise and assist migrants, thus encouraging them to go to preferred areas, and by propaganda and censorship it could discourage them from going to blacklisted areas.[29]

Some Colonial Office officials believed that

'the intention of the Bill is to discourage emigration, and to keep it under proper control . . . emigration, especially of the agricultural population, had been greatly overdone by the outbreak of war . . . the war had depleted and continues to deplete most alarmingly the manpower of the country . . . in so far as can be foreseen it will be urgently important to retain in this country – partly for industrial purposes but chiefly with a view to the conservation of the race – all men of the migrant (which is much the same as the military) age; in these circumstances it will almost certainly be necessary to discourage emigration, and to check emigration propaganda, and the Dominions must be invited to accept and co-operate in a policy of this kind'.[30]

However, the Office did not discuss the Bill with the Dominions. It had hoped to get the Bill through second reading before the 1918 Imperial War Cabinet and Conference. Thus the draft bill went to the UK War Cabinet on 11 April 1918, which approved it on 10 May. Shortly thereafter it was introduced in the House of Commons, and was being actively debated while the Imperial War Cabinet was meeting.

This was a most unfortunate sequence of events. The Dominions were annoyed to find that their representatives were expected to serve on a central control body which would have executive authority in the UK. They were furious to find that their own propaganda was to be screened. And they believed, in spite of Long's disclaimers, that the Bill was designed to restrict emigration, not merely influence its destination. In this they were certainly correct; though the Bill itself implied no particular policy, its progenitors intended that it should be so used.

The Emigration Bill envisaged permanent regulations for the passage brokers and agents. It gave permanent powers – the authority could 'blacklist' whatever non-Empire areas it liked, and could require passage brokers to ensure that would-be migrants knew of the blacklisting.[31] It could 'assist' migration to the preferred areas. W. A. S. Hewins, the

Colonial Under-Secretary, tried to convince the Dominion prime ministers that the envisaged censorship of propaganda material would produce the desired effect – a preference for Imperial territories. But he was obliged to admit that the Bill would allow the Authority to assist migration financially – even though he pointed out that any large outlay would certainly need parliamentary approval.[32] The politicians and the Colonial Office officials had wanted to make sure that the Authority would definitely have such power. They seem to have expected that the Authority would not have to use it, and would not want to use it – because it would resolve not to encourage postwar emigration, but to discourage it – even when migrants were headed for the Dominions. Long, Hewins, and the Office were prepared to go back to Parliament for *money* – if necessary. But they did not want to go back for *powers*.

Of course the Authority was also to be charged with some powers which, though permanent in form, would be transitory in fact. It was to prepare and issue material on the opportunities for land settlement in the overseas Empire, and to inform ex-servicemen of the arrangements therein. The Tennyson Committee had urged that such functions be performed. Though others had suggested that there should be one body to deal with ex-servicemen and another for emigration in general, the Colonial Office strongly favoured a single Authority, and constructed the Emigration Bill accordingly.

The Bill had a difficult time in the House, and though it passed Second Reading, was referred to Grand Committee (Standing Committee B). In this committee there was a free vote, and Government whips could not be used. Further, the committee contained few Government supporters – partly because so many of its members were absent or on war service. Hence the Bill did not move rapidly through committee. And because the committee met so infrequently, it would in any event have dealt slowly with the Bill.[33] Both in the House and in the committee, the Bill received strong criticism from the ship-owners' lobby. Though they did not object in principle, they made numerous criticisms in detail. The Office was obliged to confer with them, and to accept several of their amendments.[34] These difficulties could presumably have been avoided if anybody had thought to consult them before introducing the Bill. The ship-owners criticised the treatment of non-British migrants, and feared that the Bill's operation would divert migrant traffic from British to foreign holds.

II. EX-SERVICEMEN, UNEMPLOYMENT, AND THE OVERSEAS SETTLEMENT COMMITTEE, 1918–1920

By November 1918, the Colonial Office was taking counsel with respect to parliamentary procedure.[35] The war had ended, and, Long thought, some sort of emigration agency was now badly needed, both for policy-making and for administration. On 14 November, he established a three-man interdepartmental committee to prepare the migration information which the demobilised would demand.[36] And as soon as the unexpected parliamentary dissolution put the quietus to the Emigration Bill, he established a non-statutory emigration committee. Containing a ship-owner, a lady, an independent member, and departmental representatives from the Colonial Office, Local Government Board, Ministry of Labour, War Office, and Board of Trade, the body was to be transitional only.[37] The vice-chairman and administrative officer was to be T. C. Macnaghten, who had worked for six years in the Colonial Office on migration questions. The committee was to keep women and ex-servicemen informed about migration opportunities, to consider whether the draft Emigration Bill needed revision, to make preliminary arrangements for the eventual regulation of passage brokers, and agents, and to consider whether HMG should assist ex-servicemen, or others, to emigrate.[38] As some committee members proved uncertain about their role with respect to policy, in December Long specifically asked them to give him, by the end of January 1919, their views on two topics: what should the government's emigration policy be, and should anyone furnish information on emigration to foreign countries?[39] Thus the committee was given all those functions of the Central Emigration Authority which could be performed without statute. After some initial terminological confusion, in April 1919 it became the Overseas Settlement Committee. And as the Emigration Bill was never re-introduced, these *ad hoc* arrangements became permanent, launching the Overseas Settlement Committee on a long career of administration – and of lobbying.

In the Khaki Election of 1918, W. A. S. Hewins lost his seat, and with it his Colonial Under-Secretaryship. When Lloyd George reconstructed his government, he gave the Colonial Office to Lord Milner, who insisted that Leo Amery serve with him as under-secretary. The documents are insufficiently detailed to show exactly how much difference the change of government had made to the Emigration Committee. Under Hewins's chairmanship it began on 10 December to sit every week. Hewins presided over four sessions, in which remarkably little happened. Emigration policy was discussed, and a subcommittee was set up to deal with Long's request of 18 December. It was decided to take action to facilitate female emigration and to supply the Dominions with labour via the UK Labour Exchanges. These achievements do not look dramatic. But it would be easy to find later months in which the committee achieved no more under Leo Amery's chairmanship. And to some extent these early meetings laid foundations for the later sessions over which Amery presided. The first of these was on 14 January 1919. Thereafter the weekly session devoted an almost obsessive attention to the problems of female emigration. The committee decided to organise and subsidise the societies for encouragement of female emigration. It sent emissaries to Canada, Australia and New Zealand – all in aid of female emigration. Part of the problem was thought to be the displacement of women war workers from field and factory. Thus the missions were in part demographic, and in part concerned with demobilisation problems. This joint concern led to odd emphases. Were there openings for female homesteaders in Canada? What of chauffeuses?[40] The committee received the subcommittee report and prepared a statement of emigration policy. The labour-exchange network was developed; a labour department representative visited Canada and reported that there would hereafter be cross-listing of vacancies. Nobody asked how any such system could possibly function with sufficient speed to be of any use to anyone – even if the Antipodes were not to take part. Awkward questions *were* sometimes asked, of course. When, on 25 February 1919, the committee considered a Western Australian group-settlement scheme, several members asked whether that State could possibly absorb 1,000 families per month. Amery responded that there would be no difficulty – just consider what happened in South Africa after the Boer War. And he arranged for someone to come and tell the committee about Africa; its members might lack his own detailed knowledge. It is not clear how the other members reacted.

Nevertheless, one does have the impression that the committee gradually came to be dominated by Amery's personality. Though meetings were regular, attendance was not, and the gathering was often small indeed. Frequently the sessions must have been dialogues between Amery and Macnaghten, with occasional comments by other and more irregular attenders.

On the other hand, the committee's stance changed in the course of 1919, and one suspects that Amery too may have changed – perhaps in response to developments in the committee itself. The committee's first policy proposals were very modest indeed. Though it hoped that the Government would finance the emigration of women and children, it was not prepared to recommend state aid to emigration in general.[41] The aided ex-servicemen were supposed to settle on the land, or to have a guarantee of non-agricultural work. In recommending free passages for ex-servicemen, ex-servicewomen and their dependents, it was concerned with fairness, not with the economic situation: some servicemen would want to emigrate in any event, and it was not fair to require them to deplete their savings merely because they preferred to live in the Dominions, whom the committee had not consulted. Even then, the committee was not unanimous in favouring the policy: the Labour Ministry representative feared a labour-shortage, and acquiesced in the policy-statement only when Amery promised to have a chat with his Minister.[42]

These recommendations went to the Cabinet on 18 February 1919. On 31 March, the Cabinet decided to accept the recommendations with respect to free passage – but it did nothing about female and child migration.[43] On 8 April, Amery announced the policy in the House – explaining carefully that only those whom the Dominions would accept would be sent.[44]

In recommending this policy, the committee was flying blind, and so was the Cabinet. No one knew how many people might want to go, or how far. And travel costs were uncertain too. When asked in July to estimate the probable outlays during 1919, the committee guessed it would need not less than £5,000 and not more than £25,000.[45] But by October it was talking of £52,000 for the fiscal year 1919–20 – and £900,000 for 1920–21.[46] By then the committee was receiving 400 applications a week. And it had, rather unexpectedly, received a private benefaction as well. A National Relief Fund had been raised to help people whom the war had hurt. In March Macnaghten asked it for a grant in aid of female migration. The Government had done nothing about the committee's proposal, and yet the committee was already morally and financially committed to help the voluntary female emigration societies. In late August, the Fund made a grant of £250,000, and promised another £250,000 if needed, for the emigration of persons who had suffered in the war but who did not qualify under the existing ex-service scheme.[47]

Thus by the end of 1919 the committee was already emigrating civilians, though it was using private funds to do so. And it had begun to think again about the larger question: should the UK aid emigration in general? In July, we find the committee agreeing that 'a scheme for general settlement was considered very desirable, and such a scheme could be carried out on a contributory basis'. That is, Britain and the Dominions should share the expenses.[48]

Other bodies were thinking along similar lines. While

hopefully waiting and working for the introduction of a revised Emigration Bill, Milner and Amery had constituted the consultative committee for which the Bill provided. Starting on 5 March 1919, they met regularly with high commissioners, agents general, and other Dominion representatives, to discuss migration problems and planning. Twelve meetings were held in 1919. Several were devoted to a discussion of the new draft Emigration Bill, now retitled the Empire Settlement Bill. But others were given over to more general discussions of policy. Australian representatives pointed out that they could accept large numbers of British servicemen only if the UK would lend them the money for railway development. Canadian representatives made pessimistic noises about their Dominion's absorptive capacity. And on 7 August, the Agent General of New South Wales proposed that the UK should contribute to a joint shared-passage scheme. The Canadians were dubious, remarking that they could get enough settlers without passage-assistance. But the Agent General insisted that, for the Antipodes, only such assistance would prevent an American takeover of the territories themselves. His government had instructed him to make a definite offer: it would share in the cost of 'any Dominion agreement that might be devised to assist overseas settlement generally once the ex-servicemen had been shifted and settled. Amery was sceptical; he 'saw difficulties about anything in the nature of a joint contribution'.[49] Later he saw things differently.

It is tempting to suspect that we see here the development of detailed emigration devices and machinery which made increasingly unnecessary the Central Emigration Authority or the Emigration Bill. In the first half of 1919, this bill was still a live issue. Though opposed by the Prime Minister, Milner and Amery continued to urge its introduction; the departmental and Dominion representatives continued to worry at the draft.[50] But almost everything had happened without statute. The Central Administrative Body and the Consultative Committee were alive, well, and floating financially on the Colonial Office vote. Emigration was being assisted financially and jointly planned with the

Dominions. Impending American law would automatically discourage migration to the USA. Admittedly, passage brokers were still insufficiently controlled. And promotional literature was still uncensored. But the months of discussion may have led the politicians and the civil servants to question the workability of these arrangements. And the success of the new informal co-operation must have led them to wonder whether they needed the increasingly military-looking apparatus of the Emigration Bill. Even the power to spend, which the Bill had always included, proved not to require a new Act.

Thus the development of policies had gone along with the creation of policy instruments, though in a very different mould than the one expected. But there was still no agreement about a long-term strategy. In recommending that the United Kingdom should not aid Empire settlement *in general*, the Government Emigration Committee did not mean that it should *never* do so. And within the Cabinet there were many views, and great confusion, during early 1919. The disputes were made manifest in a chaotic conference on unemployment and the state of trade, which met in February 1919.

At this conference, Sir Auckland Geddes, the Minister of Reconstruction, pointed to four competing policies, all in circulation at once: the gold standard, trade revival, social welfare in the form of a housing programme, and colonial development – the 'imperial policy'. He argued that because the social policy would tie up so much capital, there absolutely must be large emigration. But Austen Chamberlain, then Chancellor of the Exchequer, observed that capital was painfully scarce for all that had to be done both at home and in the Empire. Lloyd George, defending the housing projects, diverted discussion to the financing of public works, asking with great pertinence why it was so easy to raise great sums for war purposes and so hard to raise small sums for peacetime projects. But Geddes dragged the discussion back to 'fundamentals': the Government must decide what is the appropriate size of the social welfare programme, and it must decide what to do about emigration and the gold standard. Both Geddes and Bonar Law argued against a return to gold, and Chamberlain agreed, while admitting that it was increasingly hard to maintain a respectable exchange rate. As for emigration, the Cabinet differed with respect to the employment prospects. It had rediscovered the point which had bedevilled planning ever since the Tennyson Report of 1917 – the impossibility of knowing what the state of trade would be. Sir Albert Stanley, the President of the Board of Trade, foresaw a few months of transitional unemployment. But Sir Eric Geddes thought this period would last from one to two years. Yet the Ministers of Munitions saw no unemployment problem, while Addison of Local Government, Churchill of the Amiralty, and the Postmaster General all feared a labour shortage, and wished to discourage emigration. In such a babel, it is no wonder that Amery was unsuccessful in arguing on a longer-term basis – the increasingly uncompetitive British economy, and the dependence both of social reform and of prosperity on Empire development. When he urged the Ministers to 'let me introduce a Bill for emigration control and get the machinery started', the Prime Minister rejected the idea all too clearly: 'It is a dangerous thing to put forward . . . it is a Bill I am against.'[51]

At this time Amery himself was not emphasising any relation between emigration and unemployment. Later in February, when urging the Emigration Bill upon the War Cabinet, he developed the same themes as at the unemployment conference. He wrote:

'The development of the population and wealth of the whole British Empire is the key to the problem of post-war reconstruction. The heavy burden of war debt upon every part of the Empire makes this development an immediate and urgent necessity. The growth of population in the Dominions, in so far as it adds directly to their strength and prosperity, and consequently to the strength and prosperity of the whole, and in so far as it increases the number of our own best customers, and purveyors of essential foodstuffs and raw materials, is so obviously desirable that it is assumed throughout this memorandum that emigration should, so far as possible, be *directed* to countries within the confines of the British Empire. On the other hand . . . it is essential that UK manpower and taxable capacity should not be weakened in the process of Imperial development.'[52]

Thus emigration should not be 'excessive', and it should be sexually balanced. Hence, though for the time being there was no need for general financial stimulation there was a case for aiding children and women who wished to emigrate.

Amery never converted Lloyd George and his Cabinet to this view of Imperial destiny. But as we shall see, he did eventually obtain a statute – the Empire Settlement Act – which gave him all he needed to concretise his vision. In a later chapter we examine the vision itself for internal consistency and relevance. Here we must continue to trace the process by which the vision was made to seem attainable.

Throughout 1920 the ideas of the Emigration Bill remained alive. Now titled the Empire Settlement Bill, it was considered by the Overseas Settlement Committee on 30 March, in a draft form nearly identical to the Bill of 1918–19.[53] Early in June, Milner asked the Cabinet to sanction the Bill's early introduction, pointing out that the Overseas Settlement Committee could not supervise passage brokers, agents, or migration propaganda, because it had no statutory powers.[54] Milner renewed his request later in July. The Cabinet now agreed that the bill should be introduced 'forthwith' – after the Parliamentary recess – once the Colonial Office and the Treasury had settled 'certain points of detail'.[55] In August these negotiations began, and they were still incomplete early in October. Late in November, the Colonial Office and the Treasury were still at work on the financial resolution and the financial white paper which would support the Bill in the House. On 18 November, an official minuted, 'I gather . . . that it is hoped to get forward with the Bill this session'. But on 6 December Amery wrote, 'no chance of Bill being introduced this session'.[56] For a few more weeks the Offices continued to work upon the Bill. But their labours were without issue.

Meanwhile, new winds were blowing. Most of them came from the Overseas Settlement Committee. For 1920–21 the Committee had requested Treasury funds to subsidise the emigration of women and children. Unsuccessful in this request, it had at least obtained a grant for a society which was to encourage the Empire settlement of females.[57] In its published report, it had requested a conference with Dominion representatives.[58] For the time being the question of such a conference was held over until the dates of the next Imperial Cabinet could be fixed.[59] But the idea was now in circulation. And in November the Committee returned to it in a Cabinet memorandum.[60]

Other pressures were created by the imperatives of the free-passage scheme. Originally requested for three years, this scheme was in fact authorised for a shorter period. At the end of 1920 it was to cease. But there had been insufficient shipping to export as many ex-service personnel as might want to go. The OSO was so understaffed that it could not process applications promptly. Therefore, it had not advertised the scheme widely, and many ex-servicemen did not know it existed. Further, the Dominions were laggard in approving applications, and showed a depressing tendency to admit only land workers and domestic servants. On 15 October therefore, Lord Milner asked the Cabinet to approve a one-year extension. In commending this extension, he sounded a note which would recur in the next two years: 'It might be borne in mind . . . that all money expended on the overseas settlement of suitable settlers . . . relieves to that extent the housing problem here and also tends to relieve in still greater proportion the problem of unemployment.'[61] On 11 November 1920, the Cabinet agreed.[62] Transmitting this verdict to the Australasian Governments on November 29, Milner sounded another note of the future. After saying that further renewals were improbable, he noted:

'I desire to take this opportunity of explaining that the adoption in future in any scheme of a similar nature must, in my opinion, be contingent upon the participation of the Overseas Governments to a greater degree than heretofore in the policy which the grant of free passages represents . . . any increase in expenditure in connection with overseas settlement could only be defended if it were shown to be required in connection with an Imperial policy of Empire development with which the Overseas Governments were in full sympathy, and in which they were prepared to share . . . the same considerations would apply to the question of extending the scheme to other classes of settlers . . . for whom there is a special demand in the self-governing Dominions.'[63]

At a Colonial Office conference, Amery had already said the same thing to Senator Millen, the Australian Minister of Repatriation.[64]

Why were such statements made? In part the reason was financial. The Exchequer was trying to reduce British Government outlays, and the Treasury strongly resisted any new or expanding programmes. In part it was disappointment: the Australian states were not working hard enough on soldier settlement, and were not treating the British settlers as generously as Whitehall had expected and hoped. But there was more than a little unfairness in the remarks, especially as they went to the Australasian Dominions alone. Both of these Dominions in fact had long assisted migrants, and they continued to do so while the British were assisting ex-servicemen to emigrate. Did the British expect that the Australasians would gradually withdraw such assistance, relying on the UK to finance programmes which were originally and properly a Dominion responsibility? There is nothing in the documents to tell us.

Thus some Dominions had been placed on notice: the UK wanted co-operation in the financing of Empire settlement. At the same time, the British Government was increasingly worried about unemployment. Long past were the disputes of 1919. The Cabinet, responding to memoranda from the Ministers of Health and Labour, had already set up an unemployment committee to consider the problem of the coming winter.[65] And on its terms of reference was migration.

The Unemployment Committee began to discuss migration on 15 October. The Overseas Settlement Committee had made representations to it, favouring settlement to help with the coming winter's troubles.[66] At the meeting, Amery testified about the mechanics of the ex-servicemen's scheme, and presented the requests of the Overseas Settlement Committee – extend the ex-service scheme for a year, and provide £25,000 to £50,000 per month 'in aid of necessitous cases not entitled to free passage'. The OSC had already been assisting such cases out of its National Relief Fund grant, but expected to run through this money by year-end. The Unemployment Committee was not prepared to consider any scheme for really large-scale emigration, because such projects did not seem to fall within its terms of reference. But it did agree to recommend two things: ex-servicemen should get free passages till the end of 1921; and the OSC should be given £50,000 per month for three months, to spend on free passages for other people during the winter of 1920–21.[67] Further, in its second interim report it recommended that the Colonial Office should negotiate with the Dominions and then 'formulate a scheme for assisted emigration on a large scale, for submission to the Cabinet'.

On 6 December, the Cabinet concurred in these recommendations, and the Colonial Office began to prepare the conference.[68] Telegrams went to the Dominions late in December:

'His Majesty's Government are anxious to consult at an early date with the Governments of self-governing Dominions as to the possibility of initiating a large-scale policy of State-aided settlement within the Empire based on mutual co-operation between Governments concerned.

'The objects in view would be to meet exceptional conditions which have arisen from the war, to distribute and use the population of the Empire to the best advantage; to develop cultivation of the land and other natural resources and to ensure that largest possible proportion of population likely to leave UK in near future should be attracted to the Dominions and available to strengthen and build up their national life, and not be diverted to foreign countries.

'His Majesty's Government trust that it may be possible to arrange special conference upon this question early in the new year. . . .'[69]

The telegram said nothing about unemployment. But it would never have been sent if the Cabinet Unemployment Committee had not recommended such a conference and scheme. The telegram itself did not link migration with unemployment. But in speeches Lloyd George had done so – and had been castigated by *The Times*, which pointed out how radical the change of position had been. In 1918 the Government had wanted to discourage emigration; now, it seemed, the idea was to encourage it.

Though I have found no evidence, I cannot believe that the Dominions did not know the background from which the telegram proceeded. This knowledge was indeed assumed by Amery, who made vigorous efforts, in 1921 and later, to reassure the Dominions. Empire settlement, he argued, was not wholly or mostly a relief for unemployment in the short-term; it was part of a long-run strategy of Empire development. This theme is already present in the telegram of 21 December. And Amery certainly meant what he said. For him, as for Milner, Empire settlement had come to form part of a very large and very long-run 'Imperial vision'. But in the Lloyd George governments few shared this vision. And of those who did, many thought the voters would not accept the measures which would make the vision real. Just as the deepening unemployment changed the minds of the Empire Settlement Committee, so it strengthened the hands of the Imperial visionaries in the Lloyd George Cabinet.

In a general way, the Dominions were ready to take advantage of such an initiative. New Zealand had just liberalised its system of nomination, and raised the number of persons it was prepared to admit. Australia had arranged for a co-ordination of immigration arrangements, by which the Commonwealth Government would recruit in London on behalf of the States. Late in 1920, Senator Millen was in London to arrange for a much-expanded immigration effort, which would, it was hoped, bring 100,000 immigrants per year. Even Canada's Prime Minister was making hopeful noises. Though Sir Robert Borden wished quality rather than quantity, he also hoped to attract persons whose ideas of government were consistent with Canadian – that is, British – ideas.[70] Admittedly, South Africa was, as usual, not interested in immigration. Further, the Dominions were having some difficulty in absorbing their own soldier-settlers, and, like the UK, were suffering the delayed postwar recession. They seemed unlikely to take many non-agricultural workers. Everything the Overseas Settlement Committee had learned confirmed its members' belief that the proper migrants would be land workers, female domestics, and children. However, it must have seemed perfectly reasonable to design a long-run scheme which would allow for these preferences, and for the Dominions' eagerness or reluctance, as well as for their different circumstances. It was some such scheme that the Colonial Office began to prepare in December 1920 and January 1921, as it awaited the Dominions' response.

In his memoirs Hewins is reticent about the period of his under-secretaryship.[71] At first sight it is hard to see how he could possibly have approved the events of 1916–20 – or the very different Empire Settlement Act which followed two years later. But in fact a good deal had been achieved by the end of 1920, and mostly along lines which Hewins approved. Admittedly, nobody was regulating passage brokers or censoring migration propaganda. No Emigration Act had been passed, and no Central Emigration Authority had been created. And the emerging commitment was to stimulation, not restriction. But a body did exist to encourage the right kind of migration. Britain and the Dominions were already discussing the question of migration planning, and were about to discuss it even more intensively. For the first time in many decades, the United Kingdom Government was spending money to assist migrants – not merely ex-servicemen, and not merely the poor law children whom the Guardians had been exporting for generations, but also ordinary citizens who wished to leave Britain. Most important, perhaps, migration policy was now seen as part of overall economic policy. Before 1914, the British Government took no cognizance of its citizens' departures. Passage brokers and Empire governments had been free to propagandise; the size and composition of populations had not been a matter for Government concern in the British Isles, and nothing had been done to manage the size of the labour force either in Britain or in the Empire. By the end of 1920 all this had changed. The Overseas Settlement Committee existed as a permanent policy-making body. Government was worried about the correct management of migration. Interested persons were installed in the Colonial Office and in the Cabinet. And whatever might be done about financial aid or the details of intra-Imperial co-operation, it was inconceivable that things could revert to the prewar situation of unconcern. By the end of 1920, migration was definitely – and permanently – on the Imperial agenda.

III. IMPERIAL CONVERSATIONS, 1921

In December 1920 there was great friction between the Colonial Office and the Treasury with respect to the Empire Settlement project. Austen Chamberlain, the Chancellor of the Exchequer, believed that Milner and Amery had exceeded Cabinet authority by cabling unduly specific and forthcoming proposals to the Dominions. To Chamberlain, the most important thing was to get a Dominion contribution to whatever emigration scheme might come forth. He envisaged British contributions towards passage and landing money, outfit, and such things; initially he had no intention of subsidising land settlement or general development in the Dominions. When he promised £2 million a year for Empire settlement, he tried to explain to Amery that this was not for land or general development, but for passage money and initial allowance. Further, he thought of a three- to five-year programme – nothing more, and certainly nothing permanent.[72]

If Amery ever understood Chamberlain's views, he ignored them when the conference met late in January 1921. In offering to spend £2 million, he reserved £1 million for passage assistance, and suggested that the other £1 million could be spent on advances to settlers – a most dubious interpretation of Chamberlain's 'initial allowance'. A Treasury official expostulated that Amery had been acting in good faith. It was doubtful if the Empire could spend as much as £2 million on passage assistance, and half of this would come from the Dominions; hence it seemed reasonable to offer £1 million for other devices. Chamberlain reluctantly assented. But he did insist that the proceedings of the conference should be confidential. He vetoed Milner's and Amery's plans for wide publicity. He insisted that final decisions should be left for the Cabinet, and for the Imperial Conference which was to meet in the summer of 1921. And he emphasised that any plans were contingent on the UK's own financial position; there could be no question of a 'pledge' to the Dominions, whose representatives, in any event, had not seemed terribly interested or terribly well-prepared. Only Australia had briefed its representative, or prepared any concrete suggestion. And the Australian idea – Senator Millen's interest-sharing plan – was anathema to the Chancellor.[73]

Amery's settlement conference met from 20 January to 4 February.[74] It must have been rather an odd affair. There was no South African representative. Only Australia had troubled to send a senior representative, or to prepare any definite proposal. From Austen Chamberlain's viewpoint, the conference was meant chiefly to elicit a pledge of Dominion co-operation and financial contribution. With this consideration foremost in their minds, Treasury officials watched the proceedings closely. But Amery had a much more grandiose vision. On his own initiative, he transformed Chamberlain's £2 million into a specific proposal – £1 million for land settlement, and £1 million for assisted passages. Already he seems to have become enamoured of Australia's broad acres, and his officials were already negotiating with Western Australia for some scheme of British settlement. The conference decided that the governments should base their plans upon land settlement.

Admittedly, Amery's own settlement proposals were

limited, and were obviously accommodated to Chamberlain's wishes: settlement schemes as such were not to be financed, but the UK might make 'landing and kit allowances' to emigrants. Hence Amery's proposal for £300 advances to the settlers themselves. In these and in the passage assistance the Dominions would share on an equal basis. The conferees welcomed the 'British offer', and agreed to refer the question to the Imperial Conference which would meet later in 1921.[75] The result distressed Chamberlain, who had acquiesced in Amery's £300 advances only reluctantly, and only after Amery had already proposed them to the Dominions. The Chancellor was also annoyed about the Millen proposal. The Australian representative had suggested that Britain should pay part of the interest on a £20 million development loan which Australia would raise to finance land settlement.

'Senator Millen's Scheme' seems to have originated at the Australian Premiers' Conference of January 1919. These conferences have been frequent in Australia for many years. They are used partly to co-ordinate Commonwealth and State policies. In January 1919, the Conference was largely concerned with soldier settlement, a subject first raised at the Premiers' Conference of February 1916. Among the Commonwealth delegates in 1919, as in 1916, was Senator Millen, who was Minister of Repatriation. The Conference was considering ways by which the Commonwealth Government would share the risks arising from soldier settlement. It had long since been agreed – since 1916, in fact – that the Commonwealth Government would lend money to the States, which would re-lend it to ex-servicemen who wished to settle on the land. The States were also to undertake whatever planning and development the settlement might require. States and Commonwealth would jointly absorb some of the interest during the first few years. By 1919 these financial arrangements had broken down.[76] Further, it was clear that there were risks in soldier settlement. Some soldiers would default, and others would not do well. A subcommittee of the conference had recommended that the Commonwealth share in this risk by absorbing one percentage point of the interest costs. It might borrow at $4\frac{1}{2}$ per cent and re-lend to the States at $3\frac{1}{2}$ per cent. But the full conference decided that political pressures would force the States to pass on any such concession by charging the settlers lower interest rates. After several alternatives had been canvassed, Mr Theodore, the Queensland Treasurer, proposed that the Commonwealth should simply pay all the interest for the first five years – the period of waiting for the fructification of investment. As this seemed excessive, he next moved that the Commonwealth should pay a subsidy of £27,500 for each £1 million of borrowing for soldier-settlement, this subsidy to be paid for five years only. The conference accepted this proposal, recognising that, as some £40 million was involved, the Commonwealth would have to find £5 million in all. As the borrowing rate was expected to be $5\frac{1}{2}$ per cent, Theodore's proposal amounted to half the interest cost for five years. It was, therefore, identical in form with Millen's later suggestion – except that Theodore's related only to soldier settlement, while Millen's related to settlement in general.[77]

Chamberlain himself vetoed the Millen scheme. Amery was keen to begin immediately upon Western Australian settlement, and he saw no reason to object to Millen's interest-sharing device. But Chamberlain believed that if the UK were to pay interest on any Dominion development loan, the Imperial Parliament would have the right to scrutinise the projects for which the loans were required![78] Whether or not they altogether agreed, Treasury officials were busily quoting this opinion long after Chamberlain had left the Exchequer. As for Western Australia, the Colonial Office and the Overseas Settlement Committee had proposed that the UK should pay a 'training grant' of £200 per settler; what was involved was '200 men of the officer class'. The Treasury, however, pointed out that the relevant funds had already been allocated to business training, and eventually insisted that even Western Australia must wait until after the Imperial Conference.[79]

No one had originally intended that the 1921 Imperial Conference should discuss emigration. When the Colonial

Office began to draft the agenda in December 1920, its officials noted four subjects that demanded attention: renewal of the Japanese alliance, naval policy, common Imperial policy in foreign affairs, and the composition and agenda of a possible Constitutional Conference. They also thought there was some case for discussing the stabilisation of intra-Imperial exchange rates, and the division of German payments for the Allied occupying army. There was no mention of Empire settlement.[80] Proposals went to the Cabinet, via an interdepartmental committee of officials, in much the same form.

In March, the Colonial Office sent the Dominions the results of the February settlement conference. Though the UK Government had yet to fix its policy with respect to the coming Imperial Conference, or to Empire settlement in general, Churchill, the Colonial Secretary, told the Dominion premiers that the matter would be discussed in June. He said, 'I trust that, as the result of the discussions, it may be possible for His Majesty's Government and the Governments of the Dominions concerned to unite in carrying out a carefully considered policy of Empire Settlement.'[81]

Here we see a striking example of a Colonial Office tactic which the other departments increasingly suspected and feared: the marshalling of Dominions' pressure in advance of an Imperial Conference. When the above telegram was sent, the whole question of emigration policy was still uncertain. In the Treasury, Sir Otto Niemeyer and other officials were composing furious memoranda. Emigration was not connected to unemployment; the Colonial Office could not be trusted; Amery was a wild man; the real problem was a credit-contraction; more spending or more guarantees would raise taxes or worsen British credit, thus discouraging industry and increasing unemployment.[82]

Churchill and Amery, however, were equally vigorous. In May, Churchill urged his Cabinet colleagues to allow the coming conference to consider and establish a definite co-operative emigration policy. He supported Amery's insistence that the proceedings of the February conference should form the basis for the coming discussions. Amery, in his turn, urged the importance of settlement on the land, and UK assistance therefore, lest the Dominions 'should reach the limit of their powers to absorb our unemployed or other classes'. Policy, he wrote, should aim at redistribution of Empire population so as 'best . . . to promote development, stability, and defence . . .'.[83]

As Treasury officials were quick to point out, there was no reason to believe that 'redistribution' would raise employment or welfare anywhere in the British Empire. Why should it be assumed that the population was not already distributed in a wealth-maximising way? Would not well-informed white workers move to their positions of best net advantage? Had they not done so in the decades before the war? At no time – either then or later – did Amery offer any reasoned refutation of the Treasury view – which was the orthodox *laissez-faire* position. His approach was intuitive. There were 'too many' people in Britain, and 'too few' white people in the Dominions. 'Obviously' it made sense to take families from Britain's 'overcrowded' cities and settle them on the Dominions' 'rich, empty acres'.

We cannot tell whether the Cabinet found these thoughts persuasive. Only on 16 June did they consider the matter, authorising Amery to proceed. He could enter into negotiations with the Dominions, 'on the understanding that caution should be exercised in regard to any immediate expenditure, and there should be no Supplementary Estimate or fresh vote during the present financial year'.[84]

The Imperial Conference did discuss emigration, but not at any great length. On 28 June, its committee on Empire Settlement met for the first time. Churchill and Amery proposed that there should first be a general discussion; a subcommittee could then go into details. For Canada, Prime Minister Meighen welcomed the idea of assisted passages, and also land settlement. But he spoke nervously of the existing Canadian unemployment problem, and of the need for careful selection. J. C. Smuts drew attention to 'the particular character of the problem in South Africa'. For Australia, however, Prime Minister Hughes was ebullient: there was unlimited need for fresh settlers in Australia –

so long as they were properly selected, and if they settled on the land. Meighen also said, rather pointedly, that the UK should pass a statute which would indicate its actual proposals. This, he thought, would incite the Dominions. Churchill ended on a suitable imperial note: 'overseas settlement should be regarded not as a means of remedying unemployment but solely as a means of building even stronger nations in the Dominions overseas'.[85]

Amery then conferred individually with the Dominion leaders. What could each country do, if the UK should legislate upon the lines of the February meeting?

Meighen was uncertain. He would need parliamentary approval before joining a passage-assistance scheme. Canada had never subsidised her settlers, and the issue might be contentious. He would also need new legislation before he could accept settlers who were not servicemen. He thought he might take 1,000 to 2,000 ex-service settlers, however. He did not think he could spend more than £300,000 per year on passage-assistance. Hughes explained that Australia could take part only if she could raise the needed loan funds in London. As to numbers, he was not much more optimistic than Meighen. He did not need new legislation, but on the basis of the February proposals he could settle no more than 1,000 men on the land each year. For passage assistance, he thought he could contribute £200,000 to £300,000 per year. Prime Minister Massey, of New Zealand, foresaw £80,000 to £100,000 on passage assistance, and from 500 to 1,000 men settled annually upon the land. Col. Mentz, the South African representative, explained that South Africa could not join any passage agreement, and that her land settlement legislation was already generous. She might, however, co-operate on other things – perhaps the £300 loan, or the cost of agricultural training.[86]

After a certain amount of formless talk, the full conference approved the recommendations of the February meetings, and commended them to the Imperial Government.[87] Nevertheless, the results had not been really favourable. South Africa would clearly not take part. Australia would do something only if credit were provided on suitable terms.

New Zealand, in spite of her recent liberalisation of migration controls, was not exactly forthcoming. And Canada was distressed about her urban unemployment. All were agreed that the Imperial Government was proposing to be generous – a fact which must have surprised the Dominion leaders. And all were agreed that land settlement must be at the centre of any workable emigration policy. But the conferees had in fact produced no policy. No Dominion had made a concrete suggestion. And on the basis of the February proposals they would settle only 1,600 to 2,300 men per year!

IV. WHITEHALL ARGUMENTS, 1921–1922

After the summer conference, the Treasury officials saw a storm cloud, but there was reason to think that the rains might pass over. Admittedly, the conference had endorsed a settlement plan. But only Australia seemed really interested. Perhaps the whole thing would go away. They were still reluctant to countenance any contribution to interest charges, or to land development. As Upcott wrote in the late spring: 'The danger is that the British Exchequer, once embarked upon a policy of promoting emigration, may be pressed, especially by Australia, to find the capital required for large programmes of this kind.'[88] They were also, in general, reluctant to spend. And there was hope that the budgetary squeeze would kill the whole idea – if not permanently, at least for two or three years. In August, the new Chancellor, Sir Robert Horne, minuted: 'Let nothing be done or said until the Report of the Geddes Committee.'[89] For the rest of the year, Treasury officials quoted this instruction to one another, and to the overseas settlement zealots.

The Overseas Settlement Office, however, had reached a different conclusion. It was not enough, they thought, to offer an advance of £300 to each man who might settle upon the land. The February proposals were not good enough, if they elicited no better response than that of July. The Office urged the Government to override the Treasury's objections. T. C. Macnaghten was unkind enough to remind other officials that, since the Government was prepared to guarantee much larger sums under the new Trade Facilities legislation, it should reject Austen Chamberlain's refusal of an interest contribution, and approve the basis of Senator Millen's scheme. The outlay would be small, and the settlement and unemployment impact would be large. Amery agreed. But as Sir Edward Harding sadly minuted, though the Government had agreed to the proposals of the 1921 conference, 'so far they have not formulated any further settlement policy'.[90]

The Overseas Settlement Office continued its pressure by a most effective route: it requested a great deal of money for the 1922–23 fiscal year. It was, at this time, being carried on the Colonial Office vote; its requests were therefore examined in that Office, before passing to the Treasury.

The Office wanted £750,000 to continue the existing free passage scheme for ex-servicemen and others. It also asked £1 million for intra-Imperial co-operation along the lines of Cmd. 1474, and £200,000 for sharing interest upon Dominion development loans.

Edward Harding's comments were caustic. He pointed out that as yet the Dominions had made no definite proposals with which the UK could co-operate. How then could one million pounds be spent in one fiscal year? And why was the committee reviving the proposal for interest-sharing when it knew the Treasury would reject it? The committee, he thought, accepted Senator Millen's statement that Australia could borrow no more. But this was not true, as she had raised £13 million in London within the preceding five months. If Australia was really overburdened with debt, should the UK connive at a further increase, for which Australia would be solely responsible after five years? Furthermore, such schemes would be a source of political danger, and they were inconsistent with the present constitutional theory on Dominion status. He concluded:

'I confess to very considerable doubt as to the wisdom of this proposal. I think it is admitted that you cannot settle men on the land en masse. If you try to do so, failure is almost certain. That this view is shared by the Commonwealth authorities is clear from the statement of Mr Hughes [at the Imperial Conference] . . . Accordingly, my own feeling is that it would be wise, in sending on the estimate to the Treasury, to say quite definitely that the Secretary of State does not endorse this particular recommendation.'[91]

Accordingly, the Treasury was told: 'Mr Churchill would prefer to reserve any expression of opinion as to the provisions suggested[92] . . . until the general policy of His Majesty's Government had been more precisely defined.'[93]

The Treasury was prepared to provide more funds for the emigration of ex-servicemen. However, in line with Sir Robert Horne's directive, they refused to make any commitment on 'the general policy of State-aided Empire Settlement until the matter had been considered by the Committee on National Expenditure'. Within the Treasury, officials were suggesting that in fact the UK was not commited to do anything; the earlier proposals must have been contingent upon her financial position, which did not now permit any new projects. Hence their vigorous effort to prevent any funding of civil emigration.[94] Macnaghten argued: 'The Treasury are quite wrong in suggesting that the free passage scheme was inaugurated with the sole object of affording assistance to ex-servicemen. . . . Obviously the provision of settlers for the Dominions was the basic reason which prompted the [Overseas Settlement] Committee to advocate this policy.'[95] Perhaps so. But the Treasury was right to point out that at no time had the Cabinet approved any *general* free passage schemes. Civilian migrants had been aided in the winter of 1920–21, but only because the Cabinet had feared temporary unemployment. That decision could not justify continuing and regular outlay without a specific decision – and, probably, a Financial Resolution.

Late in November, Prime Minister Hughes put his oar in once more. In a remarkable telegram, he asked the UK to pay half the interest on a £50 million development loan. His idea was to use the new settlers at first on land clearing, railway construction, and such things: by creating these new jobs he would make the scheme acceptable to Australian labour. As land was cleared and transport completed, the settlers would take up holdings and become farmers.[96]

The Hughes telegram was important because, coming from 'outside', it required an *answer*. But what could be said? On 30 November, the Overseas Settlement Committee considered Hughes's request. It strongly approved, recommending a short Bill which would allocate £4 to £5 million a year to overseas settlement – including the Hughes proposal. Amery, too, was personally in favour. He told Churchill that the idea meant large, quick outlays which would have a prompt impact on British unemployment, both via emigration and via work for the UK's machinery industries. His only reservation was that Britain might not be able to find enough suitable migrants with sufficient speed.[97] But the Geddes Committee had still not reported, and so nothing could be done for the present.

Was the Hughes telegram spontaneous, or did Amery suggest it? There is no documentary evidence which bears on the matter. Mr L. F. Fitzhardinge has found no relevant private correspondence. However, timing and the domestic political situation strongly suggest that the telegram was planned at the Imperial Conference. Amery and Hughes had been friends since 1907. They certainly discussed immigration in 1921. We know that Amery was not above prompting Dominion premiers to make requests which would embarrass the UK Government.

Hughes reached Melbourne from the Conference on 27 September, to encounter a busy Parliamentary session and a Cabinet reconstruction. On 11 November, Sir Joseph Cook resigned to become High Commissioner, requiring a Cabinet-building which was not finished until 21 December. Parliament had risen on 10 December. There is no evidence of any domestic political reason for the dispatch of the telegram – and no reason to infer any such reason. The Parliamentary troubles were largely provoked by the emerging Country Party, for whom a settlement scheme was irrelevant. The most plausible theory is that Hughes came back from London with a draft telegram in his pocket and that he did not get around to sending it until 24 November.[98]

Meanwhile, in London, the Cabinet unemployment committee was intermittently brooding about emigration. Late in September, at its thirty-first session, Churchill told Horne that he wanted to continue 'the scheme of overseas settlement' but the Treasury was reluctant to finance it. The Chancellor said that he favoured the scheme, and agreed to look into the matter without delay. Shortly thereafter, the committee asked the Cabinet to spend an extra £300,000 on overseas settlement – but still in the context of emergency relief.[99] Understanding that the Colonial Office was looking into the problems of a longer-term policy, it at first abstained from any broader recommendation.[100]

Late in September, the Overseas Settlement Committee began to mobilise departmental opinion. Letters went to the Treasury, the Board of Trade, and the Ministries of Labour and Health. They put the committee viewpoint all too clearly.[101] In the past, the committee stated, it had advocated State-aided Empire settlement primarily to increase the production of food, materials, and new wealth in the Empire, and to enlarge the market for British manufactures; it had also hoped that such settlement would ensure the stability and defence of the Empire as a whole Now, however, 'while not advocating State-aided Empire Settlement as an immediate and direct method of relieving abnormal unemployment in the United Kingdom, they would point out that it undoubtedly has a marked effect upon the problem. . . .' As trade might not quickly revive, the problem might continue for 'many years'. Hence, the Committee urged, there should be a UK statute which would put into effect the relevant resolutions of the Prime Ministers' Conference. What did the other departments think?

The Board of Trade was in favour:

'I am directed by the Board of Trade to state that they are in general agreement with the views of the Overseas Settlement Committee as to the desirability of promoting emigration for Imperial purposes of an economic as well as of a political character. They agree, too, that the relations of a policy of State-aided Empire Settlement to the problems of unemployment are now, and will be from time to time, of importance. The Board recognise that the general wellbeing of the Community tends to be raised by emigration from the more congested parts of the Empire to countries overseas, and that increases in the production of food and raw materials within the Empire are essentials to its balanced development. The special conditions prevailing at the present appear to the Board to make the time most suitable from the point of view of the United Kingdom for the resumption and if possible the enlargement of the pre-war current of emigration.'[102]

It would be hard to get more forceful support. But the Ministries of Health and Labour were equally vigorous. The Minister of Labour concurred with the Overseas Settlement Committee. The Minister of Health strongly favoured overseas settlement as a remedy for unemployment and urban congestion, and he wanted 'liberal assistance from public funds . . . and . . . the policy when once begun should be pressed on consistently and continuously, over a period of years'.[103] No stopgap measures for Sir Alfred Mond, the Minister of Health – and chairman of the Cabinet Unemployment Committee.

On 8 December, Mond suggested that Amery should raise the question of overseas settlement at his Unemployment Committee. Amery and the Overseas Settlement Committee did so – with a will. However, Hughes's telegram and the problem of the estimates had jointly created something of a crisis. The Treasury and the Colonial Office had tried unsuccessfully to resolve the immediate troubles through negotiation, but the issues were too large for civil servants to settle on their own. To Sir Robert Horne, the whole matter seemed to raise such large issues of policy that only the Cabinet could settle it. After a conference with Amery, he acted to put the subject of Empire settlement on the Cabinet agenda.[104]

Late in December, the Overseas Settlement Committee made representations to the Cabinet. Its arguments were by now familiar. There was a need for a long-run approach to the unemployment problem, which was 'essentially a problem of the right distribution of population'. The UK had too many industrial workers relative to her agricultural population, while she was overpopulated relative to the Dominions. Britain should export half a million people each year, for a decade. It would be an expensive task, but cheaper than the dole, or relief works. At first, the committee said, it would have trouble spending £2 million a year, but in three or four years it would easily get through £4 or £5 million. However, the emigration must be agricultural: Dominion cities would grow only as rapidly as their agricultural bases, and in any event Dominion city-dwellers would resist the import of competitors. The immediate task was simple – the Cabinet should authorise the Colonial Secretary to go into matters with the Dominions, and to prepare a short bill.[105]

Mond was less specific but equally forceful:

'I submit in the strongest manner that these Australian proposals deserve an immediate answer and that the whole question deserves immediate consideration . . . I am more and more impressed each day with a view that unemployment is a factor with which we shall have to reckon for years rather than months . . . I can see no permanent solution without a vigorous policy of migration . . . I therefore press for immediate Cabinet consideration. . . .'[106]

Amery had already begun to prepare the Bill which the Overseas Settlement Committee wanted. It was as different as possible from the now-dead Emigration Bill. Including no provision for 'control', it simply allowed the UK to spend on migration assistance, up to a limit of £5 million per year, in co-operation with the Dominions. This first draft Bill included specific provision for interest-sharing, and also for loans to settlers themselves, for passage assistance, and for many other minor projects which were dear to the committee's heart.[107] In subsequent redrafts within the OSC, most of these specifications were excised. Transmitting the new draft Bill in mid-February, the Office underlined that the Cabinet would have to approve the interest-sharing provision, and hoped that the Cabinet would also be told of the Hughes request.[108]

On 16 February, the Cabinet was still waiting to hear from the Geddes Committee. Fortunately for the zealots, the committee gave qualified approval to cautious spending on Empire settlement. Thereafter, matters moved swiftly. After deciding that £5 million was too much, the Cabinet referred the general questions to an *ad hoc* committee.[109]

The Treasury by now knew it had lost. But it continued to press for a small programme – no more than had been proposed at the 1921 Imperial Conference, and certainly no more than £2 million per year. The Australian proposal, it urged, must be rejected.[110] Amery and the OSC continued to sound familiar notes – political stability following a large overseas settlement of 'settlers, British by birth and British in spirit'; savings on the dole; creation of new markets and new supplies of primary products.[111] By this point, the publicists of Empire settlement could presumably have written the documents in their sleep.

Before the committee, Amery pressed for a £5 million ceiling, being 'personally . . convinced that Overseas Settlement was the best cure for the industrial situation'. Horne said that he had always favoured Empire settlement 'on the ground that . . . we should promote the security of the Empire, ensure larger markets for British goods, and meet to some extent the serious question of unemployment at home'. He thought the unemployment situation might well be unsatisfactory for many years to come, and if the schemes in contemplation provided an immediate remedy, he thought there was much to be said for entering upon a large and active policy of overseas settlement. The great difficulty, however, was to find the money. That is, he would swallow £2 million, but not £5 million. Since there was no dispute about principle, on 3 April the committee agreed to compromise: it would limit liabilities to £1.5 million in the first year, and £3 million for fourteen succeeding years.[112] Though Horne continued to oppose interest-sharing, the provision seems to have passed unnoticed and almost undiscussed into the final statute. The next day, the Cabinet

Home Affairs Committee agreed that the Empire Settlement Bill should be introduced immediately.[113] And it was so.

The Bill was a simple one.[114] It authorised the Colonial Secretary to make agreements with any public or private organisation in the UK or in the Dominions, for the purpose of assisting emigration to 'any part of His Majesty's Overseas Dominions'. The UK's contribution to any scheme was limited to half of the total expenses, and the Act was to expire in 1937. Treasury consent was to be mandatory; that is, for each proposal the Colonial Secretary would have to seek explicit agreement from Treasury officials. As for permitted proposals, the Act stated that 'an agreed scheme may be either (a) a development or a land settlement scheme; or (b) a scheme for facilitating settlement in or migration to any part of His Majesty's Overseas Dominions by assistance with passages, initial allowances, training, or otherwise.' The UK might contribute 'by way of grant or by way of loan or otherwise'. Interest-sharing was nowhere mentioned, but was certainly covered by the general terms of the Act.

Meanwhile, Prime Minister Hughes had become restive. On 24 March, he cabled plaintively, asking what had happened to his proposal of the preceding November. He was told that nothing could be done until the Empire Settlement Bill had been introduced and passed. But on 3 April, as soon as the Cabinet Committee had agreed on the financial limits, Churchill cabled Hughes that all was more or less well:

'. . . however . . . the amount to be set aside, particularly during financial year 1922–23, is not so large as I had hoped and pressed for, and will not permit co-operation with Australia alone on scale as large as that of your proposal of November 24. It might, on the other hand, allow of a total development as large as that suggested by you if the contribution to the several state schemes were on the basis which, as I understand from him, Sir John Mitchell has agreed with you, namely, 1/3 interest for five years from British Government, 1/3 from Commonwealth.'[115]

Hughes replied that 'the Commonwealth Government is prepared to co-operate with the British Government on the basis of 1/3 interest. . . .'[116] Better one-third of a loaf than none at all.

The Bill passed through the British House with almost no debate. Introducing Second Reading, Amery presented a detailed defence for the measure along the visionary lines which have been described earlier. Edward Wood emphasised the 'importance for every community in the Empire so far as possible to secure that its population should be made up of homogeneous elements'. Only Josiah Wedgwood opposed the measure, regarding it as a frivolous expenditure of public money which was needed elsewhere.[117] The Labour Party was not inclined to oppose; as Wignall explained, though the Labourites thought it would achieve little, they regarded the Bill as a step in the right direction.[118] And so, at long last, the UK was committed to the continuing subsidisation of emigration.

V. COMMENTS ON THE LEGISLATIVE PROCESS

This account is bound to puzzle the economic theorist who specialises in 'welfare economics' and public finance. It should also worry him. Orthodox welfare economics has evolved the idea of a 'social welfare function'. This has nothing to do with welfare in any ordinary sense. It is an analytical device by which the welfare economist is able to handle the problem of public spending. He first postulates an omniscient and disinterested Government – like Plato's philosopher king, or God. This Government coolly considers the costs and benefits of each policy – who will gain, who will lose, and how much the gains and losses will be. It then consults its social welfare function, which is simply an exhaustive statement of the *desirable* pattern of gains and losses. This statement is, of course, arbitrary: God is Calvinist. He chooses policies which, on balance, help the people He wants to help, and hurt the people He wants to hurt. Thus new projects are initiated, old ones are shut down, and continuing programmes are expanded or contracted, by reference to the facts and to the social welfare function. The external world – outside the mind of the Government – is relevant to the decision-making only in one respect: it provides *facts*.

The process we have traced is remote from the 'ideal' decision-making strategy of the welfare economist. Accident and pressure were critical; facts were absent; no one asked who would gain and who would lose; no one measured the cost of the programme against other projects which might cost the same money or achieve the same ends. But the process is also remote from the stereotypes of the decision-making process which vulgar Marxists sometimes present. Neither officials nor politicians were stooges of the capitalist interests. The capitalists, presumably, wanted as large a 'reserve army' as possible; they logically ought to have opposed emigration. We saw that, during the war itself, agricultural and other interests *were* worried about labour supply. But in the later evolution of the policy this concern was ignored. It may also be argued that Amery's strategy of Imperial development and settlement was 'objectively' in the capitalists' interests: it would create more markets and profits. However, the strategy would also serve workers: there would be more jobs at home, and many British subjects would find prosperity and security in the Dominions. So Amery hoped. And to some extent his hopes were justified.

It is true that nobody asked 'the people' or 'the workers' whether they wanted to emigrate. But on the other hand, nobody forced them to go. And experience suggested that they would certainly leave, if allowed, and if helped. Before 1914, Britain had exported several hundred thousand adults every decade. Through the ex-servicemen's scheme, more hundreds of thousands had gone. Neither politicians nor officials were wrong to expect that through subsidisation they could add many thousands of extra migrants to the flow that might in any case be foreseen. And they were genuinely concerned that the migrants should be happy. The minutes of the Overseas Settlement Committee are replete with the metaphors of gardening – 'rooting', 'transplanting', 'preparing the seed-bed', 'avoiding a hothouse environment'. They wanted the migrants to be comfortable and prosperous in the Dominions. After 1922, they tried to ensure that the transitional shocks, at least, would be as small as possible.

The emigration plans were paternalistic. In part they were meant to export the unemployed – though not the unemployables. But they were also humanitarian. Were they economically sensible? At the end of the next chapter we shall try to answer this question. First, we must glance at the evolution of the plans and programmes themselves, once the Empire Settlement Act had been passed.

Chapter 3

THE GROWTH AND DEATH OF EMPIRE SETTLEMENT, 1922–1930

I. MANOEUVRINGS AND DISAPPOINTMENTS, 1922

Having got his Act introduced, Amery proceeded briskly to generate the projects for which it would provide. He cabled personally to Prime Minister Hughes of Australia,[1] and wrote personally to the Canadian Prime Minister in the following terms:

'I do not know, though I understand you have been giving serious consideration to the whole question, whether you are as a matter of fact contemplating an active policy of immigration or of continuing and expanding the machinery of your existing soldier settlement scheme which has worked so well. No doubt if you have any definite schemes in view in which we could co-operate – though of course the amount of money we shall have available in the near future will not be very large – you will let me know. . . .'[2]

Prime Minister King responded encouragingly: co-operation between the two governments should ensure that the Empire Settlement Act would prove mutually profitable; Canada contemplated 'an active policy with respect to agricultural immigrants'; the Minister of Immigration would shortly be in touch with Amery.[3]

Official despatches went to Canada on 9 June, after the Act's passage, and to the Australasian Dominions on 22 July. It was already known that South Africa was not willing to co-operate.

The immediate response was not encouraging. The New Zealand Government reported that it could undertake no land-settlement schemes, though it proposed an assisted-passage agreement to cover 10,000 migrants. During the autumn, the Canadian Government publicly explained its immigration policy, but mentioned the Act only in connection with child migration. By December, Sir J. Masterson Smith was minuting in dismay: 'Canada has for long been an emigrants' rather than an immigrants' country. But it suggests the query whether expenditure on migration to Canada is not merely a means of increasing the population of USA.'[4] Within the Canadian Civil Service – though not in the Department of Immigration – such views were already held. They would grow in strength as politicians and officials scanned the 1921 Census results.

Only Australia showed much interest in Empire settlement. Western Australia and Victoria pressed forward with land-settlement schemes, for whose financing agreements were quickly concluded. The UK joined the Commonwealth Government in assisted-passage agreements. These reduced the fares for migrants who were 'nominated' by Australian residents and approved by State Governments, or 'requisitioned' by State Governments and 'selected' by the Australian migration agents in London. In mid-July, Prime Minister Hughes explained and defended his Government's active immigration policy.[5] London found him hypersensitive on certain constitutional points; he insisted that the States should not negotiate with the UK Government. The Colonial Office officials suspected that he simply wanted to monopolise credit for immigration in the forthcoming election.[6] But they carefully arranged matters to suit him. Even the Treasury, under protest, was induced to surrender its opposition to land-development schemes – the projects with which only Australia was concerned.[7]

Meanwhile, other government departments were pressing hard for a more vigorous export of unemployment. In June, the Minister of Labour circulated a memorandum which claimed the unemployment situation was so severe as to warrant 'a departure from the ordinary emigration policy' of caution and slow development. The country contained 300,000 young, fit, single men who had entered the army before settling down to a career; if not helped to make good, they would drift into degeneration. The Minister asked for a 'frank appeal to the Dominions', and suggested that the Cabinet should instruct the Colonial Secretary to take a more active initiative in formulating proposals. He also asked for authority to 'organize schemes for intensive preliminary training or testing without delay'.[8] Later that month, the interdepartmental unemployment committee told the Cabinet that migration was 'the only remedy' for localised pockets of unemployment.[9] In July, the Minister of Health echoed the worries of his colleague in the Labour Ministry.[10]

The Overseas Settlement Committee favoured 'any action which will accelerate the new policy of State-aided Empire Settlement'. But its members doubted whether anything more could or should be done, now that negotiations were already under way. There was some risk that an 'appeal' to the Dominions would encourage the overseas governments to seek easier financial terms, and to raise 'political and economic difficulties'. Nevertheless, the Cabinet decided to set up a committee on British trade policy and to ask for information on emigration.[11]

Amery used the cabinet trade policy committee to air his views with respect to Empire development. He urged his colleagues to spend lavishly on overseas transport – up to £10 million per year for fifteen years on shipping, an All Red Mail Route to Australia via Ireland and Halifax, airlines, train ferries, Indian and colonial railways, and irrigation. However, he saw no point in any immediate emigration initiatives.[12] On 12 August, the Cabinet was told that 'the committee have discussed the question of emigration and have been informed that various emigration schemes are now being negotiated by the Overseas Settlement Office with Dominion Governments. Until these negotiations are complete, further action by the British Government would be superfluous.'[13]

The trade policy committee lapsed with the Lloyd George Government, which took no new actions on the emigration front during its last weeks. Amery, however, continued his initiatives behind the scenes. In September, he wrote to

Prime Minister King, urging Canada to abandon its opposition to assisted-passage arrangements, and reminding the Canadian Prime Minister of the Australian settlement proposals. Putting the case for group-settlement, he explained the UK contained 'something like a million of fit, healthy, vigorous young men . . . who would make good citizens'.[14]

King does not appear to have answered, and Canada remained annoyingly unhelpful. In mid-1923, Albert Buckley, the Chairman of the Overseas Settlement Committee, explained: 'so far, Canada has shown small disposition to co-operate, and the schemes concluded with her are negligible. New Zealand does not offer much scope for migration'; South Africa and New Zealand were not participating, while 'Australia has shown far the greatest zeal and energy . . . unfortunately the progress made under these schemes is disappointing, but they are still in their infancy'.[15] T. C. Macnaghten explained:

'No Dominion is as yet prepared to co-operate effectively with the United Kingdom in State-aided Empire settlement. Canada, for example, has always got her immigrants for nothing. Her standpoint is that she wants hewers of wood and drawers of water, and a large section of her population prefers the – to our mind – shortsighted policy of introducing all classes of Americans and Europeans to that of introducing Britishers who are not willing to undertake the roughest and most menial work. Australia wants to co-operate but on cheap and therefore – in my view – inadequate lines. New Zealand does very little and South Africa naturally and inevitably stands out.'[16]

By the end of 1922, the committee was hoping for emigration '*at least equal* to the normal increase of population' – anything from 500,000 to 700,000 per year. Most of these would have to settle on the land in the Dominions. Hence the committee wanted to train the young city-dwellers of the UK. But it also wanted some further declaration of government policy – something which would jolt the Dominion governments out of their lassitude. What was needed, its members said, were 'clear and definite understandings . . . essential . . . and at present . . . lacking'. To this end, migration should be a major theme at the next Imperial Economic Conference.[17]

II. THE IMPERIAL ECONOMIC CONFERENCE AND THEREAFTER, 1923–1927

The Conference seems first to have been mooted on 20 November 1922, when Bonar Law asked the Colonial Office to prepare a summoning and agenda telegram within a week. The Office arranged for an interdepartmental committee of officials, whose draft was amended by the Duke of Devonshire, Amery, and Sir Philip Lloyd-Greame. The Prime Minister and Cabinet approved the result without change. It was cabled to the Dominions on 29 November. At Amery's insistence, the telegram placed 'overseas settlement' on the agenda, which it then shared with 'external commercial relations' and 'co-operation in the development of the resources of the British Empire'. It was hoped the conference might meet in April 1923.

The officials' draft conference agenda had not mentioned Empire settlement at all. The Overseas Settlement Committee had fought hard to win its inclusion and emphasis. The Colonial Office officials did not believe that Bonar Law wanted to put overseas settlement 'in the forefront', but of course they acquiesced in Amery's initiative.[18]

Immediately the migration lobby pinned its hopes upon the conference. The Cabinet must be convinced to press the Dominions. There must be 'an earnest heart to heart examination of the problem';[19] 'it will be very desirable . . . to elicit from the Canadian Prime Minister his real attitude and intention of his government, and this no doubt can only be done in private conversation'; Australia has already said privately that she would like to borrow £100 million for development schemes, and 'we should be prepared to meet them as far as we possibly can'.[20]

For some months these hopes might have seemed justified. In February, Bonar Law's Cabinet resolved that 'the main policy of the Government lies in the development of trade and industry in all their branches, and more particularly of Empire Development and Empire Settlement'.[21] But Baldwin, soon after Law's retirement, said Britain could not wait for Emigration and Empire Development to bring about her recovery.[22] And nobody had any new ideas. There was much chatter about the need for training, and for proper reception at the Dominion end. Reading this material, one recalls the gardening obsessions of the British: if only the seedlings were carefully transplanted into a properly prepared hotbed, they would thrive! But of course they should be moved as young as possible – before bad habits had taken hold. In a rather sick way this material is amusing, but it is hard to see how anybody could believe that such measures would do much good. During the summer, the Dominions were told that the UK Government would consider any scheme falling within the aegis of the Empire Settlement Act and its financial limits. There was no suggestion of any new legislation, or any new initiative. Further, the overseas governments were firmly informed, 'the next essential step in promoting Empire settlement on right lines lies with the Dominions,' who must make satisfactory 'arrangements for the reception, distribution, and internal supervision of British settlers . . . with the least possible delay'.[23] A more chilling invitation it would be hard to imagine.

Some British ministers may have believed that their 'financial co-operation' proposals would effectively raise emigration. Certainly this financial device came from the same quarters as the Empire settlement scheme of 1922. As we saw above, in mid-1922 Amery had urged the Cabinet to spend up to £10 million per year on Empire development. From this suggestion, the Board of Trade had gradually elaborated a much more modest proposal, by which the UK would contribute to the interest cost of public utility projects which, in the absence of such contributions, would be undertaken later, or not at all. Early in 1923 the Cabinet approved the idea; later it was placed before the Imperial Economic Conference, whose members accepted it.

By generating employment in the overseas construction trades, the co-operation scheme might have encouraged some overseas governments to 'requisition' more workers. But it is hard to believe that this would have happened to any extent: both in Australia and in Canada, there was already a good deal of city unemployment, especially in the construction trades. Anyway, there is no evidence that anyone expected it to encourage emigration; British ministers wanted it because they thought it would create more jobs in British export industries, especially the capital-goods industries.

Much more relevant is the question of preferential tariffs. Long before Australia's Prime Minister Bruce came to London and demanded men, money and markets, Amery believed that emigration depended upon Tariff Reform. People would go to grow crops in the Empire only if Britain created an artificial market for their products. Hewins, who was in Baldwin's confidence during the summer of 1923, had long held the same view. However, nobody proposed a genuine Tariff Reform in 1923. Australian insistence, and Amery's private correspondence with Dominion leaders, ensured that Imperial preference would be on the agenda. But Bonar Law had pledged himself not to introduce any basic fiscal change. Before the conference, he explained this both to Hughes and to Bruce. His own Government was willing to make some preferential concessions. But the offers were so trivial that they can scarcely have been expected to do much for emigration. Australian dried fruits and wine . . . it is hard to believe that anyone ever took such concessions seriously. Most significant of all, neither before the conference nor at it did anyone propose any preferential concession to Canada. All the deals were to be done with Australia and South Africa. Yet it was Canada whose gates the migration enthusiasts were most eager to open. They had no hopes of South Africa, and Australia was already co-operating. If Baldwin, Amery, and Cunliffe-Lister really hoped that the preferential arrangements of 1923 would do anything much for Empire settlement, they stand convicted of naïvety and foolishness.

In any event, there was no hope of help from Canada. Prime Minister King was eager to seem to welcome British migrants. In spring 1923, he asked his High Commissioner to counter a 'Whispering campaign . . . to take advantage of some appropriate occasion to make a public statement of our desire to receive in as large numbers as may find it possible to come the right class of immigrants from the British Isles'. His concern, however, was to counteract the propaganda of his political opponents, the Canadian Conservatives. Throughout the twenties, King believed that the Canadian and British Conservatives conspired together, presenting immigration proposals simply to embarrass him.[24] He would enter into agreements, primarily to spike his opponents' guns, but he would not meet the British in any serious way.

The Canadian Civil Service supported King's caution. The immigration officials explained that 'it has so far been considered the part of wisdom for the first year to exercise the greatest care in the grant of passage assistance'.[25] Dr O. D. Skelton, the Anglophobe scholar whom King brought to London as his special adviser, was especially critical of the British initiatives. He wrote:

'Immigration on a vast scale, and so rapid as to draw off the pool of unemployment in the United Kingdom, is neither possible nor desirable. At the best of times Canada adds 17,000 farms a year to her existing quota (average ten years). Half of these should come from our farming population. If we get and absorb the other half from abroad (8,000 a year) we shall do very well; in fact, we cannot again do as much. In addition, at least as many farm workers a year, 17,000, could be absorbed. In the past we have brought into this country immigrants by the hundred thousand only to discover at the next census that they had all vanished. We must build solidly in the future, and disregard paper schemes for the transfer of millions from the United Kingdom.'[26]

P. C. Larkin, King's High Commissioner in London, took the same view:

'We in Canada ought to get the cream of them [UK migrants], but personally I am not at all in favour of doing great things towards helping them to go out, for in that way we get a poor class as was shown by the vast majority of those who were brought out years ago largely to Toronto by the Salvation Army.'[27]

At the conference, which met in October and November 1923, the British Government delegation did begin a discussion of Empire settlement. But the hopes of the Overseas Settlement Committee – and of Amery, Cunliffe-Lister, and Hewins – were disappointed. The conference resolved that Britain and the Dominions should spend a little more on the training of emigrants.[28] But it generated no new initiatives. Canada remained suspicious. Australia remained as ebullient as before. Everyone was in favour of Empire settlement. But only Prime Minister Bruce was willing to do much about it. He began negotiations for a really large development loan – a proposal in prospect ever since Senator Millen had offered his 'scheme' in 1921.

The Overseas Settlement Committee had hoped to export 500,000 to 600,000 people per year. In 1923, 199,000 people left, of whom 113,000 went to the Empire. But thereafter, in spite of the conference, and regardless of Britain's efforts, emigration *fell*. Assisted emigration did rise from 36,000 in 1923 to 66,000 in 1926. But this increase was not sufficient to prevent a fall in the total, which slipped to 116,000 in 1926 and to 88,000 in 1929.[29]

The first MacDonald Government endorsed the emigration resolutions of the Imperial Economic Conference. Its members were as eager to export the unemployed as the Conservatives had been. In the House, Sidney Webb explained that the support and encouragement of Empire settlement should not be a Party matter. 'What we feel on our side of the house is a strong objection to any one in any sense being forced to emigrate' – especially by economic necessity.[30] Accordingly, the new Labour Government welcomed Australia's request for more land-settlement schemes. With the concurrence of the Treasury, the Colonial Office offered to pay one half of the interest for five years on a development loan of £20 million. It also offered to give one-third of the interest for a further five years. Australia wanted half of the interest for ten years, but the Treasury thought this unreasonable, and the Cabinet supported the Treasury view.[31]

The Canadians showed signs of interest in child settlement. For many years, the Ottawa Government had dealt with Dr Barnardo's Homes, which placed some of its orphans on Canadian farms. Within Canada's bureaucracy was a supervisor of child migration, who exerted steady pressure for the expansion of such work.[32] Some businessmen did the same.[33] However, in 1924 several Overseas Settlement officials went to Canada with Margaret Bondfield, the Minister of Labour in the MacDonald Government. Because of their observations, it was decided to send Canada no more young children.[34]

During the MacDonald Administration, the Overseas Settlement Office did succeed in negotiating a land-settlement scheme with Canada. This arrangement provided for the planting of 3,000 families on new farms. It was the only substantial farm project which Canada ever undertook under the Empire Settlement Act.[35] It shifted 3,346 families. But by early 1932, only 2,076 were still on their holdings.

These dreary results were not for want of effort on Britain's part. With the Conservative victory of 1924, Amery returned to power, presiding over the Colonial Office, and shortly over the new Dominions Office which was spun out of it. The Overseas Settlement Department was a part of the new Office. Within the Government, Amery continued to urge preferential food duties, as a necessary stimulus to Empire settlement and a sufficient cause of it. Hewins was privately advising Baldwin in identical terms.[36] But Baldwin believed he had pledged himself to impose no new food taxes. And Churchill, now Chancellor, was an emphatic free-trader.

Amery knew that Canada was taking many non-British migrants. If given to reflective thought, he might have noticed that this fact cast a great deal of doubt upon the Hewins–Amery thesis. After all, many of these non-British migrants were settling upon the land – even though their produce received no preference from Britain. In the event, he remained bemused by the Australian rhetoric of men, money, and markets – a flow of words which reflected problems in part imaginary, in part self-induced. But the Cabinet and the electorate denied him the preferential food taxes he thought he needed. Hence he was forced to work within the framework of the Empire Settlement Act. He could hope for little from New Zealand and South Africa. Australia's co-operation he already had. He needed only to convince Prime Minister King.

In 1926, Amery told the Canadian premier:

'You may see a revival of the big pre-war flow of population to Canada helping to fill all those channels of trade and revenue and putting an end to those woeful railway deficits. Numbers attract numbers and it had always seemed to me that if once a big flow could be set moving into Canada, so far from losing heavily by leakage across the American border it would by the activities it created also provoke a new flow inward from across the border. It is just because so few have come in in recent years that so many have gone out – paradoxical though it may seem I cannot help thinking there is some truth in that way of putting it.'[37]

This argument is nonsense. Canadians went to the United States because jobs were plentiful there, and real earnings were higher. North–south movement was easy, cheap, and painless during the 1920s. Given these transfer costs, Canada could retain more labour only if she could raise the aggregate demand for product, the real earnings of her workers, or both. Immigration of itself did nothing to raise either. For Canada, though not for Australia where transfer costs were so much higher, more immigration *was* very likely to encourage emigration. One could imagine development programmes which would discourage the emigration or prevent it; one cannot find any such programmes in the British or Canadian proposals of the later twenties. Indeed it was land settlement which Amery hoped to promote. And this was the worst possible kind for Canada. New farm migrants would almost certainly *lower* the average real earnings in Canada – thus actively encouraging the emigration which the Canadian government disliked. Inevitably, the new settlers would occupy relatively inferior lands; the best acres had already been settled. Hence each new settler family would produce less than the earlier arrivals. Further, the new farmers would be selling foodstuffs in the world market – an arena where price prospects were already uncertain. Their extra output would tend to lower these prices still further. Amery's instincts were wrong, and King's were right.

Of course, King could not refuse to discuss immigration. To do so would not only add fuel to his opponents' fires; it would conflict with his own image of himself as a good Imperialist. However, his own history was bound to make him careful about migration. He was, after all, the deviser of Oriental Exclusion, and the propagator – perhaps the inventor – of the standard-of-living argument as an excuse not just for protection against goods but chiefly for exclusion of migrants. Even more grating must have been the fact that he had been out of office in 1921, when the groundwork for Empire settlement was being laid at the February conference and at the Imperial Conference. Sir George Perley, eminent Conservative, had attended the former conference, and Arthur Meighen, his hated predecessor, still leader of the Canadian Conservative opposition, had attended the latter meeting. Under no circumstances could King have wholeheartedly accepted as disinterested a scheme of such unsavoury Conservative origins.

Another and more purely intellectual argument must have strengthened King's resolve to resist migration schemes. This was the hypothesis, already current in Canada during the later 1920s, that immigration merely led to emigration – at least for Canada. The hypothesis was heard mostly from the Left, who argued that there was an almost precise numerical equivalence between gross emigration and gross immigration – not year by year, of course, but decade by decade. It was tempting and natural to assert, *post hoc ergo propter hoc*, that the immigration had *caused* the emigration, squeezing out the native-born via competition in the job markets and land markets. We have no evidence that the Colonial Office had ever met this line of thought – or that King himself accepted it. But we know he heard it. In the Canadian House, his opponents frequently argued it. And in 1932 his principal civil service adviser, O. D. Skelton, was still putting the argument forceably in a memorandum for R. B. Bennett, King's successor: 'Assisted immigration should almost certainly cease; this applies to both public and organized private assistance whether rendered from the Canadian end or in the country from which the immigrant comes.'[38] The memorandum was able to draw on the evidence of the 1930–31 censuses. These facts buttressed its conclusions strongly. Of the 4.5 million migrations since 1900, 2.6 million had left, while 0.5 million of the natural increase had not been retained. What then is the point of assisted migration? In the long term the policy should be the same as the short-term policy – tight control and no assistance. Before 1932, without recent census returns, the argument would necessarily have been based on earlier censuses, and on deduction. But we have every reason to assume that King knew it, and was influenced by it.

Amery and the Overseas Settlement Department must have known about the 'excess-immigration' argument. There is no sign that they knew what King thought of the Conservative Party – though they might have guessed. However good or bad their intelligence may have been, they were obliged to continue their pressure – even to increase it – in the later 1920s. Neither tariff nor exchange rates could be manipulated. With the commitment to the gold standard went the paralysis of monetary policy. Unemployment was diminishing, but only slowly; and more people were convinced that much of the remainder was structural – confined to the old staple trades of cottons, coal, shipbuilding, iron, steel. Emigration, it seemed, was the only answer. It was no longer simply a question of exporting people so as to create export markets. The task now was to export those whom structural change had made unemployable.

In mid-1927, Churchill and Amery were wrangling about the funds which should be assigned to Empire settlement.

Amery argued that 'the thing has at last taken hold and is quickening . . . if we cannot agree on a figure to put in the estimates I shall have to ask you, or the Cabinet, to decide between us'. He did, however, come to a private agreement with Churchill – though he expected that it would be hard to keep within the £2 million for 1928–29 and the £2.2 million for 1929–30 which the Chancellor would allow him. At the 1926 Imperial Conference, New Zealand had agreed 'in principle' to a land-settlement scheme, which should be ratified and operational in 1928. Also, Britain would have to spend more under the £34 million agreement with Australia.[39]

III. CANADA AND THE INDUSTRIAL TRANSFERENCE BOARD

Later in 1927 Amery toured the Dominions, partly to discuss the working of the Australian agreement and partly to encourage Prime Minister King to take more British migrants. Reporting on Amery's Canadian discussions, the Governor-General wrote from Ottawa:

'I really think the air is much cleared, but the difficulties remain. Here there is the difficulty of winter unemployment and consequent industrial unrest, of which there is a little now, but which might quickly come if we had a lot of non-agriculturalists out here to increase the numbers. What they want to be sure of is to get people who will open up the Prairie lands for agriculture and also people for domestic service . . . they cannot risk letting industrial workers in unless they have an absolute job to come to.'[40]

Meanwhile, Baldwin had appointed the Industrial Transference Board 'to investigate immediately conditions in the most distressed areas and to see how the men can be got into other employment'.[41] On 7 January 1928, its composition was announced. And from its deliberations came a further push towards the export of the unemployed.

In mid-1928, Baldwin's Cabinet was much exercised by the Board's report.[42] The Board members were deeply disturbed to find emigration so small; its members wanted a 'steady increase in migration of all classes' which would 'create more openings here . . . and . . . create extended markets for our own products overseas'. They wanted more land-settlement schemes, more training for emigrants, and a subsidised general third-class passenger rate, which would be available to all without any formalities. In passing they were critical of the elaborate administrative machinery of the Empire settlement authorities. They thought that 'normal' emigration, outside the Act, was the best kind, and the sort which most deserved assistance. They believed that there was a permanent concentrated surplus of upwards of 200,000 men – largely miners. Neither relief works nor 'any spectacular scheme' could absorb them; the Government should adopt a multitude of small dispersing measures. Nevertheless, the Board told the Prime Minister that 'the only plan which has the possibility of giving an immediate chance of self-dependence to large numbers is migration to the overseas Dominions on a greatly increased scale. It is very many years since emigration for large numbers of people has had to be regarded from the standpoint of economic necessity, but we are compelled to draw this inference from the facts before us.'[43]

The Cabinet referred the Board report to an unemployment policy committee, which in turn set up a migration subcommittee. Believing that land in Australasia was too expensive for a really large settlement scheme, and that in Africa the settler must possess too much capital, the members of the subcommittee concentrated upon Canada as a field for emigration – both agricultural and non-agricultural. It had already been decided that Lord Lovat, the Colonial Under-Secretary, would go to Ottawa and discuss migration with Prime Minister King. What should he be authorised to offer?

Amery had already asked the Overseas Settlement Committee to elaborate a plan for the export of coalminers. The Committee reported that the UK could send 21,500 miners per year for an outlay of £28 per head, if it was also willing to provide £3 million in capital funds for land development and £300,000 in repayable advances.[44] Sir L.

Worthington-Evans had a much more visionary idea: an immense corporation should receive a Canadian land grant, import coal miners to clear it, and settle the miners on the land once they had saved enough to make suitable down-payments. He and other committee members were concerned that Canada was running out of virgin lands: if Britain did not act now, there would soon be no place for her migrants to settle.[45]

From these two starting points the migration sub-committee began its discussions. Amery opposed the corporation scheme: 'it would take years for the Corporation to collect an efficient staff'. Lord Lovat, too, 'doubted whether a Corporation could satisfactorily administer a colossal scheme on the lines suggested'. He and Amery thought it would be better if the Canadian provinces, and such existing companies as the Hudson's Bay Company and the Canadian Pacific Railway, could undertake the development work. Hence the subcommittee agreed to make no recommendation with respect to the corporation idea. But it suggested that Lord Lovat be authorised to negotiate with provinces and existing companies.[46]

Though he opposed a grandiose new corporation, Amery still supported the idea of land settlement. Before the sub-committee he argued that Canada would not accept any other proposal, and he feared that the Dominions would stop all emigration if they were asked to take many non-agriculturalists. Hence he continued to urge that emigration should be largely agricultural. He did so in the face of the growing evidence that the Canadian prairie provinces, whose consent would be essential, did not want more settlers.[47]

The Minister of Labour, Sir Arthur Steel-Maitland, was less impressed by the agricultural possibilities. He

'felt some doubt as to whether we can safely assume that large numbers of miners will come forward for overseas settlement if the agricultural qualification is insisted upon; in any event, so long as effort has to be devoted to giving them this qualification, the numbers moved in any one year cannot be considerable and cannot be adequate for our immediate and urgent needs. We ought, therefore, to consider also the question of the emigration of men who wish to seek their future in non-agricultural occupations'.

Hence he wanted to spend more on the subsidising of the general emigrant fare – if necessary, at the expense of the agricultural activities which the Empire Settlement Act emphasised.[48]

Amery repeatedly told his colleagues that the Dominions would not stand for the dumping of Britain's unemployed city-dwellers.[49] But he was not opposed to the emigration of city-dwellers. Indeed, he had already begun to discuss the possibilities with Prime Minister King.[50] His idea was to lower the transatlantic third-class fare to £10. Canada would have to agree beforehand, lest she regard the third-class passengers as charity migrants. Under Canadian law, such migrants could be excluded, or taxed heavily on landing. The subcommittee quickly agreed that, subject to Canadian approval, the UK itself should provide the appropriate subsidies, so that 'any reputable person' could go to Canada for £10. It also favoured a similar arrangement for Australia-bound migrants, though it made no specific recommendations as to rate.

When the subcommittee's suggestions came before the unemployment committee on 23 July, Churchill opposed them strongly. His lines were the traditional Treasury ones – extra spending would not create employment, and extra borrowing would merely congest the capital market, raising interest rates and tightening credit. 'Personally he did not believe that the adoption of the proposals would be advantageous. If the Cabinet decided to proceed, the money must be found by further economies or increased taxation.'[51] Nevertheless, the Cabinet did quickly approve the migration subcommittee's suggestions with respect to Lord Lovat's Mission and the £10 fare – emphasising, however, that land settlement schemes should be approved only if the Dominions paid 50 per cent of the cost, and that Lovat should make every effort to extract Dominion contributions towards the new training outlays which were envisaged.[52]

In Ottawa, Lovat conferred with Prime Minister King,

with other Canadian ministers, and with officials. He quickly won acquiescence to the British proposal of a £10 third-class fare. The Canadians were even prepared to let the British Government lend the £10 to the needy, without applying any penal conditions. However, they did insist that it would not be possible to admit large numbers of industrial workers. Canada reserved its right to regulate such immigrants, and Lord Lovat agreed to regulate the £10 loans so that Canada need only apply 'a general control'. Further, Lovat got nowhere in his request for the reservation of land for future British settlers. The Canadians were sympathetic, but pointed out that the Dominion was about to transfer all public lands to the Provinces; therefore, the federal government would soon lack the power to reserve blocks in the Ontario Clay Belt or the Peace River Country of British Columbia. Prime Minister King explained that Canada would welcome British migration as long as it was linked with land settlement – a safe proviso, since he knew that all the relevant provinces would refuse to co-operate with any large settlement plans. He told Lovat that Canada would no longer contribute to the migration of single men – though she would not object if Britain chose to do so. And neither King nor any other Canadian welcomed Lovat's 'land bond scheme'.[53]

This new device was Lovat's own variation on the old theme of a Land Development Corporation. The Canadian Government, he suggested, should borrow $50 million and re-lend it to settlers; the UK would guarantee against loss up to 10 per cent of the capital sum borrowed; there would be various special arrangements for training, work-experience in Canadian agriculture, and so on. From the Canadian viewpoint, the objections were partly political, and partly financial: as King learned from his Minister of Immigration, Canada would have to provide 90 per cent of the implicit subsidy.

From Ottawa, Lord Lovat trekked across Canada, trying to interest the provincial governments, the railways, and the Hudson's Bay Company in land-settlement programmes. Meanwhile, in London, Amery had asked the Cabinet to give him a ministerial committee which could help him implement the Government's migration policy. This committee met three times late in 1929. Its proceedings were concerned almost wholly with land settlement, and with a wrangling over its links to emigration and unemployment.

Amery insisted that it would be politically disastrous to admit that the UK wanted to export its unemployed. The Dominions, he said, would simply cut off this migration, and might even cease to co-operate in other programmes. He wished that the Industrial Transference Board had not published its report; its effect in the Dominions, he remarked, had been disastrous. Canada could be induced to accept non-agricultural migrants in any numbers only if the UK subsidised the emigration of the *employed*, and only if it provided a 'background' land settlement. After all, he declared, if *anyone* left – employed or not – his departure created a vacancy which a jobless man could fill. Worthington-Evans and Steel-Maitland, however, could not agree; they were far more concerned to export the unemployed as such and far less concerned with Canadian sensibilities. The Treasury representative, A. M. Samuel, remarked acidly that Canada did not want land settlement either, that she would certainly not accept migrants from distressed areas, and that even the £10 fare would not help very much. To protect Canadian sensibilities, Amery wished to discuss with Canadian officials the question of 'ten-pound loans': to whom, and to how many, should the UK lend the new minimum fare? Other ministers preferred to keep things vague, because they hoped to slip in as many 'undesirables' as they could; in particular, they feared that the Canadians would simply refuse to accept coal miners, whose emigration was the main point of the whole exercise. Hence they resisted codification, and they must have been relieved when Amery reported: 'the Canadian authorities would not raise difficulties with respect to the loan-assisted migration provided the arrangements were conducted quietly and without publicity, that the loans were restricted to really deserving cases'.[54] If this were done, these persons, like those who paid the £10 fare from their own resources, would be allowed to enter Canada.

With respect to this concessionary fare, it is reasonably

clear that Prime Minister King was trying to do good – but cautiously, and by stealth. There was, however, no way to float a stealthy scheme of land settlement. In late November, W. J. Egan, the Canadian Deputy Minister of Immigration, attended a meeting of Amery's migration committee.[55] He told the members bluntly that for political and financial reasons the Canadian Government could not consider the Lovat Scheme. However, he was prepared to urge on his Government the 'inversion' which he had devised. Canada would not borrow $50 million to lend it to British settlers. But why should not Britain lend $1,500 to every settler family? Canada would co-operate by placing the families – first of all, in labouring work which would teach them about Canadian agriculture, and thereafter, on suitable farms all across the Dominion. He thought that his Department could place 1,000 families per year for four years. And the Canadian Government might pay up to 10 per cent of the total losses.

Unfortunately, the Canadian Government had known nothing of Egan's bright idea. He was shortly informed by cable that his masters were most unlikely to accept it. Further, in Whitehall, the Treasury officials had been examining it with their customary cold eye. Samuel reported that so far as he could see, the Egan Plan would commit Britain to spend some £875,000, while Canada would contribute only £175,000. And only 4,000 families would be shifted! The outlays he thought disproportionate; they were also inconsistent with the 50-50 principle of the Empire Settlement Act, and with the Cabinet's own decisions of the preceding summer. Further, both the Treasury and the Dominions Office counsel thought that new legislation would be needed to validate Lovat's tenative agreements with the Hudson's Bay Company and the railways. These proposals involved no contribution by private or public body in Canada; the UK was to do all. Hence they too were outside the ambit of the Empire Settlement Act.[56]

Amery was willing – eager – to amend the Act as as to permit the UK to contribute a larger share. But the other ministers shared Samuel's dislike of the Egan Scheme, and saw no point in exploring it further. Also, no one but Amery was prepared to push such a Bill through the House at the tag end of Parliament's life. In the end, he was obliged to admit that large land-settlement proposals 'must remain in abeyance for the time being', and that, 'for political reasons,' the Empire Settlement Act could not be amended immediately.[57] And that was that. The £10 fare had been introduced. But nothing else of substance had been done to export the unemployed.

When planning the £10 fare, the Cabinet expected to spend half a million pounds in 1928–29, and £1.5 million in later fiscal years. The fare was not funded under the Empire Settlement Act, because Canada did not contribute to its cost. Amery believed that the subsidy would double the flow of migrants to Canada – if only Canada could be convinced not to exclude the ten-pounders as 'charity immigrants'. Steel-Maitland was sceptical at the beginning, and did not become less so as the autumn passed. In November, he was writing that 'unless they are prepared to go and work in agriculture, and even then only within definite limits of numbers,' miners would hardly benefit from the new programmes. The new fare might encourage 75,000 people to go to Canada – but no more than 12 per cent would come from the depressed areas.[58]

In fact, during 1929, 39,000 migrants went to Canada at the £10 rate. Another 12,000 went in 1930. Under the Empire Settlement Act proper, Canada received only 21,000 assisted migrants in 1929, and a mere 8,000 in 1930. Total migration did not double; it rose only from 39,000 in 1928 to 53,000 in 1929. Thereafter, of course, it fell sharply to 15,000 in 1930. Cheap fares were not enough to induce migrants to give up the dole, when Canada's own unemployed were numerous and ill-protected.[59]

From late 1920 until mid-1928, the British Government had insisted that the Dominions must share the costs of any settlement plans. Now, faced with an obdurate unemployment problem, and worried to find emigration so small, ministers saw things differently. Treasury opposition was not sufficient to obstruct this new departure.

Originally there had been two reasons for the Treasury

insistence. If the Dominions paid, it had been argued, they would more earnestly co-operate, and the UK would save money. The Dominions had co-operated to some extent, but in Britain there were still too many unemployed. By mid-1928 it seemed more important to shift them than to save money. In any event, ministers could – and did – compare the outlay on emigration with the saving on the dole.

Besides manipulating the ocean fare, Whitehall continued its efforts to manipulate the Candian Prime Minister. During 1928, Thomas Jones, the Assistant Cabinet Secretary, was corresponding with J. Burgon Bickersteth, the warden of the Men's Union at the University of Toronto. Bickersteth, himself an emigrant, was well connected on both sides of the Atlantic, and was believed to enjoy King's confidence. Thomas Jones was personally concerned with Welsh unemployment, and had followed the proceedings of the Industrial Transference Board. In May, he told Bickersteth that the Board would recommend emigration, and noted that Canada took more migrants from Europe than from Britain. Could Bickersteth not enter a plea with Prime Minister King? Bickersteth did so.[60] King's reply was not encouraging. He noted that Canada was spending a lot in the UK, and almost nothing on the Continent, yet getting relatively few migrants from Britain and many from Europe. For this fact King blamed the welfare state: 'the truth is that people from the Continent want to emigrate and those of a similar class from the British Isles do not'.[61] Bickersteth, who was then visiting London, returned to the charge a few days later. The Cabinet Office had told him that because Britain's birth rate had been so low during the war, there would be few migrants in ten to fifteen years. If Canada wanted more British stock, she should act immediately. Westminster did not want Canada to act against her own interests, but 'there is a very real hope that she may be able to take some action which would help and encourage the mother country', so seriously burdened with unemployed men.[62]

Such letters may have helped to gain King's acquiescence in the £10 fare. But they had no longer-run effect on Canadian policy. Late in 1928, Sir William Clark, Britain's first

High Commissioner to Canada, conferred with King in Ottawa. Clark asked whether Ottawa proposed to call a Dominion-provincial immigration conference. That afternoon, the Canadian Cabinet discussed the matter, and decided that there was no need for any conference. Britain, it believed, had asked for one only because of the impending British election. In Ontario, and in British Columbia, Canadian Conservative governments had large land settlement plans, 'and it would appear that these plans will be linked up with desires on the part of members of the Conservative Party in Britain to have something of the kind carried out in Canada'. But 'our Administration does not view with favour large settlement schemes.' In the past they had been unsuccessful, and they were 'liable to bring about critical situations in the course of development'. Further, parliamentary committees had disapproved of them. On Clark's return two days later, King told the High Commissioner that there would be no conference, and that the Canadian Conservative Party was exploiting the British emigration so as to seem more loyal than the Canadian Liberals.[63]

Thus, the Baldwin Government could never have realised its dreams with respect to Canadian immigration. The migrant ship came to grief on the shoals of Canadian politics, and of King's suspicious nature. In Australia, the perils were different, but the shipwreck was as complete.

IV. THE ANTIPODES AND LAND SETTLEMENT

Both the British and the Australian authorities were united in believing that the most valuable sort of Empire settlement was colonisation on the land. This might be by individuals or by groups. Romantics in the UK often favoured the latter pattern, which reminded them, presumably, of public school or military mess.

Any sort of developmental land settlement needed capital outlay – always on transport, and often on clearing and water supply. A recurring theme was that the settlers should earn their stakes by working for a period as labourers on these developmental works. Having saved a little during a year or two's heavy labour, and having become inured to rural life and to a particular district, workers could then take up their farmsteads, build their houses, and bring out whatever families they had left in Britain. Such schemes seemed specially attractive for two reasons, one admitted and one implicit. It was admitted that many British emigrants would come from towns – indeed, could only be drawn from towns. Such people were clearly unready for rural life of any kind. Further, it was suspected and whispered that many migrants might have been debilitated by the postwar unemployment, and by the war itself, which had prevented many boys from learning any civilian trade. For such men a period of regulated labour would be a useful preparation for the unavoidable independence of the small farm, where diligence would be essential. If the men could select the farms which they themselves had prepared, they would be already acquainted with the particular district, and with their mates, who would be settling round about. Thus contentment would be more assured, the 'transplantation' would have a better chance of success, and the drift to the cities would be restrained or prevented.

Thus the British ideology of group settlement. It appealed strongly to the Western Australian Government, which was actively engaged in settlement schemes, and which believed it had, in the timbered south-west, land ideally suited for dairy farming – if only it could be cleared. And so in February 1923, a tripartite agreement for group dairy settlement had been signed under the Empire Settlement Act.

The arrangement was suspended in June 1924, after a change of government in Western Australia. Investigation showed many defects. Migrants had in fact been placed without any training or selection. They were largely unfitted for the very hard labour which land-clearing involved. Because of this incapacity, and because the clearing work itself was badly organised and badly endowed with incentives, clearing was far more costly than had been expected. Because of the local government's haste in trying to cope with the migrants, some had been placed on land which was unsuitable for dairy farming. And there was reason to doubt that many would remain on their land after their subsistence advances ceased.

By 1930 it was clear that very large amounts had been spent to no effect. Many holdings quickly were reverting to bush. Many settlers had gone to cities, or to the developing wheat areas. At the peak there had been 4,000 settlers, but by early 1930 only 1,696 were left. Eighty-five thousand acres had been sown to pasture, and stocked with 11,000 cows, 4,000 yearling heifers, and 290 bulls. To achieve this, nine million pounds – £5,400 per settler, or £106 per pasture acre – had been spent.[64]

The other group settlement and individual settlement schemes did not reveal their defects quite so promptly as the Western Australian dairy plan. And none failed on quite so dramatic a scale, chiefly because none had involved quite so much money or quite so many settlers. Nevertheless, some Australians may have seen the difficulties from the beginning. Prime Minister Bruce later claimed to have perceived them in 1922, and to have urged safeguards as early as 1923. This did not stop him from proposing and obtaining a really big commitment from Britain – the £34 million agreement of 1925. Though not confined to land settlement, this agreement involved developmental outlays on a really large scale. And Bruce provided for a Development and Migration Commission. Established in 1926, the Commission was to scrutinise any State proposals for group settlement, or any other sort of land settlement, or any other developmental outlay under the agreement. He bound his government to accept no proposal which the Commission had rejected – unless both houses of the Commonwealth Parliament should overrule it.

In a very indirect way, the £34 million agreement may derive from the Imperial Economic Conference of 1923. To the disappointment of the Overseas Settlement Office, at the Conference Australia made no concrete migration proposals. But Bruce must have seen the way the wind was blowing. Early the next year, his government renewed the request which Horne and Churchill had rejected in 1921–22 – a large migration loan with a contribution from the British exchequer. William Lunn had acceded to the under-secretaryship of the colonies, and to the chair of the Overseas Settlement Committee. In conversation with the Premier of Queensland, he first heard of this idea.[65]

Shortly thereafter, in April 1924, R. V. Wilson, Australian Federal Senator, proposed to Lunn that the UK should pay half the interest charges on £70,000,000 for ten years; in exchange, he said, Australia would absorb one million people.

This proposal was immediately taken up with enthusiasm in the Overseas Settlement Office, whose staff thought that some new initiative was essential: otherwise, Australian migration would languish. The existing settlement schemes were proceeding slowly; larger inducements should be offered. The Treasury officials, however, were doubtful. The Overseas Settlement officials thought Britain should offer half the interest on £20 million for five years, and one-third for another five, in exchange for an Australian commitment to settle 20,000 families, or 100,000 souls, eventually causing a migration of 600,000. Treasury officials thought these figures 'very doubtful', and insisted that the loans must be directly connected with settlement: there could be no support of development in general. Though obliged by the Empire Settlement Act to acquiesce in the policy, which both Thomas and Lunn strongly supported, they suspected it and they were eager to limit the amount advanced and the interest contribution; they were also suspicious of Australia's good faith. On the last point they were not really at odds with the OSO, whose officials were already nervous about the Victorian and Western Australian land-settlement plans: they feared that the States were not spending wisely, and were not really settling British migrants on the land.[66]

On 5 May, an official offer went to Senator Wilson. Britain offered to pay half the interest for five years, and one-third for an additional five years, on migration loans of £20,000,000. Annual migration should be 2,000 families, plus 12,000 to 15,000 other assisted migrants; altogether 40,000 families or 200,000 souls should be shifted. Further, at least half of the migrant families should have no capital. This provision, dear to the hearts of Thomas and Lunn, was to ensure that the British working man could emigrate and settle under the plan.[67] The scheme itself, in Thomas's mind, was also meant to offset the Australians' disappointments with respect to imperial preference.[68] Hence Thomas wanted more generous terms – half interest for ten years, and more relaxed conditions with respect to settlement. Snowden was not willing to concede; he insisted that the whole matter should go to the Cabinet.[69]

There Snowden got his way in part. Urged by Niemeyer, he seems to have suggested that the initial offer should be withdrawn, or greatly modified. Chiefly because it had already publicly announced its adherence to a policy of overseas settlement, the Cabinet decided

'to adhere to the previous offer to the Government of Australia, that the British Government were prepared, under the Empire Settlement Act, to offer a contribution of ½ of the interest for a period of 5 years on loans not exceeding £20,000,000 (in addition to loans which may be raised by the Commonwealth under existing schemes) for developmental purposes directly connected with settlement and approved by His Majesty's Government together with ½ of the interest for a further period of 5 years; that if the Commonwealth Government should reject this offer, the question should be brought again before the Cabinet.'[70]

There followed a long and unedifying wrangle with the Australian Government. Though she never rejected the terms of the May offer, Australia pressed for ever greater concessions – more interest contributions, a compounding of payments to allow for the fact that the Empire Settlement Act would expire in 1937 while Australian loans might be floated after 1927, more contributions towards training, reception and aftercare, weaker commitments with respect to the settlement of British families. The list is endless. Australia even asked the UK Government itself to raise the £20,000,000 and advance it to the Commonwealth! It is hardly surprising that in September Niemeyer was writing,

'If Australia doesn't like the terms, they can let the matter drop.'[71] Even the Overseas Settlement Office was losing patience: 'there is not quite the right spirit in Australia in regard to Empire Settlement . . . they think they can squeeze so much out of us . . . the new requests are a try on.'[72] And in March 1925, faced with Bruce's latest demand, a Treasury official wrote: 'Oliver, I see, is again asking for more'.[73]

The negotiations did not again come before the Cabinet. As the months passed, the Treasury and the Colonial Office gave considerable ground. The change of government made little difference: Lunn, Thomas, and Amery were at one in their desire to export the British and to conciliate the Australians. Each acquiescence bred a fresh demand. At length, the Treasury gave up. Fass wrote: 'I have come to the conclusion that we are in an impossible position in trying to fight with the Colonial Office the amendments to the scheme on the grounds of policy.'[74] And R. S. Meiklejohn agreed:

'After all it seems to me that the Treasury's main concern is to secure that for every *x* pounds the British taxpayer spends, *y* persons from this country are settled in Australia. This object is secured. . . . It is to be borne in mind that the mass of our unemployed have no liking for or capacity for agricultural occupations.'[75]

Hence an official letter went to the Overseas Settlement Office on 18 March:

'My Lords have come to the conclusion that They should divest Themselves of responsibility in regard to the policy adopted in the scheme agreed by the Secretary of State. . . . They propose to leave it to Mr Amery therefore to decide as he should think fit in regard to the further modification of the Agreement.'[76]

Having been given a free hand, Amery was quickly able to close with Bruce. Shortly the new agreement was signed. It was noticeably more favourable to Australia than Lunn's offer of the preceding May.

The £34 million agreement was aimed at land settlement, but not at the financing of settlement *schemes*. Amery envisaged it as a measure which would add to the existing flow of migrants – assisted and unassisted – by providing the infrastructure for development. Projects of all sorts could be assisted if they would increase the country's 'carrying capacity', and if, in the absence of the agreement, they would have been undertaken later or not at all. The agreement provided that the UK would pay half the interest for five years, and one-third of the interest for a further five years, for all state projects the Commonwealth might approve, up to a total of £20 million. Thus it enacted the Millen proposals of February 1921. The extra £14 million consisted of the amounts arranged under the earlier agreements of 1922–24. Though it was, and is, hard to be sure, it seems that when the new agreement was signed only £2.8 million of this £14 million had been committed – almost entirely to Western Australia and Victoria.

The Agreement contained a clause by which *land* settlement schemes would involve the definite commitment to accept and establish one new farm for each £1,000 advanced on such schemes. In 1927, Bruce claimed that he had insisted on this proviso because, he said:

'When I discussed the matter first, after the 1923 Conference, it was apparent to me that certain of the land settlement schemes in Western Australia, Victoria, and New South Wales were hopeless, but I could see that there was a possibility of opening large tracts of new country in different states on a satisfactory basis.'[77]

In fact, it had been the British officials who had first proposed the figure and the requirements.[78] This clause proved an embarrassment when, late in 1927, Amery discussed the agreement with Bruce and with Australia's Migration Commissioners. He had hoped that the agreement would shift 450,000 settlers at an average of £75 each. His civil servants pointed out with some embarrassment that he really meant 200,000 *additional* settlers in a ten-year period for an assisted total of 450,000 in a decade. But Amery, by explaining his basis of calculation, made it clear that he did not mean this at all. The trouble was that at £1,000 per farm,

£34 million would not suffice if it were all spent on land settlement. Hence the British and the Australians agreed explicitly to de-emphasise land-settlement schemes even more emphatically so as to reach their assisted-migrant total! And they raised the key figure from £1,000 to £1,500 per farm.

The agreement also provided that each State should receive migrants in proportion to the capital it was advanced. This provision also gave rise to difficulties. Western Australia was proposing an immense scheme to build railways, and water projects, and to settle 3,500 farms in hitherto unexploited wheat land. Could she conceivably absorb the total immigration which the capital sum implied?[79]

Western Australia did in fact do rather well under the new agreement. By the end of 1928 she had received £2.4 million for railroads, roads, and water projects. But the 3,500-farm scheme, which would have cost at least £4.2 million, was eventually rejected by the Australian supervisory commission: the Western Australians, it believed, had overestimated the rainfall, and ignored the alkalinity of the soil.[80]

Amery was most concerned that the agreement's capital should not be frittered away on small projects which would be invisible at Westminster. He wanted big schemes, and he wanted the commission to prepare a comprehensive scheme covering a period of, 'say, 7 or 8 years' – something which he could present to Parliament and explain to the Cabinet. The expenditure implications, he said, should be made clear, and if possible the outlays should rise a little from year to year. In the end, the Commission did agree to produce a five-year plan. But the worsening economic situation and the growing Australian doubts about land settlement and development generally seem to have overcome this resolution.

Some of these doubts were already apparent at the 1927 conference. Amery agreed with Bruce, and with other participants, that market conditions did not justify any expansion of output in the Murray River irrigation districts, where surplus dried fruits and canned fruits were already generated. Wheat development and non-agricultural development were the answers – and both were explicitly included in the mandate of the Development and Migration Commission. But in 1927 the Commission had only begun its work, having been created the previous year. There was no shelf of non-agricultural projects from which it could select proposals. As for agriculture, Western Australia was ready and waiting with a wheat scheme. Though placed informally before the Overseas Settlement Department on 6 June 1928, this was, as we have seen, eventually rejected. And the other States were slow off the mark. Little was proposed, and less was acceptable. By the end of 1928, South Australia had got £500,000 for irrigation, and an afforestation scheme was under discussion. New South Wales got help for an irrigation scheme. Queensland was lent a little money for agricultural surveys. And Victoria, which had had spectacularly unsuccessful adventures with land settlement earlier in the decade, got a little more for railways but had to endure the rejection of a railway-plus-wheat scheme. The law allowed the Commission to originate schemes. But at no time does it seem to have done so. Until its abolition at the end of 1930, its labours under the agreement were confined to the screening of State proposals.

By the end of 1928, the agreement was clearly failing. As only £8,841,736 had been authorised, the agreement thus far had bound the States to accept only 86,908 migrants.

Meanwhile, by arrangement with the Australians, an official British Economic Mission had visited Australia in connection with the agreement. Its findings, published early in 1929, were dismal. Many development schemes, it thought, had been adopted because of sectional pressures, 'without due regard to their financial and economic justification'; also, often, without sufficient study. For instance, they thought that nobody had calculated whether the Murray River Irrigation Scheme would produce remunerative output. Yet in 1928, when it was already hard to dispose of the produce from the completed part, the scheme was being further developed and the irrigated area extended.[81] Faith in future British gifts – imperial preferences indefinitely extended – or in domestic market manipulation could surely go no farther. The Mission saw little scope for migration or settlement under the £34 million agreement – not at a time when Australian unemployment was high and rising.[82] And in its second report, the Development and Migration Commission gloomily agreed with the British – intensive development, not extensive settlement, was Australia's prime need.[83]

In fact, by the end of 1927, though Amery had talked optimistically of adding 45,000 migrants per year, Australia's economic downturn had already begun, and the peak migration was already past. Assisted migration had risen steadily from 9,059 in 1920 to 31,260 in 1926. But thereafter it fell – a little in 1927, and sharply in the next two years, as economic conditions worsened in Australia. In December 1929, the Australian Government began negotiations with the British Government to reduce the flow of assisted migrants. The matter was discussed with the State premiers in February 1930, when Prime Minister Scullin announced that assisted passages would thereafter be available only for boy farm-learners, domestics, and nominated members of separated families – mainly wives and children. Further, the Commonwealth Government proposed to screen the States' nominations – something it had not done since migration co-operation began in 1920 – 'to prevent an undue influx of persons for whom employment might not be readily available'. In its third and final report, the Development and Migration Commission blamed the declining migration, and the change in policy, on the depression, which, it said, 'first became noticeable in the latter part of 1927 and . . . has since become progressively worse'.[84] Understandably, the Scullin Government saw no further use for a Migration Commission, and abolished it at the end of 1930. As for the Lyons Government which succeeded to power late in 1931, it continued its predecessor's restrictionist policy: in 1932, only 175 assisted migrants entered Australia.

Table 1, overleaf, summarises the Australian experience in the great decade of Empire settlement. It reveals the utterly

Table 1 *Total and assisted migration to Australia, calendar years*

Year	Total net migration	Total assisted	of which Land settlement	Farm workers	Domestics	Boys	Other nominees
1919		245					
1920		9,059					
1921	17,575	14,682					
1922	40,209	24,258					
1923	39,766	26,645					11,015
1924	46,128	26,036					12,425
1925	39,865	24,827					14,696
1926	44,847	31,260	1,258	3,046	1,230	2,466	23,376
1927	51,645	30,123	579	2,713	1,891	2,330	22,472
1928	30,128	22,394	149	1,944	1,842	2,356	16,060
1929	11,892	12,943	8	1,386	1,265	1,391	8,789
1930	−8,454	2,683	6	84	189	176	1,615
1931	−10,037	275					
1932	−2,950	175					

Note Components of assisted migration for 1930 cover first six months only.

Source Total net migration from Commonwealth of Australia, *Official Year Book*. Total assisted migration from British Economic Mission, *Report*. Components of assisted migration from Development and Migration Commission, *Reports*. The table is incomplete because these sources do not give full information for all years.

trivial contribution of land settlement, and the continued predominance of the 'requisition' and nomination by state governments and by persons. The governments were responsible for requisitioning farm workers, domestics and 'boys'. They also nominated such other workers as they believed their economies could absorb. Thus the 'other nominations' came partly from governments and partly from persons.

Some of these nominees must have come to work on development projects which the £34 million agreement financed. Others certainly came to jobs which, by their multiplier effects, these projects had created. Unfortunately we cannot estimate either number. But it is hard to resist the verdict of contemporaries who, concentrating on the small sums borrowed, and the lesssened number arriving, called the agreement a failure. By mid-1930, eight and a half million pounds had been spent or committed; States were thus responsible for absorbing 86,434 extra migrants and had in fact absorbed 106,981.[85] More than half the money and migrants – £4.6 million and 41,200 – were committed to Western Australia.

Though much was hoped from the Australian land-settlement schemes, remarkably little was achieved.[86] Three schemes were actually undertaken – in Western Australia, in Victoria, and in New South Wales. The Western Australian group scheme, of 1923, aimed at settling 75,000 migrants on 5,000,000 acres of dairying land. There were to be 6,000 new farms, and £6 million was to be spent. By 1936 there were only 390 migrant farming families left on the site. And £10 million had been spent. Victoria had planned to establish 10,000 families with some capital, and to spend £3,000,000. The farmers were to produce dairy products, fodder, and the miscellaneous outputs of mixed farming. In 1933, 361 farmers were still on the land but after an investigation the Victorian Government agreed to compensate most of these, leaving 50 migrant families settled – at a cost of £5 million. New South Wales had meant to settle 6,000 families, and actually recruited 336, but, noticing in time what was happening in Victoria and Western Australia, it quickly abandoned its scheme before it had spent much money. In the end, therefore, the schemes had successfully settled 478 farm families, at an outlay of some £15,000,000 – rather than 22,000 farms for £14,000,000. The fatuity of the schemes only became fully apparent in the thirties. But the troubles were becoming evident by 1925. They help to explain the elaborate safeguards in the £34 million agreement.

It is worth reminding ourselves that it was the Australian States, not the Commonwealth or the Imperial Government, which eventually had to bear the dead weight of the settlement debts. The Commonwealth had raised the funds but the States were to pay interest and principal in excess of the Imperial contribution. Thus the States had spent £31,400 per farm family! Admittedly, as Kathleen Jupp points out,[87] much of this had been spent on roads, railways, and water supply schemes which provided services to other persons. But much of this social overhead capital had been designed specifically to provide services which, because the settlement did not occur, were required only decades later, or not at all.

New Zealand saw nothing so dramatic as a £34 million migration scheme – merely a succession of 'passage agreements', by which the Imperial Government shared the cost of assisting migrants via fare reductions. Admittedly, New Zealand did a certain amount of internal development during the twenties. She carried out railway, hydro-electric and drainage projects. But none of these were joint schemes under the Empire Settlement Act. The New Zealand passage agreements, like the Australian and Canadian ones, provided for loans to migrants, and for fare reductions. At certain periods, juveniles and youths could travel free, and adults paid only one-third of the ordinary fare. It was through such schemes that New Zealand shared the UK's migration bounty.

Almost all the assisted migrants were 'nominated'. That is, New Zealand citizens and businesses named individuals and undertook responsibility for them. Until 1920, the system covered only members of one's close family. But in 1920 the arrangements were liberalised, apparently because

Prime Minister Massey thought immigration good and necessary.[88] Some assistance was available, at least now and then, for those who applied, and for those who had assured employment waiting in New Zealand. Intermittently, too, the migration authorities tried to make sure that housing awaited the migrants. They were particularly eager to attract child migrants, and they devised special schemes for placing British public-school boys with New Zealand farmers.

From 1920 till 1926, New Zealand's 'quota' for migration assistance was 10,000 per year. In 1927, because a shipping strike had prevented the expected numbers from arriving in 1926, the quota was temporarily raised to 13,500. But during 1927 the government took fright at rising unemployment, and decided to reduce migration during the coming winter. In 1928, this curtailment became settled policy: passage assistance was thereafter available only for domestics, single women, separated families, and boys emigrating under one of the child-migration schemes. In 1928–29, the restriction continued even more rigorously, and in 1929–30 the authorities determined to restrain immigration indefinitely. In 1930–31, the authorities were very strict, and in 1932–33 the Government decided that New Zealand citizens could not nominate if they were residing temporarily in the UK.[89]

The results of these arrangements are set forth in Table 2. Like Australia's, New Zealand's immigration peaked in 1926 and thereafter fell away sharply. Fifty thousand assisted migrants arrived between April 1922 and April 1930 – not a large figure, and, of course, not entirely attributable to the Empire Settlement Act.

By 1927–28 it was clear that nothing could be expected from the New Zealanders. No one had ever expected much from the South Africans. But Whitehall was not yet quite prepared to give up on the Australians or on the Canadians. We have seen that in 1927, Leo Amery could talk optimistically of assisting an extra 45,000 Australian immigrants each year – a doubling of the annual flow, assisted and unassisted, to that date. And with respect to Canadian immigration, we have seen the strange and excited manoeuv-

Table 2 *New Zealand – total migration and assisted migration, 1920–1933*

Year 1 Apr–31 Mar	Total immigration from UK	Total assisted	By NZ	By UK	By both gov'ts	of whom nominated	applied	children
1920–21	14,444	9,567	4,821	5,286		4,821	n.a.	n.a.
1921–22	n.a.	7,005	3,153	3,852		3,153	n.a.	n.a.
1922–23	11,340	6,737	3,255	3,482		3,255	n.a.	n.a.
1923–24	11,488	6,752	52	49	6,651	n.a.	n.a.	2,178
1924–25	12,451	8,924	7	2	8,915	n.a.	n.a.	2,898
1925–26	10,965	7,685			7,685	6,824	861	2,652
1926–27	14,943	11,239			11,239	10,134	1,105	3,702
1927–28	6,197	3,822			3,822	3,465	357	1,319
1928–29	3,814	1,968			1,968	1,754	214	659
1929–30	3,369	1,790			1,790	1,626	164	610
1930–31	2,610	1,233			1,233	1,078	155	439
1931–32	2,258	290			290	258	32	89
1932–33	626	56			56	56	0	

Note 'Total immigration from UK' appears to be a gross figure. It has been *assumed* that, in 1920–23, all those whom the New Zealand Government assisted were in fact nominated. The Department of Immigration did not separate 'total assisted' into 'nominated' and 'applied' until 1925–26.

Source Compiled from New Zealand, Department of Immigration, *Reports* (in New Zealand, *Appendices to Journals of House of Representatives*, Annual).

rings of Mackenzie King, Lord Lovat, and Burgon Bickersteth. It is tempting to search for some common factor on the British scene – something which would account for the recrudescence of interest in migration in the late twenties. British unemployment was falling; matters were looking brighter than they had looked for many a long year. Why migration?

The answer is certainly the work of the Industrial Transference Board. But given this fact, why *land* settlement? We have seen that long before 1927 the Australian experiences were known to be dismal. We also know that the Canadian difficulties were recognised with some clarity in London. For many primary products world prices were visibly falling, and protectionism growing. How can we explain more fundamentally the continued interest in the land?

Remember that all the relevant politicians – in London and the Dominions – had grown up, and still lived, in a mental climate now long gone. To a remarkable extent they saw the world in terms of trade flows. Only for international commodity trade were there statistics. And the parts of the Empire were only too clearly articulated by commodity movements and capital movements. These people had grown up with an international economy, and they could not have escaped from its assumptions. One such assumption was that 'growth', 'development', and 'prosperity' would necessarily increase world trade, and vice versa. Another assumption related to the role of government economic intervention. In all the Dominions it had long been accepted that governments should manage their economies in the interest of development. In particular, they should borrow for public works projects that would 'develop' their lands. But they should try to ensure that the loans were 'remunerative' – either directly, through fares and use-charges, or indirectly, through a broader tax base. And such 'development' was largely seen in the context of the existing international economy. When the tariff was used for developmental purposes, it was meant to replace existing imports with domestic production. When governments borrowed for transport and utilities, they were almost always interested in export production – commodities which could find a ready market in the international economy, where the prices of the outputs and the costs of the capital funds and machinery would be determined. A more integrated and autarchic sort of 'national' economic development was certainly conceivable to them. Both in Canada and in Australia, tariffs were deliberately used in this way, and linked with railway construction and export stimulation. But this was not a context on to which planned migration readily fitted, given the assumptions and the organising abilities of the time.

A genuinely 'developmental' migration programme would have involved the export of communities, not persons and capital funds. The group-settlement enthusiasts had some glimmering of this, but they concentrated upon friendliness, not upon the diversity of occupations and activities. There was nothing inherently absurd about Lord Lovat's scheme of a new province in Canada's Peace River district. The absurdity arises only if we imagine the new province to be populated entirely by debt-burdened wheat farmers. The appropriate model for developmental migration would not be the international economy; it would be France. One would try to plant a sufficient non-agricultural population so that the local agricultural products would have a local market. Techniques of production, and economies and diseconomies of scale, would fix the size and type of the non-agricultural work force; one would then plant an agricultural population just sufficient for two things – to feed the new local population and to buy whatever imports the non-agricultural exports would not pay for.

Such a balanced plantation would not have been immune from all external disruption. But it would have been far less exposed than the totally export-oriented populations which the land settlement brought to birth. Further, it would actually have been consistent with the real aim of many Empire settlement advocates – the creation of new Britains overseas. Yet as soon as such a scheme is described, one can see why it could not have been attempted. British and Empire governments lacked the will to attempt such comprehensive planning, the ability to make the required calculations, the data which the calculations would need, the levers of power to effect acquiescence, the energy to administer any really large project, and the political support for such radical intervention.

In the settlement proposals one often finds calculations which hint at comprehensive planning. But the proponent is always placing farmers on broad acres. And the model of his calculation is always the same – and significant: it is the private land-development corporation. 'We shall obtain 100 square miles of land for £1,000 and spend £9,000 on developing it; we shall then settle 400 farmers, each of whom will pay us a capital sum of £25, in instalments, plus the market rate of interest.' *A priori* such schemes are often feasible, and desirable. But they are obviously attached to the international economy, whence the corporation will draw its funds, and into which the farmers will sell the produce from whose proceeds they will pay their £25 plus interest. Businessmen understand such schemes; they can often assess their prospects precisely because the costs and benefits are simply spliced on to the existing economy. Though optimism or electoral pressure often prevented them from getting their sums right, the Empire politicans of the 1920s were bound to conceive migration projects in these terms precisely because they thought like the businessmen of their time.

Even if politicians could have imagined a different kind of development scheme, they could not have administered it into existence. The Australian experience shows this: the actual projects demanded more administrative competence than the State governments possessed. They were unable to assess soil or rainfall; they could not forecast costs; they did not even manage to mesh the arrival of the settlers with the emergence of jobs or holdings. How could they possibly have managed to make the far more elaborate calculations, or handle the far trickier timing problems of a genuinely comprehensive settlement scheme?

In short – land settlement schemes were consistent with the attitudes of politicians who were administratively ill-supported, and who saw the economic order in late Victorian and Edwardian categories; comprehensive schemes would have been inconsistent with these attitudes, and impossible in the light of administrative realities – even if electorates would have supported them.

Further, land settlement had attractions of its own – and a respectable tradition to support it emotionally.[90] The Dominions did appear to have thriven on land settlement and export orientation. The Bible enjoined men to subdue the wilderness and make it bloom. The more visionary among the imperialists certainly saw Empire development in these terms – civilisation by means of cultivation. The intellectuals might not actually *remember* Bacon *On Plantations*, or the landed gentry the enclosures of waste, but both were part of the background that produced the emphasis which we, who consider the production and market prospects of the actual schemes, find so eccentric. Also in the background was English gardening. And so was the war, which had shown that countrymen were far healthier than city-dwellers. Far back in the shadows, there may even have been the English yeomanry – long since vanished in Britain itself, and impossible, it seemed, to re-establish there. Might one not compensate by planting sturdy peasants in the far reaches of Greater Britain? And many romantics certainly enjoyed the mere idea of planting the world with British stock. The more remote the spot at which the stock rooted, the greater their rejoicing – especially when, on their travels, they could see the results themselves. Of course it was a good thing if the settlers could live well – and better still if in the sequel British unemployment should fall and British exports should rise. But in any event land-settlement schemes would have been put forward.

But not accepted. For decades the Imperial Government had been rejecting proposals for state aid to settlement and migration. In 1907 and 1911 it had been cool to Dominion pressure. In 1918–19 it quickly lost its wartime enthusiasm for manpower management. The Government finally moved for three reasons: unemployment, the Millen-Hughes initiative, and the lobbying of Amery and the OSO. But the passage of the Empire Settlement Act opened the way for state aid not just to settlement but to romanticism.

V. THE TREASURY AND EMPIRE SETTLEMENT AND DEVELOPMENT

Throughout the 1920s, the Treasury opposed all proposals for Empire settlement and overseas development. The opposition is so consistent, and crops up in so many different contexts, that it can best be examined analytically, not chronologically. It had four foci. The Treasury knights did not agree with Amery's diagnosis of the unemployment problem. They distrusted the officials in the Colonial Office, the Overseas Settlement Office, and after 1925 the Dominions Office. They worried about the finances of the Dominions. And they were very concerned about financial management in the UK itself. At some points, as in 1923, we can trace the course of argument from subordinates' memoranda, into Niemeyer's memoranda to the Chancellor, and then into ministerial correspondence, Cabinet papers, and argument in the Cabinet itself. At other points, as in 1925–29, the influence is more diffuse. Nevertheless, there is sufficient evidence of Treasury attitudes to explain Amery's fear of Treasury obstruction. He was certainly confused about the difference between 'Treasury Control' and Treasury opinion. There is no evidence that the Treasury actually obstructed when any policy had been definitely accepted – in statute, by Cabinet, or through inter-departmental discussion. But when policies had not yet been settled, Treasury influence was consistently on the side of caution – minimum discretion to the spending departments, minimum assistance to the overseas Dominions and Colonies, maximum protection for the UK's taxpayers and bond-buyers.

The Treasury distrusted the unemployment diagnosis which Amery offered. We have seen that Amery was a sort of vulgar proto-Keynsian. He recognised what he could not properly explain: more borrowing and more real investment would generate higher prosperity, employment, and income in the Empire as a whole. The Treasury knights disagreed. In the documents there are manifold examples of the 'Treasury view': the amount of savings is limited, and so if one borrower gets more, others must take less, leaving total investment and output unaffected. Overtaxation causes unemployment, apparently by reducing the incentive to invest but possibly by reducing the flow of savings. In so far as Empire development might generate new markets, it would do so only in the very long run, because in the shorter run most of the money would be spent overseas, not in the UK. The unemployment of the early twenties was due in part to credit contraction,[91] in part to the uncertainties in a regime of floating exchange rates, and in part to the real and money wage rates. But it was wrong to link unemployment and migration: there was in fact no deficiency of emigration, as Amery thought; he used untypical years from the immediate prewar period, while a proper comparison, over longer periods, would show that postwar emigration was at least as rapid as prewar. Anyway, emigration would revive *with* trade, not before it. People would leave Britain when both Britain and the overseas areas were prosperous. They had done so in the past. They would do so again. Meanwhile, it was wrong to interfere with market processes.[92]

Even if the Treasury had accepted the diagnosis, it would have distrusted the executive ministers and agencies. Amery himself was not liked in the Treasury.[93] Niemeyer described him as a 'Mad Mullah Minister'.[94] He and his associates thought little better of Amery's officials, especially those who ran the Overseas Settlement Office. Geoffrey Whiskard seems to have commanded respect, but the Treasury officials had few good words to say for anyone else in the Colonial or Dominions Office. They thought the Office tended to put the Dominions up to things – to fly kites which would lead to Dominion demands, or to commit the UK before Treasury and Cabinet had agreed. They suspected that the Colonial Office sometimes pushed the colonies into premature development, either to satisfy some private obsession or to generate employment in the UK. They accused the officials of hastiness.[95] They were distressed by the Offices' inability 'to produce schemes which stand investigation', to understand finance, or to estimate costs and revenues accurately. This lack of concrete proposals had worried them in the early negotiations over Empire settlement. The Colonial Office wanted a Bill, but, the Treasury thought, only Australia was interested, and even she had little concrete to propose.[96] In 1929, one official dipped his pen in venom and wrote:

'As regards the Amery proposal to make the Department which is responsible for policy, responsible also for finance, whatever may be said for it in some quarters the Colonial Office would be one of the last offices to be entrusted with this dual charge. There is not a glimmering of financial sense in the place, and it is the lack of it which occasions these letters from the Minister and the failure to frame financially acceptable schemes.'[97]

When a financial department regards a spending department in this light, it is most unlikely to smile upon the plans that the spending department may concoct.

Many of Amery's dreams involved grants to Dominions, or shared-cost programmes by which the UK bore some of the Dominions' debt. Since the other Dominions borrowed rather little in London after 1919, it was Australia which was most likely to benefit from such favours. To the Treasury such arrangements raised awkward problems, both constitutional and prudential. Were grants consistent with the Dominions' dignity? What of their constitutional status? Could the UK contribute to finance their borrowings, if it did not control the spending? Further, was there not a risk of unsound schemes? If the Dominion governments were encouraged to borrow, surely they would put forward proposals which could not be properly screened in the UK and which would involve enormous waste. In any event, the Treasury would be unable to impose the proper control upon the actual spending: much of the outlay would be overseas, and almost all of it would be channelled through Dominion administrations which would be jealous of their own financial autonomy. Further, the UK Parliament might insist on its right to scrutinise the Dominion projects which its grants were financing.[98] Then there were the prudential problems. How could one avoid subsidising all Dominions loans, if one conceded subsidies on any? Would the Dominions not put all their projects under the appropriate headings so as to get the subsidy?[99] Finally, there was the particular problem of Australia. Niemeyer and other Treasury officials believed that this Dominion congenitally over-borrowed. They thought Britain unwise to encourage it to do so even more recklessly. And they foresaw a financial crash in the Australian future. Why should Britain connive to make the crash even larger and more destructive? Late in 1929, Waterfield wrote with barely suppressed satisfaction:

'Australia is in a bad way, primarily through unwise administration of the policies of protection and wage-regulation, and reckless borrowing, largely for uneconomic projects . . . the Dominion must now suffer the discomforts of deflation, and we cannot expect any appreciable flow of migration for several years.'[100]

Niemeyer's prophecies of 1923 were coming true.

Further, and most alarmingly, all the schemes for Empire settlement and development conflicted with the Treasury's own plan for financial reconstruction. The Colonial Stock Acts already gave Empire securities an 'unfair' advantage in the British capital market – an advantage which increased the Treasury's troubles in managing the UK's own debt. The more guarantees the Treasury gave, the more perfectly could Empire securities be substituted for UK securities. If the UK paid part of the interest, the Empire would issue more securities in London, further 'congesting the gilt-edge market'. It would become even harder to lengthen the term of the UK's own debt, or to re-fund it at a lower rate of interest. Also, there would be an injustice to home industry and utilities: the Dominions would be able to borrow at lower rates than Britain's own domestic railways, gas works, and electric power companies. Nor were grants any better: they necessarily fell on the British taxpayer, requiring the British Government to borrow more or tax more. Either course would tend to discourage productive activity, by reducing the supply of savings for financing private investment.[101]

Finally there was the gold standard. Throughout the twenties, Treasury strategy revolved around the return to gold – initially, before 1925, to prepare the conditions for a return, and after 1925, to preserve them. The gold standard was thought to be in the Dominions' own interests: it would automatically stabilise their currencies *vis-à-vis* sterling, and it would help their own industries, since all of them were gold producers.[102] But the more the Empire borrowed in London, the harder it would be to attain or retain the gold standard. Amery and his friends were impressed by the fact that the Dominions tended to spend in Britain what they borrowed in Britain; Niemeyer and the Bank of England were impressed by the fact that they did not spend *all* they borrowed. If loans were left on deposit, they represented an added short-term liability which would threaten Britain's gold reserves. If they were remitted to other countries, they would represent a direct drain on these reserves. In so far as the loans generated exports, these exports did nothing to help Britain pay for imports – because Britain had lent the sterling which was paying for the exports. In short, the less the Empire borrowed in London, the better for the gold standard.[103] It is hardly surprising that the Treasury and the Bank encouraged Australia to borrow in New York – or that they rejoiced to see how little Canada was borrowing in London.

The Treasury must have rejoiced when, late in 1929, the Australian Government began to disentangle itself from the £34 million agreement. By mid-1930, the Treasury and the Overseas Settlement Department had agreed that 'our policy at the 1930 Imperial Conference should be to make a final end of the absurd £34 million agreement'.[104] Though the agreement was not cancelled at the Conference, it was settled that Britain should not approve any more schemes under it.[105]

As for migration in general, an inter-departmental committee recommended that at the Conference the UK should preserve the fifty-fifty split on outlays 'which has so far protected the Treasury against extravagant demands', but should not commit themselves to any definite policy.[106] A subcommittee of the Economic Advisory Council advised the Government to stand ready to pay more; the split, it said, should be retained only for land settlement.[107] It favoured a redistribution of the white population, but thought there was little point in trying to stimulate it. And in the longer run, it saw no need or reason to do so: in its final report, it argued that emigration would draw off the better elements of the population. Britain needed an emigration policy only in the short run, 'as an emergency policy . . . in view of our postwar economic difficulties'.[108] But of course, as the subcommittee realised, it was exactly in the short run that the Dominions would not accept the migrants. The Cabinet recognised the fact too, and instructed its Conference delegates accordingly.[109]

At the 1930 Conference, the delegates' migration committee met only twice. Lunn explained that Britain did not want to force migrants on the Dominions for the time being, but that he hoped the situation would improve in time. Maloney, for Australia, said that no migrants could come for the present. The committee presented a report which, while impeccably Amery-ite in its analysis, was completely negative in its conclusions:

'Primary consideration ought to be given not to the conditions in the country which the settler is leaving, but the absorptive capacity of the country to which he is proceeding. Any increase in the absorptive capacity of the Dominions must depend in the first place on the existence of adequate markets for their products, and secondly on the inflow of capital for fresh development. Anything which will increase the absorption of the products of the Dominions must be of benefit to the Dominions and to the United Kingdom, in that it will stimulate development, encourage settlers from the United Kingdom . . . [but] mass movements . . . [are] . . . impracticable . . . [for] . . . financial, economic, and political considerations. [As for the new land settlement projects,] no recommendation can be made at present.'[110]

The Treasury had triumphed. But so had common sense.

VI. APPRAISING THE EMPIRE SETTLEMENT PROGRAMME

In Chapters 2 and 3 we have chronicled the birth and death

of Empire settlement. Through the whole saga the Australians play an oddly prominent role. At many points, especially in the immediate postwar years, it was their intervention and their suggestions which moved the project forward and modified its nature. South Africa was consistently recalcitrant, Canada lukewarm, and New Zealand cautious.

Admittedly Amery and the Overseas Settlement Office would have wanted an Empire settlement bill in any event. There was the desire, natural in the postwar period, to populate the Empire and secure its future by retaining blood stock and by filling empty places with white Britishers. In Australia there was the yellow peril and in Canada and South Africa, the French and the Boers. There was also the sentimental desire that it was splendid to have sturdy Britons scattered in far places, where they could be visited and admired. There was the romanticism about the land, which afflicted both Conservative and Labour politicians at the time. Britain, it was thought, had somehow damaged herself by allowing her agricultural population to fall so low. But land in Britain was 'too expensive' for extensive small-holding. Britain could be given a prosperous peasantry only on overseas lands – in 'Greater Britain'. For some of the leaders, like Amery himself, overseas experience coalesced with romantic bent to produce a vision. And it was all too easy to splice this vision on to the collateral dreams of Empire Free Trade, Tariff Reform, and an organically united Empire.

Further, the demographic facts might have given some independent steam to an Empire settlement movement. In discussing this matter, one cannot avoid the impression that the leaders thought they were breeding animals. Britain had too many women, and the Dominions had too many men. Left to themselves, they would impregnate lesser breeds – coloured women or continentals – and the result would be less British. Meanwhile, in the UK itself, thousands of women were condemned to permanent spinsterhood. What better idea than to export the women? In the Dominions, they could work for a time as domestic servants – work they would not undertake at home, in spite of the 'servant shortage'. But soon they would marry and raise up sturdy young stock – yeoman, merchants, and if necessary, cannon fodder.

Besides these demographic realities, there was a pseudo-demographic myth – the 'overpopulation' of Britain, and the 'underpopulation' of the white Dominions. At its simplest, this myth merely asserted the obvious – Britain was much more densely populated – and drew a conclusion – that it was desirable or essential to redistribute population. We cannot assert unequivocally that this was nonsense. One can construct models in which the average real income would be higher after a 'redistribution' than before. One can also make enough assumptions to justify a corollary: that without redistribution Britain would be unable to feed her 'teeming millions'. However, the assumptions are strange, and grossly unrealistic, because they involve so many rigidities, and foreclose so many automatic or discretionary adjustments in the British economy. Amery and his friends never specified their assumptions, and in this matter they never tried to justify themselves with any detailed analysis of economic processes.

If 'redistribution' would raise average real income, why need government assist it? Would not people move on their own account? Such has always been the *laissez-faire* criticism, and it deserves a moment's thought. The individual may have trouble financing a long journey, even though he knows that he will be much better off at the other end. Further, he can have only the most imperfect knowledge of real opportunities overseas. Also, he may be reluctant to leave the relatively developed social services – especially the dole – in the UK. Finally, he is interested in earnings after taxes, whereas output is gross of taxes. To some extent, therefore, the government may be justified in subsidising emigration: the subsidies offset the reluctance which may come from one or more of these four sources, achieving a redistribution which genuinely does raise total Empire output – and therefore average output and income per head. However, this argument does not make any case for a particular kind of development in the receiving country.

Certainly there is no case for land settlement, if the workers would be more productive in some other use. If moderately productive British factory workers are transformed into rather impecunious Australian dried-fruit farmers whose incomes are supported artificially through the British preferential tariff system, the individuals themselves *may* lose. Australia will certainly gain, because she will be producing more than before. But Britain will lose, and so will the Empire as a whole: that is, the loss of potential output in Britain will exceed the gain of actual output in Australia. In short, there is an *a priori* case for subsidising migration in general, but not for subsidising land settlement in particular.

The same, roughly speaking, applies to the subsidising of child migration. Recall that such subsidies were not invented in 1922. Poor Law Guardians had been exporting pauper children for decades. In Canada, Doctor Barnardo's Homes had long been welcoming orphans from the British Isles. In Western Australia, the Fairbridge Farm School already had a considerable history. From the philanthropist's viewpoint, all these efforts were justified because the child would have a better chance overseas than at home. But would he? Again, we can imagine British arrangements which would better have protected his standard of living and opened wider horizons. But he could not, of course, become a peasant proprietor in the British Isles. And that was the status which the philanthropists hoped he would attain – in Greater Britain. The visionaries shared the philanthropists' hopes. But they also thought that it was good to transplant early. The seedling would root better in the new land if he could be shifted before his habits were set. In particular, the urban child was relatively likely to grow into a successful and contented overseas peasant; British adults were much more likely to pine for city life, either in the Dominions or back in Britain. For all these propositions there were advocates as eager in the Dominions as in Britain. But no one could know, in fact, whether the transplantation of children would raise Empire output. And no one had traced the fortunes of child transplants; for all anyone knew, they might be thoroughly urbanised. Anyway, the above considerations established no *a priori* economic case for the migration of children as against adults. One would have to show that a given outlay on child migration would raise the present value of total output more than the same outlay on adult migration. And the outcome is uncertain, because the adult migrant is immediately productive, and the child is not.

The philanthropic arguments had circulated for many years. They had caused the foundation of numerous voluntary societies for helping migrants in general, and for subsidising the emigration of women and children. If one found the case persuasive, one gave money to these bodies. There is, however, no reason to believe that such arguments would have produced the Empire Settlement Act – or anything like it. The actual development depended upon three things: Australian pressure, manipulation from Amery and his Overseas Settlement Committee, and the growing unemployment problem of 1920–22.

Australian pressure mattered both for the timing of developments, and for their content. Consider land settlement. If only because of gardening and estate management, any British scheme would have given some place to 'plantation'. The report of the Tennyson Committee pointed in that direction. But without Australian pressure, its actual place would have been much more restricted. It was only in Australia that really grandiose settlement projects were begun under the Act, and only there do they seem to have created any permanent settlements. Further, Australia invented the idea of interest-sharing. This idea delayed the progress of the Empire settlement proposals as a whole, because the Treasury and certain ministers opposed it so strongly. On the other hand, the Act provided for it, and in the later twenties it absorbed a good share of British outlays under the Act. Remember too Hughes's telegram of 24 November 1921. Whether or not it was concerted with Amery, the telegram may have been crucial in the sense that it forced the Cabinet to act: Hughes was not a person one could ignore, but before he could be answered, the British Government had to establish its policy.

No one can be sure whether Churchill and Amery would have forced a Cabinet decision without the Hughes telegram. As the Treasury and the Colonial Office were already at loggerheads over the Overseas Settlement Estimates, perhaps the Cabinet would have been forced to take some decision. On the other hand, Amery had found it very hard to bring any measures forward. Lloyd George opposed the old Emigration Bill, and he seems to have thought that domestic reform should take precedence over the subsidising of emigration. Further opposition could have been expected as the Government became ever more nervous about its finances, and as Treasury views were ever more vigorously put forward. Churchill supported emigration, but his real interests were elsewhere – in Mesopotamia.

Before Amery joined the Government, nobody was really pushing hard on the Empire settlement front, and the Government had been given no coherent reason for spending on emigration, or even for planning it. Hewins and Long, because they wanted an essentially irresponsible 'control', may have done more harm than good. Further, they offered no coherent ideology into which Empire settlement could be fitted. Amery supplied this lack, in a fashion particularly apposite to an under-employed economy. Admittedly, many of his themes could be found in the Report of the Dominions Royal Commission. But no one seems to have noticed them there. And the Commission, in any event, had not thought that Britain could or should do much. Amery harnessed the vision to a programme. Empire settlement could cheapen imports, create markets for exports, develop 'scarce' raw materials, and improve Imperial self-sufficiency. It would also reduce unemployment.

The link between Empire settlement and unemployment is a peculiarly slippery one. First of all, the evidence suggests that if there had been no unemployment problem neither Amery nor Hughes would have got very far. It was because of unemployment – and largely through the Cabinet's Unemployment Committee – that the critical steps were taken. First, the idea was a temporary measure to export a relatively few people in a bad winter. Then, as more and more ministers began to suspect that unemployment might not pass quickly away, the emphasis shifted to longer-run measures. For this, Amery was ready with an interpretation. He knew that short-term, emergency programmes would not work. The Dominions would not accept such devices; they even insisted on screening the soldier migrants for suitability. If Britain were to gather up the *visibly* unemployed and ship them abroad, the Dominions would simply refuse to admit them. Further, Amery's work with voluntary societies, whose representatives worked with the Overseas Settlement Committee, must have convinced him that an organisation was needed. Migrants must be selected, perhaps trained, guarded, and planted out in the new land. And the necessary organisation could not be bodied forth at a moment's notice. But a permanent apparatus could handle all things better. In co-operation with the Dominions, it could help select and train the types of migrants which the Dominions wanted. It could make arrangements with the voluntary societies. It could tailor and adjust the aid to the Dominions' prejudices – especially their obsession with land workers, female domestics, and child migrants. How would such migration help unemployment? Even if the actually unemployed did not leave, Britain's labour force would shrink, and so the unemployed would face a better job market. Further, as the Dominions developed, Britain would sell them more. And if migration could be linked with immediate large investment, as in the Australian settlement schemes, British heavy industry would get an immediate stimulus. In other words, British exports would rise long before the child migrants had grown up, or the female migrants had married and bred.

The author believes that Amery's diagnosis, and the underlying unemployment itself, were essential to the Cabinet's acceptance of the Empire Settlement Bill. And we must admit that Amery was not talking nonsense. The Dominions, especially in the Antipodes, were heavy buyers of British goods. It was sensible to argue that if they could produce more Britain would certainly export more. Further, Amery was right to think that overseas investment would immediately generate orders for British heavy industry. Finally, since Britain was so large an importer of food and raw materials she obviously stood to benefit from any measures which, in the longer run, would increase the supplies of primary products and lower their prices.

Nevertheless, the diagnosis and prescription were one-sided. Why must investment be overseas investment? Domestic investment of equal amount would have given an equal or greater stimulus to British output and employment. If the investment were of appropriate sort, it would even relieve that 'congestion' and 'over-population' which Amery and his friends so disliked. True, it would do nothing directly for British exports. But from 1919 until 1925, the pound was a floating currency. There was no good reason to worry about the balance of payments. If domestic investments had stimulated imports, it would also have encouraged a downward flotation of sterling which, in turn, would have stimulated exports while helping to *restrain* imports. The unemployed of Britain were not absolutely and permanently redundant. Deficient aggregate demand at current prices and wages had cost them their jobs; reflation – accidental or deliberate – would give them new ones. And in exporting population, Britain was permanently reducing her *own* productive capacity.

On the other hand, we must see Amery's diagnosis and prescription in their historical contexts. Everyone wanted to get back to the gold standard at the pre-war exchange rate. Meanwhile, everyone worried when the pound floated downward. Irrational though this worry was, it influenced everything. Also, the role of domestic investment was not understood. The 'Treasury view', though not universally accepted, was influential: it was thought *impossible* to raise investment 'artificially'. Government deficits and public spending congested the securities markets and raised the cost of finance for private users, thus *discouraging* trade. The country 'could not afford' decongesting and job-creating investment. The export of capital and labour was not the only way for Britain to recover. But at least, at a time when most realistic policies were proscribed, it worked in the right direction. When we see things from this angle, we must congratulate Amery for the Empire Settlement Act.

But what did the Act really accomplish? We know it helped many people to emigrate – 345,400 from 1922 to 1931. Total emigration was only 885,000 during the same years. On this emigration the UK spent considerably less than the £3,000,000 per year which the Empire Settlement Act allowed. Seldom have so many moved so far for so little. Unfortunately, these figures tell us little about the Act's impact on the British economy. To some extent, the Act replaced or supplemented the assistance of other bodies – poor law guardians, organised private charity, and the Australian and New Zealand Governments. Further, many migrants would have gone even if they had not been aided; though the authorities gave grants and loans only to certain occupational groups, as defined by the various passage agreements, they imposed no means tests. Hence, one cannot identify the net movement for which the Act alone may claim credit.

The same obscurity shrouds the Act's impact on Dominions settlement. We know that most of the assisted migrants were children, agricultural labourers, would-be farmers, and domestic servants. Australia and New Zealand were only intermittently willing to assist 'nominated' migrants, who were going to cities under someone's sponsorship. Canada never assisted the non-agricultural male migrant. Hence, at first sight one might think that the Act succeeded in its purpose of settling broad areas and equipping them with farm labourers and farm wives. However, we also know that in all the Dominions there was a large subsequent drift from the land. Only in Canada did any follow-up investigation occur: there it was found, in the later 1920s, that half of the single farm labourers, whom the Act had assisted, were not working in agriculture. The same sort of thing seems to have happened in the Antipodes. Further, in the 1930s, when there was net immigration to the UK, some of the remaining agricultural workers and settlers must have returned to Britain. Therefore, one can say only that to some indeterminate extent the Act did raise the farm populations of the Dominions, and that to an equally indeterminate extent it also raised their city populations.

Only one thing is sure: the Act had almost no effect on rural or urban white populations in Africa. Only a few hundred settlers moved under the Act to South Africa, Rhodesia and Kenya. The racial troubles of these countries cannot be blamed on the Empire Settlement Act.

Further, though in principle the Act could have encouraged settlement in other colonial or dependent areas, in fact it did not do so. Thus, it had no link with the production of non-edible primary products – gold, copper, rubber, sisal, tin – or with tropical foostuffs – tea, coffee, sugar,[111] cocoa, palm oil. Only in the production of lead and zinc, where Canada and Australia were major world exporters, may the Act have had some marginal effect on production, by increasing labour supplies in these two Dominions.

As for temperate foodstuffs, the Act clearly operated to lower world prices by raising world production. The Dominions produced wheat, butter, cheese, meat, wine, dried fruits, fresh fruits, and canned fruits. By encouraging the opening of new lands, and by supplying settlers, farm labourers, and wives, the Act tended to increase output, especially in Australia. It is, however, impossible to say what output would have been in the absence of the Act. We can neither construct nor quantify a model which would estimate world production and prices in the absence of the expansion which the Act induced. Nor can we definitely identify the areas where settlement and output depended on the Act. In Canada, three thousand farm families were scattered across the country, and no one knows where the farm labourers were used. The same is true of New Zealand. In Australia, Empire settlers were mingled with native Australians on the wheat lands of Western Australia and the fruit and dairying lands of the south-eastern states. All we can do is to 'make a qualitative assessment' – that is, to guess.

I find it hard to blame the Act for much of the wheat-price collapse which was so painful in the late twenties and early thirties. All over the world, production was rising, and countries were restricting their imports; in Canada, Empire wheat settlers were few relative to the growth of the agricultural population, and in Australia the new wheat areas were, at least at first, very unproductive. Hence I conclude that in the absence of the Act world wheat production would have risen almost as much, and wheat prices would have fallen almost as much, as in fact they did. But I am not prepared to say the same of butter, dried fruit, mutton, and lamb. Here the problem is Australia, where 'closer settlement' meant forced expansion of these products, and where, after 1926, artificial marketing plans stimulated domestic production by supporting the local price and dumping the surplus abroad. Without the Act's assistance, Australia would probably not have attracted so many producers into these high-cost, non-competitive, and inefficient industries. In the event, however, her production grew rapidly – far more rapidly than her domestic consumption. And her marketing practices ensured that her production would have maximum price-depressing effect on world markets. Hence, in the early 1930s, the growing fury and concern of New Zealand and Denmark with respect to Australian butter, and of New Zealand and Argentina with respect to Australian mutton and lamb.[112]

If these guesses are correct, they suggest a sad irony. During the 1930s, the British Government tied itself in knots as it tried to protect its domestic dairy farmers and livestock breeders while negotiating favourable trade agreements with competitive overseas suppliers – Denmark, the Argentine, Australia, and New Zealand. But it seems that the price conditions which upset domestic producers and terrified overseas governments were in part the result of the expansionist policies which the UK itself had adopted a decade before. The result must have pleased Amery, and others who, like him, had hoped for a self-sufficient Empire. But it can hardly have pleased anyone else – least of all the harried ministers who worked so hard on food treaties between 1932 and 1938. It is as well that Amery could contemplate the fruits of Empire settlement from outside the Cabinet room.

Fortunately for everyone, there was more to Empire settlement than land settlement.[113] In all the Dominions, few of the new agricultural labourers and farmers actually stayed on the land. Like the women domestics whom the politicians cherished, they soon moved to other work – even before 1929. In any event, many of the subsidised migrants – the 'nominated' and 'requisitioned' workers – were not destined for agriculture at all. In spite of the planners' hopes, Empire settlement actually speeded the drift to the cities of Canada, Australia, and New Zealand.

With the benefit of hindsight, we should rejoice that the migrants did not all stay on the land. Agricultural prices were already falling in the late 1920s, and were shortly to fall further. Machinery was already reducing the demand for farm labour, and throughout the Empire the average size of farm was rising. It was in cities, in mining, and in construction work that labour was needed. As long as there was reasonably full employment, migrants would do better in such work, and they ought to have been seeking it. The Act and the related programmes were successful, in spite of Amery's intentions, in so far as they speeded the urbanisation of the Empire.

Admittedly, there were problems in the Empire's cities. Poor relief was ill-organised and ill-financed. The Dominions' economies were cyclically unstable. Their prospects depended heavily on investment activity, and on primary-product prices. Both were variable. Hence unemployment was never absent, and sometimes was serious – even before 1929. Besides, to the Empire's politicians there were two disadvantages in urban immigration. Organised labour was strong in the cities, and its leaders did not want more competition for the existing jobs. Further, cities were likely to attract the urban socialists of Britain. The homesteading farmer could not become unemployed. He created traffic for the overexpanded railway systems of Canada and Australia. He was less likely to be radicalised by the activities of leftist agitators. So Empire politicians thought. Unfortunately, the experiences of the 1930s showed that there were worse things than unemployment. A price-collapse would pauperise the cash-crop farmer just as efficiently as unemployment would pauperise the construction worker. When destitute, farmers became as radical as city dwellers.

Consciously or unconsciously, the politicians of the 1920s had wanted land settlement because they hoped it would bring social peace and stability. It could have done so only if it had been designed to produce subsistence farmers, growing their own food and not depending upon any market – domestic or external. But the settlement-schemes were not designed to produce subsistence farming, and nobody meant them to do so. Prime Minister Bruce had made the point in 1923: the men would come, and the capital would flow, only if the markets existed. On this score, as on most matters, Amery and the other London visionaries were at one with the Australian Prime Minister. To these politicians, subsistence farming was as inconceivable as the 'balanced agricultural-industrial development' which we described earlier in this chapter. We can understand why they saw things the way they did. We can even admit that, on balance, the Empire settlement schemes did a great deal of good, and very little harm, in human terms – though in connection with land settlement they certainly wasted resources scandalously. But nonsense remains nonsense, even when spouted in a good cause.

Chapter 4

BULK PURCHASE, IMPORT BOARDS, QUOTAS, AND THE IMPERIAL CONFERENCE OF 1930

The 1930 Imperial Conference met in London for more than a month in the autumn of the year. With respect to economic policy it is best known for Bennett's tariff demands, Snowden's opposition, and the deadlock which led directly to the Imperial Economic Conference at Ottawa nearly two years later. But there was more to the 1930 Conference than Bennett's 'ten per cent preference' and Thomas's 'humbug'. This chapter examines some of those other aspects. As the dispute over bulk purchase, the MacDonald Government's vacillations over import boards, and the confusions about an 'Empire wheat quota' did not have much to do with the later events at Ottawa, they are treated here, not in the next chapter.

In the 1928 election, the Labour Party advocated 'import boards' and 'bulk purchase'. The former meant government purchasing agencies which could arrange for the import and distribution of basic foodstuffs and raw materials. The latter meant large international contracts for the supply of such goods. After its partial victory, the Party found itself lumbered with this plank. Lacking a clear majority, and divided within itself, the Cabinet was unable to act on either front. Nevertheless, circumstances obliged the Government to give constant if embarrassed attention to both subjects. The principal pressure did not come from within the UK. Instead, it came from Australia, and it was mediated through the Imperial Conference framework which the UK had created in preceding decades. The 1930 conference was not even a UK idea. Canada had taken the lead in proposing it, and even before the gathering we find Labour ministers regretting the whole business in so far as it forced them to think about these two embarrassingly divisive and knotty problems. In this chapter we trace the interaction between the UK and the Dominion Governments with respect to both. First, however, we must briefly consider the devices themselves.

Both bulk purchase and import boards harked back to the later years of World War I, and to the immediate postwar years, when the British Government itself had planned many importations and had itself contracted for enormous amounts of certain raw materials – meat, wheat, wool, butter, leather, and so on. It is easy to see why some socialists would like these schemes. Avoiding the 'anarchy of the market', the import boards could 'physically plan' their buying in light of 'national needs', thus ensuring 'adequate supplies', to meet demands. And if one is 'planning' one's purchases in this way, one logically ought to place very large orders – 'bulk purchases' – if possible, for long periods. The result is 'security'. Physical planning and mass buying should be more economical – because distribution costs would be lower, and because administrative overheads and profits could be kept down. At least, so many socialists hoped – not least Dr Christopher Addison, the renegade Liberal whose first governmental experience had been in Lloyd George's administration, and who presided over the Ministry of Agriculture and Fisheries in Ramsay MacDonald's. If such costs could be shaved, the boards would be able to pay a better price to suppliers, charge a lower price to consumers, or do both. They might also discriminate between various buyers and sellers.

Now that we have had more experience with large enterprises, both nationalised and capitalist, we can see how fatuous these hopes actually were. Bigness usually means heavier overheads, not lighter. Physical planning is extremely difficult, and usually wasteful, even if the planners admit that the quantities 'needed' are related to the prices at which goods are offered. There is, in fact, no such thing as an objectively determined physical national 'need'. And supplies, too, respond to prices. Thus planning in terms of 'shortage' and 'surplus', though natural in a wartime environment where the market system has been disconnected and where there really are some definite national goals, is not appropriate for a peacetime situation where one economy is connected with others through manifold trading links, and where the authorities have eschewed both ration tickets and overriding objectives. However, as socialists still find these matters hard to understand, we should not severely criticise the simple Labourites of 1929 for getting them muddled. Nor should we laugh at their entirely *a priori* belief that the distributive trades were unduly wasteful – that with clever socialist organisation, preferably monopolistic, an import board could do better both for producers and for consumers. But it is much harder to see why they were so vague about the bargaining situation which the boards and the bulk purchases would create. Since so many Labour leaders were experienced in trade union bargaining, they surely ought to have seen that their scheme would politicise the pricing and purchasing of basic foodstuffs. Where would the boards buy? At what prices? How much would they decide to sell? At what prices? No scheme could be more fruitful of conflict – both domestic and international. The only excuse must be the following. Import boards and bulk purchase represented a verbal escape from the dilemma in which the Labour Party found itself. Committed to free trade, and unwilling radically to redistribute property, it could hope to benefit the producing and consuming masses only by squeezing profits and distributive margins. And the boards and the bulk purchases must have seemed useful squeezers.

The Labour victory of 1929 carried this bundle of confusion intact into the Ministry from the platform. During the transit it attracted attention elsewhere, especially in Australia, where another new Labour Government, even more confused and much more grasping, quickly proposed that import boards and bulk purchase should be discussed at the Imperial Conference of 1930.[1]

The UK had not previously included this subject in its conference draft agenda.[2] Originally, Whitehall had simply proposed a general review of trade – 'including the effect of successive tariff changes on [the Empire's] constituent parts, and also of the other factors, such as cartels, etc.,' which might affect trade. The officials reported that there was no reason to fear a Dominion initiative with respect to tariffs, because both Canada and Australia were moving so rapidly towards protectionism. The advisers, and their ministers, proposed to press for some sort of 'imperial economic machinery', which could somehow co-ordinate economic development – especially the industrialisation of the Dominions. This was a natural idea for a government which favoured rationalisation at home. But it gave no warning of the suggestion which the Australian telegram contained.[3]

The Dominions Office promptly asked Australia to make more specific suggestions. Exactly what did Canberra want to include? Prime Minister Scullin responded that the Australians thought they might like to talk about bulk purchase, price stabilisation, and equalisation of labour conditions. This response was insufficiently specific to satisfy Whitehall. On 16 July, Australia formally asked that the agenda should include 'the question of bulk purchase of Dominion products and price stabilisation'.[4] But she still made no concrete proposals.

The Australian request forced the UK Government to think – if possible, to formulate a policy. There is no sign that such matters had been really seriously considered before 7 May, in any context. Thereafter cabinet ministers and officials brooded long upon them. It was, of course, impossible for Labour to create boards and purchase schemes, because it could not count upon Liberal support for any such measures. Nevertheless, by early July Dr Addison was urging his colleagues to invent an agricultural policy – one which would include import boards. His main concern was to achieve security for the *home* cereal producers who were already suffering from the collapse of grain prices. Given the Party's free trade commitments, and the country's treaty obligations, only import boards or 'quotas' would do the trick.

What were these 'quotas'? Throughout the 1920s, continental countries had been forcing their millers to buy stated proportions of their grain from domestic sources. This percentage was called a 'quota'. Nowadays it is often called a 'mixing scheme'.[5] For some time, officials in Britain's Ministry of Agriculture and Fisheries had wanted a similar device. Addison, whose previous governmental experience had been as a Liberal, in the very dirigiste atmosphere of Lloyd George's government, fell romantically in love with agriculture, self-sufficiency – and the quota. By early July 1930, he was convinced that his staff had evolved a workable quota plan, and he was urging his Cabinet colleagues to approve the idea. But he badly wanted import boards too, writing, 'in order to prepare the way I suggest that the principle should be considered by the Cabinet forthwith with a view to some announcement that the Government will submit this question to the forthcoming Imperial Conference'.[6]

It is more than a little odd to find a Labour minister espousing agrarian protectionism. The wheat 'quota' would be bound to raise the price of British-grown wheat so long as this wheat was guaranteed a proportion in excess of that which would prevail in free competitive conditions. The whole point of the import board, so far as domestic agriculture was concerned, was also to pay the domestic farmer a higher price than he would otherwise get. But in the long run, as Ricardo had pointed out a hundred years before, all such measures would raise agricultural rents! On inframarginal land, a larger surplus would accrue; further, the highest price would encourage the extension of cultivation to less favourable land, which would come to yield a rent which it would not otherwise have earned. Hence the principal beneficiaries of agrarian protectionsim would inevitably be the landlords! Farmers might benefit even in the long run if a larger output permitted some better organisation of production which could not be drawn off as a rent increase.

It is hard to see what such improvements might be. Some would also benefit in the sense that the agrarian sector would be larger with protection than without it: that is, there would be room for more farms and more farmers. In so far as farmers attached positive value to farming, this change would be worth while even if the landlords drew off all the extra rent which the protectionist policies had created. But it remains odd to find socialists espousing a policy which keeps the agricultural population larger and more prosperous than it would otherwise have been. After all, British farmers were not peasants.

At first, no one expected the quota to affect wheat prices. It was meant to give 'security'. For home producers Addison soon asked a price guarantee. Even without any such guarantee, a quota would be bound to raise the average price of British grain so long as the quota percentage was sufficiently large to expand production. This must be true because agriculture is an increasing-cost industry. And expansion was exactly the point: British farmers were to be encouraged to grow more wheat.

One would like to be able to say that other Labour ministers opposed Addison's scheme because they saw these implications. Unfortunately, they seem to have understood it as little as Addison did. Their objections were partly practical, and partly principled – the high principles of *laissez-faire*.

Besides his colleagues, Addison was fighting the civil servants. Only in the Ministry of Agriculture did any officials support quotas, bulk purchase, or import boards. Later in the summer, Whitehall's senior officials produced two memoranda in which the devices were examined. The officials were tactfully negative about them all, concluding: 'only a preferential method is likely to achieve the object desired by Australia, and this presupposes either import duties . . . or an Import Board or Boards empowered to pay a preferential price for Dominion and home grown produce.'[7] If forced to choose *something*, they preferred the wheat quota.

Addison also had to fight the Economic Advisory Council. Sir John Simon presided over a Council committee on agricultural policy. On 15 July, Simon told the Cabinet that his committee saw no reason to give agriculture any long-run special protection. As for temporary protection, the committee members disagreed about its necessity, and did not suggest what measures the Government might take.[8]

Finally, Addison was obliged to fight the redoubtable Philip Snowden. In a pointed memorandum the Chancellor underlined the divergence between Addison's policy and the Simon Committee's suggestions.

'The minister's policy is to offer agriculture . . . subsidies and protection. Mr Simon's Committee would adhere to free trade principles for agriculture so long as protection is not given to other basic industries. The question of Import Boards ought to be considered on its merits and not merely as a means of subsidising the producer. We have not yet had the arguments fully before us, and I think that the whole subject should be examined by a committee of officials . . . .'[9]

Yet the Imperial Conference would open in less than ten weeks.

In his devotion to socialist principles the Chancellor was second to nobody. But like all free-traders he kept the consumer welfare firmly to the fore. Hence he opposed the wheat quota, and he doubted if import boards and bulk purchase were really practicable. Was there *really* so much to be saved out of distribution costs? He did not think so. If there was not, then the boards could help producers – at home or abroad – only by squeezing consumers. The producers would get more because consumers would pay more. And this was unattractive to a consumption-oriented socialist like Snowden. Further, the pricing of bulk purchase contracts would lead to interminable wrangles – as indeed had happened in World War One, and afterwards. If the boards did not pay the current market price, they would be accused of exploiting someone. But if the market price was to be paid, then the boards and the bulk purchases would make no difference: the final result would be the same as if the 'chaotic market' had been left to itself. Snowden was not even inclined to admit that suppliers might extract some psychological gain from the security of a long-term bulk purchase contract: if the prices exceeded market prices on such contracts, then the suppliers were exploiting the consumers, and if the reverse occurred, the suppliers would rightly protest that they were not getting a fair price. In other words, they would not be prepared to take a lower price in exchange for a secure price and market.[10]

One might have expected that Snowden's opposition, and his arguments, would have sufficed to defeat Addison, yet the Cabinet proceeded to set up a wheat quota committee, which recommended an emergency quota arrangement, 'pending the working out of the full party policy of an Import Board'.[11] The officials went off to confer with the grain and milling trades, and to elaborate quota plans, both for home wheat and for Dominion. However, at no time did the Cabinet formally adopt any specific proposal. And the Imperial Conference was coming ever nearer. It was to open on 1 October.

By early September, the Cabinet's Imperial Conference Policy Committee had still not considered the basic question of import boards and bulk purchase. It had only managed to approve certain descriptive briefs which were to guide ministers. As these documents came from the same hands that had treated Addison's dreams so roughly in the early summer, it is hardly surprising that the final briefs – circulated to the Cabinet on 6 August – should follow the same line. The officials had high hopes for the Empire Marketing Board – that invention of the Baldwin Government which tried to create a 'non-tariff preference' by advertising Empire goods and by subsidising research on their preserving and transport. They had come to favour a wheat quota. But they still did not like import boards or bulk purchase.[12] They believed that the Australian proposal – or any scheme of bulk purchase – necessarily implied a board with monopoly powers to import and to buy all home production. Further, they said, if the UK consumer was to be protected against overseas 'rings', and if the UK producer was to benefit through economies in the purchase and handling of overseas products, the monopoly board must be free to buy anywhere – at the lowest price. They did not think that monopsony buying and central administration would save much; hence, they noted, buyers' and sellers' interests would necessarily conflict. If the boards bought at the best price, the Dominions would not benefit. And price bargaining would necessarily create bad blood between London and the Dominion governments. Further, if a board should be created for one product, like wheat, the Dominions which produced little wheat would press for extension of the system to the products in which they were interested. Thus there would be a natural tendency for the system to expand until it embraced almost all British food production and importation.[13]

By early September, a committee of officials had approved a Dominion wheat quota.[14] In effect, another percentage for Dominion wheat was to be placed on top of the basic percentage for home wheat, and millers would be compelled to produce flour from wheat in the assigned proportions. Faced with the need to offer *something* at the impending conference, and perhaps suspecting that the Dominions would submit tariff demands which could not be granted, the officials – and some Cabinet members – seized upon a, Dominion quota. A logical extension of the home scheme, it would be popular but costless – because there would be no price guarantee on the Dominions' grain.

Though the officials did not explicitly oppose the import boards, the thrust of their report certainly was that the boards would be useless, pernicious, or both. But the Cabinet could not be expected to discuss this or any other matter in August. Perhaps to force examination of the questions the officials had raised, on 11 September Snowden circulated a cabinet paper in which he raised 'certain fundamental issues'. What was the goal of an import board – higher prices for producers, or lower prices for consumers? If the former, would home producers benefit as well as Dominion suppliers? What of repercussions on trade with non-Empire countries if the Board favoured Empire suppliers? And how would its price-bargaining affect Imperial relations?[15]

Addison responded with an alarmingly concrete proposal – an import board for the purchase of imported and domestically grown wheat of millable quality. It would be the sole importer, and sole buyer, of all suitable home-grown wheat. It should enter into bulk purchase contracts for forward delivery at fixed prices, or at formula prices. It 'might' give Empire countries the first chance to supply UK needs. But it should buy from the Dominions 'so far as possible at world prices', and it 'should have regard to the interests of our trade in other countries'. It would, however, pay home farmers more than they would otherwise get, distributing the subsidy over its sales of imported flour. And its basic idea would be to arrest the decline in *domestic* agriculture.[16]

At last, on 17 September, the Cabinet reached the question of import boards. And the verdict was negative:

'It was realised that it would be as difficult for the Dominions to offer a secured market for the manufactures of the Mother Country without detriment to their world trade, as it would be for the United Kingdom to purchase their requirements from the Dominions to the detriment of their trade with foreign countries, such as, for example, the Argentine. . . . The Prime Minister summed up the discussion by stating that while theoretically there was a great deal to be said for an Import Board it would in fact be extremely difficult to establish one on a full-sized scale. . . .'

The Cabinet still could not decide whether to accept or reject a wheat quota, either for home or for Dominion grain. It agreed that the President of the Board of Trade should formulate the UK's requirements for any import board, 'the first of such requirements being that the Board must be established primarily in the interests of the UK. The Board would be free to purchase in any part of the world'.[17] And as the Chancellor later noted, the Dominions would not like any bulk purchase scheme in which the board simply paid world prices.[18]

On 8 October, a week after the Imperial Conference began, the Canadian Prime Minister made his famous offer. Prime Minister Bennett said:

'first we must approve or reject the principle of preference. . . . I offer to the Mother Country and to all the other parts of the Empire, a preference in the Canadian market in exchange for a like preference in theirs, based upon the addition of a ten percentum increase in prevailing general tariffs, or upon tariffs yet to be created.'[19]

He went on to propose that an economic conference should meet at Ottawa in six months, to work further upon its adoption.

This proposal sent the UK Government into a state of shock. Thanks to Snowden, the Cabinet was quickly able to resolve not to impose any new tariffs. Hence it could not respond to Bennett's offer – which, in any event, its advisers thought worthless.[20] It was prepared to discuss bulk purchase and import boards, but only on conditions which ensured that the Dominions would reject them. It was willing to discuss a wheat quota – but not to *impose* or *propose* one. The conference ended on 14 November, with the Dominions accusing the UK of treachery, and the Dominions Secretary rating Bennett for 'humbug'.[21]

Though it has attracted relatively little attention from historians, the question of Russian trade and competition was as disruptive of the conference as the tariff question. It was, moreover, closely linked with the idea of an Empire wheat quota.

As Soviet export capability and effort had revived in the late 1920s, Soviet competition became increasingly worrisome to those few countries whose exports competed with Soviet goods, especially in the UK market – Russia's chief foreign outlet for timber, wheat, and other primary products. The Soviet export drive centred on a few such products – timber, wheat, salmon, and coal. Canada had reason, or thought it did, to worry about all four. Australia brooded about wheat. Britain herself feared Soviet coal competition in Europe, and even in Canada. Post-revolutionary chaos had withdrawn Soviet goods from most export markets. But the first Five-Year Plan generated large demands for foreign exchange, and these demands forced the USSR to squeeze an export capability out of the painfully limited productive capacity of its primary-producing industries. These Soviet efforts coincided with the years 1930–32, when first Australia, then Canada, and finally Britain herself were trying to modify the UK's trading patterns for their own ends. How could Australia and Canada win bigger shares of the UK market, in the face of this Soviet competition?

At the 1930 Imperial Conference the Dominions' worries were brought sharply forward.[22] The Australians and the Canadians complained about wheat, and the Canadians about timber. Hence Prime Ministers Bennett and Scullin were eventually though temporarily converted to the idea of a wheat quota. Since the quota involved no price guarantee, its only merit was as an anti-Soviet device. J. H. Thomas had strongly advocated it for exactly this reason: it would permanently end the threat of Russian wheat dumping, thus cheering Prime Ministers Bennett and Scullin.[23]

Originally Bennett had disliked the wheat quota for ideological reasons. But academic and political advice had helped to change his mind.

In May, the UK representatives in Canada had begun to predict that the Canadian Government might have to ask for a privileged position in the British wheat market.[24] By the beginning of 1930 it was already clear that the Canadian co-operative wheat 'pools' would not realise enough from their wheat sales to cover their own marketing costs and the payments which they had already advanced to their farmer-owners. The pools were in fact insolvent – sitting upon enormous heaps of wheat whose market price was steadily falling. Provincial governments had extended some guarantees, but it was doubtful if these would suffice.[25]

How would a quota help? In the short run, we now understand, it would mean nothing at all: by displacing foreign wheat from Britain to other markets, it would worsen marketing conditions in these markets to exactly the same extent as it would help them in Britain. But Bennett's principal adviser, D. C. MacGibbon, told the Prime Minister that the quota would lower the price the foreigner would get; it would thus, in the long run, discourage foreign production, leaving more scope for Canadian grain exports.[26] A seductive thought for a politician who faced an immense glut of prairie grain! Other advisers were more concerned with political repercussions: Bennett should accept the idea of a wheat quota because if he rejected the scheme he would seem uninterested in prairie wheat interests – 'with adverse political effect in Canada'. So argued H. H. Stevens, Benmett's minister for trade and commerce.[27]

But in the course of the proceedings Bennett became enamoured of the quota, largely because it could be used against Russian grain exports, and partly because it might help move Canada's grain surplus.[28] At the last plenary session, he announced that Canada 'was prepared to consider the possibility of accepting the system as a solution of the problem of marketing our Empire wheat in the UK'.[29]

The New Zealand representatives began with ideological objections, which, unlike Bennett, they did not shed in the course of the conference. But among the Australians the climate of opinion was very different. Australia had lived for years with regulated markets. From 1916 till 1920–22, Britain had taken all Australia's meat, wool, and butter exports under fixed-price bulk purchase contracts. The Australian meat industry, it seemed, had never been really prosperous since these contracts were discontinued. Prime Minister Bruce himself had raised the question of bulk purchase at the 1923 Imperial Economic Conference. And by 1930 the Australians had devised internal controls for the marketing of butter, cheese, currants, raisins, canned fruits, sugar, and wine. For wines, canned fruits, and dried fruits, minimum prices were also prescribed. Sugar prices and production were controlled, but the other schemes did not control production at all: they merely tried to manipulate marketing in such a way as to maximise the producers' total revenue, via a two-price system. Domestic prices were consistently higher than export prices, and domestic supplies were limited to maintain this differential, the excess output being dumped on the British market. All these schemes antedated Scullin's Labour Government and all were strongly supported by Australian producers. So long as production was not controlled, managed marketing had no terrors for the rugged individualists of Australia. Hence it is not surprising that Prime Minister Scullin approved the wheat quota.[30]

When Scullin's Government had first proposed to discuss price stabilisation and bulk purchase at the Imperial Conference, it does not appear to have considered a wheat quota. Indeed, it seems to have had nothing definite in mind. On 28 June, the Prime Minister had rather plaintively asked his civil servants what their views were; London, he wrote, would like to know.[31] By 16 July nothing much had been written, though a few memoranda had been forwarded to the Australian Cabinet on 19 July. At last, however, when the Australian ministers set off for London, they had been equipped with a thick and strongly favourable memorandum. This document still ignored the quota, concentrating instead on bulk purchase. Not only was bulk purchase the only alternative to tariff-preference for currants, sultanas, lexias, prunes, sugar, canned fruits, jams, jellies, and wine, the officials thought; it would also be of material assistance for wheat, flour, butter, cheese, eggs, beef, mutton, lamb, hops, apples, and other fresh fruit – in other words, for every one of Australia's food exports.[32] 'Probably the scheme would not apply to such products as wool, skins, hides, tallow, timber, or metals, as there is no general demand by those interested for their inclusion at present.'[33]

By the time they drafted this memorandum, the Australian officials had clear – and extraordinary – ideas of what bulk purchase would mean. Details would have to be left to subsequent negotiations, but obviously there must be controlled trade in each and every Dominion, and controlling authority in the UK. Bulk sales, the officials wrote, 'would probably enable the producers in Australia to accept reductions on present prices as a result of savings in commissions and other payments'. But 'at present the price obtainable in Great Britain . . . is below cost' in some cases. 'It would be necessary in these cases for some provision to be made by the British Government when any advantage is gained by the British consumer through the purchase of Australian products below cost of production . . . a freight subsidy or other concession shall be made to the selling authority in Australia, for the ultimate benefit of the producer. It is not suggested that the British Government should be required to make up losses incurred in the country where the goods are produced from causes such as poor harvests, defective quality, or other cause. The financial assistance would only be required because of the loss consequent on, say, the dumping of the foreign article on the British market, or through a special cutting of prices to meet Australian competition.'[34]

These opinions are extraordinary because they imply, in effect, that Britain should underwrite whatever standard of living the Australians thought their farmers and farm labourers should enjoy. Unfortunately, there seems to have been little to suggest to the Australians how badly they had misread the British attitude. Indeed, early in June Scullin had received a letter from F. L. McDougall, the Australian agricultural expert long resident in London. McDougall then said that he thought the UK Government might now look with favour upon bulk purchase. And later in the same month, McDougall reported a talk with J. H. Thomas. McDougall had asked whether the UK Government would consider tariff preferences and bulk purchase. The Dominions Secretary had replied that 'as far as he was personally concerned, he would exclude nothing'.[35] It is hardly surprising that the Australians came optimistically to London.

After a fortnight of wrangling on the subject of preferential tariffs, the British conference delegation proposed that quotas and import boards should be *investigated*. The principal Empire delegates agreed to set up a 'Committee on Economic Co-operation' to consider the various schemes. It soon became known as the Quota Committee.[36] Philip Snowden later described its proceedings as follows:

'In response to Mr Bennett's request for concrete proposals . . . we submitted for consideration the questions of bulk purchase, quota, and import boards. Committees were appointed to examine these proposals, and for a month they wasted time in preparing reports on them which every member of the conference realised would bring forth no practical results. After six weeks of this time-wasting procedure, the conference ended with practically nothing accomplished.'[37]

The Dominion ministers soon came to believe that Britain had made a 'proposal'. Though it is hard to see how this impression could have arisen from the delegates' words on 13 October, it is easy to see how the subsequent deluge of staff papers could have created it. Whitehall prepared documents which the Quota Committee was invited to consider. One emphasised the ominous surpluses which overhung the world wheat market. Another outlined schemes for UK and Dominion wheat quotas.[38] The Cabinet, however, could not make up its mind. On 24 October, Ramsay MacDonald asked his colleagues to let him say that the UK would introduce a quota for Dominion wheat. The President of the Board of Trade had already told the Cabinet what the Quota Committee would propose.[39] But the Cabinet could not agree on this or any other device to save the conference, and decided to hold the matter over until its next meeting.

J. H. Thomas proceeded to circulate a memorandum which argued, *inter alia*, for the acceptance of the Dominion wheat quota. The Dominions understood that the UK would not impose any new food taxes. But what could the UK offer? 'It is wholly insufficient for us to rest on this purely negative policy.' If the wheat quota were not accepted, the Dominion governments would conclude that the UK had been 'fooling them for the last fortnight'.[40]

But Thomas's plea was unheard. On 28 October, the Cabinet reviewed the history of the quota, reminding itself that it had felt unable to decide on the question beforehand and that it had favoured 'a noncommittal attitude' at the conference. It had hoped and still hoped that such matters as import boards and bulk purchase should be referred at, or by, the conference to 'such inter-imperial machinery as may be created'.[41] And there was, it seemed, no more to be said.

The Conference Quota Committee, however, had a great deal more to say. Early in November it produced its report. The members recognised that a wheat quota would not raise prices, and might even depress them if it encouraged UK production. Nevertheless, they favoured a minimum quota for Dominion wheat, regardless of this fact, so as to give security against dumping, especially by Russia. They thought it would be administratively impossible to have quotas for individual Dominions. As for other commodities, they saw little hope of working a quota system: for administrative reasons, quotas would have to operate at the point of import, and this would contravene Britain's treaty obligations, especially to Germany. Import boards with monopoly power to purchase all imports and all home production would avoid most of the legal and treaty difficulties, they thought. But they would cause intra-Imperial friction 'on such questions as price, variation in quality, and allocation of purchases'. A board could stabilise prices by entering into long-term contracts. But its monopsony power might be used to reduce the prices the Dominion suppliers would get. Bulk purchase schemes would stand exposed to great losses if other producers should dump. But for canned fruit and canned fish they would merit further exploration. For fresh fruit the committee favoured a quota but saw little hope of dealing with poultry and dairy products by any of the proposed devices.[42]

When Ramsay MacDonald told the Cabinet of this report on 11 November, the members still refused to commit themselves to a wheat quota at the conference[43] . . . even though MacDonald emphasised that the other delegations were accusing the UK of bad faith. This accusation was openly made at that day's meeting of prime ministers and heads of delegations. The Dominion representatives repeated that they thought the UK had actually *proposed* a wheat quota. If, as the quota report showed, it would benefit the wheat-exporting Dominions, why did the UK not agree to it? The unfortunate British ministers could only say that the 'suggestion had been only one for examination, that their representatives had throughout made it clear that the UK Government was not necessarily committed to the proposal. . . .' And MacDonald, following Cabinet policy, tried to refer quotas and bulk purchase to the Imperial Economic Committee.[44] But he was not allowed to get away with this;

the next day it was agreed that the UK Government would further consider a wheat quota. And all other parts of the quota report – import boards, bulk purchase, and quotas for commodities other than wheat – were simply referred to the Empire governments for consideration.[45]

No wonder Snowden thought that six weeks had been wasted. And no wonder the Dominion governments were annoyed – apart altogether from their disappointment with respect to preferential tariffs. The UK had really made only one positive proposal – barter agreements.[46] But for ideological reasons Prime Minister Bennett disliked these, and other Dominion leaders were unenthusiastic. Snowden had rubbed the Australians' noses in the implications of a bulk purchase arrangement: he told the heads of delegations that it would involve the placing of forward contracts in the cheapest markets, and that 'if import boards were on business lines they could be of no assistance to the Dominions'. Doubtless it was this remark which led Bennett and Scullin to fear that the UK would simply use bulk purchase to *lower* their producers' returns. Certainly the British would have enormous monopsony power.[47] And if Snowden had a bulk purchase scheme, doubtless he would have used it in this way.

After the conference had dispersed, barter agreements vanished without trace. Little more was heard of boards or bulk purchase. In November and December 1930, they were unhelpfully discussed in Parliament.[48] And early in 1931, ministers and officials considered both in connection with the coming Ottawa Conference, only to reject them.[49] Price guarantees were also examined, but not extensively – though the Labour Government's Ottawa committee was prepared to recommend a price guarantee at least for butter.[50] However, the Cabinet decided that it was in no way committed to these butter proposals.[51] Indeed, by year-end the Cabinet members themselves seem to have begun to forget their own actions and decisions. We find the minutes recording that it had been hoped the 1930 conference 'would be able to deal finally with the question of a wheat quota, but in the event the settlement of this question had been left over until the Ottawa Conference'.[52]

I. WHEAT QUOTAS, 1930–1932

In May 1931, the Cabinet committee on the coming Ottawa conference recommended that the UK delegates be empowered to offer a percentage quota for Dominion wheat. They wanted a simple mixing scheme without any price guarantee. J. H. Thomas thought that this was the 'one constructive scheme of any importance which the UK could put forward at Ottawa'.[53] But after the 1931 election had confirmed the National Government and given it a doctor's mandate, a new Cabinet committee had again to turn its attention to the inherited complex of devices. On 23 November it reported that bulk purchases and import boards were impracticable. They should not be further considered. However, the Dominions should be offered a wheat quota – still without price guarantee.[54] In June 1930 Baldwin had committed the Conservative Party to a different sort of wheat plan for the British producer – a guaranteed minimum price on a fixed maximum wheat output. The scheme may have originated with Amery, whom Baldwin had asked for advice on agricultural policy. Amery then suggested a price-guaranteed plan.[55] In December 1931 and January 1932, Sir John Gilmour carried this proposal through Cabinet – with some opposition from Labour and Liberal members. In spring 1932, it was enshrined in the Wheat Act. But nobody ever envisaged that the scheme would be extended to the Dominions. It would, in any event, have been impracticable to do so. The Wheat Act imposed a levy on all flour, and used the proceeds to subsidise domestic wheat farmers, so that they received a price in excess of the market price. The arrangement worked only because Britain imported most of the grain her millers ground. But the Dominions produced far more grain than Britain could use. Hence if the Wheat Act system were extended to Dominion grain, Britain would consume only Dominion and UK wheat – apart from small quantities of special qualities that might be needed for mixing. There would be no foreign grain to pay the levy, and the guaranteed price would apply to the entire wheat consumption of the UK. Hence the Wheat

Act, though related to the Conservative Party programme, had little to do with previous inter-governmental discussion, and nothing to do with the quota proposals which the National Government realised it was obliged to produce for the Ottawa Conference.

Early in November 1931 Sir John Gilmour, the new Minister of Agriculture and Fisheries, told his Cabinet colleagues that the *home* wheat quota was being studied departmentally. Later in the month he asked authority to announce that the home quota was government policy. The result was a lengthy and vigorous discussion – necessarily rather formless, as the Minister had neglected to work out the mechanics of his scheme. The minutes state, 'while the policy of a British wheat quota was felt by some members of the Cabinet to be open to criticism from a political point of view . . . they did not press their objections to the point of rejection.' At length the Cabinet agreed that the Minister could make his announcement – but that he should circulate the details of his proposal as soon as possible.[56]

Early in December, ministers saw a preliminary proposal – 'in essentials identical' with Baldwin's ideas of 1930. That is, it provided for a guaranteed price on a definite quantum of home-produced wheat, and a carefully concealed levy to finance this guarantee. In January, Gilmour presented a more elaborate scheme, which he had devised with the co-operation of the millers and the grain trade. 'The discussion of the scheme revealed doubts as to whether it was not wider in scope than the Cabinet had contemplated, and as to whether it would not involve a more perceptible increase in cost to the consumer'. The proposals went to an *ad hoc* committee, which later recommended that they be accepted. Following another long and formless discussion in which Empire and foreign repercussions were nowhere mentioned, the Cabinet agreed to approve these recommendations. In mid-February, without any further debate, it authorised the immediate introduction of a suitable Wheat Bill.[57]

In the end only British farmers much cared what the Act actually said. But we must briefly note its provisions, both to conclude our account of *minimum-use* quotas, and to record the first appearance of another device, the deficiency payment in levy-subsidy form.

Introducing the second reading of the Wheat Bill, Sir John Gilmour explained that the Government had four aims to enhance the prices of home-grown wheat; to create a secure market for this wheat; to avoid Exchequer subsidisation; and to give no encouragement for the extension of cultivation to unsuitable land.[58] Hence the Bill proposed that millers and flour importers should make 'quota payments'[59] on their entire throughput, in amount sufficient to cover the 'deficiency payments' on the annual 'anticipated supply' from domestic farms. This supply could vary from year to year, but could never exceed 27 million cwt (6 million quarters). Deficiency payments would be made to the extent that the ascertained actual price might fall below 10s. per cwt. The bill fixed no quota percentage of home-grown wheat in milling, and said nothing about the Dominions. But it had the effect of ensuring that all home-grown wheat would be bought for milling at the going rate. Farmers would get 10s. per cwt. for the 'anticipated supply', and the actual market price on any excess supply.[60] To make absolutely sure that nothing could go wrong, the Act established a Flour Millers Corporation, whose chief function was to make a market; it could be ordered to buy any millable UK wheat, up to a maximum of 12½ per cent of the 'anticipated supply'.

Unlike the early proposals for minimum-use quotas, the Wheat Act scheme could not easily accommodate Dominion supplies. Even if the British Government had been willing to extend the levy-subsidy scheme to cover Dominion wheat, the scheme would have broken on the rock of Dominion output as the Dominions produced more wheat than the UK consumed. Any such scheme would soon exclude all foreign wheat from the British market – leaving no source on which the necessary levy could be collected. By introducing a bill of this sort, the National Government should have recognised that it would have to have two *kinds* of wheat quota – a home assignment with a price guarantee, and a Dominion one with none.

Long before July 1932, when the Ottawa Conference was to assemble, the wheat quota had become a dead issue in the Dominions. Canadian and Australian opinion was hardening against it, as producers and dealers saw little gain and some possibility of loss.[61] Besides, they now had reason to expect a more attractive and intelligible alternative in the form of a preferential tariff.[62] Further, both Canada and Australia had chosen to press for more direct and forceable measures – including prohibitions – to control Soviet competition in the British grain market.

In December 1931, Bennett had said that a Dominions wheat quota was a *sine qua non* for success at Ottawa. But he was trying to discover what Western farmers thought of it.[63] The more he learned, the less politically attractive did the device seem. Amery was telling him that the British themselves did not take the quota seriously.[64] And his own staff was discouraging.

In a 'Memorandum on Wheat and Flour . . . with Special Reference to the Quota',[65] the Canadian officials admitted that if the percentages were right a quota would be of value to Canada whenever all producers had substantial carry-overs. 'It appears certain that a quota would have reduced somewhat the Canadian carryover.' But in normal years the quota would have as many disadvantages as advantages. Because the British market could not absorb all the Empire's marketable surplus, the quota, like imperial preference, could not yield a higher price. Further, it would be hard to administer, fraught with difficulty for Canadian millers, open to price-manipulation, and conducive to the spread of a particular barrier to international trade – a barrier, already extensively used in Europe, which Canada should be trying to eliminate, not to spread.

Another memorandum reached similar conclusions. Examining the various types of trade controls, its authors concluded that preferential tariffs were best, because they were simplest, least subject to arbitrary change, and least disturbing to private business. All the other devices – quotas, barter, bulk purchase, import boards – 'are expedients . . . forced upon the world . . . they do not give any promise of permanency. Essentially they are "makeshift" contrivances for a topsy-turvy world.'[66]

This report must have gladdened Bennett's heart, as he certainly preferred tariff manipulation to anything else. In Australia the new United Australia Government and its officials were equally critical of the wheat quota. So was the informed public. In March 1932, a young Australian economist slated both quota and preferential tariff.[67] And in identical terms, in June, the Development Branch of the Australian Prime Minister's Office concluded that the wheat quota held no attractions for Australia, as it would neither raise the price she would get nor increase the total vent for her surplus.[68] Preferential tariffs they thought equally unattractive.

Prime Minister Lyons had already conveyed his feelings to Bennett:

'In view of the great importance of wheat exports, would appreciate direct exchange of views with your government with view to co-operation. We . . . find practical difficulties which in our view nullify value of suggested concessions by means of quotas or even preferential tariffs. Fact that in any circumstances half the Dominions wheat must be sold outside the Empire would govern price levels including that protected by quotas in British markets. This would prevent any benefit accruing to Empire wheat growers. . . .'[69]

Admittedly, the Australian wheat problem was not the same as the Canadian. Bennett was obliged to cope with an enormous stock of unsold wheat on which large sums had been lent. He was as much concerned to move this inventory as to achieve better prices on future production. But Lyons's telegram must have told him that if at the coming Ottawa Conference he simply pressed for a large share of the British wheat market, he would get no support from the Australian delegation. Further, the more he learned of opinion in his own western provinces, the less political mileage did the wheat quota appear to contain.[70]

All this was vaguely known in Whitehall. Nevertheless, the officials were still at work on a Dominion wheat quota. Late in December 1931, Thomas had made it publicly clear that at Ottawa the Government intended to offer one – so long as the *quid pro quo* was adequate.[71] In January 1932, Sir John Gilmour obtained the co-operation of the home millers' trade, which thereafter participated actively in the planning.[72] In March, an interdepartmental committee decided that the administrative difficulties were far greater than had been foreseen. But high commissioners in the Dominions were told that the quota was still a live proposal.[73] At this point, Sir Geoffrey Whiskard, a senior official in the Dominions Office, wondered whether the Dominions would not rather have something else. What of a prohibition against Russian wheat? Or a duty of 2s. per quarter? Both, he presumed, were politically impossible.[74] In early May, following further elaboration, an official committee made a definite recommendation.[75] In June, Thomas met the millers three times. Of the four schemes then in play, the only acceptable ones involved a separate quota for each Dominion, and probably offered little attraction to any of them. Whiskard wrote:

'I am not sure that the fact that the scheme is not particularly attractive to the Dominions need trouble us much. We have for long been aware that it is unlikely that the Dominions would be much interested in *any* quota scheme . . . on the other hand we are pledged to produce *a* scheme, and if it should appear at Ottawa that we could not produce any scheme Mr Bennett might be relied on to make capital out of that fact, even though it is very unlikely that he would be prepared to offer any very substantial concession in return for any scheme. In the circumstances I think the best course is to put up Plan A . . . for acceptance by the Cabinet, explaining that we must have some scheme . . . and that this is the best scheme that can be produced, and that in the circumstances we should not ourselves put it forward at Ottawa, but should have it ready to produce if it should be asked for.'[76]

Fortunately the details of these schemes need not concern us, as little more was ever heard of any of them. On 27 July, at Ottawa, the British delegation discovered that it agreed neither about the principle nor about the mechanics of a wheat quota. Faced with Bennett's agricultural demands, which spoke of preferential concessions either by tariff or by quota, and which included wheat,[77] the other delegates sent Chamberlain and Gilmour to modify an earlier scheme, so that it might be submitted first to Bennett and then to other delegations.[78] Bennett received it the same day, and it was later passed to the Australians and the Indians. But the Canadian Prime Minister quickly made it clear that he would rather have a duty on foreign wheat – even though he admitted that it would not actually help Prairie farmers. And S. B. Bruce, the leader of the Australian delegation, thought that a quota would do more harm than good because it would upset the Liverpool futures market.[79] As the UK did in the end agree to tax foreign wheat, and to protect the Dominions against Russian competition, it is not surprising that the wheat quota sank without trace.

Chapter 5

PREPARING FOR OTTAWA, 1930–1932

I. THE BEGINNINGS

The Imperial Economic Conference of 1932 met at Ottawa from 20 July until 20 August. At the time, it was widely viewed as the culmination of British political and fiscal developments whose origin was in 1902, or even earlier. Julian Amery has recently written of it in these terms – as a long-delayed vindication of Joseph Chamberlain's work for tariff reform.[1] More recently, political historians and biographers have examined the conference itself largely as a stage on which negotiators disported themselves.[2] Economic historians recognise that the conference decisions established a framework within which Empire trade and economic diplomacy were to be conducted for many years. In the next chapter, we examine the conference proceedings, with the aid of official documents which have only recently become available. In the present chapter, we survey the process by which the British Government prepared for the conference – both before and after the fall of the Labour Government. The present section contains some reflections on Imperial conferences in general, a sketch of the relevant events from the 1930 Imperial Conference of October and of the steps – few and halting – which the Labour Government took after November 1930, in preparation for the coming meeting at Ottawa. In the second section, we turn to the National Government; a brief account of its protectionist tendencies serves as introduction to a more detailed account of the preferential proposals which were in circulation during the winter of 1931–32. This section also contains some reflections upon the National Government's unemployment policy. Was it sensible to impose protective tariffs when the exchange rate was already floating? The third section traces the course of the preliminary negotiations themselves. The question of Russian trade and competition was important both before the conference and at it. Since this question, like the monetary issue, arose partly in connection with the agenda, it is scrutinised in the fourth section. The fifth treats the process by which conference agenda were generated. It proved convenient to treat the question of monetary discussions in this section. Finally, the sixth and last section summarises the position which Cabinet and delegation had reached on the eve of their departure.

At the Imperial conferences which preceded the Ottawa meeting, there had been a series of arguments about British tariff policy. The Dominion governments systematically and consistently pressed reluctant British ministers to impose duties on foreign foodstuffs while allowing Empire goods to enter Britain duty-free. The 1923 meetings, when Baldwin's Government was willing to impose some new duties on foreign luxury foodstuffs, constitute a partial and slight exception to the general pattern: Dominion importunity, and UK intransigence.[3] The agenda of the conferences were lumbered, especially in 1923, 1926, and 1930, with many economic topics. Compared to the tariff reform question, all these topics were insignificant – and were perceived to be so. With respect to constitutional evolution the Imperial conferences were certainly fruitful. With respect to economic relations, they almost certainly did more harm than good.

The tariff discussions were always oddly one-sided. Dominion ministers felt free to attack Britain's agricultural free trade. But British ministers could not attack the growing protectionism of the Dominions. Canada and Australia were strongly protectionist; after 1922 India was following their examples, though with some circumspection; after 1925, South Africa was eager to do the same. To British manufacturers and politicians this protectionism was very worrying, especially during the 1920s, when sterling was overvalued and unemployment was severe. Admittedly, the Dominions charged lower duties on many British goods. But these 'preferential' concessions did not always mean very much. The preferential rates themselves were often prohibitive, or nearly so. Yet, at the conferences the UK never felt able to discuss Dominion protectionism.

The reasons for this reticence were never fully stated. But they may be inferred. British ministers might have feared that the Dominion ministers would treat a criticism of Dominion tariffs as a challenge to fiscal autonomy – one of the marks of 'Dominion status'. They certainly knew that Britain had little to offer the Dominions so long as she kept to free trade. Finally, they were determined not to bargain over tariffs.[4] Within the Empire, preferential concessions were to be unilateral free gifts; there would be no bargaining over Imperial preference, and each part of the Empire would give its fellows what it could. Within the Dominions Britain's trade commissioners could and did make representations. After 1928, when the UK began to plant high commissioners in the Dominions, her diplomats certainly did the same. But Imperial conferences were meant for harmonious discussions, not for trade negotiations.

Partly for this reason, the Dominions Office and the MacDonald Government had tried to keep the tariff issue off the agenda of the 1930 London Conference. The delegates would face weighty constitutional issues, they should not waste their attention on economic arguments which would certainly be fruitless. Though some of MacDonald's ministers inclined towards protectionism, his Chancellor of the Exchequer was an unyielding bastion of free trade orthodoxy. Philip Snowden even disliked the existing concessions which Britain gave to a few Empire goods. And the Labour Party itself was committed to complete free trade – an 'untaxed breakfast table'. With the duties on sugar, coffee, tobacco and canned fruit would go the preferences thereon. Churchill had already done the larger part of the job when, in 1929, he abolished Britain's tea duty. Snowden proposed to complete the work of abolition as soon as he could spare the revenue. But neither he nor the Dominions Office could keep the question from arising. Australia's Labour Government insisted that it wanted to discuss bulk purchase, price stabilisation, and import boards. Canada's Prime Minister, R. B. Bennett, startled the conference soon after its opening by offering 'a 10 per cent preference' in exchange for British taxes on foreign food.

As J. H. Thomas had feared, the result was deadlock. On 13 November, the Conference Committee on Economic Co-operation, having made little progress, recommended that within twelve months there should be an Economic Conference at Ottawa 'to examine fully the various means by which inter-Imperial trade may best be maintained and extended'. The next day, at the final plenary session, R. B. Bennett moved 'the adjournment of the Economic Section of this Conference to meet upon a date within the next twelve months to be agreed upon'. He continued, 'I wish, on behalf of the Canadian people to assure you of their most hearty welcome'.[5]

In London, the 1930 Conference was barely over before a new Cabinet committee began to consider the Ottawa meeting.[6] However, the committee met infrequently – only five times between November 1930 and April 1931. Urgency should not have departed, as only on 6 June 1931 was it announced that the conference would be deferred until 1932.[7] But long before this delay had become necessary, the committee – and the Cabinet – were paralysed by the same disputes and rigidities which had caused the 1930 Conference to end so inconclusively.

At its first meeting the committee agreed that the Agriculture Ministry should consider the wheat quota, that an interdepartmental committee should consider bulk purchase, import boards, and intra-Imperial cartelisation, and that the Board of Trade should draw up a schedule of useful tariff concessions and circulate them for comment to the ACOC, the FBI, and other trade organisations. At later meetings it tentatively approved a butter-price guarantee, rejected any other manipulation of the butter trade, passed a wheat-quota scheme to another committee, and resolved that at the coming conference the UK delegates were to seek reductions of preferential rates but that 'In no circumstances were the United Kingdom delegates specifically [to] advocate a policy of increased rates in the general duties.' Finally, at its last meeting, it agreed by a majority to recommend that the delegates be empowered to offer a wheat quota. This decision followed an appeal from Thomas, who argued that the wheat quota was 'the one constructive scheme of importance which the United Kingdom could put forward at Ottawa'; unless it were preferred, the 'proposed conference would do more harm than good'.[8]

In the Dominions, meanwhile, the politicians hoped for little from the coming conference. Havenga had already expressed his reservations to Bennett.[9] In May 1931, the UK representative reported from South Africa that Havenga was willing to attend, but saw little point unless the UK should modify its fiscal position.[10] The Canadian Trade Commissioner was reporting from South Africa to Ottawa in the same terms.[11] Indeed, he believed that South Africa would attend the conference only to negotiate an agreement with Canada.[12] The New Zealand Government saw little point in attending, because His Majesty's Government in New Zealand, in the light of economic discussion at the last Imperial conference, felt bound to assume that there was no possibility of any effective consideration at Ottawa of a general system of Imperial Preference embracing the UK.[13] And even after the National Government had been formed, Bennett wrote: 'The difficulty is that the [United Kingdom] Government is so divided in its views that it is difficult to see how a conference in London will accomplish anything, and unless there is something accomplished at the next Conference, we have reached the end.'[14]

II. THE NATIONAL GOVERNMENT, PROTECTION AND UNILATERAL PREFERENCES

With the change of government in the UK there came a renewed push on the Ottawa front. In a general way, the shape of the negotiations was already obvious. Indeed, it had been clear since the Imperial Conference of 1902. The Dominions would ask for protection in the British food market; Britain would ask for the same in the Dominions' markets for manufactures. Efforts would be made to include India in the preferential system: the subcontinent had never accepted the principle of preferential tariffs, and still gave only a few incidental concessions to British goods. Southern Rhodesia, too, would seek concessions – and might even offer some. But what was needed was a detailed confrontation on particulars – individual commodities and rates. Given the complexities of the Dominions' tariff structures, such confrontations could better be handled by experts, before the conference itself had assembled. Or so the British administrators thought.

The Labour Government's preparatory committee had asked the Board of Trade to prepare 'schedules' of concessions which Britain might request – one for each Dominion, and one for India. Whitehall conferred with the Association of British Chambers of Commerce and the Federation of British Industries, to discover which tariffs in which Dominions were most objectionable to British exporters. The Board of Trade and the Dominions Office also began to gather data about non-tariff practices – arbitrary valuations for the assessment of duty, tariff surcharges to offset the depreciation of sterling, 'primage duties', and delays in customs administration.

During the last four months of 1931, as the UK's new government moved rapidly toward a protectionist policy, it became meaningful to think about Ottawa – what would be demanded, and what could be offered. The Cabinet preparatory committee was re-formed – chiefly, at first, to guide J. H. Thomas, who was proposing a negotiating tour of the Dominions. Largely at his urgings, the Cabinet approved the idea of pre-conference negotiations on 2 December.[15]

Thomas himself did not travel to Canada and the Antipodes, apparently because his colleagues did not trust him. But the committee continued its labours, preparing in December some *ad hoc* suggestions on British food duties. It would not contemplate a meat duty or a wheat duty, even for the sake of granting a preference, but it looked more kindly upon the traditional dutiable foodstuffs – luxury fruits, tinned and dried fruits, and such like. However, these proposals soon became mixed with the similar but not identical suggestions which the Cabinet Committee on Agricultural Policy was simultaneously producing. Under much tighter protectionist control, it was disinclined to tolerate free entry for Empire foods. And it wanted a wider range of duties.

During the same weeks of December 1931, Sir John Gilmour, the Minister of Agriculture, was maturing a scheme for the protection of British wheat – the 'quota' with guaranteed price which Baldwin had proposed more than a year before. Britain was already committed to offer a 'quota' at Ottawa – but not to guarantee any particular price. Indeed, the *domestic* quota would work only because Britain imported so much of her wheat consumption. By imposing a small levy on this wheat, the Government could find the money for 'deficiency payment', raising the farmers' price above the world level. But the Empire produced more wheat than Britain consumed: if such deficiency payments were offered, only Empire wheat would enter the British market, and there would be no dutiable imports from which deficiency payments could be funded. Hence the Government's consistent determination that though it would offer the Dominions a guaranteed share of the British wheat market it would not guarantee or support the prices they would obtain therein. From November 1931 until July 1932, Whitehall officials laboured to devise a scheme which would satisfy the Cabinet, the millers, and the Dominions. But neither the officials nor anyone else took these labours very seriously: long before summer 1932, they knew that Australia and Canada had lost interest in so valueless a device.

By the end of 1931, conference planning had merged with the general scheming for British protectionism. Many Conservatives were attracted by the idea of a three-decker tariff, like Canada's, which offered Preferential, Most-Favoured-Nation, and General rates. Empire countries would pay the least, and foreign countries could be awarded the intermediate rates if they made sufficiently generous concessions. But the Liberal and Labour free-traders and the moderate Labour protectionists were unhappy about this proposal – and also about the wheat quota and about the extreme agrarian protectionist proposals which were coming from the Agricultural Policy Committee.

During the Christmas recess of 1931, MacDonald went to Scotland, but Runciman stayed in London. There he negotiated with Chamberlain and the other protectionists, and with Snowden and the free traders. He convinced Chamberlain to accept the Liberal idea which Keynes had already publicised in March 1931 and which MacDonald's Labour Ministry had considered in August – a general 10 per cent 'revenue tariff'. Runciman's initiative, which all factions eventually accepted, was the basis of the Import Duties Act of February 1932.[16]

In January 1932, the Cabinet's Balance of Trade Committee also recommended a 10 per cent tariff. This Committee had been set up in response to the concern about the trade balance – a concern which several politicians had expressed at the 1931 election. Much of this concern may have been artificial – a Conservative attempt to win their Liberal and Labour colleagues to protectionism. But Chamberlain himself seems to have been genuinely worried about the balance. And so were Treasury officials.[17] The Economic Advisory Council had shown that in 1930 the UK had indeed run a large current-account deficit, and that she would run another in 1931. On 16 December, the Cabinet Committee was established to brood on the problem.[18]

When one's currency floats, there is no logical reason to worry about the balance-of-payments implications of a current-account deficit. One knows that the price of one's currency will adjust so that supplies of foreign exchange equal demands for it. Indeed, these adjustments, and related adjustments in the economy at large, will tend to eliminate the deficit itself, unless capital movements are sufficiently large to move the exchange rate in the wrong direction. The pound had been a floating currency since September 1931. Why, then, did Chamberlain and the Treasury worry about the state of the national trading accounts? Certainly there was a naïve worry that the country was 'living on capital' – dissipating its foreign investments to maintain current consumption. But this was not the whole story. In private, Chamberlain would admit that the depreciation of sterling was helping British exports. But he feared that these effects would dwindle. The sterling prices of imports would rise, and other countries would also devalue, float, or impose quotas.[19] As Sir Richard Hopkins explained, there was a good reason for worrying about the balance of trade if one cared about the level at which a floating pound would float. The Economic Advisory Council had thought, in September, that a depreciation of 25 per cent would not be excessive. Hopkins thought that for the export trades the best rate would be between $3.80 and $4.10. He argued that a tariff would raise the exchange value of a floating pound, but that sterling must not be allowed to float too high. On the other hand, an unduly low rate would be disastrous: it might cause panic and would certainly lead to 'a rise in cost of living, and a fall in value of our investments abroad, mostly in sterling, toward rubbish values. Our real problem is to secure a balance of payments consistently with a reasonable exchange value of the pound.'[20] Another Treasury memorandum argued that sterling must be supported, so as to retain London's financial business, and to help create a sterling bloc. Its author also worried about the fact that Britain's overseas assets, including her war-debt credits, were denominated in sterling, but that she owed dollars to the USA. He thought that depreciation would necessarily turn the gross barter terms of trade against Britain, and he observed that it would certainly lower the foreign purchasing power of the sterling interest on Britain's foreign assets. If other countries were to fix their currencies to sterling – 'which we presumably want' – *vis-à-vis* such countries there would be no gain from further sterling depreciation, because their monies would go up and down along with the pound.[21]

These arguments are not without force. But it is perverse to try to raise one's exchange rate if one has millions of unemployed. As Professor Mundell has shown, when a country has a floating exchange rate a new tariff is likely to be contractionary – that is, it will increase the number of unemployed, reducing national output and income, other things being equal.[22] If the exchange rate is fixed, an import tariff will unequivocally expand domestic production and reduce foreign receipts of the domestic currency. Thus unless foreign governments retaliate, it will improve both employment and the current-account balance. But if a tariff is imposed along with a floating exchange rate, the tariff-induced upward float of the exchange rate will encourage imports and discourage exports, offsetting some or all of the stimulus which the tariff itself would give employment. The National Government itself believed that it was following an anti-unemployment policy. With respect to its own goals, therefore, we must find its measures inconsistent. But these considerations did not worry most of the politicians who made up the Cabinet Committee on the Balance of Trade, or the officials who advised them.

The Committee majority recommended a general revenue tariff to remedy the imbalance of trade. In response to Cunliffe-Lister's urgings,[23] it urged that something be done to Anglo-Russian trade. The USSR was selling far more to Britain than she was buying; could not this imbalance be adjusted?[24]

The Committee did not recommend any specific preferential margin. Its calculations were made on the assumption that the Dominions would be granted a rebate of one-third from the general 10 per cent levy. But it did not recommend that this or any other rebate be granted automatically. Instead, it suggested, 'some intimation should be given that the whole ten per cent. would form the subject of discussions at the Ottawa Conference, and might be modified, or even suspended altogether, if an adequate return could be obtained'.[25] As for the colonies, it proposed 'special arrangements . . . including total exemption from duty of some imports therefrom in certain cases'. It had not considered Indian goods, but thought 'it could be arranged . . . for preferences to be given to Indian products on lines similar to those proposed for Dominion products'.[26]

These recommendations supplemented the suggestions which had already come from the Cabinet Agricultural Policy Committee. It had proposed general protection for British agriculture. It also thought that the Dominions should be granted a reduced rate of duty – but not free entry – for their butter, cheese, honey, raw apples, raw pears, oranges, grapes, other raw fish, canned fruit and salmon, crayfish, crab, lobster, and dried and preserved fruit.[27] It had no specific recommendations on wheat and flour, presumably because Sir John Gilmour was already at work on the Wheat Bill.

Finally, the Cabinet's Ottawa Committee had already recommended that on a wide range of foodstuffs the UK should impose preferential tariffs – 'provided that an adequate *quid pro quo* is obtained'. The committee excluded from consideration canned and dried milk, eggs, dead poultry, bacon, ham, beef and mutton, lamb, tinned meat, live edible animals, and maize. But it proposed a mixture of *ad valorem* and specific duties on foreign butter, cheese, honey, raw, canned, and dried apples and pears, oranges, grapes, other raw fruit, canned fruit, pineapples, fish and dried and preserved fruit. The agricultural representatives thought that it would be dangerous to allow free entry for all such Dominion goods: cheap Dominion food might be bad for home agriculture. Hence, the committee was prepared to contemplate the taxing of these Dominion goods – but at a preferential rate.[28]

The Cabinet noted the reports of the Ottawa Committee and the Agricultural Policy Committee. It never approved them. But these, like the Balance of Trade Report, formed part of the background from which the Government proceeded, late in January, to divide with respect to protection,[29] and to decide on its preferential strategy. The Import Duties Bill was in draft. Should there be free entry for Empire goods in hope of a *quid pro quo*? No preferential concessions for the present, pending the results of the conference? Or some other arrangement? And what of tea and India?

When the Bill first came before the Cabinet, it contained a clause which would allow the Treasury to fix a lower rate of duty, or no duty, on goods consigned from and grown in any Dominion, India, or Southern Rhodesia.[30] Thus at first the duty would be charged or lowered on the goods of those countries which would sign helpful Ottawa agreements. However, Chamberlain quickly became convinced that the result would be 'disastrous'. Rather than strengthening Britain's hand at the Ottawa Conference, he argued on 3 February, it would destroy the point of the conference. He proceeded to telephone both J. H. Thomas, in Geneva, and R. B. Bennett, in Ottawa.

Bennett, in turn, consulted his Cabinet, and told Chamberlain that the best idea would be to impose a general non-preferential tariff but not to levy it on Dominion goods until after the conference.

Thomas consulted the Dominion high commissioners who were also in Geneva. Explaining the Import Duties Bill, he said that the new fiscal policy was solely intended to break down the tariff walls of other countries. As for Ottawa, it had been decided to offer a wheat quota and other advantages, but not whether to put preferences into the Import Duties Bill. Did they think that Britain would be justified in taking the risk of giving the Dominions free entry immediately and awaiting a satisfactory *quid pro quo* at Ottawa? The Australians and New Zealanders said 'yes'; the South Africans and Irish said 'no'; the Canadians said 'perhaps'.[31]

Thomas told Chamberlain that he did not like the Bennett–Chamberlain 'solution', but the majority[32] of the Cabinet accepted it, fearing 'anything calculated to destroy the atmosphere of the Ottawa Conference'. And so it was decided to grant preferences in the Bill – but only until 15 November. If the conference did not produce meaningful concessions, this provision would lapse, and Dominion and Indian products would no longer enjoy the duty-free entry which the Act secured to the colonial Empire.

Among the many products in which the Dominions were interested, the Bill proposed free entry for some – notably copper, wheat and meat – and a 10 per cent duty on others – notably butter, flour, aluminium, lead and zinc. To these products much economic diplomacy would soon direct its attention. Would Britain reduce her free list? Would she raise her duties on foreign supplies, while charging no duty on Dominion goods?

Introducing the proposal in the House, Chamberlain underlined that one of the reasons for protection was to offer advantages to the Empire 'in return for the advantages which they now give, or in the near future may be disposed to give, to us'.[33] Hence, he explained, so as not to prejudice the Ottawa discussions, the Government had decided to defer the application of the new duties to goods from the Dominions, India, and Southern Rhodesia. They would be imposed non-preferentially on 15 November if the Ottawa results were not satisfactory.

The Import Duties Act did not impose any new levy on tea. In 1929, Churchill had abolished Britain's tea duty – and the preference that went with it. Chamberlain and others assumed that the question of a preferential tea duty would be an important issue in the Anglo-Indian negotiations. By 15 January, the Cabinet's Ottawa Committee had recommended such a duty.[34] Chamberlain, however, wanted to wait until the Budget to impose this duty; Cunliffe-Lister and others thought that tea should be taxed at 10 per cent under the Import Duties Bill.[35] Chamberlain got his way: only when he made his budget speech did he announce that henceforth foreign tea would pay a duty of 4d. and Empire tea a duty of 2d.

The question of a tea duty, and the general question of preferential margins, were not solely questions of negotiating strategy and of protectionism: they were also questions of revenue. Whatever their other functions, the new duties were consciously intended to raise money for the balancing of the government budget. Preferential concessions meant loss of revenue, even on current volumes of trade; if preferences succeeded in diverting Empire goods to the British market, the new duties would bring even less revenue. What concessions could the British budget digest? Early in January we find the Treasury estimating the yields of the new duties which the Ottawa Committee and the Agricultural Policy

Committee had suggested: assuming a 10 per cent rate on foreign goods and a 6.7 per cent rate on Empire goods, the officials foresaw revenue of £11.1 million.[36] The Customs officials believed that a 10 per cent general tariff would have yielded £61 million on 1931's imports, even if wheat, meat and food products were exempt. A one-third preference, they thought, would reduce the yield to £54 million, and complete exemption to £38 million. The sacrificed £16 million would go largely to India (£3 million), Australia (£2 million), and New Zealand (£2 million); the other Dominions would gain one to two million pounds each.[37] Thus the concessions of the Import Duties Act – indefinite free entry for colonial produce, and conditional free entry for Dominion produce – were considerable sacrifices from an economy-minded Chancellor. It is hardly surprising that he made them only at the last possible moment.[38] With respect to tea, he and his advisers experimented almost until Budget Day: repeatedly they calculated the revenue effects of various rates and preferences. There is no evidence in the Treasury papers that they consulted the India Office or the Indian Government with respect to these rates and margins.

Thus a mixture of motives seems to have been present in the preferential devices which Britain introduced early in 1932. With respect to tea, revenue considerations dominated both general rate and preferential margin, even though the preference itself was granted unilaterally as a bargaining counter in the coming negotiations. With respect to the Import Duties Act, the final version granted the Dominions much more generous preferential concessions than Chamberlain or his colleagues had originally contemplated. Here, questions of negotiating strategy won out, defeating the Chancellor in his search for revenue, and also defeating the elements in the Conservative Party and the Cabinet which wanted more agrarian protectionism.

With respect to British industry the Import Duties Act was, of course, protectionist; besides imposing a general levy, it provided for increases if the Import Duties Advisory Committee should recommend higher protection in particular industries. But there is no sign that the Cabinet or its advisers feared any competition from Empire or Dominion manufactures. Hence they cannot have imagined that they were trading employment for bargaining position: in conceding free entry to the non-agricultural produce of the Empire and the Dominions, they were sacrificing neither revenue nor jobs. The Dominions did send some manufactures to the UK before 1932. But almost all of these were 'McKenna goods' – cars, watches, and optical equipment. When the UK introduced Imperial preferences in 1919, it lowered duties on Dominion and Empire goods which were subject to the McKenna duties of 1915. But it did not admit these goods duty-free. And the McKenna structure of duties continued, in tandem with the new levies of 1932. Thus the UK had *not* granted free entry to those Dominion manufactures which had already demonstrated their ability to compete in the British market. It was in Canada that these goods were made. One wonders whether the Canadian Government and its advisers noticed the significance of the British package: conditional free entry for primary products, but, with respect to manufactures, no meaningful concessions.

With respect to agriculture and food products, the governmental moves of early 1932 must have been less effective bargaining counters then the National ministers expected. Britain was so large a buyer of so many foodstuffs, and of tea, that any new British duty would certainly tend, at least in the short run, to be 'shifted backwards'. That is, world prices would fall, at least a little, because British buyers, facing a higher retail price, would buy less of the newly-taxed good. To India, therefore, the new preferential tea duty actually meant *lower* tea prices. Thus the tea duty was an extraordinary thing for a British Government to do to an Indian Government from whom it hoped to win tariff reductions, and whose advisers it knew to favour vigorous price-*raising* policies.

The White Dominions emerged rather better from the National Government's tariff innovations. By imposing new duties on so many foreign foods, the Import Duties Act ensured a fall in world prices for dairy products, dried fruits, canned goods, and other lesser foodstuffs – though not for wheat or meat, on which no duties were imposed. Since foreign countries supplied Britain with large amounts of all these foods, the British retail price would be determined by the new and lower world price, plus the duty. Because the Dominions did not export enough of these goods to supply all British demand at the relevant prices, Dominion suppliers, paying no duty, would get this British retail price, minus marketing costs and distributors' profits. As this price would exceed world levels, and as world prices would be unlikely to fall by the full amount of the new British tariffs, Dominion producers would get a higher price than foreign suppliers, and a higher price than before the tariffs were imposed. But because the tariff itself lowered world prices, their gain would be very much less than the preferential margin the new system created for them.

Wheat was not taxed under the Import Duties Act. Even if preferential duties had been imposed, they would have done the Dominions neither harm nor good. Because Canada and Australia produced more wheat than Britain would import at any relevant price level, a preferential duty would simply have diverted Dominion wheat to Britain, repelling identical amounts of foreign wheat on to other markets. The world supply–demand balance, world prices, and British internal prices would not change. Hence the apparent absence of a wheat duty, though perhaps politically annoying to Mr Bennett, was of no economic significance. Much more important, and certainly damaging to the Dominions, were Britain's 'deficiency payments' under her new Wheat Act. This measure guaranteed a price for a quantum of British-produced wheat, and imposed a levy on flour to provide the funds for this system. When market prices were below the guaranteed level, British farmers would receive deficiency payments from the fund. Though not called a duty, and though not built into the Import Duties Act, the levy was, of course, an import duty, and the net effect of the Wheat Act was to raise the UK prices of wheat, bread, and fodder. We have already described the result in connection with tea: a higher retail price meant smaller sales, and a lower level of world prices. Further, the guaranteed price was definitely intended to expand British wheat production – at least a little. So the British market would be taking less wheat from other countries – Dominions and foreigners – simply because her domestic supply was being artificially increased.

If these aspects of the new British agrarian protectionism were understood in the Dominions, it can hardly have disposed Prime Minister Bennett and S. M. Bruce to look with favour upon the coming negotiations. Nevertheless, because the import duties concessions were so explicitly temporary, the British negotiators would at least be able to say, 'what we have done we have done; if you do not make some concessions to us, we shall do something even nastier'. As we shall see, this threat was certainly made, both before the conference and during it.

III. PRELIMINARY CONVERSATIONS

1. *The General Arrangements*

Early in December 1931, the Cabinet's Ottawa Committee acted to start a process of preliminary negotiations which continued spasmodically for months. Both Thomas and Chamberlain were determined to map the ground thoroughly before the conference.[39]

The committee resolved to send each Dominion a 'schedule' of goods on which Britain would like tariff concessions. The Board of Trade had been at work on these schedules for some months. On 10 December, the Dominions Office told the overseas governments that the schedules would soon be on the way. It also proposed a format for the exploratory talks. Each Dominion might nominate London representatives to discuss the material in Whitehall; overseas the Dominions might nominate expert advisers to discuss the schedules with Britain's High Commissioners, representatives and senior trade commissioners. The Office emphasised that the discussions would be 'wholly non-committal on both sides, and directed merely to clearing the way for the conference'.[40]

By 13 January, South Africa had not answered this message. Other Dominions, including the Irish Free State, had agreed to discussions overseas in London, or in both places. By 23 January the Dominions Office had decided that in South Africa, its representative Sir H. Stanley might negotiate as he liked. At the end of the month the Permanent Under-secretary of the Dominions Office wrote: 'the negotiations here and in the Dominions [are] an essential preliminary to a further report of the Ottawa Committee to the Cabinet as to the prospects of an arrangement with the Dominions.'[41]

In February, the Dominions Office suggested that the London discussions should treat British concessions, and the overseas conversations should stick to Dominion concessions. This was an attempt to generalise the pattern that was emerging in the Anglo-Australian talks – and to discourage any comparing of offers and requests.[42]

Nevertheless, things went slowly, and Whitehall became alarmed. In May, ministers and officials agreed to prod the Dominions, where, they feared, the Import Duties Act had been misread. Accordingly, on 9 May, the Dominions Office sent a vigorous telegram. Britain would continue free entry for Dominion goods only if the Dominions made extra concessions. She would find it very difficult to grant concessions with respect to goods still on her free list. Only if the Dominions made concessions of outstanding importance would Britain consider imposing or raising her duties on foreign goods. In particular, it was essential for the Dominions to tell Britain what they would give merely to retain their privileges under the Import Duties Act. Meanwhile, it was important to press on with the negotiations.[43]

This telegram so annoyed the Dominion governments that they nearly broke off negotiations. In Wellington, Canberra, Pretoria, and Ottawa, the UK must have seemed grasping and unreasonable. Within each Dominion there were sound political reasons for the delays. Australia and New Zealand had fiscal crises. Canada had a parliamentary session. Further, all the Dominions already gave tariff concessions to Britain. The Import Duties Act simply equalised these. Why should the Dominions give *more* simply to retain their rights of free entry?

In each Dominion the UK 'schedules' and the 9 May telegram set off a different sequence of pre-conference discussion and bargaining. It is time to trace these sequences separately.

2. *Talks with South Africa*

In the preliminary negotiations, South Africa was not very forthcoming. In 1925, her Nationalist Government had abandoned its old preferential tariff system. The new one granted substantial preferential concessions on some items, and none on others. The general principle, which the South African finance minister still espoused in 1932, was one of reciprocal concession on a simple basis: Britain and South Africa should so balance their preferences that both would be sacrificing the same tariff revenues. In 1931, the South African Minister of External Affairs told the British Trade Commissioner that he would like to re-introduce a general preferential discount, combined with a three-column tariff of the Canadian sort.[44] If South Africa had such a tariff structure she could concede the 'intermediate' rates to co-operative foreign countries while granting the lower 'preferential' rate to Britain and the Dominions. But Dr Havenga, the Finance Minister, was strongly attached to the 1925 system. Hence, when South Africa introduced an exchange-dumping duty in November 1931, he refused to give the UK any special treatment.[45]

In May 1931, Canada's Trade Commissioner reported that Havenga would try to avoid sending a delegation to the Ottawa Conference 'unless for the specific purpose of concluding [a] trade agreement with Canada. . . . If we [Canadians] initiate preliminary discussions with South Africa they will probably commit the conference in anticipation of completing [the] agreement'.[46] Such discussions did go on until early 1932. But the South Africans were very reluctant to begin preliminary conversations with Britain, either in London or in Cape Town and Pretoria.

South Africa received Britain's requests on 2 February 1932. Discussion began on 14 March. But by 5 July nothing definite had emerged. The 9 May telegram does not appear to have had any impact on the South Africans. They had grouped Britain's many requests into three simple categories: 'yes', 'perhaps', and 'no'. When Dr Havenga and Mr Fourie reached London from Cape Town on 6 July, more serious conversations began at once. Havenga explained that South Africa was eager to co-operate in diverting her imports from foreign to British suppliers. But, he said, she could do less than the other Dominions because she had already done more under her 1925 tariff, which already granted free entry to British cottons, iron and steel. Britain, too, could offer little to South Africa, except on meat.[47] Havenga had already told the Canadians that if Britain could do nothing for wool, maize, and meat the negotiations were pointless, because the remaining preferences were of little or no value to South Africa.[48] In a meeting of officials, a South African pointed out that the existing British preferences on wine, brandy, and fruit affected only small areas in South Africa, and that in these areas the Nationalist Government was not strong.[49] Meat, however, came from the solidly nationalist farmers of the Veldt.

3. *Talks with New Zealand*

New Zealand was equally reluctant to talk seriously before the conference itself. In April, Wellington cabled a request for an increase in all existing preferential margins, and for new preferences. The requests covered thirty-five items, including all sorts of meat, butter, cheese, wool, eggs, processed milk, and fresh fruit. According to the New Zealand Government, all were equally important.[50] On 7 April, Sir Horace Wilson discussed these requests with New Zealand's London representatives. Later that month, a Dominions Office official wrote that New Zealand must immediately be denied any wool or cheese concessions.[51] However, these London discussions quickly merged with the much more extended Anglo-Australian talks which dealt with the same products. It seems that New Zealand's hopes with respect to meat were not dissipated until well after the conference itself had begun.

At the New Zealand end, things moved equally slowly. The officials and ministers had promised to examine Britain's requests by mid-May. However, the 9 May telegram annoyed them so much that they broke off negotiations. One minister told the Trade Commissioner that his first reaction had been to cancel all preferences forthwith. On 19 May, the New Zealand Cabinet reported its reaction to the circular telegram. After regretting that the extremely difficult parliamentary session had prevented them from considering the requests more promptly, the ministers explained:

'His Majesty's Government in New Zealand have for some time been doubtful whether any real progress can be made by discussions affecting rates of duties on commodities unless conducted between representatives of Governments actually present at conference. They are now strongly of that opinion. Your telegram raises important questions of principle.'[52]

Hence, they suggested, to obviate hard bargaining by correspondence, there should be no more discussions either in London or in Wellington.

In London, New Zealand's representatives were anxious to continue the talks.[53] In Wellington, the British Trade Commissioner continued a gentle pressure. On 28 May he was asked to explain things to the New Zealand Cabinet. In the event, the Dominion's Government allowed the conversations to proceed. The experts met on 22 May. But the New Zealand Government insisted that the Trade Commissioner must not report on the talks' progress. When the New Zealand officials asked him what they might offer to retain free entry and to win a duty on foreign meat, the Commissioner suggested they might have to widen the preferential margins by ten percentage points. Later in May he wrote that the New Zealand Cabinet was divided on this suggestion.[54] Early in June he met J. G. Coates and W. Downie Stewart, the New Zealand ministers who were to journey to Ottawa. They said they would make large concessions to get certain meats off the free list. The Government would do everything it could to help Britain; ministers kept asking what concession might be sufficiently spectacular to make Britain impose a duty or quota on foreign meats. The Trade Commissioner wrote:

'The nature and extent of the delays which have taken place make me wonder whether they were intentional delays. I recently ascertained, however, privately, that the real cause was friction in the Cabinet and between permanent officials, mainly, I think, on matters of precedence. However, progress is being made.'[55]

As talks proceeded in Wellington, so they resumed in London. On 21 June and 4 July there were two general chats about Anglo-New Zealand trade. The New Zealanders argued that because they already gave the UK so much they should not be asked to give more merely to retain free entry for their butter and cheese. Britain should ask more of the other Dominions before requesting anything of New Zealand.[56] Wellington had authorised its London representatives to discuss preferences in general terms, without specifying definite rates of duty. The conversations, however, were centred on New Zealand's requests – especially upon meat, butter, and wool. Sir Horace Wilson, on the British side, was rather deflating. Though one must not annoy the Danes, Britain *might* raise the duty on foreign butter. Quotas were not inconceivable, though Britain did deplore them. Only in exchange for very great benefits – 'some outstanding concession' – could the UK impose duties on foreign meat and wool. The New Zealanders replied, rather sadly, that there was not much scope for an outstanding concession.[57] And there matters rested until the delegates reached Ottawa.

4. *Talks with Canada*

Neither in South Africa nor in New Zealand had the governments ever expected much from the coming conference. In Canada things were different. Prime Minister Bennett set great store by it.[58] If it should fail, there would be a Canadian-American accommodation.[59] But if Britain would commit herself to the 'principle of preference', and extend it to national products, Canada would charge no duty on British goods which Canada did not produce. What could be fairer?

Before he could proceed, Bennett had to know what the manufacturers would tolerate. Also, he had few reliable officials.[60] Hence, late in December 1931, he asked the Canadian Manufacturers Association for help. The 'CMA' was to ask its members on what goods they wanted free entry, preferential concessions, and higher duties. In particular, it was to discover which goods were not produced in Canada.[61]

The Association quickly discovered that it could not trust its members. 'If they think they may be making some particular class of commodity at some future time, [they] do not hesitate to declare they are making it already!'[62] Eventually, on 17 June, it produced a list of 9,553 articles 'of class or kind not made in Canada'. For these, it said, free entry was conceivable. But it did not subdivide the list by country of origin, suggesting that the Department of National Revenue could do so.[63]

This was not the sort of help which Bennett had wanted. The list was too inchoate, and it came far too late.[64] Long before 17 June, the High Commissioner, Sir William Clark, had been pressing for some comments on the British 'schedule'.

The schedule contained 253 items. It was dispatched on 14 January.[65] On 20 February, Sir William Clark attended a Canadian Cabinet meeting, and presented the document to the Canadian Ministry. Clark himself thought the Cabinet 'sympathetic',[66] but Bennett noted nervously that 'in many cases, reductions in the Preferential Tariff would be essential. .... Not merely increases in the General.... Stability was [also] essential'.[67]

After this flying start, absolutely nothing occurred. In March, Frederick Field, the Trade Commissioner, reported nervously that the preparations were going slowly. The Cabinet Committee had not yet met.[68] The Tariff Committee did not meet until 19 April.[69] Late in March, Clark reminded Bennett that Britain would like some word on the schedule, and on the concessions for which Canada herself might ask.[70] On 7 April, Bennett sent the schedule to the CMA, which had reported on 225 items by 4 July. In May, Clark gave Bennett a supplementary schedule of sixteen items. Eventually the Department of National Revenue itself produced a list of 7,000 items not made in Canada. But none of this material reached the UK officials.

On 11 May, two days after the circular telegram had arrived, Clark managed to talk to Bennett. He found the Prime Minister inclined to hide in lofty principle, and to avoid 'mere vulgar details':

'Did he mean by all this that we were to have no discussion on our schedule before the Conference? He hastily repudiated the suggestion. . . . I frankly find it extremely difficult to say where we stand. . . . Similarly, I find it very difficult to make up my mind as to what Bennett is really after . . . I sometimes wonder whether Bennett isn't deliberately playing for delay in order to have little or no time for pre-conference examination of tariff schedules. Then at the Conference he would trust to luck . . . and try to get away with it by putting forward his principles . . . you will see from all this that the first impact of your circular telegram has not been very promising of results so far as Bennett is concerned . . . but Bennett after all is a businessman, and when he thinks it over, will no doubt see our point of view – thought it may not convince him. At any rate, I will do my best to keep up the pressure here as opportunity serves . . . but the *vis inertiae* has been really formidable.'[71]

In June, Clark found Bennett still 'toying with the possibility of evading the issue in a cloud of sonorous principles'.[72] Late in May, the Trade Commissioner got a copy of the CMA list through private channels. The Government, however, did not transmit the list officially until the Conference had actually opened.[73] At the end of June, Clark managed an hour's talk with Bennett. He still would not discuss the schedules, but now admitted 'he could offer little and so will ask for little'.[74] He found Canadian manufacturers intransigent and unhelpful, the Prime Minister admitted. Clark concluded, correctly, that the schedule would not be discussed before the Conference opened.[75]

Bennett was equally dilatory with respect to his own requests. In December 1931, he had accepted the British plan for parallel discussions in London and overseas. But he seems never to have informed or instructed his own High Commissioner in London. Further, he sent his own requests to London only on 11 July – two days before the British were to sail for Quebec. He wanted concessions for wheat, flour, meat, cattle, dairy products, tobacco, fruit, vegetables, timber, pulp, and base metals. He named no rates of duty or preference, explained either a duty or a quota might serve his purpose, and reserved the right to extend his list.[76] These requests cannot have surprised the Whitehall officials, but they came too late to be useful.

In one area, Bennett did acquiesce in serious pre-conference discussion. J. H. Thomas had long favoured intra-imperial 'rationalisation' – the planned division of production between home and Dominion factories. Tariffs could be used if necessary to support such planning, but the basic agreements should come from the industrialists themselves. During March 1932, Field reported, the Canadian officials were willing to allow the Canadian iron, steel, and cotton trades to negotiate directly with their British counterparts. In June, two industrial delegations came to Montreal. The iron and steel trades reached an agreement which seemed likely to increase British exports. The mill-owners were less successful. Sir William Clark reported:

'They found themselves up against a complete brick wall . . . I am convinced that the Canadian textile representatives did not mean business. [H. H.] Stevens . . . held out no hope of any let up in the present extreme protectionist treatment of cotton goods.'[77]

5. *Talks with Australia*

Only Australia played the game as London wanted it played. Yet in Australia, as in New Zealand, local problems absorbed ministers' time and attention. The Commonwealth Treasurer must have found it hard to concentrate upon the tariff when New South Wales, the richest State in the country, was going thoroughly and messily bankrupt. Nevertheless, both in Australia and London there were active negotiations. Thus the Australian offers and requests had been thoroughly canvassed long before the beginning of July.

Australia, like Canada, had sharply increased her tariffs in 1930. Further, to her ordinary tariffs she had added an emergency 'primage' duty whose purpose was to raise revenue but whose effect was to give yet more protection. In addition, the Australian pound was now pegged well below the British. In sum, these measures had painfully constricted British sales in Australia. On the other hand, after sterling left gold in September 1931, the Australian and British pounds together floated downwards *vis-à-vis* the dollar. British goods gained an advantage over American exports both in Australia and in New Zealand, whose pound was also pegged to sterling. Further, since the London conference of 1930 the Australian Government had changed. The Scullin Labour administration had collapsed in disorder. Its successor, the United Australia Party, had just won an election campaign in which it had promised to reduce tariffs and to heed its Tariff Board. In February 1932, the promise was repeated in the Speech from the Throne, and several duties were soon reduced a little.[78]

All these developments encouraged Whitehall to hope. Further, in Australia as in Canada, Britain was well represented. Sir Robert Dalton, the Senior Trade Commissioner, had lived in Melbourne for many years. Like Frederick Field and Sir William Clark in Canada, he had informal access to the local politicians. Dalton was chronically inclined to expect the worst. But at first, even he reported cheerfully from the Antipodes.

London's Australian 'schedule' was dispatched on 7 January. Besides the usual list of goods on which unspecified concessions were asked, the Board of Trade was anxious to change the terms for 'bylaw items' and 'deferred duties'. The former were goods on which the Australian Customs collected preferential and ordinary tariff rates of zero and 10 per cent, even though the statutory rates were much higher. The latter were rates well in excess of zero which for the time being were not being collected at all. Both bylaw items and deferred duties could be assimilated into the ordinary tariff system at any time, by ministerial order. Further, on bylaw items the preferential margin was not very large. Hence the Board of Trade was anxious to 'conventionalise' Britain's right of free entry, to increase her margin of preference on bylaw goods, and to incorporate the resulting rates and goods into the ordinary tariff schedule.[79]

In January, the Australian Government established an Ottawa subcommittee. Its three members were S. M. Bruce, H. S. Gullett, and Mr Hawker. Bruce and Hawker were to represent Australia at the coming conference. All three shortly approached Dalton, asking what ought to be done. Bruce and Hawker agreed that Australia's tariffs must come down; Gullett seemed much more protectionist, and very much more inclined to bargain. He also stressed that Australia would eventually want to bargain with foreign countries too.[80]

On 9 February, the British 'representative', W. C. Hankinson, passed London's 'schedule' to the Australian Government. For some time nothing was done with it. Meanwhile Dalton was becoming gloomy again. Britain's Import Duties Act had weakened Australia's resolve by granting Dominion preferences. Australia's protectionist manufacturers were winning the Cabinet's ears.[81] Nevertheless, with the Cabinet's blessing, Dalton and senior customs officials conferred regularly and intensively until late April. Once in that period the subcommittee met Dalton, but its members were too busy to examine the schedule. As Hankinson explained: 'We have tried repeatedly to get a move on but in the existing political situation it has been impossible to arrange further meetings with the sub-committee in the last few weeks.'[82] Dalton, however, was less inclined to blame politics:

'It would appear that the [sub-]committee is unable to make

up its mind either as to the strength that it can display or as to the activity which it would take if the way were open. . . . Mr Abbott himself[83] is apparently very much concerned about the indication in the United Kingdom Government's telegram [of 9 May] that unless something is done very soon the preferences in the United Kingdom may be taken away. On the other hand, I understand that the subcommittee is a little inclined to underestimate the significance of this statement. . . .'[84]

The 9 May telegram was much resented in Australia, where the Government thought the UK had also been dilatory. On 25 May, Hankinson and Dalton met the Cabinet subcommittee for the first time in many weeks. The atmosphere was 'by no means so friendly as that of all our previous conversations'.[85] The subcommittee proposed to cable an offer of modest preferential margins. In private, Dalton and Hankinson urged Bruce and Hawker to defer its despatch. On 30 May, Dalton and Hankinson convinced the subcommittee to make a more generous offer. The ministers pointed out that they had already submitted many items to their Tariff Board. They hoped the Board would suggest reductions,[86] but could not prejudge its findings. They also explained:

'all these preferences would be conditional upon the grant of equally comprehensive concessions . . . and also upon the value of the preferences which might be granted by other Dominions to United Kingdom goods in return for benefits comparable to those which may be conceded to Australia.'[87]

What were the Australians conceding? It will be recalled that London had listed goods, but had not made any requests or suggestions as to the form any concessions might take. Dalton himself had invented the idea of a 'formula' and a more generous 'sub-formula' which would fix the preferential margins. Since he envisaged a three-column tariff, Dalton thought that the Australians would still have something to offer foreign countries. The higher the duty on British goods, the wider the percentage margin between this duty and the next highest tariff rate. It was this device which the Australians adopted.

Ideally the formula or the sub-formula would apply to the whole Australian tariff.[88] In practice, the Australians restricted it. Many protective duties were sequestered because the Tariff Board was already looking at them, or because the Ministry intended that it should. The 'bylaw duties' were to be treated separately. So were the 'deferred duties', under which free entry continued only at the Ministry's pleasure. So finally were the primage duties. Nevertheless, the offer was not ungenerous, and it was a far more concrete proposal than any other Dominion was able to make. Further, by 25 June, the Australian Government had reported on about half of the items in the original 'schedule'.[89]

In return, Australia asked Britain to impose duties and quotas on Argentine meat. To Bruce and Gullett meat mattered for several reasons. They knew a wheat duty or a mixing plan would not help them.[90] They also knew Britain could do nothing to help the wool trade. But meat was different. In Australia, the export industry produced a low grade frozen lamb and an even lower grade frozen beef. For some time, only institutions had bought the beef. But Argentine chilled beef was now so cheap that it was demolishing even this export market. Yet in Australia the industry was failing. If it could gain a better price or a larger vent, there would be rejoicing in every State of the Commonwealth.

Gullett's Department of Markets was hard at work on the meat question. It admitted that it did not know at what price meats would be 'payable'. Nevertheless, it calculated that a 1d. duty on foreign chilled beef would raise the Australian producer price from 1.8d. per lb. to 3d. In corned beef, a 25 per cent preference would be needed to exclude the South Americans.[91]

In other directions, the Department of Markets was comparably greedy. It wanted a butter quota, to freeze Britain's imports of foreign butter at the 1931 level, and also duties of 1½d. per lb. on foreign butter and 1d. per lb. on foreign cheese.[92] For dried fruits, it wanted the British to increase the preferential margin from 7s. 6d. per cwt. to 10s., and to raise the duty on Greek currants from 2s. per cwt. to 10s. per cwt. as soon as possible. For wine and brandy it wanted a reduction in the preferential duties and an increase in the duties on foreign goods. It had similar suggestions for canned fruits, eggs, poultry, tallow, and fresh fruit. In making these suggestions, it showed a mixture of concerns. Sometimes it simply wanted a 'payable' price, and sometimes a more profitable one. In a few cases, it was worried about surpluses. In some it hoped a preference would cause more production and more planting.[93]

Gullett must have had these memoranda in mind every time he asked Dalton and Hankinson to tell him what Britain would offer Australia. Presumably F. L. McDougall had the same information at hand as he pressed Australia's case in London, where preliminary talks began in March.

Early in April, McDougall saw J. H. Thomas. Australia and New Zealand, he said, would ask for 'something on meat – perhaps a beef quota and a tax of say ½d. per lb. on foreign lamb and mutton.'[94] A week later, McDougall told Sir Horace Wilson that Australia wanted concessions on meat, barley, fruit, wine, brandy, grape juice, lead, zinc, butter, cheese, dried milk, eggs, frozen poultry, honey, flour, and peas.[95] Again McDougall stressed the importance of meat. In early June he asked Sir Horace Wilson to tell him at the least whether Britain would discuss the meat question at Ottawa.[96] Later that month he expanded his meat plan.

Australia wanted free entry for Empire meat, 1d. per lb. on foreign frozen lamb, ¾d. per lb. on foreign chilled and frozen beef, mutton, and pork, 20 per cent on foreign canned meat, and 'qualitative restriction on foreign imports'.[97] She also wanted quotas to control foreign butter and canned fruits. And she wanted very specific margins and duties on foreign eggs, butter, cheese, fruit, apples, pears, canned fruits, dried fruits, wine, malting barley, and dried peas. Finally, she asked Britain to stabilise for fifteen years the preferential margin on dried fruit.[98]

In effect, this was Australia's traditional shopping list.

She had asked for similar things in 1922, 1923, and 1926. But by 1932 her need was more desperate. World prices had fallen, but Australia's farmers were producing more than ever. Ten years of rural 'development' had exacerbated a problem which had first appeared in 1922.

The 1932 requests arose directly from Australia's eccentric agricultural structure. The Commonwealth produced many labour-intensive crops under high-cost conditions. The crops were so 'managed' as to encourage growth and exports, almost entirely to Britain. Yet these Australian farmers could compete only if they were sheltered by Britain's preferential tariff. And Australia's schemes of export-dumping encouraged farmers to produce more than the British market could absorb at 'payable' prices. The Australian producer could prosper only if Britain would progressively squeeze foreign meat and luxury goods out of her own domestic market.

In the preliminary talks the British gave the Australians little or no satisfaction. Sir Horace Wilson kept saying that only a most extraordinary concession could conceivably justify a meat duty. On the lesser foodstuffs, Britain was in fact prepared to give a great deal – in some cases, more than Australia had asked. Yet it seems nobody told McDougall, or Bruce, or Gullett. It is hard to explain this reticence, which can hardly have smoothed the negotiators' paths. No wonder Canberra thought that London was dilatory and evasive.

6. *The Non-Ferrous Metals*

Canada was very concerned about Britain's non-ferrous metals duties. So was Australia, which exported lead and zinc, and Northern Rhodesia, whose great copper mines were about to open. In February 1932, Britain's Import Duties Act imposed a 10 per cent levy on foreign aluminium, lead and zinc, but not on foreign copper. Dominion and colonial metals entered free, as did all metallic ores and concentrates. Thus British refineries paid no duty on their raw materials. However, on 15 November Dominion aluminium, lead, and zinc would begin to pay the 10 per cent levy unless a good bargain could be struck at Ottawa.

Further, the Empire copper producers in Canada and Rhodesia were eager for a British duty on foreign supplies.

In July 1932, the President of the Aluminum Company of Canada asked R. B. Bennett to press for Empire free trade in aluminium ore, metal, and fabricates. He claimed that the free entry of aluminium into the UK was essential to the success of the Canadian aluminium industry.[99] The Canadian Prime Minister was also in close touch with J. J. Warren, the President of Consolidated Mining and Smelting. 'Cominco' produced lead and zinc in enormous quantities. In June, Bennett asked Warren to advise him on base metals, and Warren reported that the Empire could be self-sufficient in lead, zinc, and copper.[100] The International Nickel Company of Canada was pressing Bennett for Empire free trade in nickel, nickel-copper alloys, and platinum.[101] 'Inco' was also an important copper producer. In London, the Colonial Secretary was receiving representatives from well-placed Conservatives with respect to Rhodesian copper.[102]

These requests cannot be understood unless we remember American tariff policy, the structure of world trade in non-ferrous metals, and Britain's need for cheap raw materials.

The Empire copper producers were afraid that if the United States were to introduce a copper duty, the great American refiners would dump their excess output on the British market. In March 1932, a duty was enacted, and on 21 June 1932 the United States did impose a duty of 4 cents per pound. Immediately the Empire copper producers committee asked Britain's Import Duties Advisory Committee to impose a duty on foreign copper. As Sir Auckland Geddes led the copper producers, they were assured of a sympathetic hearing. Warren kept Bennett informed of these negotiations.[103] Both Canada and Northern Rhodesia shortly added their voices to the request for a British copper duty.

For many years there had been international cartels in the non-ferrous metals. These had operated with varying degrees of success and stability. They were both feasible and attractive because there were so few refiners of the non-ferrous metals. Hence the metals trades were highly organised and very international. Governments could and did deal directly with the firms or with the cartel committees.

Britain produced none of the non-ferrous metal ores, but she had refineries, and she used the finished metals in large quantity. Both refiners and fabricators insisted that if they had to they would pay duties, their costs would rise and Britain's exports would fall.

In effect, the Empire producers were asking Britain to support or replace cartel organisation with a tariff system that would give them the British market. American tariffs were important because they had shut Empire producers out of the US market while increasing the risk of American competition in Empire markets. But Britain could not tolerate any duty which would raise her production costs. Hence the Empire producers were prepared to give some assurances. The Canadian copper producers promised that they would supply Britain at the world price even if there were a tariff.[104] Cominco shortly gave the same promise with respect to lead and zinc. The Australian firms followed the Canadian example.[105] Walter Runciman had already practically told Bennett that if there were any attempt to raise metals prices because of the tariff, neither duty nor preference would last long.[106]

During the Ottawa Conference, producers and users continued to discuss the regulation of the Empire markets in copper, lead and zinc. But their preliminary negotiations had already fixed the terms which were finally written into several Ottawa agreements. British firms could buy at world prices; foreign metals would pay a duty, but only as long as Empire producers could supply all British demand at world prices. Only for metals did the preliminary talks actually yield results. And they did so only because the producers dealt directly with the several governments.

IV. THE PROBLEM OF RUSSIA

So far as the UK was concerned, the problem of Russian trade and competition first joined the Empire's diplomatic agenda at the 1930 Imperial Conference, when R. B. Bennett announced that he was worried by British purchases of Russian grain, especially wheat, and also by Russian salmon offers.[107] He initially wanted a preferential tariff to keep out such foreign goods. The Australians, too, were concerned about Russian wheat sales. Philip Snowden explained that the stories about Russian wheat dumping were 'grossly exaggerated'.[108]

Four days later, William Graham, the President of the Board of Trade, echoed Snowden's words. He told the Dominion leaders that Britain had deliberately expanded her trade with the USSR who was selling wheat cheaply because she urgently needed cash and credit. The conference, he thought, might consider making 'representation' to Russia and also the extension of Britain's domestic wheat quota proposal to cover Dominion wheat. He made these suggestions, he said, because 'he gathered that the main Canadian anxiety was with respect to the wheat position, and especially the question of Russian dumping'.[109] Prime Minister Forbes of New Zealand later said that he too was worried about such dumping.[110] Thus before the 1930 conference had ended, the six Dominions had expressed their concern about the Russian problem.

The upshot of these worries was the abortive quota discussion which ended so acrimoniously on 12 November 1930. The Russian question then dropped out of sight for a few months. But it did not go away. Indeed, so far as one can tell from the documents, it seems to have grown larger and larger in Canadian official and entrepreneurial minds. By the end of 1931, as we shall see, Bennett and his advisers were especially concerned with Soviet competition in the British timber market, where Canadian lumber, newly excluded by tariff increases from the USA and ill-adapted for traditional British uses, would have to win its way. Unfortunately for the Canadians, the USSR was putting an increasing quantity of timber into the British market – admittedly less than in 1913, but very much more than in the 1920s. In 1931, she supplied one-quarter of the UK's needs. Further, the Canadian wheat surplus had not diminished, and Canada's co-operative wheat pools were tottering towards bankruptcy, dragging three provincial governments and perhaps several great banks in the same direction.

The documents which have survived in the Bennett Papers suggest the Canadian Prime Minister and his advisers had only the vaguest idea of Soviet export planning. They do not seem to have understood the basic difference between Soviet and Western trading motivations.[111] Western industrialists, especially in 1931–32, were looking for foreign markets to absorb products on more favourable terms than the home market could offer. The USSR was exporting only enough to earn the foreign exchange which her domestic plans required. In 1930–32, the Soviet planners and the party were discovering that they had underestimated the input requirements of the first Plan. Further, we have every reason to suspect that they had not foreseen how sharply agricultural collectivisation would reduce farm output. Exports, therefore, had to be painfully extracted from a domestic economy which could readily have absorbed the timber, wheat, and coal. It was a national tragedy for the Soviet Union that her heavy import-needs were coming just when the world's commodity markets were so unrewarding. Because prices were so inconveniently low, the USSR presumably had to export more than her planners wanted – more than they exported later in the decade, when Soviet productive capacity was higher and when world commodity prices were considerably more attractive than in 1930–34. Since the Soviet problem was to earn a necessary quantum of foreign exchange per year, high prices and small export volumes were in the Soviet national interest so long as they yielded at least this quantum. Canadian concern eventually led the British to take measures which tended to serve that interest.

While Canada competed with the USSR in Britain, the USSR competed with Britain on Canadian anthracite markets. And just as the Canadians feared one Soviet export, so the British feared another. Fortunately for Britain, the Bennett Government was prepared – for its own reasons – to place a unilateral embargo on Soviet goods.

On 24 January 1931 H. H. Stevens sent Bennett a memorandum on the subject of Soviet timber. Not only was Stevens Minister of Trade and Commerce; representing a Vancouver seat, he naturally tended to serve as a channel through which the views of the lumbering industry could reach the Prime Minister. The Montreal Forestry Association, he reported, feared that Soviet lumber would shortly enter Canada, and had just asked the Government to ban it. The Canadian Lumbermen's Association was about to meet in Toronto and it was to be asked to present a similar resolution. Though reluctant to do so, the Association executive 'feared that if they refuse it will be misconstrued in Quebec. They are prepared, should the Quebec Government's representative appear there, to announce to the Convention that the Federal Government had already taken action along these lines.' Stevens pointed to the 'obvious endeavour of the Quebec Government to make political capital at the expense of the federal authorities',[112] and brought the question forcibly before Bennett.[113] On 27 February, Canada prohibited the import of Soviet coal, pulp wood, wood pulp, timber, lumber, asbestos and furs.[114]

Early in 1932, in an effort to formulate policy for the coming Ottawa Conference, an official Canadian committee summarised their worries about the Soviet Union. Noting that the principal competition was in lumber, wheat, coarse grain, and canned salmon, they then said:

'The question, after all, of Soviet competition is a wider and deeper one than "forced" versus "free" labour, "dumping" verusus "no dumping". In the last analysis the issue appears to be drawn between two economic systems in which the duties and rewards of the workers and the function of the state with respect to trade are conceived in fundamentally different terms.'[115]

True, doubtless, but rather too vague to be very helpful! The committee proceeded to write that it was very worried about Soviet competition in the UK, whose government should be asked to introduce preferential tariffs 'or some other means' –

preferably a quota – to contain this competition. The committee recognised that preferences would not raise farm prices for wheat and coarse grains, but they thought that they would give Empire suppliers 'an advantage' of unspecified type. The Forest Service officials were especially worried about Russian competition in Britain, where, they believed, Canada could not compete with 'the prices set by the Soviet Government'. In fact, the Soviet Government did not fix prices: Soviet timber sold in Britain under a 'fall and rise clause', by which, if market prices differed from contract prices, the USSR would receive the former instead of the latter. The Canadian Forest Service had got its facts crucially wrong – but perhaps nobody in Ottawa noticed.[116]

On the general question of Canadian Government policy at the conference, the Canadian officials' 'general economic committee' suggested:

'It would not be inappropriate to invite the United Kingdom to denounce the commercial agreement which at present assures Soviet products of Most Favoured Nation treatment . . . by maintaining an adequate spread between the maximum and preferential tariffs, it would be quite possible to institute a de facto embargo on the principal Soviet exports competing with Empire producers without departing from the normal and recognized forms of international trade.'[117]

Other advisers, however, did not agree.

The Canadian Government made sure that Whitehall would know how their concerns were developing. On 9 January 1932, the Canadian High Commissioner, Howard Ferguson, complained about Russian timber, fearing that the Soviet exporters were out to capture 'the entire British timber market'. He said that, in the interest of a worthwhile Empire trade agreement, Britain should do something.[118] On 16 January he reported that Ottawa had asked him to 'protest against the consummation of the contemplated arrangement' between British and Soviet timber traders. On 5 February, he forwarded a memorandum which proposed prohibition of Soviet timber, cancellation of the most-favoured-nation clause, and/or a quota – much the same proposal which the Canadians would later make at the Ottawa Conference. Thomas, however, took the view that the UK had not been asked to give an understanding that tariffs and Dominions' preferences would not interfere with the Russian timber deal. Anyway, he wrote, no such commitment could be made prior to the conference.[119]

Late in June Sir William Clark reported that Bennett was increasingly worried about the problem. Discussing the coming conference, 'he hinted that as Russian anthracite had been excluded from Canada greatly to our advantage, so Russian timber and wheat might be similarly excluded from the United Kingdom. *I got the impression that we shall hear more of this*.'[120]

When the draft conference agenda reached Whitehall from Ottawa on 24 May, it contained a specific reference to concerted measures against Russian trade. The British jibbed at so explicit a mention, but admitted that the matter would have to be discussed. In agreeing to the excision of Russia *expliciter*, Canada took pains to underline the common understanding on this matter.[121]

The Australian Government, though less worried than the Canadian, was none the less seriously concerned, especially about wheat. In London, the senior Australian trade representative raised the matter when chatting with the president of the Board of Trade on 27 May 1932.[122] Australian officials had already begun to press for quantitative restriction or prohibition. Further, the Australian Government was trying to concert its strategy with the Canadian. Prime Minister Lyons had cabled Bennett in the following terms:

'We have informed our London representatives that restriction of imports of Russian wheat desirable because of disorganisation of markets by Russian sales methods and also because large Russian surplus generally in the same year as heavy West European crops and consequently low import quotas of Germany, France, Italy. Our representative in London has been instructed to explore possibility of heavy discriminating duties or other restrictions by anti-dumping regulations.'[123]

By these means the British Government had been placed on notice that they would need a Russian policy to take to Ottawa.[124] In fact, they went without one.

At the end of May, an *ad hoc* Cabinet committee on Soviet trade produced a forthright report: Britain should denounce its temporary trade agreement with the USSR so that it should have freedom to negotiate at and after Ottawa.[125]

Receiving this recommendation, the Cabinet decided to do nothing. The reasons are obscure, but two considerations seem to have been most relevant: the desire to get more mileage at the conference by offering denunciation as a concession, and the recognition that, at least for the time being, Britain was running a trade surplus with the USSR.[126] As the Cabinet had first established the trade-with-Russia committee simply because Sir Philip Cunliffe-Lister worried about the large trading imbalances of 1930–32, the latter consideration may have been the most telling. In addition, MacDonald must have been reluctant to abandon the trade links with Russia which the Labour Party, under his leadership, had so long desired. In any event, the British delegation sailed for Ottawa in an odd state of mind: for its own reasons it was prepared to denounce the existing Anglo-Soviet trade agreement, but it had not considered what kind of concession it might make to meet the demands which it knew Bruce and Bennett would put forward.[127]

V. THE AGENDA AND THE MONETARY QUESTION

The several governments received the conference's final agenda only on 7 July – less than a fortnight before the conference was to open, and long after the delegations had left Australia, New Zealand, and South Africa. These delays were not the fault of Whitehall. As host, Canada was to produce the agenda. Hence the delays resulted entirely from the incompetence of the Canadian bureaucracy, as supervised by O. D. Skelton, the local version of Sir Maurice Hankey, and from the vacillations and obsessions of R. B. Bennett, the Canadian Prime Minister.

During the 1920s, a definite formula had evolved with respect to the generation of agenda for an Imperial conference. The convening government – always before 1932 the UK – would set up an agenda committee which would generate proposals. After Cabinet scrutiny, these would be cabled to the Dominions, which would be asked to suggest changes, additions, or deletions. All the suggestions of any one Dominion would be reported to all other Dominions. After further discussion in the UK Cabinet, and often after renewed interchanges with the Dominions, revised agenda would be prepared and disseminated – first by cable to the Dominions, and then by question in the House of Commons.

As Canada was the convenor of the Ottawa conference, it was up to her to prepare, discuss, and disseminate the agenda. At earlier conferences, the process had begun months before the conference – often as much as a year or more in advance. On this occasion, nothing happened until well into 1932. And it is not clear that anything would have happened until the opening plenary session if the UK had not pestered the Canadian Government.

On 11 March, in response to an inquiry from New Zealand, the Dominions Office cabled Sir William Clark, the UK High Commissioner in Ottawa, asking him to find out what had happened to the agenda.

It was already known in London that as late as 25 February the essential Cabinet committee did not yet exist, though interdepartmental committees had began rather casual work. This was still the case on 19 March.[128] Clark's enquiries revealed that Bennett wanted a short, working conference, which would concentrate on trade and currency.[129] The latter subject, predictably, chilled both the Treasury and Neville Chamberlain. Bennett also wanted to discuss inter-Imperial rationalisation and propaganda. Clark also learned that nothing had been done about formal agenda. Bennett proposed to construct the document himself after the end of the Canadian parliamentary session – in May![130] On 18

May, Bennett told Clark that he had the agenda before him, and would shortly send them to London.[131]

In March, Clark had provided Whitehall with scarifying accounts of Ottawa's incompetence, and of Bennett's sloth:

'Having now had a good deal of experience of administrative machine here, I would like to add that I am convinced it is advisable to aim at all possible simplification of the business of the conference. . . . PM does not seem as impressed as one would wish with the desirability of getting on with matters. . . . In the last week I have had further evidence of the degree of unpreparedness here in respect of the Conference. A committee of civil servants is, I believe, functioning, but no Cabinet committee has yet been appointed by the Prime Minister, and he is resisting pressure applied by His Excellency [the Governor General] and by important business men who are beginning to be anxious about the possibility of a Canadian breakdown. The fact is that the Prime Minister is waiting as usual until he can find time to deal with matters himself, and he talks of there being ample time after Parliament has adjourned. This is taking serious risk as the session may be prolonged beyond the first week in May. . . .'[132]

Later the same month, Bennett showed alarming signs of vagueness. Clark reported that the Canadian Prime Minister wanted to confine the conference to 'principles rather than details'. Clark pointed out that the principles would be valuable only if properly applied. The Prime Minister quickly agreed that the preliminary tariff talks should continue. But the conversation led Clark to suggest that Bennett's 'new theory' of the coming conference had been 'influenced in part by his difficulties in getting down to preparatory work'.[133]

By 12 April the Canadian Cabinet had at last discussed the broader questions. Departmental committees were at work. The Canadian Manufacturers' Association had been asked in December to prepare a list of goods not made in Canada, on which tariffs might be cut. But not until 12 April, when Bennett asked R. W. Breadner of the National

Revenue Department to chair an officials' tariff committee, did the Canadian authorities begin to prepare for the sort of conference the British were determined to have.[134]

On 24 May Bennett cabled his draft agenda to London, to the other Dominion capitals, and to New Delhi. He wanted the conference to discuss trade and money. It was also to brood on the problem of Russia, and to negotiate trade agreements.[135] For reasons which we shall discuss in a later section, London would not tolerate an overt mention of the USSR. The Dominions Office, prompted by Thomas himself, also wanted the conference to discuss methods for ensuring economic co-operation between conferences, and to examine the Imperial Economic Committee report on industrial co-operation.[136] But the real problem was the monetary section. It made both Office and Treasury very unhappy indeed. To see why, we must glance backwards at the evolution of British official thinking with respect to sterling, the Empire, Ottawa, and the international pegging of exchange rates.

Britain left the gold standard on 21 September 1931. The pound then fell quickly and precipitously, touching $3.40 in December 1931. In early 1932 it rebounded, rising to $3.70 in April, but thereafter it fell steadily for the balance of 1932. Not since 1919–20 had the pound fallen so far or fluctuated so greatly. After six years of gold-standard 'stability' and 'normal' exchange relations, such changes were especially worrying and confusing to Empire politicians, who neither understood the forces which produced the fluctuations nor enjoyed the result – an unpredictable margin of protection for their home industries.

The questions of Empire money and exchange rates were old ones. They had agitated Leo Amery and the Colonial Office in 1920–22. In 1923, the Imperial Economic Conference had suggested that Empire governments might stabilise intra-Imperial exchange rates, building their London reserves to do so. With the resurrection of the gold standard both questions became otiose. But in 1930, at the Imperial Conference, the Australian Prime Minister insisted he wanted the Ottawa Conference to consider financial matters: 'he thought it was particularly important that all parts of the Empire should agree upon a united view on the gold problem'.[137] Neither Thomas nor Snowden liked the suggestions. The former thought agreement unlikely. The latter feared the discussions might unsettle the gold standard or annoy foreign countries. No other Dominion premier spoke to the question, which was, in any event, uninteresting so long as the UK remained on gold.

In December 1931, Walter Runciman arranged that if necessary, the Dominions Office should take up questions of money and silver policy direct with the Treasury.[138] It seems that J. H. Thomas first suggested the Ottawa Conference might have to deal with such matters.

So far as I discovered, it was also J. H. Thomas who first wondered at what level the pound should float. Early in January 1932, he asked Chamberlain about monetary policy at the coming Ottawa Conference. He wrote:

'I am, of course, well aware of the dangers and difficulties of any proposals for anything like a common monetary policy within the Empire. On the other hand, disparities between exchange . . . may obviously be of even greater significance . . . than tariffs. The question, difficult as it is, can hardly be avoided.'

He feared Canada would raise the question of silver, and asked what Britain should now do to define its policy, lest any of the other Ottawa participants might want to talk about money, credit, and the exchanges.[139]

Chamberlain did not answer in haste; on 3 March Thomas was obliged to write again.[140] But work went on within the Treasury, which had been charged with responsibility for the monetary side of the conference operations.

Ralph Hawtrey had already told Chamberlain that because Britain was off the gold standard, she was insulated from the American depression.[141] Sir Richard Hopkins shortly produced two more extensive memoranda. These defined the policies which were to be followed until the outbreak of war.

It is impossible, Hopkins explained, to know what the exchange rate or the price level ought to be. Hence, though the pound should be stabilised from day to day, and eventually taken back to a gold base, there would be no point in 'lengthy discussions at Ottawa . . . much of its [i.e. British] policy cannot yet be framed, and some of its thoughts cannot be openly expressed'. As for exchange rates, it would be helpful if Empire countries would peg to sterling, and build up London balances for exchange equalisation, but this would be a matter for the Dominion governments themselves. If sterling could float at a 'relatively stable' level, Canada and South Africa would eventually join the sterling area. 'Nevertheless, there is no reason why the British Government should not definitely adopt a sterling basis for the currencies of the Empire as an object of policy, and invite the Dominions to concur in it.' The result would be an 'Imperial sterling standard', with Dominion and colonial monetary balances in London. Finally, as to action: 'The Treasury . . . suggest that, after discussion at Ottawa in which the objective would be declared and its general colour defined, the [sterling area] would be best left for a time to grow. A sane management of sterling will do more than many conferences to secure the end in view.'[142]

Hopkins did not explain why a sterling bloc was a good thing. Nevertheless, we may find a hint in one of his earlier memoranda. Writing for the Cabinet, he explained that though a floating pound might seem to eliminate all concern about the balance of trade, it did so only if one did not care about the level at which sterling would float. But that, he said, 'is what we are not willing to do. . . . Our real problem is to secure a balance of payments consistently with a reasonable exchange value for the pound'.[143]

Meanwhile, Leo Amery was doing his best to excite trouble on the monetary front. For years he had been a monetary reformer. In the early twenties, he had espoused Mr Darling's schemes of Empire exchange and credit. This espousal had won him nothing but the contempt of the Treasury officials. In 1932 he was out of office, but late in January he wrote to R. B. Bennett: ' I trust you will not let the Treasury here veto the fullest discussion at Ottawa of the currency question . . .'[144]

Late in February, the Canadian House of Commons resolved that the Canadian Government should 'initiate and support measures for the stabilisation of the currencies of all British countries'. Hence nobody was surprised when Bennett told Sir William Clark that the conference should emphasise currency as well as trade.[145]

Chamberlain decided that he wanted to know in what form the Canadians would raise the question of currency.[146] Clark thought that the Canadians had nothing concrete in mind, but Thomas asked him to find out for certain.[147]

For more than two months, there was no word from Ottawa. In mid-April, Bennett told Clark that he expected the UK delegation would make the most contribution.[148] At the same time, the Government of India weighed into the lists. Delhi supported Canada's idea of a discussion of 'fundamental issues of whether there could be a concerted currency policy amongst the Empire countries'. It hoped Britain would accept 'the principle that sterling policy shall be regulated with deliberate purpose of producing a certain level of prices', taking account of Empire countries' interests.[149]

This was more than the Treasury could stand. Later that month its officials wrote that it was impracticable for Britain to admit the Dominions to the management of sterling. The coming conference was not likely to say anything definite about sterling management, and so 'the outcome of the discussion on currency policy at Ottawa is likely to be somewhat negative'.[150]

When the Canadian Prime Minister cabled his draft conference agenda to London on 24 May, he said:

'The Canadian government . . . are convinced the measures for the development of inter-Imperial trade must, to a considerable degree, be dependent upon the stabilisation at appropriate levels of our several currencies. It is recognised that in some respects these questions will not admit of satisfactory settlement on exclusively Imperial lines. The

Canadian Government, accordingly, feel it would be premature to proceed with detailed plans for concerted action in this field until it is clear as to the policy which will be adopted at the forthcoming Conference in Lausanne.'[151]

In the agenda, under Monetary-Financial Questions, he included: 'Consideration of desirability and feasibility of taking steps to restore the general price level and to stabilise exchange, including consideration of monetary standards.'

It was vital to stabilise exchange rates, though as yet the Canadian Government had nothing specific to propose.[152]

Following the usual practice for Imperial Conferences, Bennett repeated his telegram to the other Dominions. In response the New Zealand Government urged that the agenda papers should include 'currency and price level, central banks, and kindred problems'. It feared that the UK would omit or ignore these matters.[153]

Whitehall was not happy with the Canadian suggestion for the agenda. It replied that it would prefer the following words: 'Consideration of existing inter-relationships of various currencies and monetary standards of the Empire and of means to be taken to promote and secure exchange conditions most favourable to mutual trade.' And it commented: 'We . . . are of opinion that favourable conditions for framing any definite plan of stabilisation may be found not yet to exist.'[154]

The Canadians insisted that they wanted to fix 'wider terms' than the British wording would allow. They demanded, and got, the following:

'Consideration of existing inter-relationships of the various currencies and monetary standards of the Empire, and of the desirability and feasibility of taking steps to restore and stabilise the general price level and to stabilise exchange.'[155]

Once the agenda had been settled, the Treasury prepared another memorandum which was, in effect, a comment upon their monetary aspect. The arguments were the same as before. It would be a good thing if prices were to rise.

But though monetary manipulation would help to raise them, it would not suffice. Hence it would be premature to restore the gold standard or peg the pound, because the underlying disequilibria still remained. Interest rates, however, had fallen, and should remain low, while credit should be sufficiently easy to be 'adequate to meet the requirements of expanding trade and industry provided that no speculative movements occur'. With respect to the conference itself, a pencilled Treasury note said the interrelationship of Empire currencies was a 'minor' question. The author urged that there should be no discussion of the price-level and stabilisation. 'All the economic and currency experts will want to propose every kind of scheme. If the matter is referred to them we shall have nearly as many recommendations as there are experts, with a very unsettling effect on sterling and on confidence.'[156]

Amery and the New Zealand Government had expected the Treasury to bury the currency question. Both had been right.

VI. THE RESULTS

Only in non-ferrous metals did the pre-conference negotiations move the Empire countries towards agreement. Nor had the conversations helped the UK to decide upon its own policies, or to choose between the several courses its delegates might follow at Ottawa.

When the British delegates sailed, they knew somewhat more about the Dominions' concerns than they had known eight months before. The problem of meat had been thoroughly canvassed. The four major Dominions had declared their concern with it. The Australians in particular had explained how important they thought it. New Zealand had been equally importunate and South Africa's interest was far from slight. Yet the British had done nothing with respect to meat policy. They knew what they would be asked to do. But they had not even discussed what, if anything, they could concede. With respect to Russian trade, the same thing had happened. Only from Australia had Britain learned what concessions she might expect. Even in monetary policy, little had been done. Certainly Chamberlain knew what he did and did not want to do. But he had not told the Cabinet, which had never considered what monetary commitments Britain might or might not make at Ottawa. The officials did their best to lay out the alternatives and to clarify the issues. But the politicians ignored their efforts, and committed themselves to nothing. The delegation sailed with full power to negotiate – and in full confusion about the terms it might or might not accept. They were more or less committed to work for tariff reduction. However, for several ministers this commitment was weak and equivocal, especially with respect to home agriculture. They wanted to reduce tariffs within the Empire, not raise them against foreign goods. Yet they ought to have faced the fiscal problem. Most Empire countries could not afford to reduce any tariffs unless they raised some. Even if they were not protectionist, they could not forgo any customs revenue.

Eight months before, Chamberlain and Thomas had hoped that the conference would assemble to ratify agreements which had already been completed. In the event, nothing went as planned. When they sailed for Quebec, the delegates were divided. Their hopes were unrealistic. Their plans were unmade. The conjuncture was unfavourable. No agreements had been drafted. Indeed, no one yet knew whether the conference would yield a single, multilateral trade charter, or a set of bilateral agreements. It has become fashionable to blame R. B. Bennett for the troubles at Ottawa. Certainly, as we shall see, the Canadian Prime Minister was neither a tactful host nor a skilful diplomat. But surely some of the blame belongs with the British. The UK delegation set sail in great disarray. Only if self-sacrificing saints had led the Dominion governments, could trouble have been avoided.[157]

Late in May 1932, the British and American governments had begun the conversations which, after further processing at the Lausanne Conference and at Geneva, would later cause the League to convene a World Monetary and

Economic Conference. The Dominions were told of these conversations early in June 1932, when Sir John Simon spoke of a prospective conference on 'methods to stabilise commodity prices'.[158] Yet in the preparatory discussions one finds no evidence that anyone considered the possible interactions between Ottawa, Lausanne, and the prospective world gathering. Before the Ottawa Conference began, the Lausanne Conference had already asked the League to arrange for a meeting at which monetary policy, tariffs, and trade barriers would be examined. But the British delegates left for Ottawa almost immediately after the end of the Lausanne Conference. They had no time to brood upon Imperial trade relations in the light of a world conference which might never take place. Furthermore, the Treasury officials refused to think about this more remote meeting until the nearer one had reached some conclusions. After Empire trade and Empire money had been tidied, there would be time enough to think about world trade and world money.

Chapter 6

THE OTTAWA CONFERENCE

The seven British delegates sailed for Quebec on 13 July. In some respects the conference may be said to have begun on shipboard, as the ship also carried other delegations – the South African, New Zealand, Southern Rhodesian, and Indian. Further, the British ministers were able to undertake some of their own preparatory work. As we saw in the last chapter, the full Cabinet had given them absolute powers to negotiate. They knew that the Dominions were planning to ask for higher and additional food duties. And they were most concerned to prepare general resolutions which the full conference might accept. In the event, their efforts on this front were largely wasted: in its early days the conference was not prepared to pass any such resolutions, and the final statement owed little to the delegates' shipboard labours. Nor did they advance towards a common mind on the subject of food duties. But in negotiation they were able to make some progress.

After a preliminary meeting on 20 July, the conference proper opened with a plenary session on 21 July, and concluded with the fifth plenary session on 20 August. Besides these full sessions, there were six meetings of heads of delegations. The second such meeting, on 21 July, set up five committees – on Promotion of Commonwealth Trade, Customs Administration, Commercial Relations With Foreign Countries, Monetary Questions, and Methods of Economic Co-operation. The formal business of the conference was centred on the meetings of these committees, the plenary sessions, and the gatherings of heads of delegations, but the substantive business was effected almost entirely through bilateral discussions, varying in formality. Thus on the average, the British delegation had three bargaining conferences per day – in addition to the formal meetings. Often the delegates had to proceed directly from one set of negotiations to another. They also had daily conferences with their official industrial advisers, and were doubtless exposed to a certain amount of informal lobbying as well. Ottawa swarmed with unofficial representatives – self-selected, or mandated, like Leo Amery, or the officials of Canadian industrial and commercial bodies. Further, the delegates had frequent conferences with Sir Horace Wilson and with the senior officials who had accompanied them to Ottawa. There were departmental advisers from the Board of Trade, Treasury, Inland Revenue, Customs, Dominions Office, Foreign Office, Colonial Office, Ministry of Agriculture and Fisheries, Department of Overseas Trade, Empire Marketing Board, and Cabinet Office. The UK Trade Commissioners for India, Canada, Australia, South Africa, and New Zealand were also present. One hundred and sixty-nine documents were circulated to the delegates, who held 81 meetings, in addition to the 11 meetings of heads of delegations and plenary sessions, and the 20 committee meetings – 112 gatherings in all. Fortunately the Ottawa weather was far cooler than it usually is in July and August. If the summer had been as torrid as usual, the conference might have broken up in failure. Nevertheless, this was an extraordinarily demanding conference, not only for the advisers and secretarial staff but for the delegates themselves. In appraising the results, we must allow for the conditions under which the conference business was done.

Before the conferees assembled, nobody had decided exactly what they would do, or how. Would there be a single multilateral agreement? A series of bilateral agreements? Either way, time was short: all the Dominions were present, and so were India and Southern Rhodesia, while the UK herself was negotiating on behalf of the dependent Empire. Would the agreements be specific or general? London wanted the former, but Bennett was believed to want the latter. And most important – how would the day-to-day business be carried out?

Britain's industrial advisers continued to hope that the conference would commit itself to some broad statement of principles. But as the days passed, it became ever clearer that the agreements would be bilateral, and that the bargaining would be painful. After the heads of delegations had agreed on 21 July to set up five committees, the next day the Committee on the Promotion of Trade within the Commonwealth established ground rules for bilateral tariff bargaining. The results of these bargainings are the main work of the conference.

In later sections of this chapter, we trace the conference's bargaining work along topical lines: 'domestic competition' and Dominion concessions, the Russia problem, the question of meat, and other British concessions. The final section evaluates the conference as a whole. The next section treats the more important aspects of the committee work.

Before turning to these matters, we must pause to examine the interaction between the delegation and London. Through the High Commissioner's Office, daily news-cables went to the Dominions Office. But these were extremely brief. And they were both optimistic and arid. Further, they were not circulated to the Cabinet or even to the Prime Minister. Nor was there any transatlantic discussion of policy, strategy, or tactics. Admittedly, the UK delegation was a very strong one – Baldwin, Chamberlain, Hailsham, Gilmour, Thomas, Runciman, and Cunliffe-Lister. It might be argued that all the relevant ministers were in Ottawa – that, in effect, the Cabinet itself had come to Canada. But this was far from the case – as the delegates discovered soon after their return. Everyone knew that on trade and tariff policy the Cabinet was deeply split: five months before, its members had publicly 'agreed to disagree'. Hence it is surprising that there was so little surveillance from the London end. Thomas and Chamberlain had wanted a free hand. And certainly that was what they got.

While in Ottawa, Baldwin's delegation cabled two lengthy 'appreciations' to London. The first, on 4 August, was circulated to the Cabinet, which noted it but did not discuss it. The second, on 15 August,[1] could not be circulated, because the Cabinet had dispersed for the summer recess. It would seem that only MacDonald read it. And he does not appear to have understood it.

In this 'appreciation' the position was sketched clearly, but one major consideration was omitted.

'We shall probably have to take our definite decision today (Monday). . . . Our policy throughout has been to try to secure agreements that embody the principle of the progressive lowering of tariff barriers . . . we have laid great stress on the principle that duties against British goods in Dominions should not be at a higher rate than is necessary to put the UK Manufacturer in the position of a domestic competitor . . . and that Tariff Boards in Dominions should be instructed to review duties in accord with that principle and that we should have right of audience. . . . We shall insist on this as the most important term in our agreements.'

There followed a summary of the concessions by the various Dominions.

'Bearing in mind the need for bringing the Conference to a satisfactory conclusion and on the assumption . . . that the tariff and other concessions are of sufficient immediate and prospective value to warrant the expectation of increased markets for UK goods, we feel justified in making agreements. . . . Apart from the Russian question, Canada has made it clear that she expects a duty of 2/– per quarter on wheat. Our difficulty in accepting this was great [but was mitigated by Bennett's world-price undertaking]. Before we left London it was apparent that meat would be the principal question at issue, and everything that has happened here has emphasized this. . . . Australia in particular has reiterated that all her proposals are conditional upon satisfaction in regard to meat. They asked for duties on lamb, mutton, beef, and bacon. We have said we are unable to agree to this. We have prepared a scheme for temporary restriction of mutton and lamb in 1933 pending a conference of meat interests. . . . Over and above the trade advantages

. . . there is the intangible but very important gain to sentiment and confidence (which might well extend far beyond the Empire) in the course of which the Empire had shown unity of purpose and had translated ideals into specific agreements. We hope, too, to be able, to preface the specific agreements by conference conclusions which will form another intangible but very important asset through the adhesion to general principles of a kind that could be represented at home and to the world as committing the Empire to a policy intended to diminish the barriers to trade and to restore world prosperity. We are unanimously satisfied in the circumstances that the concessions we have been able to secure justify us in making agreements on these lines.'[2]

MacDonald's response, vague in the extreme, also reveals that the British Cabinet as such never considered the major changes in fiscal policy which the Ottawa agreements involved:

'Only those who have been through the whole negotiations can value present situation. I have greatest confidence in my colleagues' judgement and though I must reserve a final decision for myself until I know whole scheme and its possibilities my inclination will be to back you up. Had I been able to get any important Ministers on telephone today for a consultation I should have done so; but all are scattered. Must therefore content myself by strongly urging you all to remember feeling in this country about food taxes and possible reactions in Cabinet. Do your honest best to secure a rational conclusion and I shall do mine to find reasons for keeping us together though one cannot conceal difficulties.'[3]

The delegation had already recognised[4] that 'it was inevitable owing to the rapid changes in the situation in the last days of the conference that decisions should be taken in Ottawa by the UK delegates without prior agreement of their terms and with their colleagues at home'. Thus MacDonald had simply acquiesced in their prior understanding of the situation. However, one wonders whether he would have done so had the delegates sent him the calculations from Baldwin's memorandum of 7 August. This document,[5] circulated to the British delegation but apparently not discussed by them, contained an estimate of the *immediate* trade increases which the agreements promised the UK. At present levels of Dominion imports, UK exports might rise by 1.8 million pounds a year – excluding Canadian and Indian purchases. In a 'good year', 12.5 million might be expected, including 6 million to India but no figure for Canada, whose final concessions were still undetermined. The outside estimate for new Canadian purchases, given the *first* list of concessions, had elsewhere been presented as 10 million dollars;[6] later concessions raised the estimate to 15 million. Of course, these estimates were of the roughest kind, and in some cases we are not told how they were made. But they certainly do not imply a massive growth for British exports. Even setting aside the question of the import content in UK exports – a question which nobody raised at the conference except in connection with the definition of Empire content – it was obvious that so far as immediate impact was concerned, there was no great employment potential in the agreements.

The modifications after 7 August and after 14 August did little to change this picture. Thus the UK delegates were putting their faith in the Dominions' future tariff policies. Hence it is not surprising that Britain wanted long-term agreements with no escapes; the agreements were binding for five years, and could not be denounced during that term. However, it is very surprising that, in view of the Dominions' past records, they made no provision for arbitration, or for sanctions. The agreements include no such provision, and there is no sign that the UK delegates ever pressed for them.

Besides these two cables, the records reveal one telephone conversation between Thomas and MacDonald. It did not affect the conference or its outcome. Some scholars[7] have mentioned a further transatlantic consultation. They claim that it was crucial to the results: that, without MacDonald's last-minute intervention, there would have been no Anglo-Canadian Agreement. This exchange has left no trace in the official records of the UK delegation. It is discussed below, in the third section of this chapter.

I. COMMITTEES

The five committees of 21 July were formed to carry forward the common work of the conference. But the reports were not binding on anybody, and were totally without force or significance. Not surprisingly, the conference's real work was done elsewhere. Indeed once the bilateral pattern of bargaining was set, there was little work for the Committee on the Promotion of Trade within the Commonwealth. Other committees met more often; one even gave rise to a subsequent committee meeting in London. But only the monetary committee is of any great intellectual interest.

The Committee on Trade Relations was the venue for various discussions – export bounties, anti-dumping duties, trade with Russia, and 'Empire Content'. However, the final form of the trade-with-Russia decision, eventually embodied in the Anglo-Canadian Agreement, was fixed through bilateral discussion, not through this committee. Empire content was a vexed question for two reasons. Britain and the other Dominions were worried about Canadian branch plants, and Britain was worried about cottons in relation to the Dominions' content regulations. If Canada exported a car, how much of the value was Canadian work? Presumably one did not want to call something an Empire product merely because it was painted or bolted together on the northern side of the Great Lakes. Similar problems arose for British industries which processed imported raw materials. Cotton textiles were the most threatened. The price of raw cotton often changed relative to the price of the finished product, thus changing the percentage 'Empire Content' – because the cotton came mostly from the USA and from Egypt. During the late twenties, all the Dominions had been changing the rules with respect to Empire content. The effect, in all directions, was to increase the likelihood that an Empire manufacture might not qualify for the preferential tariff rates. The committee recommended standard valuation procedures, and hoped that the percentage of Empire content could be fixed at 50.

The Committee on Customs Administration was the venue for a discussion of the many arbitrary practices Dominions had begun in the early thirties. The chief offender was Canada, and the committee report was strongly critical of Canadian practices. In effect, the committee members urged Canada to reduce the uncertainties to which her practices gave rise, and to stop valuing Empire goods arbitrarily for customs purposes. Both the Canadians and the Irish registered reservations, and only the anodyne parts of the report were published. However, Bennett did publicly agree to avoid uncertainty, reduce delay and friction, and provide machinery for settling disputes.[8] Privately, he promised to suspend the arbitrary valuation of British goods at the customs house, and he later amended Canadian customs law accordingly.

The Committee on Commercial Relations with Foreign Countries did no significant business at its two meetings.

The Committee on Methods of Economic Co-operation met five times, and it also did little. In effect, it was a dumping ground for various topics which had intermittently occupied British ministers, civil servants, and Imperial conferences for more than a decade. Thus it brooded upon standardisation, films, radio, grading, shipping, 'industrial co-operation', and intra-Imperial co-ordination.

Before the Ottawa Conference assembled, Whitehall hoped that there would be a discussion of 'methods of co-ordination and promoting economic co-operation between Imperial conferences, and development of suitable machinery'. But the officials suspected that Canada and other Dominion governments might object. Nevertheless they thought there should be 'some body of sufficient authority and status to prepare and present the considerations which should be borne in mind by Ministers in reaching decisions between and at their conferences'. They hoped also for a sort of standing conference, with frequent meetings of ministers, to work out detailed policies of 'Imperial Economic Co-operation'.[9]

Already there were several intra-Imperial bodies which worked on economic affairs. The Imperial Economic Committee concerned itself chiefly with foodstuffs and transport. The Imperial Shipping Committee studied ocean transportation and ports. The Empire Marketing Board promoted Empire foodstuffs in the British market. Only the last of these had any executive power: funded by the British Treasury, it could spend on posters, films, other advertising, and research. These bodies, and others, had little to do with one another – and, indeed, little to do. The Whitehall officials, and some ministers, were thinking of something different – an office which would have on-going administrative functions.

Predictably, Canadian officials were annoyed. One wrote, 'Thomas is making a dead set for setting up a permanent and unified Empire secretariat in London'.[10] Dr O. D. Skelton, Bennett's Under-Secretary of State for External Affairs, had long opposed any such plan. He thought it a means whereby Britain would control the Dominions; he saw no way by which Dominion delegates could be responsible to their home governments.[11] Bennett's Minister of Trade and Commerce[12] thought otherwise. But he did not have the ear of the Canadian Prime Minister.

Hence the committee recommended that 'An Imperial Committee on Economic Consultation and Co-operation should meet and consider the future of the various Imperial bodies, especially the Empire Marketing Board and the Imperial Economic Committee.'

This new committee began to meet in the autumn of 1932. Skelton was in the Chair. It reported in April 1933, recommending the abolition of the Empire Marketing Board but the retention of the Imperial Economic Committee.[13] Of its findings, a Whitehall official wrote:

'It is no secret that the United Kingdom Government would

have been prepared to go much farther in the direction of the establishment of machinery for economic co-operation than the Committee recommended, but it is understood that the Report represents the maximum on which unanimity was possible.'[14]

Thus finally expired the dream of an imperial economic general staff – killed, and rightly, by a fact: that economic policy is political, not just technical.

The Committee on Monetary and Financial Questions was potentially the most important and most creative part of the entire Ottawa Conference. In the event, thanks to Chamberlain and to his Treasury coaches, this body was as meaningless as the other four.

The Monetary Committee met four times. In the Chair was H. H. Stevens, the Canadian Minister for Trade and Commerce – a man well known for his opposition to deflationary policies and monetary orthodoxies. Chamberlain represented the UK. He had approached this committee with some uneasiness. The South Africans were known to be firm in their defence of monetary orthodoxy and the gold standard. The New Zealanders, though opposed to domestic 'inflation' of the money supply, had been rendered desperate by the fall in export prices. The Australians, too, were desperate for a rise in the price level. And in Canada the Cabinet was known to be at cross-purposes. Stevens was an expansionist, but Bennett was using surreptitious exchange control to keep the Canadian dollar at or near par with the American. And the Canadian Government was so strongly opposed to British devaluation, which had undercut the protective effect of Canadian tariffs, that it had imposed 'exchange-dumping duties' which offset some of the fall in the pound. Chamberlain could hardly have forgotten that before the conference met, Bennett had wanted to discuss 'exchange stabilisation' as well as measures 'to restore and stabilise prices'. And the British officials certainly knew that Bennett was vaguely interested in schemes for an Empire Bank which somehow would stabilise exchange rates. In their addresses to the committee on 28 July, the Dominion and

Indian ministers made their worries all too clear. And they hoped for much from the UK.

On 19 July, Chamberlain consulted the other UK delegates about the statement he was to make to the Monetary Committee. He explained to them that price increases were certainly desirable, but that the Empire countries could not themselves achieve this desideratum where there was a *world* market – as for wheat. However, where the UK was the only significant buyer the world market was a *sterling* one. And for such markets the conference might be efficacious, if its participants would agree to control *output*. There was general agreement with this line, and the next day Chamberlain presented it to the committee.[15] He explained that the UK also wanted to see higher primary prices, stable exchange rates, and easy credit and low interest rates. British monetary policy, he said, could and would be used to keep credit cheap and plentiful. But it could not be used to raise commodity prices: for this, production control would be essential. And the UK could not stabilise her exchange rate or return to the gold standard: no one yet knew what the right rate would be, and the world's monetary system was still disturbed by the disorders which had forced Britain to leave gold the preceding year. Hence there could be no question, for the present, of stabilising exchange rates either within the Empire or outside it.

To the delegation's relief, the other conferees swallowed this line. Cabling Ramsay MacDonald on 3 August, the delegation explained:

'There was consensus of opinion that unless wholesale commodity prices rose, primary producers in all the Dominions would be faced with disaster and might even be unable to meet their obligations to us. Little or nothing has been heard of Empire Super Bank, Empire Currency or Silver, and it is gratifying that crude inflationary proposals have not been put forward. . . . Our attitude toward quantitative restriction can to some extent be inferred from statement of Chancellor of Exchequer on monetary policy in course of which he suggested as regards commodities whose world price is governed by sterling market price that the regulation of supply would be preferable to the regulation of imports into the United Kingdom. . . .'[16]

And the Monetary Committee's final report was in line with Chamberlain's address.[17] From this fact, Chamberlain and others took hope for the future of price-raising production controls at the coming World Economic Conference – already scheduled for 1933.[18]

Chamberlain was badly confused about the relations between debt service and the prices of primary products. It was true that if Australia and New Zealand could get higher prices without cutting back their exports they would have larger sterling receipts with which to pay interest on their sterling debts. But if the higher prices are obtained through export restriction, the answer is not clear. Only if the demand for the good is price-inelastic over the relevant range of price movement will total sterling receipts be larger with smaller volume and at a higher price. For many industrial raw materials – tin, rubber, copper – this condition of price inelasticity might probably be satisfied, because these materials represented so small a fraction of the costs of the goods in which they were embodied. For some foodstuffs – tea, sugar – demand might also be price-inelastic, because these foods have no close substitutes and because they absorb little of the householder's budget. But for meat, dairy products, and wheat, demand was certainly price-elastic over any relevant range. These foods bulk large in family budgets and they have various substitutes. Hence quantitative restriction would probably not have raised the sterling receipts of Australia, New Zealand, or Canada. If foreign supplies alone were cut back, while Dominion supplies were allowed to remain unchanged or to increase, then of course the Dominions would receive more sterling, even if demand were elastic. But initially Chamberlain envisaged no such scheme: Empire suppliers, too, were to cut their supplies. And what of British capital in Argentina? If we make room for Antipodean meat at the expense of Argentina, we may ensure solvency for the Antipodes and default for Argentina.

Finally, even if demand is inelastic, or even if all the weight of restriction falls on the foreigner, the improvement will be increasingly difficult to hold: the higher prices will tend to increase supplies, from the UK, the Dominions, and foreign countries, creating a larger and larger problem of administering and policing the supply control.

Chamberlain was not alone in believing that prices ought to be higher. The general price collapse had certainly done dreadful things to primary producers and financial institutions all over the world; it is hard to avoid the conclusion that it had also depressed real output, employment, and investment. But Chamberlain was wrong to believe in output control. The right way to raise prices was through monetary and fiscal expansion – not output restriction.

On 12 and 17 August the conference met in plenary session and approved the five committees' reports. On 20 August, having concluded the final trade agreements late the preceding night, the conferees adopted the conference report and passed a series of innocuous resolutions which drew upon these reports. It would be a good thing, they announced, if there were more uniformity with respect to Empire content rules, and if prices could be raised and exchanges stabilised. Customs administration ought to be more certain, and less prone to friction and delay. More should be done with respect to industrial standardisation. Pious hopes, without force or significance. As contemporaries realised, the Conference's real work had consisted of the negotiating sessions at which the bilateral trade agreements had been hammered out. To these discussions we now turn.

II. DOMESTIC COMPETITION AND DOMINION TARIFF CONCESSIONS

In this section we trace the UK's efforts to extract concessions from protectionist and nervous Dominions. The larger part of the section treats the search for tariff concessions of the ordinary type – reductions in rates, 'conventionalisations' of rates, fixings and increasings of preferential margins. However, this search soon became entangled with another sort of importunity: the British delegates, discouraged with respect to immediate conventional concessions, soon began to press the Dominions for commitment to a principle. British goods should enter Dominion markets as if they were produced therein; tariff boards should operate to ensure that they would enter upon the appropriate terms. Hence we trace the disputes about this arrangement, which soon came to be called 'domestic competition'. At the end of the section, we turn to ancillary but very important matters – customs administration, 'primage' and other special levies, and exchange-dumping duties.

The conference proceedings began in a glow of optimism. In his opening speech, Bennett proposed 'that the United Kingdom have free entry into Canada for her products which will not injuriously affect Canadian enterprise'. He explained that he meant an extension of the free list, retention of existing preferences, and increased preferences in respect of selected articles which Britain was 'especially equipped to supply without injuring efficient Canadian enterprise'. In exchange, he asked for the retention and extension of Canada's preferences in the UK – essentially the concessions under the McKenna Duties and the Import Duties Act. For New Zealand, Coates offered to lower duties and widen preferential margins, so long as the UK could do something about foreign meat, dairy products, and fruit. For Australia, Bruce said nothing about Australia's offers, but claimed he was ready to help. Like Coates, he hoped that prices would be raised, partly through closer Empire union and partly through monetary policy. Chatterjee, too, wanted higher prices, but offered some hope for the extension of preferences in the Indian tariff. Any such concession would be of immense importance: India had never accepted the principle of preference, and by 1932 she had granted preferential duties only on a few British cotton and iron goods. Even Havenga, while stating that South Africa could do relatively little on the preferential front, admitted that lower duties and higher preferences 'were our duty today'.[19]

Presumably Bruce could be silent about Australian concessions because the subject had already been so thoroughly explored at Melbourne. Robert Dalton, Britain's senior trade commissioner, had already convinced the Australian ministers to accept a 'formula' and a more favourable 'sub-formula' for preferential margins. The formulae fixed margins which widened as the British preferential rate rose, more steeply increasing the rate on foreign goods. Thus when British goods paid up to 14 per cent duty the margin would be 12½ per cent; foreign goods would thus pay from 12½ per cent to 26½ per cent. At the top end, where British goods paid 30 per cent or more, foreign goods would pay 20 per cent more than British – that is, 50 per cent or more. The 'sub-formula' established a margin of 15 per cent when British goods paid up to 19 per cent and 20 per cent when they paid more.[20]

Nothing so concrete had emerged from the other countries. But even the Australian offer was less specific than it seemed. To what goods would it apply? The Australian Ministry was already pledged to refer all variations in 'protective' duties to its Tariff Board. Hence the delegation could not agree to a universal application of the formulae. And nobody could be sure what duties were 'protective'. Hence the Australians soon resisted the extension of the formulae to any substantial part of their tariff.

India, too, was unable to lower duties or install preferences in any wholesale way. She too could change 'protective' duties only after reference to her Tariff Board. Fortunately, her tariff practice clearly identified 'protective' duties, separating them from 'revenue' ones. Unfortunately for the British, for some years the Indian Government had been levying 'protective' duties on cottons, iron, and steel – exactly the products for which Britain most eagerly desired concessions. At most, the UK delegation might hope for some commitment with respect to the future: might India agree to refer her protective duties to the Tariff Board once again? A preferential tariff was consistent with the principle of Indian protectionism: if British goods were less competitive than Japanese, the right course, according to India's fiscal theory, was to tax British goods less heavily than Japanese.

Thus the sky was less sunny than it seemed at first. And it soon clouded over completely. Bennett had still made no concrete offers, and he seemed disinclined to do so. As for the other Dominions' offers, they did not amount to much. Australia's offers seemed insufficient to justify the temporary preferences under the British Import Duties Act. Bennett's opening speech was encouraging, as it appeared to offer free entry 'for those United Kingdom commodities which Canada did not now produce'. However, the speech was alarmingly unspecific.[21]

Professor Kottman has recently argued[22] that the sky was never sunny at all. Some months after the conference, Bennett told a journalist that he and Bruce had colluded to 'defeat . . . any tariff reductions'.[23] Kottman reports that because Bruce hoped to float a conversion loan in London, he let Bennett carry the burden of the opposition to British requests. There is no reason to doubt that Bennett and Bruce colluded with one another and with Leo Amery. Further, Kottman is right to say that both wanted to raise tariffs against foreign goods, and that both were reluctant to reduce tariffs against British. However, the situation was more complex than his narrative suggests. Bennett was genuinely willing to give Britain free entry for all goods not made in Canada. His initial problem was to find out what these goods were.[24] Bruce was prepared to concede something on preferential margins; his problem was to meter his concessions so as to extract the maximum concessions with respect to meat. And Bruce certainly did not leave the running to Bennett; though the latter Premier's behaviour was more objectionable, the former's was equally vigorous. The British perhaps disliked Bennett more than Bruce.[25] But by the conference's end they were equally disgusted with both.

On 23 July, the UK delegates discussed the various Dominion proposals for the first time. It was pointed out that the Australian Government was already pledged to tariff reduction by its election promises, regardless of Ottawa's outcome. Dalton thought her specific offers would raise Britain's exports by £0.5 million so long as imports were at the

1931–32 level, or by £1.25 million in any year when Australian imports reached £100 million. If the Australians could be persuaded to extend their offers of 'formula' margins to cover the whole tariff, and if a more generous sub-formula could be extracted for forty items, the above figures would rise to £1.14 million and £2.86 million. New Zealand already bought so much from Britain, and granted such generous preferences, that even if her ministers were to do a really generous deal in exchange for lamb duties, Britain's exports would not rise by more than £1 million. The Capetown Trade Commissioner remarked that Havenga would find it difficult to reduce the duty on British goods: 'revenue and other considerations' would impede him. Frederick Field, the Senior Trade Commissioner in Canada, pointed out that Bennett had as yet offered nothing, but that it would not be worth much if he simply extended his free list. If he merely continued the existing preferential tariffs, Britain would gain no extra trade. As for the selective tariff cuts, it remained to be seen what he would offer. In any event, he would probably do nothing for bituminous coal.[26]

Unless Chatterjee and Bennett were to prove extraordinarily generous, the conference would have little immediate impact on British output and employment. But the British delegates kept telling themselves that its main purpose was to create jobs.[27] Even in 1931, British exports had been £391,000,000, and we now know that in current prices her 1931 Gross National Product was £4,649,000,000.[28] Relative to these large figures, what use were the Dominions' offers? How much employment could they create? And given her reservations about protective tariffs, what could India contribute?

Nevertheless, from this meeting Chamberlain extracted some comfort. Field had suggested, 'There would be better prospects of success if gradual reduction were agreed upon. To Chamberlain this was a new point, at least new to me.'[29] In fact, the idea was not new. Bennett had put it to Clark and Field long before the conference. But the civil servants of the Dominions Office seem to have kept it to themselves – perhaps because they believed the task to be immediate tariff reduction. Nevertheless, when he finally heard it, the idea seems to have grown in Chamberlain's mind, quickly becoming a plan for 'competitive' tariffs. The development of the idea may have been encouraged by Chamberlain's contacts with the Indian delegates; India's protective tariffs had long been framed on the appropriate lines.

What was the plan? The Dominions were to submit their customs duties to impartial tariff boards, which would decide what duties would suffice to offset Britain's lower costs. The Dominions would agree to impose only these 'scientific' tariffs on British goods, which would then enter the Dominions with the status of 'domestic competitors'. That is, the tariff would be offsetting but not protectionist. Further, the Dominions would promise not to increase their tariffs on British goods without consulting their tariff boards.

Canada's laws provided for an impartial Tariff Board, but Bennett had yet to set it up. Australia had had a Tariff Board for a decade. So had India. New Zealand and South Africa lacked both boards and statutes. But perhaps they could be convinced. . . .

On 25 July, Chamberlain 'reminded the meeting that . . . the offers which the Dominions were likely to make could not be translated into anything substantial, either as regards the trade figures or the employment which would result'.[30] Thus the best hope was for a long-lived agreement which would provide for 'progressive decrease in the duties protecting the home manufacturer in the Dominions'; such a package 'could be made to look very much more attractive than anything in the way of immediate results which it might be possible to secure'. And the other delegates agreed with Chamberlain – an odd action, given the fact that bilateral negotiations had not yet begun.[31]

The Board of Trade officials urged another device. They suggested that the delegates should press for an agreement on *eventual* maximum duties for UK goods.[32] Rates could fall towards this level by specified annual percentages. But this suggestion seems to have vanished without trace. On 26 July, the delegates agreed that Baldwin should tell the other delegates:

'The United Kingdom delegation would urge upon the Dominions that the rates of duty charged should be so graduated as to give to the products of the United Kingdom a reasonable chance of competing on even terms, and that the rate of duty against United Kingdom products should be fixed for protective purposes no higher than is necessary to give a reasonably efficient industry in the Dominions a fair chance.'[33]

In discussions with Bennett, the UK ministers claimed that his public pronouncements had already committed him to the principle of domestic competition. Bennett himself agreed, and claimed that in formulating his tariff offers he had been guided by it. It would be embodied, he said, in any Anglo-Canadian agreement.[34] These protestations comforted the ministers as they awaited Bennett's actual proposals. Only on 4 August did he give them a list of concessions. Presumably it had been hammered together from the materials that his civil servants and the Canadian Manufacturers' Association had earlier gathered.[35] It was less than satisfying to Britain's representatives. Their advisers told them that Bennett's offer would mean $6 to $10 million in new exports – not the $55 to $80 million that Bennett had promised. Further, Bennett made his offer conditional upon some solutions to three questions: currency, unfair competition, and dumping. He would let British firms appear before his new Tariff Board, but insisted there was no need to embody the domestic-competitor principle in the agreement. His putative Tariff Board, he said, already provided for it. Nor would he bind his Government to accept any Tariff Board rulings.[36]

It is not surprising that Britain's delegates thought Bennett untrustworthy. They pressed him strongly, both for immediate concessions and for a clearer commitment to the principle of domestic competition. On 9 August, Chamberlain again emphasised its importance in a private talk with Bennett. The next day, the Canadian Prime Minister conceded the point, and the draft agreements thereafter embodied it. The British had already told him that his immediate proposals 'were no use'.[37]

Relations of a sort were re-established by 10 August, and negotiations resumed. But to the end Bennett tried to evade a more definite commitment with respect to the Tariff Board, which, he argued, would provide all that the UK wanted. But the British delegates knew that Bennett had just abolished the old Tariff Board, as soon as it had given a judgment in line with the principle of 'domestic competition'. Further, he had yet to constitute the new Tariff Board, though his Government had provided for one. J. H. Thomas reminded the meeting that some little time ago the Canadian Tariff Board took evidence from the UK woollen manufacturers, and, after a very careful investigation, made a recommendation based so far as could be judged on the principle of the 'domestic competitor'. The Canadian Government had then stepped in, suppressed this recommendation, abolished the Tariff Board, and passed new legislation for the establishment of a new Tariff Board, which Board was to be actually constituted after the conference terminated. This was not a very promising start for the new policy.[38]

The industrial advisers did not believe that Canada really intended to implement the principle, whatever Bennett might say or sign.[39] Would it not be better to break off negotiations? Baldwin could not contemplate a break, or failure.[40] But on the 18th, Thomas suggested that the delegates beard Bennett before his own Cabinet, suggesting that no agreement be made. The UK would continue to grant Canada duty-free entry.[41] But it was Bennett in general, not domestic competition in particular, which had driven Thomas to make this suggestion. The next day, after a long and angry meeting at which the British delegates had confronted Bennett, Stevens, and Weir, Bennett gave way on the question of domestic competition – perhaps because he knew that the proposals were unenforceable unless he should choose to enforce them. The result is embedded in the Anglo-Canadian Agreement.[42]

Canada promised to increase her duties on British goods only after a report by the Tariff Board, and in accordance with the facts it might find. She would protect only industries 'which are reasonably assured of sound opportunities for success'. Protective duties would not exceed 'such a level as will give UK producers full opportunity of reasonable competition on the basis of the relative cost of full and efficient production'. Canada would refer particular tariffs to the Board on Britain's request, and would, after a Board report, invite Parliament to fix tariffs 'in such manner as to give effect' to the principle of reasonable competition. British firms were to have right of audience before the Board.

Having won a sort of victory with respect to domestic competition, the British continued to press Bennett for immediate concessions, especially with respect to textile duties. They proposed a schedule which would reduce some preferential rates and increase some intermediate and general rates. It devoted special attention to reductions of preferential rates on cottons, woollens, linens, iron and steel, and binder twine. In the end, they did win an agreement which fixed margins of preference for five years, reduced preferential rates on 132 items, and increased intermediate or general rates on 83.[43] This was a more favourable outcome than they had expected on 4 August – and probably more favourable than Bennett had hoped to achieve. But on textiles and ironwares they made much less progress than they had hoped.

Bennett, like any politician, faced political pressures on his home front. Unlike any other delegate, he was in his own country, with a Cabinet in continuous session. The Cabinet was deeply divided with respect to the negotiations. Further, some of its members represented sectional interests that had much to fear from an Anglo-Canadian agreement. Cotton and coal were especially strongly protected in the Bennett Cabinet.[44] And some cabinet ministers did their best to convince Bennett that the British delegates' industrial advisers – and Ramsay MacDonald himself – were not to be trusted.[45] In effect, the Canadians saw the British ministers and advisers as mirror images of themselves.

Bennett was also exposed to lobbying from the Canadian industrialists who had supported his campaign, and who were, of course, strong protectionists. Hence his reluctance to give way on cotton duties, and his extraordinary manipulation of the iron and steel proposals long after he and the British had agreed on the terms of the new duties.[46]

Nevertheless, Bennett was not as stupid or greedy as his Liberal and Socialist critics have claimed. His manners were certainly deplorable and his preparation incomplete. But he did recognise the facts of life so far as negotiation was concerned. His officials had explained[47] that Canada could retain free entry under the Import Duties Act only by making substantial concessions. He did not really want to protect Canadian cotton manufacturers at all costs.[48] And throughout the conference he was receiving advice – partly from his civil servants and partly from his confidants – urging him to adopt exactly the strategy which in fact he followed.[49] Also, Leo Amery's activities must have confused him and his ministers. Though the British found him slippery, evasive, and changeable, with respect to the details of the tariff scheme, in the end he made extra concessions – enough, the British officials thought, to divert an extra $5 million in trade.

A very sore point was the Canadian proposals with respect to iron and steel duties. It will be recalled that, before the conference met, Britain's Trade Commissioner had arranged Anglo-Canadian industrial discussions. The textile magnates had been unable to agree on any division of the Canadian market. But the iron and steel industrialists had done better: the Canadians had agreed that the British could have the Canadian market for certain shapes – especially the wider steel plates. This steel agreement was the only 'rationalisation' of which the conference could boast. And it would raise British steel exports by £750,000 – if suitably supported by Canada's tariff structure. The Canadian manufacturers were not prepared to accept any reductions in the British preferential rates. But they acquiesced in free entry for some British steel wares, and higher tariffs on foreign steel goods, whenever the types were not produced in Canada.

When the British steel makers examined the Canadian official proposals of 4 August, they thought their Canadian sales would *fall* by £40,000. They concluded, 'The agreement between British and Canadian steel makers has apparently been ignored'.[50]

The iron and steel issue now appears to have been a misunderstanding. Canadian officials were certain that the agreement would not divert any *tonnage* to the UK. 'That was why, in speaking to you on the phone yesterday morning, I stated that, if you could see your way clear to drop altogether the so-called Joint Agreement, you could do better by Britain than you could by following them.'[51] Further, the Canadian officials believed that the agreement had not involved any commitments as to tariff rates – while the UK delegates and ironmasters thought that it had. However, the Canadian officials did admit to Bennett that the proposals which they had given him, and which he had transmitted to the British, did not contain all that was agreed at Montreal.[52] Hence it is hardly surprising that Bennett gave way when the British delegates complained. This concession was withdrawn by Bennett at the last minute. It was only restored because the British pressed very hard indeed. On 18 August Bennett proposed to impose higher duties on wide British steel plates, because a Canadian manufacturer had told him that such plates could be made in Canada.[53] It was this, plus Bennett's evasiveness with respect to Russia and domestic competition, that led the UK delegates to consider withdrawal. Some scholars report that only a cable from Ramsay MacDonald prevented the British from doing so. One scholar cites a *1962* interview with H. H. Stevens and the others cite no evidence or source.[54] Other scholars mention no message, no telegram, and no appeal to London.[55] The official British records do not contain such a cable. Given the care with which the officials recorded all transatlantic correspondence, it is hard to believe that a cable of such importance would have escaped unrecorded. It seems more likely that Mr Stevens, recalling the conference thirty years on, remembered a rumour about another cable and telephone call – an earlier interchange relating to *Australia* – and transposed it to the matter in which he was most concerned.[56] Nevertheless, we must admit the possibility: a message from MacDonald may have given Bennett the time to make the final concessions and commitments which were so much more favourable to Britain than those he had proposed on 5 August.

These commitments were not made until the last possible minute, and they were diluted by desperate concessions on the UK's side. On the morning of 19 August, Bennett had become more conciliatory than he had been for several days. He was willing to accept almost all of the particular tariff rates which the UK delegates had suggested. He was willing to do something about 'domestic competitor' status, and to regularise though not abolish the exchange-dumping duty which offset the benefits of the floating pound. By that afternoon, the delegates had accepted a very vague and non-binding clause with respect to the exchange-dumping duty.[57] But they appeared to have won at last with respect to the Tariff Board and 'domestic competitor' status.[58]

At 5.34 p.m. on the 19th, Thomas sent MacDonald a glowing private cable. 'Success now assured. Bennett apologised fully this morning. Got steel schedule restored and magnificent clause on domestic competition. No meat duty. Agreement with all. . . .'[59] At midnight, however, the Canadians were still discussing. They had noted that the draft agreement committed them to stabilise the *rates* of duty on many goods. After long discussion,[60] the British agreed to the addition of a phrase which expressly allowed Canada to reduce duties so long as preferential margins were maintained, and also to raise the intermediate and general duties.[61] This was a serious concession: it meant that Canada could bargain away the preferences by reducing her intermediate or general tariffs, or destroy the value of the preferences by raising the British preferential rate along with her intermediate and general rates. But without this final concession the agreement would probably not have been signed.

We have explored the Anglo-Canadian negotiations at such length because the tale is so tangled, and because they show how the search for immediate tariff concessions was linked with the request for 'domestic competitor' status. The Australian negotiations show the same links, but they were much more straightforward, because the Australian Government had already made concrete offers. Hence the British tried to improve these offers – to extend the sphere of the 'formula' and 'sub-formula', and to reduce the number of duties which were reserved as 'protective'.

The Australians first heard of 'domestic competition' on 2 August. Bruce favoured the idea from the beginning, and in view of later developments we may assume that his agreement was principled. His colleague, Gullett, also acquiesced, perhaps because he knew Canberra could evade any terms. Also, both ministers could argue that their United Australia Party was already committed in principle to domestic competition: had it not promised to lower duties, and to refer protective duties to the Tariff Board?[62] On 12 August they agreed upon a text. Hence the Anglo-Australian agreement, like the Canadian, contains clauses which are meant to regulate the future development of the Australian tariff.[63]

The Australians promised to protect only industries which were reasonably assured of success. They agreed to impose no new protective duty, and to raise no existing duty, except as recommended by the Tariff Board, before which UK producers were to have audience. With respect to 'full opportunity of reasonable competition', they made the same promises as Canada. And most important, they agreed that their Tariff Board would quickly review all existing protective duties. The Canadian Agreement required Ottawa to acquiesce in any British request for review; the Australians agreed that they would themselves undertake a comprehensive review.

Convinced that the first Australian proposals were not good enough to justify a continuation of free entry,[64] on 2 August the UK delegates decided to ask for a more generous preferential formula. They wanted Dalton's 'sub-formula' to cover the whole tariff.[65] In exchange, they proposed to offer concessions on brandy, wines, sugar, and fruit. But Australia was to reduce its preferential tariffs – not raise its foreign rates.

Bruce was prepared to 'give anything which seemed

possible, within reason . . . short of wiping out her own industries' – so long as he was satisfied with respect to Britain's meat-concessions. Subject to this proviso, he soon conceded substantially what the UK wanted.[66]

But during the next two weeks, Bruce twice threatened to break off negotiations if the British would not satisfy him on meat. Thus the meat quotas were the price the UK paid for a substantial widening of Australian preferential margins. The British did not get all they wanted: in the end, Bruce and Gullett insisted that the formulae should not apply universally. But the exclusions were fewer than the Australians had at first proposed.

The Australians did not bind themselves with respect to duty. They merely committed themselves to maintain certain margins between preferential and other rates.[67] They even retained the power to reduce margins to specified amounts on specified goods. These provisions were included because Australia wanted to reserve some bargaining power *vis-à-vis* third countries. If preferential margins could not be reduced, what could Australia offer the USA, or Germany, or Belgium? This provision was weaker, from Britain's viewpoint, than the parallel article in the Anglo-Canadian Agreement.[68] This clause bound the Canadian Government with respect to maximum preferential *rates* as well as minimum margins.

Like the Canadians, the Australians were exposed to pressure from lobbyists, and from politicians at home – though the pressures must have been less acute. The eminent protectionist, J. N. H. Hume Cook, attended the conference as an adviser. He had conferences with Gullett and Bruce, but was not privy to the detailed proceedings or results of the conference. Fearful that Bruce and Gullett would give, or had given, higher preferential margins by lowering the preferential duties instead of raising the general rates, he conferred and discussed regularly with certain officials – especially Messrs Abbott and McKay, of the Australian Customs. He regularly advised on the question of free entry for particular British goods. If any good was actually made in Australia, he opposed free entry. And he strongly opposed the British textile producers when they asked for a 'fighting chance' in the Australian market.[69] There is no way to tell how influential these lobbyists were. But one has the impression that, compared with R. B. Bennett, the Australian delegates were relatively uninfluenced by them. Gullett himself, however, was a protectionist. And the United Australia Government, though less protectionist than the Labour Government which had preceded it, was very far from free trade. It would not have dared to risk many unemployment-creating tariff-cuts.

South Africa was not very interested in the Ottawa Conference, and she was totally uninterested in 'domestic competition'. In 1925 her government had deliberately embarked on a policy of selective, protected industrialisation – largely to absorb her poorer whites into decent urban employment. Early in the game, Dr Havenga, her chief delegate, announced that he would have nothing to do with Chamberlain's idea. Nor would he offer any concessions: the UK must first suggest something. On 5 August, he explained that South Africa would maintain her existing preferences but would offer little or nothing more. Though South African tariffs were low, and though few were overtly protective, the preferential margins were also small – three to five percentage points, and they were granted 'selectively'. Chamberlain explained that he had hoped for a preferential margin of ten percentage points, and told Havenga that Britain would not continue free entry unless recompensed.[70] It gradually became clear that the South Africans attached great importance to the meat question. Though they did not yet export chilled or frozen meat, they hoped to do so; meat-export would help the Boer farmers, for whom life was increasingly hard. Hence the meat negotiations form an essential background to the Anglo-South African talks. On 7 August, the UK delegates decided that 'we should be more likely to arrive at a satisfactory settlement if we begin by asking for 15 per cent.'[71] But on 15 August, Havenga refused to extend even 10 per cent preference to woollens, linens, socks, agricultural machinery, iron and steel, hardware, motors, or paper.[72] He continued to worry about the disruption of South African trade with foreign countries.[73] The British delegation had hoped[74] that 10 per cent margin would give the UK an extra £1 million in export sales. Havenga's concessions were worth almost nothing. Yet in spite of earlier threats to remove South African products from the free list, they closed with Havenga on this unsatisfactory basis . . . perhaps because, in the end, he did a little for iron, steel, and machinery.[75]

From New Zealand, also, little was obtained – but little was asked. This Dominion already drew most of her imports from Britain; she already gave large preferential margins; her tariffs were low; her fisc could not stand a loss of customs revenue.

New Zealand did not have a Tariff Board, and did not want to set one up. But she quickly agreed to the principle of 'domestic competition'. The Anglo-New Zealand Agreement provided for an *ad hoc* Tariff Tribunal, which would examine all protective duties; the New Zealand Government promised to reduce duties 'as speedily as possible to such a level as will place the UK producer in the position of a domestic competitor'; it agreed to protect only industries which had good prospects.[76]

Coates explained in late July that he would offer 'almost any preference' in exchange for British concessions on meat, butter, and other New Zealand products. But the UK delegates thought it was out of the question for them to entertain New Zealand's requests, given the small pay-off they would obtain from *any* conceivable New Zealand concession.[77] Hence Chamberlain explained to Coates that he was prepared to continue free entry for New Zealand produce if New Zealand would continue her *existing* preferences on British goods.[78] He was prepared to concede a higher duty on foreign butter, but resisted Coates' requests for a quantitative restriction of foreign lamb and mutton. The Anglo-New Zealand negotiations, like the Anglo-Australian, nearly came to grief on the meat question. At length, in exchange for the higher British duty on foreign butter, and for Britain's restriction of foreign frozen meat, Coates agreed to reduce preferential duties on certain specified goods, to exempt UK goods from customs surtaxes, and to maintain the existing preferential margins of 20 per cent. Where margins already exceeded 20 per cent, he promised not to reduce them below 20 per cent without London's consent.[79]

The Anglo-Dominion negotiations involved constant discussions between delegates at the highest possible level. Indeed, to a remarkable extent the story of the conference is an account of Chamberlain's dealings with Bennett, Bruce, and Coates. The Anglo-Indian discussions, in contrast, were left much to the officials who accompanied both Indian and UK delegates. By 30 July these discussions had produced a draft agreement, which the delegates approved, welcoming 'the outstanding feature of the negotiations, namely, the acceptance by India of the principle of Imperial Preference'.[80] However, as the policy of domestic competition took shape, there were further Anglo-Indian discussions. On 3 August, Chamberlain and Baldwin asked Chatterjee for 'competitive entry' to the Indian market for iron and steel products. In exchange, they were prepared to offer free entry to Indian iron, steel, and other manufactures. They also offered to impose higher duties on foreign raw materials which competed with Indian goods. The Indians, in turn, asked for Britain's good offices with respect to Australia, whose Government accorded Indian goods no preferences. Chamberlain, who had already raised the matter with the Australians, promised that the point should be borne in mind; on 9 August he again reminded Bruce of its importance.[81] But the delegates themselves do not seem to have considered Indian questions until 17 August. By that time, the officials had completed an Anglo-Indian agreement but the Indians would not sign it until at least two major Dominions had also signed their own agreements. Hence the Indian agreement also hung fire until the very last minute; it too depended upon the successful outcome of Britain's wranglings with Canada and Australia. Only on the evening of the 19th was it finally initialled.

The Anglo-Indian Agreement did nothing for British access to the subcontinent's textile markets. But India did agree to consider the protective duties on cotton and artificial silk in the light of a Tariff Board report. She also promised to introduce a preferential margin of ten percentage points for a specified range of cotton and rayon goods – if the Tariff Board did not recommend protective duties for these goods.[82] In exchange, Britain promised to help increase Lancashire's consumption of India's raw cotton, Britain agreed to continue free entry for Indian iron and steel, subject to a satisfactory arrangement with respect to Indian duties on British galvanised sheet, and granted an even lower duty for sheet rolled from Indian-made bar. The scheme was to last until the Tariff Board could next examine the Indian iron and steel industry.[83] India also conceded a 10 per cent preferential margin on many manufactures, and a 7½ per cent margin on a few others – cars, buses, chassis, and vehicle parts. However, the agreement specifically precluded preferential margins on 'protective' duties, and on many other categories.[84] Thus, although India had accepted 'the principle of preference', she had not adopted any general scheme thereof – and had exempted the industries which her politicians and officials were concerned to protect. Further, she could not simply cut her duties on British goods. The Indian central budget depended heavily on tariff revenue; it was already in deficit; Whitehall had been urging Delhi to balance it. Hence the Indian Government could create new preferential margins only by taxing some foreign goods more heavily. On both sides the officials recognised this fact, which was noted in some of the early position papers. Hence the British gained much less than at first sight one might believe.

At Ottawa the UK also negotiated trade agreements with Newfoundland and Southern Rhodesia. The Newfoundland discussions are of little importance, and the Southern Rhodesian mattered only with respect to tobacco. Therefore, the former are ignored, and the latter are treated in a later section. There were no Anglo-Irish discussions.

In the preceding pages of this section, we have traced negotiations with respect to concessions on the more obvious fronts: preferential margins and rates on particular British commodities. However, the UK delegates were just as concerned to extract concessions on three other fronts: customs administration, 'primage' duties and surcharges, and exchange-dumping duties. We conclude the second with a glance at these matters.

With respect to customs administration, both Canada and Australia had annoyed the UK. Australian tariff law provided for many 'deferred' duties – lower rates which were to be levied as long as Australian industry did not produce the good in question. At any time the Australian Government could remove an item from the deferred list, replacing a relatively low duty with a much higher one. British officials and negotiators were anxious to end this uncertainty. The Anglo-Australian Agreement did not mention deferred duties. But in private, the British delegates were assured that so far as possible, the duties on the relevant items would not be increased above the 'deferred' level.

As for Canada, there were analogous problems. Canadian law provided for lower duties on goods 'of a class or kind not made in Canada'. But Canadian customs officials could and did decide arbitrarily whether or not a given shipment or item should pay these lower duties or the normal and higher ones. Further, it was up to the overseas exporter to prove that his shipment was *not* of a class or kind made in Canada. In addition, and quite separate, was a provision for arbitrary valuation. Bennett had introduced into Canadian tariff law a clause whereby the customs officials could fix the valuation of an import. In the last resort, the value could be 'such as the Minister shall determine': as a penultimate resort, valuation could be, and often was, the fair market value *in Canada*. Such a provision of course could defeat any *tariff* concession. A protectionist administration could value any import in a discouraging or prohibitive way; by so doing it could eliminate whatever competitive advantage the British producer might otherwise enjoy in virtue of the exchange rate, his own sterling costs, or the preferential tariff. Both in public and private he moved to make these promises effective.

The Conference Committee on Customs Administration took a dim view of this arbitrary provision – Section 43 of the

Canadian Customs Act. On 15 August, Bennett's Minister of National Revenue asked Bennett if he might placate the British on this Committee by agreeing to amend Section 43 so as to exclude British goods. As Bennett agreed, the Minister told the British delegates, and the resulting confidential correspondence formed part of the conference bargain.[85]

All the Dominion governments depended heavily upon customs revenues. As trade shrank, so did these revenues. Australia, New Zealand, and Canada had responded by imposing 'primage duties' – universal levies at low rates, whose aim was fiscal not protective.[86] New Zealand's primage duty was 3 per cent; Canada's and Australia's were 5 per cent. Though the rates are low, these levies did have some protective effect,[87] and by raising import prices in the Dominions they somewhat reduced the volume of British exports thereto. Hence the British delegates were eager to dispose of the primage levies as fast as possible. Unfortunately, the finances of the Dominions were not strong enough to permit immediate repeal. The best the Dominions could do was to promise to remove the primage as soon as their finances would allow.[88] Similarly, Canada and Australia agreed to remove various surcharges and prohibitions 'as soon as practicable'. What was 'practicable'? An answer could be given only by specifying all other revenues and all outlays in each Dominion's budget. In principle, the Dominions could replace primage and other surcharges with other tax revenues. Or they could cut government expenditures. But no one could have expected the Dominions to submit their future budgets to Whitehall scrutiny. And at Ottawa no one tried to introduce such examination. The UK had to be content with an earnest declaration of intent: the Dominions simply indicated that they did not mean these levies to be permanent. But, since this commitment was so vague, they could easily give it – and then ignore it.

On exchange-dumping duties the UK delegates achieved something. Both South Africa and Canada had introduced special levies to offset the depreciation of floating currencies – in particular, the depreciation of sterling since September 1931. South Africa refused to give up this levy or to make any special commitment with respect to it. However, with respect to South Africa the issue soon became a dead one: late in 1932, the South African Government devalued *vis-à-vis* gold and soon stabilised her currency on sterling. Canada was a more important market, and the oddities of her exchange-dumping duties were linked with the general arbitrariness of her customs practices: by proclamation, the Canadian Government could and did vary the rate at which sterling prices were to be converted into Canadian dollars for customs valuation. Hence the Canadian Government was making a major concession when it promised 'to give sympathetic consideration to the possibility of reducing and ultimately abolishing the exchange dumping duty in so far as it applies to imports from the United Kingdom'.[89] In the months after Ottawa, the Canadian Government tried to honour this commitment. Gradually it brought the arbitrary valuation into closer alignment with the market exchange rate. Through the High Commissioner, the Dominions Office exerted constant pressure in this respect. However, for Canada as for South Africa the problem proved to be temporary: once the American dollar had been floated and devalued, sterling rapidly moved to a premium over the former gold par, and Canada's exchange valuation, which had discouraged British exports between September 1931 and mid-1933, actually began to encourage them!

Exactly how much did all these tariff and non-tariff concessions mean? At the time, the UK representatives knew the qualitative answer: very little. In the last section of this chapter, we summarise their own estimates, and present some crude calculations of our own. To conclude this section, we merely note some of the dangers which their bargaining might reasonably claim to have averted.

Both Canada and Australia were uneasy about their existing preferential systems. In the twenties, Australia had moved rapidly towards a protectionism which, the British believed, hindered British exports while appearing to grant preferential concessions. London had every reason to fear that, though the new United Australia Government was committed to tariff reduction, it would so arrange its affairs as to further handicap the British export trade. The tenor of the dispatches which passed through the Dominions Office would tend to increase this fear. Furthermore, Australian politicians had often threatened to abolish their existing preferential margins. One cannot be sure that they meant this threat seriously. But they repeated it at Ottawa, and they were certainly eager to negotiate trade agreements with third countries – if necessary, at the expense of their existing concessions to the UK. Hence the British delegates were to some extent bargaining for the retention of an existing preferential system; they were also trying to prevent Australia from sliding deeper into protectionism. With respect to Canada the same two considerations applied. Bennett's Conservative Government was strongly protectionist, and closely linked with protected industry. Canada's preferential system had been a Liberal invention. Bennett, like Bruce, wanted trade agreements with third countries – especially with the United States. If Britain did not satisfy him, he might well have reduced or abrogated the preferential margins for the sake of such agreements. Admittedly, the Canadians had a three-column tariff: foreigners' goods could be admitted at the intermediate rate, leaving the preferential rate and margin unchanged. But eager foreign bargainers might well insist on a reduction in the intermediate duty, or in the preferential margin. The Anglo-Canadian Agreement, and the Anglo-Australian, should be seen as defensive measures – attempts to prevent the two large Dominions from behaving in even more inconvenient and uncomfortable ways.

There was little Imperial warmth in the conference bargaining. The UK delegates had long since resolved that they would make concessions only in exchange for adequate *quid pro quo*. In so deciding, they had departed from the pattern of past Imperial conferences. Indeed, before 1932 most of the intra-Imperial preferences had been unilaterally extended. Inter-Dominion negotiations had led to tariff concessions between Australia, Canada, New Zealand, and the West Indies. But between Britain and the Dominions, preferences had been extended as free gifts on one side or the other. By 1932, such days were gone for ever. To extract new concessions and to retain old, Britain had to meet the Dominions' demands on many fronts. For Canada, the important issues were wheat, timber, and Russia. For the three southern Dominions, what mattered were meat and dairy products. Canada and Southern Rhodesia also cared about tobacco. All the Dominions had some interest in a variety of lesser foodstuffs.

All these demands were more or less traditional. Since 1902, Canada had wanted Britain to tax foreign wheat. Since 1921, Australia had been asking Britain to do something about foreign meat and processed fruit. Since 1930, the 'Russian threat' had been on the Imperial agenda. But it was still hard for any British Government to swallow a wheat duty or a meat duty. And many minor foodstuffs were as politically sensitive, at least to some ministers. Hence the British delegates hoped to extract the maximum concessions for their own exports, while raising their own food duties as little as possible. Matters would have been simple if the Dominions and India had had no industry, and if Britain had had no agriculture . . . or if Empire supplies could meet all British requirements. If retaliation could have been ignored, Britain could then have conceded prohibitive tariffs on foreign food, timber, and metals, while demanding free entry for her manufactures. But Empire Free Trade was 'not on', and nobody thought it was.

What of British agriculture? It needed protection from the Dominions as much as from foreign countries. The Wheat Act had already looked after the corn-grower. Many other prices were at satisfactory levels. But lamb and mutton prices were not. Hence Chamberlain's efforts to make the Dominions accept quantitative control: meat was a problem for the UK herself, and for meat, cheapness was no longer enough. But timber should be kept cheap, in spite of Canadian importunities. Britain herself produced some, but not much, and not enough. Nor could the home supply be quickly increased. Hence Anglo-Russian trade should be regulated no more than necessary to keep Canada quiet. As for dairy products, the Dominions were far, and Denmark was near;

perhaps a higher duty on foreign butter, or even a quota, would help the British cowherd. The problem of pig-meat was already in hand: bacon imports were to be controlled by quota, and a domestic industry was to be created. The emerging agrarian protectionism of the UK was as much a part of the conference fabric as the established industrial protectionism of India and the Dominions.

All the above is an *ex post* rationalisation of the negotiating course which the UK delegates adopted. At no point did they organise their thoughts explicitly on these or any other coherent lines. But in the negotiations we can detect all the above strands – free trade, cheap food, cheap timber, food taxes, and the agricultural interest. Within the delegation the division was predictable: Thomas and Runciman opposed food tariffs, while Chamberlain, Baldwin and Hailsham acquiesced joyfully in them. But all were aware of the political background. Would the National Government survive? And what would happen in Parliament and in the constituencies? Once stated, these concerns need not be repeated. However, they should be remembered as, in the next three sections, we trace the process by which the British delegates were induced to concede so much.

III. MEAT AT OTTAWA

The British officials had prepared some proposals which their ministers might offer the Australians with respect to meat.[90] But on shipboard the delegates decided they could not put these forward. Chamberlain proposed, instead, voluntary and multinational arrangements for the control of production. In the form of an International Meat Conference, this idea was to have a long and tangled life in later negotiations. It was referred to the officials for study, and may have formed the basis for the control scheme to which Britain eventually committed herself. Later, the delegates also decided to reject the Australian request – a mixture of duty-free quotas for foreign meat and penal duties on excess shipments. However, they were not prepared to discard the idea of a meat duty. Still, they assumed that 'We should entertain the idea only in return for very valuable concessions.'[91] And so they landed with no meat policy. In a private letter, Baldwin recorded that none of them could see what they would do about meat. Amery believed that Baldwin and Chamberlain were already willing to tolerate duties both on wheat and meat. But Amery was not a delegate.[92]

Once the conference began, there was a lull before the question of meat came up. The Dominions had gone off to co-ordinate their demands. After some days, they jointly asked Britain to impose a duty of ¾d. per lb. on all kinds of meat except lamb, which was to pay 1d. per lb. They wanted a 43 per cent cut in Britain's purchases of foreign lamb and mutton, a 10 per cent cut in foreign chilled beef, 40 per cent off foreign frozen beef, and similar cuts for bacon and frozen pork. Dominion meat was to be free of any quantitative control. Canned meat was to pay an *ad valorem* duty of 20 per cent – roughly the equivalent of the specific rates which were proposed for other meats. Poultry was to pay 2½d. per lb.

These requests were of interest chiefly to Australia and New Zealand. Neither shipped chilled beef to Britain, but both believed that cheap Argentine chilled beef had damaged the British market for their frozen beef – a lower quality product – and for their sheepmeat. South Africa was concerned to invent a chilled-beef trade. Canada exported no dead meat to the UK, and sent very little bacon; British sanitary embargoes kept out her live cattle.

Just as the running on Russia was left to Prime Minister Bennett, so S. B. Bruce applied most of the pressure with respect to meat. On 27 July he began his attack.

We now know that Bruce's requests were more moderate than his own Department of Markets had recommended. Further, this Department had suggested lower duties and fewer quotas than the Australian meat industry had proposed. Finally, Bruce was asking for no more than his official, McDougall, had requested in London two months before. Nevertheless, his words were not welcome. He described the importance of the Australian lamb and mutton trade, and of the Canadian bacon trade. The hope of the future, he said, lay in an intensified production, especially of fruit, dairy products and meat – all products which the Empire imported on balance. If only the UK would act to extrude foreign products from her market, Australia could increase her production of these products. Further, as her solvency would then be assured, she could service her overseas debt, which was mostly held in the UK. Bruce therefore asked for many things: to aid Canada, a duty and a restriction on foreign bacon; to prevent the substitution of South American chilled beef for Antipodean frozen beef, a duty and restriction on foreign chilled beef – even though the Dominions as yet did not export any; to restore profitability and encourage expansion in the Australasian sheep industries, a duty on foreign mutton and lamb, as well as a 45 per cent cut in foreign shipments.

The British delegates did not comment on Bruce's requests. But in private they did not know what to do about them. Chamberlain was pressing ever more strongly for voluntary supply restriction by producers. Before his colleagues, and before the monetary committee of the conference, he developed this theme at some length.[93] But it was anathema both to Australia and to New Zealand. Further, Canada lacked the legal authority to impose export controls, and Prime Minister Bennett was known to oppose them on ideological grounds. Nevertheless, though the UK delegates had still not definitely decided against meat duties, they did decide on 2 August that Chamberlain was right about restriction. It should exist, should be voluntary, and should be operated by the suppliers. Lamb and mutton might be tackled first. Meanwhile, it would be proper to 'discuss' duties on foreign butter and meat.[94]

J. G. Coates was leading the New Zealand delegation. He would offer almost any tariff concession if only he could ensure that New Zealand's goods could retain duty-free status at British ports . . . if only Britain would act against foreign meat, butter, and other produce. But Britain's delegates knew that New Zealand in any event had little to offer. Hence they thought New Zealand's requests were out of the question. They asked for very little, and simply offered Coates the voluntary restriction scheme. The New Zealand Finance Minister was far from happy. As he later explained to Baldwin, the whole effort of his country had been devoted for fifty years to the supplying of the British market; how could he consider any proposal for the restriction of supply?[95]

Bruce responded more encouragingly. When meeting the UK delegates on 3 August, he said he would give the scheme favourable consideration. But he undoubtedly received the impression that if Australia would offer enough concessions Britain would also impose a duty on foreign meat. Given a quota and a foreign tariff, he said, 'in exchange, Australia was prepared to give anything which seemed possible . . . within reason . . . short of wiping out her own industries'.[96]

Since the entire point of the British initiative was to win large Australian concessions, this response was gratifying. But it rested on a misconception. And Bruce continued to press for a preferential beef duty in the form of a quota duty – the device which the UK delegation had rejected weeks before.[97] Bruce argued that the cheap Argentine chilled beef had lowered the price of Australasian frozen lamb and mutton; hence the former must be restricted if the price of the latter was to rise.

The South Africans, meanwhile, had shown themselves well disposed to voluntary restriction of lamb and mutton. This was not surprising, as they exported neither. However, they did want help with the export marketing of chilled beef – a product they were just beginning to ship. Therefore, they continued to press for a duty on foreign chilled beef.[98]

Gradually the British delegates were being forced to make their decisions, and then to explain their policy. On 4 August, Chamberlain told Coates that he was prepared to consider a duty on foreign mutton and lamb. He did not like the New Zealand plan for quantitative restrictions, because Britain would have to impose and manage them. But he put the same proposal he had offered the Australians, and the exporters should voluntarily control their exports of mutton and lamb. Coates at first resisted the idea, but once he was convinced it would not lead to bulk purchase, he agreed to explore it with the British and the Australians.[99]

On 5 August, after agreeing that the British and Australian experts should jointly formulate a restriction scheme, Baldwin exploded:

'the real answer to the Australians was that they had, by over-production, themselves flooded the market, and broken the price in the case of mutton and lamb, and that the break in price was not due to South American chilled beef exports . . . it seemed not improbable that the Australian representations were based on political, not economic considerations.'[100]

The officials were inclined to support a voluntary restriction plan.[101] So, it seems, were most or all of the ministers. If lamb and mutton imports were restricted, British sheep raisers would certainly benefit. But what of the duty? The delegates brooded long and hard over Chamberlain's sheepmeat ideas, and also considered the whole meat question at length – without result.[102]

Meanwhile, the British were still trying to convince the New Zealanders that it was a good thing to regulate exports. On 9 August, Baldwin told Coates how important export quotas were. Cunliffe-Lister noted their success in raising sugar and tin prices. Both men pointed out that Britain was flooded with Antipodean lamb and mutton. No wonder their prices were falling! Production quotas with steady increases in the Dominions' shares were the obvious answer. But foreign supplies could not be cut off all at once. What of Argentina? Britain, they said, was prepared to regulate pigmeat imports. She would also tell the chilled-beef producers that their trade faced regulation if it should threaten the mutton and lamb producers. Coates rather sadly asked if it would not be enough to restrict *foreign* sheepmeat. He was told brusquely that it would *not*.[103]

The next day it became clear that there would be disaster on the Antipodean front unless the meat question could be resolved to Australia's satisfaction. Bruce and Gullett told Chamberlain and Hailsham that they would accept the proposed general agreement, including the critical concession of domestic competitor status for British goods in Australia – but only if Britain's meat programme were satisfactory. They insisted on at least one of three things – a heavy duty, a severe restriction of foreign meat, or a combination of moderate duty and moderate restriction.[104]

On 14 August, the UK delegates decided that they could not propose a meat duty. Some of them favoured it in principle, and were certainly prepared to concede one for the sake of conference 'success'. But Runciman and Thomas, having already given way on wheat duties, and believing that the conference had been thoroughly rigged against the British, would not give way to Chamberlain's importunities.

That night, Baldwin went to Bruce and told him there would be no meat duty. Bruce was furious. Not unreasonably, he accused the British of bad faith. And he threatened to withdraw the Australian delegation.

Baldwin, it would appear, talked Bruce into remaining at the conference. At least, so Bruce appears to have told Baldwin's most recent biographers.[105] But the Australians maintained that they would have to start all over again, considering *inter alia* the preferential margins which British goods already enjoyed under their existing tariff. The New Zealanders had reported that they could not possibly go home and ask their citizens to produce less.[106] Could the conference be allowed to fail?

They were reaping the fruits of their long vacillation with respect to their meat programme. Though they had almost certainly not meant to mislead Bruce, by coquetting with the idea of a meat duty, and by refusing to state that such duties were impossible, they had certainly misled him in fact.

On 15 August the British delegates cabled their conclusions, concessions and forebodings to Ramsay MacDonald.[107] His reply was non-committal; it reminded them that excessive protectionism would split the Cabinet, but told them to do the best they could.[108]

These remarks were unhelpful. Chamberlain and Hailsham were sure that the New Zealand and Australian delegates would accept a restriction plan only if Britain also taxed foreign meat. Should the UK ministers reverse their decision of the preceding day?

Nobody wanted the conference to break down. Thomas pointed out that there was a real risk the Australians would simply go home and default on their external debt. But, though he believed that it would be disastrous if the conference were to collapse,

'it was impossible to proceed on the present lines. He [Thomas] paid a very warm tribute to Mr Chamberlain and Lord Hailsham for the manner in which they had conducted the negotiations with the most splendid loyalty to their colleagues, and in the face of every possible kind of insult and discourtesy. He [Thomas] declined any longer to be blackmailed. No one had suffered more from Mr Bennett than he had . . . he could not shut out from his mind the thought that in the whole of this matter the real source of trouble and friction was Mr Bennett himself . . . the United Kingdom delegation had been giving way to the demands of the Dominions in every possible direction, and the point had been reached when it was only possible to defend the concessions which we had made by an appeal to sentiment, and by urging that we must not look to the immediate future for any return, but that we were sowing the seeds of a great harvest which our posterity would gather in. The United Kingdom delegates had now reached the stage when they were being held up to blackmail, and ransom. The limits of all possible concessions were long past. . . . He [Thomas] could not assent to the proposal that the decision of the previous day not to impose a tax on meat, should be reversed.'[109]

Runciman agreed with Thomas: both would acquiesce in the delegation's other decisions but would not accept Chamberlain's proposal for a meat duty. Chamberlain himself

'expressed his great gratitude to those of his colleagues who were not members of the Conservative Party for the manner in which they had acceded to the wishes of their colleagues up to the present, and he felt he could not possibly ask them to go farther than they had already done . . . however, the idea that the Conference should break down filled him with despair . . . while there was no excuse for the way in which the United Kingdom Delegation had been treated, he thought it was an intolerable position that Australia should be allowed to go out of the Conference on this issue. He did not believe that Mr Bruce had abused his position. Throughout he had been studiously moderate and had tried, within his limitations, to be reasonable.'[110]

In the rather formless discussion which followed, Runciman said that though it was impossible to make a balance sheet of the agreements, 'if one could be made we could not defend our concessions in LSD terms'. It was decided that Thomas should telephone the Prime Minister and ask his views.

Baldwin's biographers[111] strongly imply that Baldwin, in private conversation, persuaded Thomas to telephone MacDonald. Whatever Baldwin may have recalled, this cannot have happened: the delegates' meeting began at 10.45 p.m. and the decision to call MacDonald at 7 a.m. was taken during it. Whatever the role of Baldwin's conciliatory talents, they were exercised at this meeting, not before or after it.

On the morning of 16 August, Thomas telephoned and cabled MacDonald. Fearing that his telephone was tapped, he was obliged to be vague.[112] And MacDonald was not very helpful. Explaining that the telegram had been very complicated, he reminded Thomas that five ministers would resign if a meat tax were imposed. He then said that he 'had been unable to communicate with other Cabinet Ministers in the UK, and that he fully realized the extreme difficulty of the position. He hoped that the delegates would do their best to arrive at some solution which could be unanimously accepted'.[113] He would cable his views. But when these came, they were vacuous.[114]

This telephone call is presumably the origin of the legend, reported in several recent studies and biographies, that to prevent a breakdown, MacDonald intervened some days later, in the negotiations *with Canada*.[115] The primary source for this legend seems to be H. H. Stevens' recollections. But Stevens himself was not at the centre of the negotiations. And it is easy for a rumour dimly remembered from 1932 to have displaced itself by a few days in 1962, when Stevens recorded his recollections. In any event, even with respect to Australia and meat, it is certainly not true that MacDonald told the delegation to accept Dominion terms rather than return empty-handed. His message was in much more equivocal terms – as much concerned with the Cabinet as with the conference.

Meanwhile, it was beginning to appear that, after all, the Australians might not insist on a meat tax. Perhaps they were losing faith in the advice of Amery, who was still urging the Dominions to press for a 3-cent meat duty.[116] The Australian concession was first adumbrated on 16 August, and confirmed by Bruce on the evening of 17 August. This fact makes the personal mock-heroics of 15 and 16 August, as reported in various biographies,[117] quite irrelevant to the final arrangement. The British delegation, thanks to its internal dissensions, had gained a critical forty-eight hours. On the 16th, too, Chamberlain convinced Coates to think better of the meat scheme. And the next day the New Zealander said that he was not going to rupture negotiations on the issue of a meat duty.

By the 18th, the Australians and the New Zealanders had gone to work on the quota plan. They hoped to draw it so as to make Australian opinion accept it.[118] In the process, they rendered it unacceptable to the UK delegates, who asked Chamberlain to prepare a new scheme in which the UK would itself regulate the imports of foreign lamb and mutton, while leaving the Dominions to regulate their production, for a definite short period – probably twelve to fifteen months.

Until this point, Bennett had been allowing Bruce to make the running on the meat front. The British had already decided to remove the veterinary controls which had long prevented Canada from shipping live cattle to Britain. On

18 August, they also guaranteed Canada a quota of duty-free and unrestricted entry for up to 2 million cwt. of bacon every year – far more than Canada had ever sent to the UK.[119] The same day, Bennett staggered them by demanding that they place restrictive quotas on foreign bacon as well. In any event admittedly the British proposed to restrict foreign bacon shipments. But it was Britain's own producers, not the Canadians, who were meant to gain. Canada in any event supplied less than 1 per cent of British bacon needs. They refused to make this further concession, and Bennett backed down accepting the British consolation prize – a bacon quota of 2.5 million cwt.[120]

On 19 August, Bruce again raised his ante. He declared that he would go home without an agreement unless the British would restrict their imports of foreign lamb and mutton by 35 per cent after eighteen months, instead of 24 per cent after twelve months. He also insisted that the UK should regulate its imports of foreign frozen and chilled beef.[121] Much earlier the Australians had asked for this, but the British had not considered it. The British gave way on both fronts.

At long last it was possible to initial the agreements – the Australian at 11.30 p.m. on the 19th, the New Zealand at 10.15 p.m. on the same night, and the Canadian at 1.30 a.m. on the 20th.[122] Meat had not been crucial to the success of the Anglo-Canadian talks. It had mattered to New Zealand, but Coates would probably have been grateful for any concessions he could obtain. And he had had no trouble with respect to dairy products: on both butter and cheese the British delegates had quickly agreed to raise the duties against foreigners. For Australia, however, the meat question was absolutely central. If Britain had not been willing to impose meat quotas, there might well have been no Anglo-Australian trade agreement. If one had been signed, it would have been even less advantageous to the British.

Exactly what had Britain conceded? The delegation had successfully fought off the Australasian pressure for a meat duty. But it did agree to control imports of foreign chilled beef, frozen beef, veal, mutton, and lamb for a five-year period. Foreign chilled beef was to be restricted to the level of 1931–32. Foreign frozen beef, veal, mutton, and lamb were to be cut in stages of 65 per cent of the 1931–32 level – the 'Ottawa year' of later controversy. Britain promised to impose no duties on Empire meat until mid-1936, and no quotas until 1 July 1934 at the earliest. On their side, Australia and New Zealand agreed to limit their shipments during the calendar year 1933. Finally, the Dominions were promised a rising share of the British meat-import market.

Canada was promised free and unrestricted entry for up to 2.5 million cwt. of bacon per year. She was also freed from certain veterinary controls on her shipments of live cattle, though she was given no guarantees with respect to permanent freedom from quota. The South African delegates, who wished to expand their very small chilled-beef trade, were promised that Whitehall would use its good offices with the meat companies to make sure that facilities would be available.[123]

In Schedule H of the Anglo-Australian agreements, Bruce and the British recorded their further agreement on various matters of principle. Frozen-meat prices were too low; it was essential to take steps to raise them; Britain would arrange for the regulation of frozen meat and chilled beef with this in mind; British policy was first to secure development of home production, and then to give the Dominions a bigger share of British meat imports. During 1933, Britain and Australia would consult about the best permanent policy to raise prices and improve marketing.

All these arrangements have a makeshift look. Certainly they did not precisely satisfy Australia's pre-conference hopes, or New Zealand's. They may or may not be thought to satisfy Britain's own agricultural interest: there was, after all, little point in restricting foreign meat merely to make room for unrestricted Empire meat. For Chamberlain, the result was a qualified victory. He would certainly have liked a meat tariff, but he had also sought a quota. In opposition, as Chairman of the Conservative Research Department, he had arranged for the working-out of a quota plan.[124] In the delegates' meetings, and before the monetary committee of the conference, he had strongly pressed for production controls as price-raising devices. Within a year he would exhort the World Economic Conference in similar terms. And he had drafted the various quota proposals which the conferees had examined. Bruce urged quotas on the UK. Coates supported Bruce. But Chamberlain made quotas palatable to the other British delegates.[125] And from his point of view there was hope for the future: had not Australia agreed to confer with the UK, in 1933, on more permanent controls?

Whatever Chamberlain may have thought of the meat clauses, we can now see that from every point of view they were unfortunate. The Australians had no intention of co-operating with the British in a permanent cartelisation of the British meat-import trade. The Canadians and South Africans were uninterested in the device, and the New Zealanders were never convinced about it. As for the temporary and voluntary restrictions, during 1933, only the New Zealanders ever made any serious effort to control their shipments. Hence the agreements did nothing to protect the British shepherd. But they did a great deal to antagonise the Argentine – the chief target of the Australians' trade-diversionary tactics. Further, time was to show that in exchange for their meat concessions the British had obtained remarkably little either from Canada or from Australia. Finally, within weeks of the conference's end, the meat arrangements had embroiled ministers and officials in a tangle of continuing dispute – on-going discussion about quotas, modifications, demands, and counter-threats. These discussions were neither edifying nor productive.

In mid-1932, a protectionist Britain would have done far better to impose a preferential meat duty. As Britain was the only large buyer of meat, in the short run, the duty would have been largely shifted backwards – on to Empire and foreign producers. There is every reason to believe that in 1932 the Australians were too confused to understand that *they* would pay the meat duty – even if it were preferential. If meat prices did not rise in Britain, the Government would have extracted from overseas producers a fund which could have been used for subsidy. For wheat, the arrangement already existed; the Wheat Act had been on the statute books for more than six months. For meat and butter, it would later be suggested.

General meat quotas would raise the price Britain paid for meat imports, turning the terms of trade against her. Preferential meat tariffs would turn these terms of trade in her favour. In granting the Dominions virtually unrestricted entry, while imposing quotas on foreigners but levying no duties on anyone, the British delegation had acquiesced in the pessimal package. To make matters worse, they had got very little for their acquiescence. In a few months the various chickens would come home to roost.

IV. OTHER BRITISH CONCESSIONS: WHEAT, FLOUR, DAIRY PRODUCTS, METALS

On 22 July, it was decided that the Dominions which produced particular goods would first discuss matters among themselves, and formulate common proposals which they could then submit to the UK delegates. There were to be five groups – dairy products, meat, fruit and vegetables, cereals including flour, and metals and minerals. It was also agreed that these discussions on UK concessions would go on simultaneously with conversations about Dominion concessions. The Dominion representatives then met, formulated their demands, and passed them to a co-ordinating committee of officials, which met seven times between 29 July and 5 August. The result was a group of 'agreed reports', which were the basis for discussion and bargaining between the UK and the Dominions during the last three weeks of the conference.

With respect to a wheat duty, Prime Minister Bennett made the running. Only Canada and Australia were significant wheat-exporters; the Australian Government was convinced that a preferential wheat duty would do nothing to help its farmers; Bennett also understood this fact, but for political reasons he needed a British concession on wheat. In turn, the UK delegation understood that though a preferential wheat duty would divert trade it would neither help Empire producers nor hurt British consumers. Admittedly, for the free-traders in the delegation a wheat duty was embarrassing – especially as Bennett had asked for the same duty that Joseph Chamberlain had proposed thirty years before.

On 26 July Bennett presented his demands. He wanted Britain to accept the 'principle of preferences' on natural products.[126] In particular, he wanted a duty on foreign wheat – 2s. – per quarter. Discussing his demands the next day, Baldwin and his colleagues discovered that they still did not agree either about the principle or about the mechanics of a Dominion wheat quota – the alternative device on which so much staff work had gone between October 1930 and July 1932. Gilmour and Chamberlain went off to modify the officials' preferred device;[127] Bennett received it on the 27th, and it was later passed to the Australians and the Indians. But it sank without trace; Bennett wanted a wheat tax, and nothing else. The Australians knew Britain could not help them with respect to wheat.[128] But Bennett continued to press for a duty.

With respect to a wheat tax, the British delegates were divided. They thought the request purely political and not at all economic. By 12 August they had still not decided whether to give in. And they could not decide about the related question of a flour duty.[129] But by now they believed that a duty on foreign wheat implied a duty on foreign *and Dominion* flour. When Bennett was told of this, and of the proposed quantitative regulation of the bacon trade, he became very angry; there was believed to be a real risk that he would withdraw all the Canadian offers.[130] Admittedly, these offers were worth only $10 million in extra export trade. But even that was too much to cast away. Hence the British quickly conceded his demand with respect to wheat.[131] And they informed Ramsay MacDonald of their decision.[132] Nevertheless, they were cheered by Bennett's undertaking: they could remove the duty if the supply prices of Canadian wheat should rise above the world price.

There remained the question of flour. For some days Chamberlain maintained that if Britain were to tax foreign wheat she must also tax Empire flour. This statement roused Bennett to fury. At length, on learning how strongly the Canadian Premier felt, the British agreed to give way. By 18 August they had done so.[133]

This last-minute concession may have had something to do with the more conciliatory attitude that Bennett then took up. Within the next twenty-four hours he agreed to a form of words on his exchange-dumping duty. He also increased his tariff concessions raising the British 'gain' from $10 million in extra exports to $15 million or so.[134]

What could be more horribly protectionist than a wheat tariff? Probably it was this new duty which has fastened the protectionist label so firmly on the conference. But in fact the wheat duty mattered far less than the meat arrangements, which were genuinely trade-diverting and price-lowering. In 1902, the Empire had been a net importer of wheat. At that time, a preferential wheat-duty would have raised producers' receipts by roughly the amount of the preferential margin – unless the duty itself lowered the general level of world wheat prices. Hence in 1902 it made economic sense for the Dominions to demand a duty on foreign wheat, and for consumption-minded politicians to oppose it. However, long before 1932 the situation had changed. Canada and Australia produced more wheat than Britain imported. In the new situation, one of two things might happen. The Dominions might form a 'ring' to control their wheat exports, extracting from the British the higher price which the preferential margin made possible. By eliminating competition they would be able to gain from the preferential system. But if they allow free competition to continue, the British price for Dominion wheat would remain at world levels. Quality differences aside, only Dominion wheat would enter the UK. But some Dominion wheat would be sold in foreign countries. And the foreign wheat, displaced from the British market, would simply displace the Dominion wheat which would in the absence of preference flow to the same foreign market. Hence the preferences would simply divert the flows of wheat without affecting prices, costs, or returns.

Neither the Canadians nor the Australians seemed likely to devise an efficient 'ring'. But the British delegates insisted that they should be allowed to remove the duty on foreign grain if any such ring should be formed. Thus the grain duty was a concession in form though not in fact.[135] Both British and Canadian delegations understood this fact very well. But on flour they were much more strongly at odds.

Bennett wanted free entry for Dominion flour. But if Dominion flour were to come in free, while foreign wheat was taxed, would not the British millers object loudly? So some British delegates argued. The delegation as a whole strongly resisted Bennett's flour demand, giving way only when they saw how important Bennett thought the point. Of course their resistance was based on a confusion. British millers could buy wheat at the same price as before; hence the wheat duty did nothing to raise supply prices to British millers, and so it did nothing to change the competitive position of British millers *vis-à-vis* Dominion millers. Even with free entry for Dominion flour, their position would be the same as if neither foreign wheat nor foreign flour were taxed.

For dairy products and minor foodstuffs, the principal suppliants were Australia and New Zealand. The Indian delegates did not ask for a new preferential tea duty. But they did request a new duty on foreign linseed, and the UK delegates agreed. Britain also promised to raise her duties on foreign rice, castor and other oils, and magnesium chloride. The southern Dominions were much more importunate. They wanted quotas on foreign butter, prohibitions on foreign apples, seasonal duties on citrus fruits, higher duties on dried fruit, cheese, honey, canned fruit, poultry, fish, and various fresh fruits.[136]

In December 1931, the Ottawa Committee had recommended various concessions on such foods. Hence it is not surprising that the delegates gave way without much fuss.

They granted higher butter duties, though they refused

to restrict foreign supplies as both the Australians and New Zealanders wanted. 'If absolutely necessary' the British were prepared to envisage a producer-operated scheme which would voluntarily restrict production.[137] The Australians still asked the British to impose a quota on foreign butter. The historian must wonder why it was a good thing for sheep-raisers to limit production, but a bad thing for dairy farmers to do the same thing? Were butter prices then high enough to satisfy British dairy farmers? Were Britain's butter imports much larger, relative to home consumption, than her sheepmeat imports? Or did the delegates simply believe that Australian and New Zealand dairy farmers could not be trusted to control their output? Whatever the reasons, Chamberlain stood firm against a foreign butter quota. Combined with Britain's meat concessions, an increase in the butter and cheese duties was enough to calm Australia and New Zealand.

The South Africans got their way with respect to the new duties on dried and canned fruit – items in which the Dominions hoped to outsell the Americans. But the new butter, cheese, honey, and fruit duties were lower than the Dominions had jointly requested. And several goods, particularly poultry and fruits, were left untaxed in spite of the Dominions' requests.

The UK delegates conceded new or higher duties on foreign butter, cheese, apples, pears, canned fruits, dried fruits, eggs in shell, condensed milk, milk powder, honey and flat white maize – South Africa's basic food export. There were also new seasonal duties on peaches, nectarines, plums, grapes, oranges, and grapefruit. The canned and dried fruits were of special interest to Australia, whose governments had brooded upon their fruit industries since 1921. South Africa gained from the maize duty. The butter and cheese concessions were of value chiefly to Australia and New Zealand.

Unlike the wheat duty, these new food imports were definitely price-raising in the UK and definitely hurt foreign countries – chiefly the United States, Denmark, and smaller Baltic nations. The Dominions exported less than Britain imported. Hence, at least in the short run, the ruling British price would be the world price plus the duty on foreign goods. Because the duties would almost certainly be shifted backward, the British price would certainly not rise by the full amount of the new duty. But at least in the short run – until Empire production rose and/or foreign exports fell – the duties would definitely help Empire producers. That is, the duties would raise their prices and also their total sterling earnings. The duties might also raise the prices of these goods in the Dominions' *internal markets*. Under competitive conditions, domestic prices would rise to the new higher levels which could be earned in the export trades. But the Australian food trades were anything but competitive; nearly a decade of regulation had severed the link between domestic and export markets.

All the Dominions were guaranteed free and unrestricted entry for three years with respect to their own eggs, poultry, butter, cheese, and other milk products. However, the UK reserved the right to impose duties or quotas thereafter.[138] As protectionist pressures mounted in the UK, these promises were shortly to cause enormous trouble. The Australians and New Zealanders immediately began to try to produce themselves out of bankruptcy: export 'surpluses' soon mounted, and all were sold in the UK, which had promised free entry until mid-1935. Having made the promises, how could Britain protect or help her own dairy farmers? The British delegates must have known that they were running a risk; we saw in the last chapter that Sir John Gilmour had long been pressing for a preferential system that would tax Empire foods at a non-zero rate. But it is easy to understand how, given the New Zealand delegation's desperation and the Australian delegation's combativeness, the British were unable to retreat from the free entry that the Import Duties Act allowed.

Besides raising some duties on foreign goods, the UK promised the Dominions not to reduce the existing duties on foreign tallow, canned meat, sausage casings, casein, meat extracts, dried peas, seeds of grass and clover, copra, sugar or milk, various gums, barley, wheat, flour, macaroni, dressed poultry, eucalyptus oil, wattle bark, asbestos, some dried fruits, some preserved fruits, whale oil, whale products, crayfish, fresh hake, oyster shells, ground nuts, goatskins, lucerne seed, kaffir corn and meal, maize products, box wood, potatoes, ostrich feathers, fresh fish, marine shell, canned salmon and other fish, timber, zinc, and lead. They also bound themselves to maintain stated preferential margins on some wines – a commitment that raised the British wine duty by 1s. per gallon. And for all the items that were dutiable under the Import Duties Act, the Dominions were guaranteed free entry. Similarly, India was guaranteed the existing margins of preference on tobacco, tea, coir, cottons, leather, jute manufactures, and some minor items. No one seems to have foreseen that Indian cottons would one day be sold in the UK itself! Britain also promised free entry for Indian iron and steel – a matter of enormous importance for the Tata Works, which believed that for pig iron and certain castings it could compete in Britain's home market. And India too was promised free entry for all the other items which temporarily entered duty-free under the Import Duties Act.

This binding of duties and margins is called 'conventionalisation'. At Ottawa none of them were disputed at all hotly. In themselves such commitments were not protectionist. They were a natural recompense for the Dominions' own commitments with respect to guaranteed margins. However, because they limited Britain's freedom to bargain with foreign countries they could be – and were – attacked. If Britain could not reduce the duty on foreign butter, for example, she had little to offer Denmark. In Cabinet and in the House, this line of thought produced many bitter attacks. However, later events proved that the agreements had not significantly impeded Britain's bargaining power – at least for a year or two. She was quickly able to extract favourable trade agreements from Denmark and the Baltic States – the countries most affected by the binding of preferential margins. Only later, when the British Government wished to become still more protectionist, were the agreements an embarrassment – because they prevented Britain from moving as rapidly towards protectionism as her government then wanted.

In short, present-day critics are obliged to argue that if Britain had conventionalised fewer duties and margins at Ottawa she would later have won even more concessions from more foreign countries. In light of her later negotiations, and of world-wide trading habits during the 1930s, it is hard to believe in this double conditional.

For the Australian and New Zealand politicians, of course, Britain's promises were extremely valuable. Both delegations could go home and say that the UK had guaranteed free entry for unlimited quantities of dairy products; the Australians could also report that Britain had helped her perpetually sick fruit industries.

In Australia, dried and canned fruit were desperately important, and extremely sensitive politically. During the twenties, thousands of family farms had been established to produce the raw materials for these simple processing industries. No one believed – or had ever believed – that the industries were internationally competitive. They were protected at home; they could export only because of the long-established British preferential tariffs, and because Australian governments connived at two-price systems which dumped 'surpluses' in the British market. But on the success of the fruit schemes a great deal depended – irrigation schemes, mortgages, the policy of closer settlement. Similarly, Australian butter production had been placed on an export basis through a mixture of protection and export subsidisation: since the mid-twenties Australian butter exports had been subsidised from the proceeds of a levy upon domestic sales. And Australian dairying, like Australian fruit-raising, was tied up with closer settlement and the family farm. Both, in turn, were linked with the idea of a largely agrarian and wholly white Australia.

For New Zealand the issue was less emotionally charged, but it was comparably important. The New Zealand Government was an anti-socialist coalition, under strong attack from a *dirigiste* Labour opposition. The leaders of the Government were committed to a system of free markets and international division of labour, by which New Zealand concentrated on primary foodstuffs, kept her tariffs low, and imported manufactures, largely from the UK. The dairy provision seemed likely to help New Zealand dairy farmers; equally important, they vindicated the government's ideological stance.

The discussions about tobacco began on shipboard, before the conference had properly begun. The Rhodesian delegation, like the South African, was sharing a ship with Baldwin and his fellow ministers. The Rhodesians pressed for an increased tobacco preference, and for a renewed stability in the preferential concession; a stabilised preference would encourage development, whereas a changeable preference would not. They were told that considerations of revenue made the question very difficult.[139] However, they continued to press for something on tobacco.

By 10 August it had become clear that Canada was also interested in tobacco. So was India. Chamberlain then decided it might be necessary to change the earlier decision. But it was agreed not to increase the tobacco preference – merely to stabilise it for ten years. The Rhodesians were informed the next day, and Bennett learned the day after.[140]

Thus in the Indian, Canadian, and Southern Rhodesian agreements, the UK promised not to reduce the existing preferential margin of 2s. ½d. per lb. – so long as the rate on foreign tobacco did not fall below this rate, in which case Empire tobacco would enter free of duty. The margin was stabilised until August 1942. This arrangement was later to give trouble in the Anglo-American trade talks of 1936–38: the USA wanted the margin reduced, and, on being denied this concession, pressed hard for a British commitment to reduce the preferential margin after August 1942 – in spite of the fact that by 1942 the Anglo-American trade agreement would already have expired!

With respect to non-ferrous metals, the UK and the Dominions did little more than validate the agreements which the few Empire producers had made among themselves. In copper, Canada and Southern Rhodesia were specially interested; in lead and zinc, Canada and Australia. The lead and zinc producers were negotiating in London with the UK users, who were afraid that they might be obliged to pay a higher price than their competitors in foreign countries. The Canadian Government had asked for a higher duty on lead and zinc, and for a UK market for her copper, now excluded from the United States by the new American copper duty. Canada, however, was prepared to supply the UK at the world price, while the Australian producers wanted a price higher by the amount of the tariff. Early in August, the Australians agreed that they would settle for the existing 10 per cent tariff, with free entry. Thus the final agreements included a new duty on foreign unwrought copper but they did not raise the existing duty on foreign lead and zinc. The agreements presumably strengthened the hands of the Empire producers in their dealings with the great American producers of copper, lead, and zinc. Thus they must have affected the pattern of world trade in these commodities – if only by influencing the cartel agreements.[141]

V. RUSSIA AND TIMBER

In the last chapter we saw how Prime Minister Bennett warned the UK to expect trouble over Anglo-Soviet trade. At Ottawa he duly made such trouble. Then and later, British ministers were not sure whether he really meant what he said, or really wanted what he demanded – a prohibition on British imports of Soviet timber, or, failing, quota control of these imports.

So far as one can tell from the documents which have survived in the Bennett Papers, though the Canadian Prime Minister and his advisers knew of the Soviet Five-Year Plan they had only the vaguest idea of Soviet export planning. They do not seem to have understood the basic difference between Soviet and Western trading motivation. Western industrialists, especially in 1931–32, were looking for foreign markets to absorb products on more favourable terms than home markets could offer. Canadian timber interests were especially alarmed at their prospects: new American tariffs had excluded them from the United States market to which, for several years, most of their exports had gone. Meanwhile, the USSR was exporting only enough to earn the foreign exchange which her domestic plans required. In 1930–32, the Soviet planners and the Party were discovering that they had underestimated the input requirements of the first Five-Year Plan. Further, we have every reason to suspect that they had not foreseen how sharply agricultural collectivisation would reduce farm output. Exports, therefore, had to be painfully extracted from a domestic economy which could readily have absorbed the exported timber, wheat, and coal. It was a national tragedy for the Soviet Union that her heavy import needs were coming just when the world's commodity markets were so unrewarding. Because prices were so inconveniently low, the USSR presumably had to export more than her planners wanted – more than they exported later in the decade, when Soviet productive capacity was higher and when world commodity prices were considerably more attractive than in 1930–34. Since the Soviet problem was to earn a necessary quantum of foreign exchange per year, high prices and small export volumes were in the Soviet national interest so long as they yielded at least this quantum.

In the preceding chapter we saw something of the importance which Canada had attached to the Russian question in pre-conference discussions.[142] We also saw something of the advice which the Canadian Prime Minister was receiving from the Canadian Forest Service[143] and from his officials.[144]

At Ottawa, as expected, Soviet trade bulked large in the Anglo-Canadian conversations. Bruce allowed Bennett to make the running on this subject. At first, the Canadian Premier used the Committee on the Promotion of Trade within the Commonwealth as a forum. A subcommittee also discussed Soviet trade, but did not report – presumably because the bilateral negotiations had pre-empted the subject.[145]

The question of timber was linked with the question of Russia. The British had brought a timber delegation – largely composed, the Canadians believed, of people active in the

Anglo-Soviet timber trade.[146] The Canadian lumber interests were present in the city, lobbying vigorously, and they were regularly consulted about the various proposals. Bennett also saw members from lumbering constituencies. At the time, it was widely believed that Bennett was using the question of Soviet trade purely for domestic political gain. The *Canadian Forum* said that he was playing up the 'Russian bogey . . . for our innocent patriots and Christians'.[147] All the evidence suggests, however, that Bennett must have thought the problem was real. Certainly his industrial advisers, civil servants, and Cabinet colleagues were all telling him that it was.

Though united in diagnosis, Bennett's advisers differed somewhat with respect to prescription. H. H. MacMillan, later a BC lumber magnate, strongly favoured a quota division of the British market, and urged Bennett to seek one.[148] But the chairman of the Economic Committee of the Canadian Lumbermen's Association reported that, for the sake of a preference and some other controls over Russian goods, he would, if necessary, forgo an import quota.[149] Howard Green, another Vancouver MP, complained on 12 August of Soviet pricing practices, and of the way in which Soviet sales were organised. He told Bennett, 'no 20 per cent preferences or quota can compete with such outrageous conditions. Can not the English Government regulate such contracts?'[150]

Canada had originally asked for a 10 per cent duty on Scandinavian timber, a 20 per cent duty on all other foreign timber, and free entry for her own. She had also suggested that the UK should take 30 per cent of her timber imports from Empire countries – as against 5 per cent in 1926–30. Stevens supported this request because it put all foreign countries on a level – 'thus removing any suggestion of a prejudice against Russia': he foresaw $40 million in new Canadian trade, a considerable offset to the lost American timber market.[151] Bennett also asked for a quota restraint, if necessary. The British were prepared to raise the timber duty, but found the Bennett package 'out of the question'.[152] They were sceptical of a high duty, pointing out that the

Russians and Scandinavians might simply absorb it, and doubting whether any politically tolerable duty would shift much trade, given the oddities in Canadian timber sizing and preparation. However, as pressed as they were they prepared to raise the duty on foreign timber.

Early in the negotiations Bennett himself, and other members of his Cabinet, had doubted that Britain would actually honour any commitment the delegation might make with respect to Soviet trade.[153] Nevertheless, he and Bruce had begun to press for a cordon around the USSR. The British delegates felt unable to agree, largely because in the UK such a prohibition would create unemployment, raise the price of timber, and imperil £7 to £8 million in export credits.[154] However, they had no objection to some formula which would satisfy Bennett – if one could be devised. Their own inclination at first was towards anti-dumping legislation 'of a special character' – though their industrial advisers assured them that only a worldwide cordon would contain Soviet competition.[155] However, the British officials urged that until the UK announced its plans for Soviet trade, Bennett was unlikely to make any definite offer of concessions on other fronts. Hence on 27 July, a week after the conference's opening, the British delegation approved Neville Chamberlain's plan for an anti-dumping duty which, though aimed at Russia, would apply to all countries. The next day Bennett welcomed Chamberlain's scheme.[156] But by 3 August the British themselves had discovered new difficulties, and the UK delegates were discussing the problem worriedly though inconclusively.[157] Principle was not at issue; the problem was to devise a way of satisfying the Canadian Prime Minister. By this time the Australians seem to have decided to leave the matter in the Canadians' hands; they themselves were preoccupied by the questions of meat duties and quotas. By 5 August, Chamberlain and Runciman had devised a formula which proposed actions that the UK might take whenever the Import Duties Advisory Committee might conclude that Soviet sales were undermining the imperial-preference scheme.[158] On 11 August as part of the effort to get more generous concessions from Bennett, this formula was broached. There were many redraftings and some second thoughts on the British side, as well as much intrigue on Bennett's. The British delegates believed that Bennett had not been telling his Cabinet the truth about the British formula. They were also annoyed by his continued pressure for a simple prohibition of Soviet timber – a demand which the British ministers would not consider.[159] H. H. Stevens, Canada's commerce minister, opposed the British formula, claiming that it argued against a preference, a quota, or any other form of resistance to Soviet goods. He called it 'a grossly anti-imperial document'.[160] Nevertheless, in the end, it was this formula, somewhat modified, which made it possible to conclude an Anglo-Canadian trade agreement.

The UK also promised not to reduce her duties on foreign timber, and she guaranteed free entry for Canadian timber. These commitments, plus the new British duty on foreign wheat, formed part of the fence against the Russians – though nobody expected them to be effective.[161] It was in Article 21 of the Anglo-Canadian Agreement[162] that Bennett put his faith. And the outcome won him golden opinions.[163]

VI. EVALUATION

When the Ottawa Conference ended on 20 August, the conferees resolved:

'the nations of the British Commonwealth having entered into certain Agreements with one another for the extension of mutual trade by means of reciprocal preferential tariffs, this Conference takes note of these Agreements and records its conviction; that by the lowering or removal of barriers among themselves provided for in these agreements, the flow of trade between the various countries of the Empire will be facilitated, and that by the consequent increase of purchasing power of their peoples, the trade of the world will also be stimulated and increased; further, that this Conference regards the conclusion of these Agreements as a step forwards, which should in the future lead to further progress in the same direction, and which will utilise protective duties to ensure that the resources and industries of the Empire are developed on sound economic lines.'[164]

Economists now know that in principle the conferees might have been right. In a world of unemployment, a partial customs union may so stimulate employment and output within its membership that, in spite of higher tariffs against foreign goods, it will import more, both in volume and in value, from the rest of the world. But the delegates had no good reason for their simple faith. And it now seems unlikely that the agreements had any such positive effect. They did not do much for the level of economic activity in Britain and the Dominions; they contained measures of quantitative restriction against foreign goods; they introduced new tariffs which were almost certainly shifted backwards, on to the foreign suppliers. *Vis-à-vis* foreign goods, the British delegates had conceded some increases in their own tariffs, and acquiesced in, or actively sought, many increases in Dominion tariffs. They had achieved something – but not enough – by way of immediate tariff-cuts on their own goods.

The British delegates, and their officials, had originally hoped for something very different – a general reduction in the tariff and other barriers to inter-Imperial trade, and no significant increases in the barriers against foreign goods. But the realities had defeated them. At a time of general unemployment, no Dominion government could possibly make unemployment-increasing tariff adjustments. Yet the British strategy made sense only if the Dominions could be expected to make such adjustments. Whenever a Dominion industry actually manufactured a good, and where the industry actually needed the protection of its national preferential tariff, a cut in that tariff would necessarily shift employment from the Dominion to the UK. If, as part of the bargain, the UK should concede higher duties on foreign foodstuffs and raw materials, the Dominion would benefit from higher sales and higher prices in the British market. However, this agricultural expansion would not necessarily absorb the extra urban unemployment. Certainly in agriculture or forestry themselves there would be few new jobs. There would be indirect effects. Because the agricultural population would be much better off, it would demand more city manufactures. Even so, in the cities unemployment might still rise. And the Dominions, all highly urbanised, could not ignore this possibility.

'Domestic competition' was no real escape, either. The proposal rested on a fallacy – the idea that all British producers operated at a single relatively low cost-level, while in each Dominion all producers operated at a single but higher cost-level. In fact this was not true. Different firms had different costs, and, within a firm or an industry, unit costs depended upon the scale of output. Further, a higher price would always extract a larger output from any particular set of industrial plant and equipment. Hence there could be no unique 'competitive' tariff. The higher the tariff on a British commodity, the more of it the Dominion would produce, and the more men would work at its production. Logically, therefore, one could fix the 'competitive' tariff only after someone – tariff board or government – had fixed the industry's output and employment, both in the Dominion and in the UK. One may talk evasively about 'reasonable charge' and 'efficient production' but one cannot avoid this fact. Hence one cannot expect a government in an unemployment world to honour a pledge of 'domestic competition', unless the implied tariff leaves industrial employment unchanged. In effect, this means that tariff boards will cut tariffs only when it can be shown that domestic producers are 'profiteering' – given that their actual output, their profits, are 'excessive' relative to their capital. In such cases, boards and governments might lower duties without expecting any extra unemployment.

In fact, if the profiteering monopolist has rising short-run or long-run marginal costs, he might be expected to reduce output and employment in this situation. If this is noticed, the board or government is likely to seek some slimy evasion. For instance, it may claim that higher tariffs are needed so that the industry can supply more of the market; low tariffs imply higher costs because of smaller scale, while high tariffs imply lower costs because of the larger scale. This argument makes sense only if the board and government want to protect the manufacturers' profits, or if the tariff is temporary. Once the firms have 'grown up', and are actually operating at the larger scale, they no longer need the high protection. They will be able to hold their larger market share, and make normal profits, without it. But if the protection is temporary, there is force in this argument. And so 'domestic competition' has a time dimension too: a tariff structure may evolve in a 'competitive' way even though at any moment it gives 'excessive protection'.

The conference should have worked on exchange rates, not tariffs. By devaluing their own currencies *vis-à-vis* sterling, the Dominions and India would have raised the domestic-currency receipts of their primary producers. Demanding more goods at all relevant prices, these primary producers would have generated more demand for local factories to satisfy. Given the elasticities of demand for their products, they would have earned more, lightening the burden of their external debt and raising their own real incomes. They would also have tended to export more sterling. British exporters, though hindered by the devaluation, would benefit from the higher real incomes of the Empire primary producers.

The Dominions and India could surely have devalued without trouble: no foreign country would have retaliated, and probably no one would have objected. Indeed, New Zealand and Australia had already devalued, thus benefiting both primary producers and domestic manufacturers. But the United Kingdom had forced India to retain the old parity between rupee and pound. Bennett preserved the fiction of the gold standard by means of clandestine exchange controls. He wanted a stable exchange rate against sterling.[165] But no one at the conference seems to have suggested that Canada could *devalue*[166] with advantage.[167] And at the conference South Africa strongly resisted devaluation – though late in 1932 the

South Africans in fact did devalue. In effect, by clinging to the old gold parities both Canada and South Africa had *appreciated* their currencies *vis-à-vis* sterling, which in 1932 was floating far below below its old gold content. It would be hard to imagine a measure more obviously calculated to increase their trading difficulties and weaken their commercial links with the sterling bloc. Because they had devalued *vis-à-vis* a downward-floating pound, Australia and New Zealand had doubly devalued *vis-à-vis* the dollar and the gold bloc countries. This arrangement must have enormously increased Britain's trading edge in their markets.

No one knows what would have happened if Chamberlain had said, 'We think you all ought to devalue your currencies *vis-à-vis* sterling. This will help you and hurt our trade. Please, therefore, reduce your preferential duties, at least a little.' It is a great pity that he did not. Instead, as we have seen, he used the monetary discussions to produce anodyne formulae, and to support his quota schemes. Perhaps the very suggestion is anachronistic. It is far from clear that any of the governments possessed the sophistication to see what devaluation could do. Most professional opinion, and most economists, thought that it was evil to manipulate the currency. Certainly Chamberlain and his party could much more readily imagine Empire economic integration and reconstruction through tariffs. Monetary devices came from cranks, carping Liberals, and out-of-office Tories like Amery. Nevertheless, we can now see, with the aid of hindsight, that a monetary conference would have done far more to raise Empire employment and to reintegrate Empire commerce than any tariff could possibly have done.

Similarly, hindsight now tells us that the agreements were for the wrong term. With respect to meat and dairy products the UK made commitments for varying terms which almost immediately caused severe difficulty in the management of UK agricultural prosperity. In these respects the terms were too long. However, for working out a policy of 'domestic competition', many years would have been needed; the five-year terms of the Anglo-Dominion agreements were far too short, even though, after 20 August 1937, the agreements would run on indefinitely unless denounced. The UK delegates underestimated the time which was needed for tariff boards to do their work, and for governments to act on their recommendations. When, after the conference, Liberal politicians criticised the agreements for tying Parliament's hands, they were essentially right, even though their constitutional grounds were frivolous: with respect to agricultural policy, the agreements were a great nuisance. But with respect to the industrial integration of the Empire the critics were badly confused: only very long-term agreements could have achieved the results for which Chamberlain and his colleagues hoped.

Considering the record of the conference, one is reminded that no British minister or civil servant in living memory had been involved in such trade negotiations. As long as the UK was essentially a free-trade country, they could not happen. Surely it is extraordinary that such neophytes should attempt to construct seven major trade agreements in thirty-one days. Depending on his mood, the historian may thus explain their particular failures by remembering their inexperience, or admire their general and administrative success in obtaining agreements at all. By the end of the conference, the exhausted British delegates certainly seem to have been pleased not so much with the agreements' *terms* as with the documents' *existence*.

The British delegation had been trying to divert trade so as to create employment. Early in the negotiations, it seemed that the new Indian trade might be worth £3 million,[168] the Australian £2 million, the New Zealand less than £1 million, and the Canadian £2 million – a total of £8 million in a year (1929) when British exports were already £729 million and British output £5,108 million. Obviously no such concessions would do much for employment in the UK. Hence the delegates' desperate efforts to do better. On 7 August, Baldwin circulated a memorandum which painted a slightly better picture. In a 'good year' he thought, the concessions already offered the UK an extra £12.5 million in exports – of which India would account for half.[169] To this must be added the Canadian concessions which Baldwin omitted – originally valued at $6.8 million, and raised through negotiation to $15 million, or about £4 million. Australia, too, improved her offer thereafter, adding £1.3 million to the 1931–32 level, or £2.75 million in any year that Australian imports might reach £100 million.[170] Something must also be allowed for South Africa's later concessions in this way. But if the delegates had made such adjustments, they would have got a total of £18 million – not a large sum, even if one were to ignore the large import content in this extra export flow.

Of course no such figure should be taken very seriously. In most instances we do not know exactly how the delegates and their advisers made their calculations. We do know that they could not possibly have made them correctly, because they lacked the statistics on which accurate estimates might have been made, and they did not have the conceptual framework within which the statistics might properly have been used. Unfortunately, though we now understand the problem better, we find it equally difficult to prepare a correct estimate of the agreements' trade-diverting effects. To each Empire market, British exports were determined by several things – habit, trade connections, consumer preferences, incomes in the Empire country, British export prices relative to competitors' export prices, the composition of production and demand in the Empire country, the price of sterling to that country's importers, domestic prices, and trade barriers – including exchange controls, quota restrictions, and tariffs. If we pretend that during the interwar years there were no changes in habits, trade connections, and preferences, we could in principle carry out an econometric analysis of intra-Empire trade so as to analyse the separate effects of these various determinants. For all the independent variables, statistics exist or can be constructed. Unfortunately, because there are so many independent variables and so few observations in the interwar period, we could not have much confidence in the results. Hence it is not worthwhile to undertake the calculations.

Fortunately there is a simpler approach which, though crude, cannot mislead us very much. In the interwar period there were certain patterns in the sources from which British imports and Empire imports were drawn. We can guess at the trade-diverting effect of the Ottawa Agreements by examining the percentage of British imports drawn from the Empire, and the percentage of Empire imports drawn from Britain and from the Empire. The statistics show clearly that, in 1931–33, the trading patterns noticeably altered. More of British imports came from the Empire; more of Empire imports came from the UK. We know that these changes can be attributed partly to the Ottawa Agreements, partly to changes in exchange rates, and partly to other changes. By attributing all of the observed share-changes to the Agreements, we will *over-estimate* their effect. This does not matter so long as we clearly understand the implication: the Ottawa Agreements certainly did not do as much for Empire trade as the following figures suggest.

Through the interwar period the Empire drew a decreasing proportion of its imports from the UK. However, in 1932–35 the proportion was slightly higher than one might have expected in the light of the declining trend. The difference seems to be about three percentage points, which implies the following increase of UK exports – £13 million in 1933 rising to £28 million in 1937. These figures are 3.5 per cent and 5.4 per cent of UK exports during these two years. They are also 5.4 per cent and 6.6 per cent of Empire imports from foreign countries. To approximate their impact on employment and output in the UK, we must deduce the import content of the extra exports, and also allow for the 'multiplier'. Assuming the multiplier to be two,[171] we find that the Ottawa Agreements increased British output by £26 million in 1933, and £56 million in 1937 – 0.5 per cent and 1 per cent of total British output in these two years.

As for British imports from the Empire, relative to total British imports, these were remarkably stable throughout the twenties, but rose sharply in 1932 and continued to rise thereafter. Projecting the 1922–30 percentage through the thirties, we find that the Agreements raised British imports from the Empire in the following amounts – in 1933, £46 million and in 1937 £98 million. These were 11.4

per cent and 16.5 per cent of British imports from foreign countries in these years, and they were 7.2 per cent and 10.3 per cent of total British imports.

It would seem that foreigners had some ground to complain of the Ottawa Agreements. However, these trade-diverting effects were small relative to income and employment not only within the Empire but outside it. Further, much of the trade diversion did not involve any loss of income or employment to foreign countries. When Britain exported more manufactures, the result was clearly to transfer income and employment from foreign countries to Britain. But when Empire countries sold more of their primary products to Britain, in general they had less to put on foreign markets. Thus Empire goods replaced foreign goods in British markets while foreign goods replaced Empire goods in foreign markets.

In fact the agreements did not prevent foreign countries from increasing their sales both to the UK and to the Empire. From 1933 to 1937, Empire imports of foreign goods rose by 76 per cent in value terms, and in the same terms the UK imports of foreign goods rose by 52 per cent. Only in 1932–33 was there a decrease in foreign receipts. We might attribute this decrease to the agreements: UK imports fell by £25 million but her imports from foreigners fell by £26 million, instead of the £21 million which we might have expected on the basis of 1922–29 patterns. Similarly, Empire imports fell by £13 million, but the Empire bought £14 million less from foreigners. Patterns of 1922–27 and of 1933–37 would have produced a decline of £7 million. Thus the impact effect of the agreement might have been £12 million – £5 million less in sales to the UK and £7 million less in sales to the Empire. Relative to world trade and output these figures are infinitesimal – even at the depth of the Depression.

In several respects these crude calculations are unsatisfactory. First of all, they ignore the real possibility that, by stimulating confidence in future profit prospects, the Agreements encouraged businessmen and primary producers, both in Britain and in the Empire, to build more plant and build up more stocks. Within Britain and the Empire the agreements can hardly have encouraged business pessimism; in so far as they made people more optimistic, they must have had an additional impact, raising output and employment in Britain and the Empire by more than our figures suggest. Conversely, if they made foreigners more pessimistic they must have discouraged real investment abroad. Secondly, the calculations probably do not capture all the interactions between the British and Empire economies. Because the Agreements lowered tariffs within the Empire relative to tariffs on foreign goods, they integrated Britain and the Empire more fully in a dynamic sense. That is, *whatever* might happen to stimulate output and employment, *anywhere* in Britain and the Empire, more of the stimulus would be retained within the 'Ottawa area' than if the Agreements had never existed. Thirdly, as already explained, they attribute too much to the Agreements themselves. In particular, they ignore the realignments of exchange rates which occurred between 1930 and 1932. These realignments would all have worked in the same direction as the Ottawa Agreements. Australia and New Zealand devalued *vis-à-vis* sterling. After the UK floated sterling, the British pound fell *vis-à-vis* the dollar. Even after the dollar was floated and devalued in 1933, sterling continued to enjoy a competitive advantage *vis-à-vis* the gold bloc countries everywhere. These realignments increased the competitiveness of British manufactures compared with American, French, and probably German manufactures[172] in all three countries. They also made Britain a more attractive market for primary producers in many parts of the Empire. So far as Britain was concerned, their effect was reduced after the devaluation of the American dollar, and further reduced after the tripartite stabilisation agreement of 1936, under which France also devalued. Nevertheless, British goods continued to enjoy a competitive advantage compared to foreign goods though not to domestic goods, in those Empire and foreign countries which had devalued and stabilised their currencies *vis-à-vis* sterling. Thus in so far as the Empire became a somewhat more integrated trading unit during the 1930s, the credit must go to the new exchange rates as well as to the Ottawa Agreements.[173]

In an earlier section of this chapter we noted that the conference adopted a mild and non-committal resolution on money, credit, and the foreign exchanges. The UK promised to keep short-term credit plentiful and cheap; for all purposes interest rates would be 'as low as financial conditions permit'; though the 'ultimate aim of monetary policy should be the restoration of a satisfactory international monetary standard', it was not possible for the present to operate such a standard. The Empire countries could create 'an area of stability . . . in relation to sterling', and they could avoid 'wide day-to-day fluctuations between sterling and gold'. But the world could not return to a gold standard until the great nations had agreed to satisfy the UK with respect to certain conditions: 'a rise in the general level of commodity prices in the various countries to a level more in keeping with the level of costs, including the burden of debt and other fixed charges; and an adjustment of the factors political, economic, financial and monetary, which have caused the breakdown of the gold standard in many countries and which, if not adjusted, would inevitably lead to another breakdown of whatever international standard may be adopted'.[174]

When made, this statement was of little importance. The UK could maintain the policies of cheap money and floating currency to which she was already committed, while maintaining that she would ultimately return to gold if only other countries would amend their ways. In later months, the statement proved unexpectedly useful. In the long discussions which preceded the World Monetary and Economic Conference, British officials used it systematically as a definition of British monetary policy. When, in June 1933, the World Conference first assembled and then collapsed, Chamberlain and his advisers employed it first to pacify the Dominions and India, and then to distinguish British policy from the gold policy of France and from the monetary experimentalism of President Roosevelt. This was not the most dramatic 'Ottawa aftermath'. But it may have meant more to British recovery than the tangled perplexities which we explore in the next two chapters.

Appendix I

Telegram to London
(Text as approved at Meetings of UK Delegates on Sunday, 14 August 1932, at 9.30 p.m. and on Monday, 15 August at 10 a.m.)

(Cyphered and sent 3.45 p.m., 15 August 1932)

PART I

Hitherto the discussions have been entirely on a non-committal basis, conducted with a view to eliminating and as a far as possible evaluating the limits to which the respective parties can wisely go. We shall probably have to take our definite decisions today (Monday) and we sent you this telegram so that you may know in advance.

2. Our policy throughout has been to try to secure agreements that embody the principle of the progressive lowering of tariff barriers and it will be seen from what follows that this principle has been accepted by both Canada and Australia. In our negotiations with the Dominions we have laid great stress on the principle that duties against British goods in Dominions should not be at a higher rate than is necessary to put the United Kingdom manufacturer in the position of a domestic competitor in the Dominion market, and that Tariff Boards in Dominions should be instructed to review duties in accordance with this principle and that British Industries should have right of audience. Our Industrial Advisers agree with us as to the vital importance of securing the acceptance of this principle; and we shall

insist on this as the most important term in our agreements.

3. We hope to secure from Canada and from Australia declarations to the effect (1) that it will be an instruction to the Tariff Board that, as regards commodities which are the product both of Canada and the UK, all protective duties shall be reduced as speedily as possible to such a level as will give the United Kingdom producers full opportunity of reasonable competition on the basis of the relative cost of economical and efficient production; (2) that protection by tariffs shall be given only to those industries which are reasonably assured of sound opportunities for success.

We have also been able to secure some immediate tariff changes over a wide field, including iron and steel of all kinds, chemical, glass, linens and chinaware. We secure, too, the immediate establishment of a Tariff Board to which will be referred the textile items, with power to our manufactures to give evidence, the Board acting under the general declaration set out in the preceding paragraph. In the meantime, as an immediate indication of changed tariff policy, there will be reduction of 33⅓% in all specific duties on cotton goods and a reduction of 25% in all specific duties on woollen goods, these changes extending to hosiery and ready-made clothing. They are not in themselves of much direct benefit, their chief value being to indicate a downward trend.

Canada will also agree that Customs administration in Canada shall be governed by such general principles as will ensure (a) the avoidance of uncertainty as to the amount of Customs duties and other fiscal imposts payable on the arrival of goods in the importing country; (b) the reduction of delay and friction to a minimum; and (c) the provision of machinery for the prompt and impartial settlement of disputes in matters appertaining to the application of tariffs, e.g., by reference of such disputes to an arbitrator or some independent body.

4. In addition to the declarations set out in paragraph 3, Australia has agreed to an improved formula under which extended preferences will be given over the greater part of imported goods other than those covered by the protective

tariff. The formula will also be applied to by-law items, which are of considerable importance.

Australia also agrees that all existing prohibitions and surcharges on United Kingdom products, including primage, shall be completely abolished at the earliest possible moment.

5. New Zealand has been willing to give us extended preferences, but having regard to the very wide preferences she already gives us, and remembering her precarious revenue position, we came to conclusion that, in her interests, and, indeed, in ours, it would be unwise, except in a limited number of cases, to accept further preferences, which for the most part could be obtained only by putting up already high duties on foreign goods. We shall, however, be in a position to re-open the matter with New Zealand as and when her revenue position improves.

New Zealand agrees, in the meantime, to remove certain surcharges on imports, the effect of which is to give us increased preference.

6. South Africa's preferences up to now have been of a meagre character. We are endeavouring to obtain extended preferences.

7. Southern Rhodesia made certain changes in our favour earlier in the year, and would be prepared to make others. As with New Zealand, however, extended preferences could be given only by raising the general scale of duties all round, and we have concluded that this would be unwise. We are at liberty to re-open the matter when the revenue position improves.

8. Our telegram No. 242 of 3rd August gives information about tentative agreement with India. It is undoubtedly of great value, not merely because of the prospect it affords of increased trade, but because of the political value of a trade agreement which confirms and confers benefits upon many Indian interests.

PART II

9. Bearing in mind the need for bringing the Conference to a successful end and on the assumption (which we think can

properly be made) that the tariff and other concessions which we can secure through the various trade agreements (see Part I of this telegram) are of sufficient immediate and prospective value to warrant the expectation of increased markets for United Kingdom goods, we feel justified in making agreements on the following lines. In the first place, we should continue free entry for Dominion goods after 15th November, 1932. Secondly, we should agree to increase up to 15 per cent. the duties on a number of articles already having a duty of 10 per cent. These are apples, butter, cheese, eggs, canned fruit and a number of minor articles. The agreement with India provides for the addition to free list of a few articles, the most important of which is raw jute. To help the agricultural interests of India and to gain their support to the agreement (see para. 8 for its value to us), we should add linseed to the articles coming under the 10 per cent duty. White maize will also become dutiable as part of the agreements with South Africa and Southern Rhodesia. Certain minor changes will be made in revenue duties on wines, dried fruits and coffee.

10. At the outset Canada stressed the importance of Russian dumping, and this dominates Canadian view, especially affecting timber and wheat. We have examined the possibility of prohibitive duties to counteract sales proposed at prices which would frustrate preferential arrangements, but conclusion reached is that this would involve Government responsibility for fixing detailed minimum prices and would be otherwise impracticable or objectionable. Canada has pressed for the establishment of complete embargo, which is her own policy. We have said that we could not adopt such a policy, but we recognise that our preferential arrangements must not be frustrated by deliberate price wrecking by state action and we are seeking solution which appears likely to take form of power to prohibit entry of particular classes of goods from any country pursuing such a policy.

This would entail notice to Russia to terminate existing agreement, but we should propose at same time to negotiate new agreement in substitution for old.

11. Apart from Russian question, Canada has made it clear that she expects a duty of 2/- per quarter on wheat. Our difficulty in accepting this was great, but it has been greatly mitigated since we have obtained from Bennett an undertaking as to world prices, it being part of the arrangement that the United Kingdom Government will be at liberty at any time to remove the duty in the event of the price demanded for Dominion wheat in the United Kingdom being above the world price. We regard this condition as of first importance, and, indeed, vital to our case.

12. *Base Metals.* It will be necessary to continue the duty on lead and zinc, commodities in which India and Australia as well as Canada are interested, but the continuance of the duty will be subject to undertaking as to world prices on the lines of that given in the case of wheat (see para. 11 of this telegram).

Copper. In the case of copper we should be prepared to impose a duty provided we were satisfied as to undertaking as to world prices on above lines.

13. Before we left London it was apparent that meat would be the principal question at issue, and everything that has happened here has emphasised this – Australia and New Zealand heading the pressure for duties and for restriction on all classes of foreign meat, with Canada concerned so far as regards bacon. Australia in particular has reiterated that all her proposals are conditional upon satisfaction in regard to meat.

They have asked for duties on mutton, lamb, beef and bacon. We have said we are unable to agree to this. We have prepared a scheme for temporary restriction of mutton and lamb in 1933 pending a conference of meat interests for the purpose of considering arrangements for the more orderly marketing of meat supplies for the United Kingdom, and hope to obtain Australian agreement.

PART III

14. Over and above the trade advantages indicated in preceding paragraphs, there is the intangible but very

important gain to sentiment and confidence (which might well extend far beyond the Empire) that would follow a 'successful' Conference, in the course of which the Empire had shown unity of purpose and had translated ideals into specific agreements.

We hope, too, to be able to preface the specific agreements by Conference conclusions which will form another intangible but very important asset through the adhesion to general principles of a kind that could be represented at home and to the world as committing the Empire to a policy intended to diminish the barriers to trade and to restore world prosperity.

We are unanimously satisfied in the circumstances that the concessions we have been able to secure justify us in making agreements on these lines.

Parliament Buildings,
Ottawa.
15th August, 1932.

Public Record Office,
CAB 32/102,0(UK)(32)49.

Appendix II

5th August, 1932.

Since Mr. Bennett met the U.K. Delegation on Tuesday I had not ceased to feel hotly about the bullying manner adopted by him towards us, and his insulting references to U.K. businessmen and their 'lack of enterprise'.

At 2.30 p.m. Friday, August 5th, he took me into his room when I told him that as we had many points of contact I felt we could talk with less reserve than could some of our colleagues. Thereon I warned him that he was heading straight into a failure and we stood at present that failure would be apparent to us by Sunday night. He was taken aback but I repeated and emphasised this warning.

I pointed out to him that our public in the United Kingdom of all parties would examine critically any agreements reached by us, and one test would be applied to all our transactions: how much extra employment did the extension of our trade in the Dominions represent. The Canadian proposals imposed some burdens on our people; how much new trade was to come to us? In the case of iron and steel, I reminded him that I had said at our joint conference that British manufacturers could not expect to get $40,000,000 more (according to Mr Bennett's prophecy); that it was a gross exaggeration and was based on a mere newspaper paragraph. Now I found from the Steel organisation, which negotiated the iron and steel agreement, that $750,000 was nearer the mark. I showed him Sir William Larke's letter to Sir Horace Wilson. Mr Bennett said that this was surprising to him, and he was not at the moment equipped to refute it. I reminded him that he was doing nothing for cotton or woollens – all the things that mattered were left out of the list of benefits he proposed to confer.

He was elusive, and it was most difficult to get him to concentrate on points under discussion.

He harked back to former controversies, and said he fully understood my position then and now. I had to make clear to him that I was pursuing a large and long course, of which Lausanne, Ottawa and the World Economic Conference were the sequence. I begged him to take the long view. He thereupon got on to an exposition of his Tariff Board Act of 1931, and Section 4 of the Act and its six or seven sub-sections. I asserted that for me as well as the others there could be no question of wheat and meat and other similar duties unless we got real value in return. What had he done to enable us to evaluate his position? Nothing. At an early meeting of the Delegations I had secured from him across the room that Dr. Coats, his statistician should be available for reaching the evaluation. He had not been lent to us, and we had duly received Mr. Bennett's figures which we could not and would not accept.

In employment our Ministry of Labour figures showed roughly (excluding coal and agriculture) 2,500 directly employed for a year per £1,000,000 of trade. How could we on a gloomy afternoon in November commend all round duties to the House of Commons on the ground that in return we had secured employment for 25,000 men at a time when we had 2,750,000 on the unemployed register? We would be laughed out of the House. He no doubt had his own troubles but not more telling than that.

This was my reason for warning him that he was heading straight into failure – that his figures would not stand close examination, and the Canadian Government's programme was so devised as to give our unemployed in exchange for increased duties on food, etc. nothing but derisory help: and we were not going to be such fools as to tumble into such a blunder.

When I appealed to his enthusiasm for Imperial policy he responded warmly, and seemed to be disturbed by my assertion that if we committed the error of accepting their proposals we would break up our National Government. None but a National Government in England could carry the policy, and if this one failed the course of Imperial unity would either be ruined at once or set back for 30 years. He expressed agreement volubly.

His mind harked back to his own difficulties which he said lay not so much with his colleagues as with his Civil Service, and he mentioned in particular 'Old man Breadner'. (Mr Breadner had at one time been the agent of the Canadian Manufacturers' Association.) He rambled over a great deal of ground, saying he was glad to feel free to talk to me, and that he trusted Hailsham, Chamberlain and me.

I tackled him hotly about his depreciation of our British businessmen and I told him that this was warmly resented by us. Our manufacturers and exporters were the most enterprising and successful in the world and had achieved their success and won their way (even over tariff walls) without assistance from tariffs, and that was in striking contrast with the Canadian who had been nurtured in a protective hot house. We had won the very first place in manufacturing export, beating all the world, and this was not an evidence of incompetence and lack of enterprise. He was impressed and said he would take some public opportunity to say so. I said I felt keenly his injustice to our people, and his commendation ought to be as public as possible.

To the 'domestic consumer' principle he asseverated his adherence and when he said his policy might be a blow to his supporters if it fell on them all at once I said that this was a good reason for adhering to Chamberlain's long term (say ten years) agreement with a progressive decrease in tariff barriers between us each year. He thought ten too long. I remarked that his country like ours found tariffs led to lobbying, and even a corrupting influence on politics: the advantage of a long period was that the businessmen would for say seven years attend to business and only in the last three organise a lobby or a party fund. He said there was much in that, but he swung off to other subjects.

I told him that the long-term policy was the only justification I could offer to myself or my public for agreeing to duties which otherwise I could never accept. There are two ways of dealing with our problems – one the small and meaner method of bargaining like a horse-dealer, the other the statesmanlike outlook on both the present and the future. He would surely wish to go down to history as a statesman. The time for decision and action was very short.

Having been with him for well over an hour I left, carrying with me, I fear, a very indefinite impression of what his views were on individual problems or what was to be the real tendency and final decision that would spring from this shallow restless mind.

W.R.

University of Newcastle-upon-Tyne
Runciman Papers
Box 3
File 'Ottawa'

Chapter 7

OTTAWA AFTERMATH: MEAT, BUTTER AND THE DOMINIONS, 1932–1938

I INTRODUCTION

In an earlier chapter we traced the abortive efforts of the Labour Government to invent a mixing scheme for home wheat which its own members would accept, and to devise one for Dominion wheat which the Australians and Canadians would enjoy. We saw that in the parlance of the time, wheat mixing schemes were called 'quotas'. In this chapter we turn to another sort of 'quota' – the quantitative control which sets maximum physical limits on the imports of some one good. For brevity we shall call these restrictions 'import quotas' or 'quotas' *simpliciter*, remembering that they have little in common with the mixing schemes we discussed above. Both quotas and mixing schemes, if correctly constructed, will raise prices and domestic production by exactly the same amount as a tariff of suitable height. Thus all three are protective devices, tending in the short run to raise farmers' incomes and farm outputs, and in the longer run to inflate rents and land values, while permanently keeping domestic farm output higher than it would otherwise have been.

Before 1933 the British Government had no general power to impose import quotas, and very little power to control the production of her own farms. Externally, the problem was an Anglo-German commercial agreement which permitted import controls only if domestic production was simultaneously controlled. Under the Ottawa Agreements Act, the UK took power to impose specific cuts in foreign meat imports – the reductions which had been arranged at Ottawa.[1] But not until the Agricultural Marketing Act was passed in 1933 did the Government take any general power to restrict import by Order.[2] And even then the power was limited; it could be used only when there was a scheme for reorganising some branch of domestic production, and when the scheme's success depended on controlling the imports of the particular product.

During 1932–33, import quotas were beloved by the civil servants in Britain's Ministry of Agriculture and Fisheries. We have seen that they, and they alone, wished the British delegation to concede Australia's request for a meat quota. However, Neville Chamberlain also loved quotas. While in charge of the Conservative Research Unit, he had sponsored a study of their working. He was anxious to protect British agriculture. And he was persuaded of the conventional wisdom of the time: only through price rises could prosperity be restored. These price rises, he hoped, could be attained through a planned management of output – an international cartelisation of primary production, in which producers would organise to regulate the volume of output. Since Britain was a food importer, such arrangements would of course hurt her consumers. But they would help her farmers and landowners. For some products, such as meat, Britain was the only significant buyer on world markets. In these cases she could take the lead in the planning of cartelisation. But for most products she was not sufficiently important to run the show on her own. In any event, Chamberlain did not want Britain to do the managing. The idea, he thought, was producer-control – not importer-control.

Neither Chamberlain nor anyone else seems to have understood precisely what this arrangement might mean for Britain. Both quotas and tariffs would tend to raise retail food prices and producer returns in British agriculture. But, as I argued in the last chapter, in the thirties a new British meat or butter tariff would almost certainly be shifted backwards: that is, overseas producers would absorb it, British prices would rise very little, and British farmers would gain little or nothing, while the Exchequer would receive a large revenue – which, in effect, overseas producers had paid. Because the duty would be shifted backwards, it would not attract any real resources into agriculture; therefore, it would not misallocate Britain's own productive resources. Hence on grounds of national self-interest and on budgetary grounds, Chamberlain ought logically to have wanted a meat tariff and a butter tariff, not production control – so long as he could devise some other way to help British farmers.

Production control would generate no revenue. It would unequivocally raise everyone's price. Foreign and Empire as well as British producers would thus 'gain'. But British and overseas producers would be forced to produce less. Their total revenues might rise or fall, depending on the elasticities of British demand for the relevant foodstuffs. Most observers now believe that for the goods in question – meat, butter, other dairy products, eggs, bacon – these elasticities are and were quite large. That is, a low price would have yielded more total revenue than a high price. In other words, primary producers – in Britain and overseas – would have probably been worse off with production control than without it. And they would have found even more difficulty in servicing their debts. No amount of market manipulation could really have helped them as a group. But if any single national supplier managed to gain a sufficiently large share of the allowable output, that supplier would of course be better off . . . at the expense of other producers. Hence any system of production control was bound to turn into a very nasty battle about the division of the market.

Chamberlain hoped that Britain could evade these battles by allowing her overseas suppliers to arrange things for themselves. Unfortunately, Britain was bound to be involved, because she herself produced some of the perishable foodstuffs her people consumed. It was logically impossible to omit British farmers from any system of production control. At the very least, for each food the British Government would be obliged to fix domestic production and *total* import, thus implying a market price, and letting overseas suppliers dispute the division of total imports. We might expect Britain to ensure that her own farmers would enjoy a larger total revenue with the scheme than without it. Hence overseas producers would have even less to divide than if the scheme did not exist. Chamberlain, we know, worried about the balance of trade and about the sterling exchange rate. In principle, this sort of production control could affect the market price of the floating pound. But if we make the reasonable assumption that overseas food producers tended to spend in Britain the sterling they earned in Britain, such controls would equally affect sterling supplies and demands, leaving the balance of trade and the exchange rate unchanged. The same is true of a backward-shifted food tariff. Things would be different if there were no automatic matching of sterling earnings and sterling spendings. For instance, if New Zealand earns less sterling because of a butter quota but maintains her sterling outlay by reducing her purchases from other countries, sterling will tend to appreciate, *vis-à-vis* all other currencies – including the New Zealand pound.

Chamberlain and his advisers may be excused for their failure to speculate on such matters. First of all, many of Britain's traditional suppliers were so tightly connected with Britain that it was reasonable to expect they would match sterling receipts; and payments. Secondly, in the thirties no government was willing to let market forces determine the pattern of its bilateral balances – with Britain or in other directions. As governments were already beginning to bargain about bilateral balances of trade and payments, there was and is little point in speculating about the course of events in the absence of such bargaining. Nevertheless, British food policy deserves some of the blame for the spread of trade and payments controls during the 1930s. To help British farmers and to speed world recovery through price increases, Chamberlain and Runciman were trying to manipulate world foodstuffs – both production and international trade. These operations did disrupt some traditional patterns of trade and multilateral settlement. Inevitably, these disruptions increased governments' unease. More bilateral balancing, more payments agreements, more interferences with other trade flows – these were the inevitable results of the commodity negotiations to which the

British Government devoted such tender loving care at Ottawa and for nearly a decade thereafter.

These negotiations passed through three distinct phases. First was the attempt to enforce the Chamberlainian policy of quantitative regulation and producer control. Next, the UK tried to convince her trading partners to modify the trade agreements of 1932–33 so as to allow the taxing of Britain's meat and butter imports. The negotiations, which began in 1934 and ended late in 1936, were of limited success. In ministers' minds, these new duties were to form sequestered funds for the subsidising of British meat and butter producers. This 'levy-subsidy' plan, a generalisation of the 1932 wheat arrangements, was definitively abandoned only in 1937–38. The Cabinet then made its peace with the Exchequer subsidies which it had first granted as temporary measures in 1934, but which it had so often prolonged in the subsequent months and years of negotiation. In the next five sections of this chapter, we trace the process by which the arrangements of August 1932 were transformed into the very different structures of August 1939. First, however, we must glance at the intra-Imperial discussions of primary products which surrounded the World Monetary and Economic Conference of 1933.

By early 1933 it was reasonably clear that a world conference would meet at London. In February, at a meeting of high commissioners, Bruce urged that there should be a parallel conference of the countries which were interested in primary products. The Treasury feared that such a conference would simply resolve itself into a series of demands for help; the real solution to low prices was sensible monetary expansion. The Foreign Office agreed with the Treasury, but Chamberlain did not. In May, he told the high commissioners that 'monetary manipulation' would not raise wholesale prices; there must, he asserted, be some regulation of supplies. Both Runciman and Elliot concurred. Hence Thomas and Chamberlain agreed to arrange some pre-conference discussions on primary products – not a world gathering, but an intra-Imperial discussion.

Bruce had asked for a permanent committee to work out

primary-products policy. So had New Zealand's High Commissioner, Sir Thomas Wilford. But when Thomas and Chamberlain summoned a meeting for 4 May, they said it would discuss only 'the question of possible regulation of supplies of primary products'. It would begin on the 'economic' side of the World Conference agenda. Once the Dominions' experts reached London, the Treasury would be glad to talk of monetary manipulation.

At this time, in May 1933, the Board of Trade was still pressing for an International Meat Conference, which would devise a plan to regulate Britain's meat imports. Chamberlain told Bruce that he contemplated a series of conversations with foreign governments, on the basis of a general policy agreed with the Dominions beforehand. In planning his 4 May meeting, the Chancellor may have thought that British and Dominion officials would devise this general policy. If so, he was disappointed. The new committee did little and meant nothing. Because the UK had no policy, its officials could not act. Hence the committee devoted itself to general conversation, and to the gathering of statistics. During May 1933 it met twice; it did not meet again.

The meetings of Commonwealth delegations superseded these meetings of officials. During the World Monetary and Economic Conference the Empire representatives met thirteen times. The attendance varied somewhat, but it normally included Chamberlain, Hailsham, Cunliffe-Lister, Simon, Elliot, Bennett, Bruce, Forbes, Smuts, Havenga, Strakosch of India, and Connolly of the Irish Free State. To a considerable extent, therefore, the meetings reassembled the membership of the Ottawa Conference itself.

The delegates worked briefly and inconclusively on matters of quantitative control. On 22 June they had a general discussion of the subject, and on 10 July, having talked of wheat and sugar, they set up a 'production and supply committee'. Among its members were Bruce, Bennett, Elliot, Forbes, and Havenga. Elliot urged the others to face the facts: abnormal pressure of supply was lowering British prices, and hurting both home and overseas producers. Bennett and Bruce were prepared to discuss regulation, but

Bruce said that the Australian Government was not willing to discuss any general regulation of production and marketing; with respect to wheat it had agreed to converse, but only because Canada and the USA held such immense stocks. Havenga would not agree to anything which would damage the special safeguards which he claimed Britain had given the nascent South African meat industry. And Forbes insisted that if Britain had to restrict her meat imports, she should cut only the foreign supplies, while allowing the Dominions to send even more than before. The positions, like the personnel, had not changed since the Ottawa meetings of the previous August.

The committee later agreed that the interested governments should separately discuss cheese, condensed whole milk, eggs, apples, meat, and livestock. At its last meeting, on 26 July 1933, it actually managed to record some definite conclusions. Britain and Canada would continue their talks about oats. New Zealand and Britain would settle cheese between themselves. As for processed milk, Britain would cut foreign imports to 80 per cent of the level of June–December 1932, while the Dominions would try to keep their shipments at the June–December level. For eggs, similarly, in principle there would be a standstill in Empire shipments and a 10 per cent cut in foreign shipments. But for butter and meat, as might be expected, nothing was settled. There would be further talks about meat. And about butter the committee recorded no decision at all.[3]

Chamberlain and Elliot did not restrict their efforts to these private intra-Imperial conversations. Addressing the World Conference in full plenary session, Chamberlain urged quota-controls upon it. Arbitrary and protective restriction he deplored. But he thought much better of quotas which were merely meant to raise wholesale prices. These, he thought, might be production or marketing quotas, and they should be based upon international agreement. 'The UK delegation', he declared, 'would be prepared to co-operate in the regulation of wheat supplies and supplies of other foodstuffs on the part of the principal food-exporting countries with a view to restoring and maintaining a reasonable level of prices.'[4]

The conference did bring forth a wheat marketing scheme, but it mounted no general assault on the problem of glut, though it did commend output-restriction. Britain would have to save her own livestock producers, with little help from foreign countries. This she proceeded to do.

II. EARLY ADVENTURES WITH QUANTITATIVE CONTROLS

1. *Meat*

The Ottawa Agreements, as we saw in the last chapter, committed the British Government to a specific programme of import controls for meat. Argentine chilled beef was to be kept at the 1931–32 level. Foreign frozen beef, mutton and lamb were to be controlled ever more stringently, so as to reduce Britain's purchases to 65 per cent of the 'Ottawa year'. Australia and New Zealand would control their shipments to Britain during 1933, and after mid-1934 Britain would be free to impose whatever quantitative control she might choose. During 1933, it was agreed, Britain and Australia would try to discover means to ensure 'an improved price situation and orderly marketing'.[5]

Because the Ottawa meat arrangements were so hastily constructed, they quickly produced misunderstandings. Canada, for instance, consistently maintained that because the Anglo-Canadian Agreement did not specifically reserve the right to limit Canadian livestock shipments after 1 July 1934, the agreement in effect guaranteed Canada free and unrestricted entry for five years. And South Africa argued that there had been an 'understanding' to the effect that she could count on an unrestricted market for up to 100,000 carcasses of chilled beef per year.[6] Australia wrangled interminably about the meaning of 'expanding share'. Did it mean a share of consumption, or a share of import? Was the UK bound to guarantee a rising share, or merely to arrange matters in such a way as to permit and encourage the share to rise?

Further, the agreements had been made without any adequate view of the restriction which Britain's own stock-breeders would require or demand. Thus it was immediately necessary to supplement the agreements with various improvisations. For example, at Britain's request the Australian dominions voluntarily agreed to cut their lamb and mutton shipments by 10 per cent in November and December 1932.

Finally, quota controls quickly thrust the civil servants into protracted and infuriating wrangles for which they had neither experience nor liking. In these wrangles there were no fixed points, except the Ottawa agreements and the later trade treaties with the Argentine and other foreign countries. Because the quotas were usually quarterly, the wrangles were not annual but constant.

To administer the quotas and mediate the disputes, there had begun to appear by the end of 1932 a network of interdepartmental committees. Usually the Ministry of Agriculture and Fisheries fixed the total allowables, and division was made by the Foreign Office, the Dominions Office, and the Board of Trade, all of whom were responsible in some degree for negotiations with overseas governments. Diplomats soon became involved; thus from late 1932 J. H. Thomas regularly discussed the meat situation with the Dominions' representatives, trying to make them accept 'reasonable' quota figures. And the officials quickly became aware of the immense intra-Imperial friction which the quota system engendered. The Dominions were at one in wanting the UK to cut foreign quotas. But they fought furiously to cut one another's throats. In particular, Canada made no serious effort correctly to estimate her future shipments of bacon or live cattle. Figures were provided, but never had anything to do with the actual arrivals in British ports. Yet these estimates were needed if the British authorities were correctly to determine the quotas for other countries – countries whose goods could, under treaty, be subjected to quota control. Neither Canada nor Australia had any domestic machinery by which they could control *exports*; hence it was often possible to get a paper agreement about allowables but it was usually impossible to enforce it – except with respect to Argentina and New Zealand. In the former country, the great meat companies, and in the latter, the export control boards, operated the restriction.

Whether or not an agreement was really enforceable, its mere attainment increasingly had dreary side-effects – sometimes simple fury overseas, sometimes the risk of retaliation against British manufacturers, and sometimes a demand for a *quid pro quo*. These side-effects were especially alarming in Australia. The British gradually became convinced that the Government had no intention of honouring its Ottawa commitments with respect to manufacturers. They were increasingly reluctant to give the Australians any excuse for their dishonourable actions.

None of these depressing developments had begun when, late in 1932, Walter Elliot told the House of Commons that the UK had embarked on a general quota system for meat. He explained that because lamb and mutton prices had collapsed, the UK had got Australia and New Zealand to arrange for quota controls of these meats for eighteen months. He had managed to associate Argentina with this lamb and mutton control, which was relatively easy to operate because in the whole world there were only three exporter countries and one importer country. But he hoped that the scheme would show how more complicated commodity patterns could be planned too.[7]

Early in 1933, Walter Runciman approached the Australian and New Zealand High Commissioners, S. B. Bruce and Sir T. Wilford, to propose the general meat conference which the Ottawa Agreements had adumbrated. But Bruce and Wilford thought so little of the idea that nothing more was ever heard of it. Instead, the UK went ahead on her own: she opened negotiations with the Argentine.[8]

Even at Ottawa an Argentine agreement had always been envisaged.[9] But it was especially necessary afterwards because the Ottawa Agreements had so infuriated the South Americans, who feared even more severe cuts in their meat shipments. Before Ottawa, the Argentinians had been prepared to denounce their treaties with France and Italy, so as to be able to give a tariff preference to the UK. After Ottawa they certainly did not want to do so and trade relations quickly worsened. Further, because of the Argentine exchange control, British-owned railway and utility companies had great trouble in making remittances from the River Plate to London. However, the Argentine Government was eager for some guarantees with respect to the emerging quota system. Could the British guarantee that there would be no further cuts?

From the negotiations emerged an agreement which gave the Argentinians most, though not quite all, they had hoped for. The UK agreed not to increase any meat or wheat duties. She promised to impose no quota controls on Argentine wheat, maize, wool, and various other products. And for meat quotas she made the following promise:

'The Government of the United Kingdom . . . will not impose any restriction on the imports of chilled beef into the United Kingdom from the Argentine below the quantity imported in . . . the year ended 30 June 1932, unless . . . it appears . . . to be necessary in order to secure a remunerative level of prices in the United Kingdom market, and no such restriction will be maintained if it appears that the imports so excluded are being replaced by increased imports into the United Kingdom of other kinds of meat (other than experimental shipments of chilled beef from other parts of the British Commonwealth of Nations) with the effect of neutralising the desired effect on prices . . . If . . . the Government of the United Kingdom consider it necessary that imports into the United Kingdom from Argentina of chilled beef should be reduced in any year to an amount more than 10% below the quantity imported in the year ended the 30th June 1932, they will consult . . . with a view to arranging for a reduction in the imports of chilled and frozen meat from all sources. The government of the United Kingdom will not reduce the imports of chilled beef from Argentina to an amount more than 10% below the quantity imported in the year ended 30th June 1932 unless the imports of chilled beef (other than shipments of an experimental nature) or of frozen meat into the United Kingdom from all the meat exporting countries, parts of the

British Commonwealth of Nations, are also reduced by a percentage equal to the percentage reduction of Argentine chilled beef below 90 per cent of the quantity imported in the year ended 30 June 1932.'[10]

Thus in certain circumstances the United Kingdom could unilaterally restrict the Argentine shipments of chilled beef – but only by 10 per cent. And any additional cuts would have to imply a reduction in Dominion shipments also. As for Argentine frozen beef, mutton, and lamb, Britain promised to make no cuts beyond the 35 per cent reduction of the Ottawa Agreements, unless she also cut imports from the Dominions.[11]

While negotiating with the Argentinians, the British officials were also devising trade agreements with Denmark, Sweden, and other Baltic states. Here the problem foods were not beef or lamb, but bacon, ham, and butter. In a series of trade agreements, the UK proceeded during 1933 to guarantee these countries' food trades in particular. She promised not to increase her duties on butter, eggs, or cream and she guaranteed free entry for bacon and ham. As for quotas, she promised not to regulate the import of bacon, ham, poultry, eggs, or cream, except in so far as quotas were needed 'to ensure effective operation of a scheme or schemes for the regulation of the marketing of domestic supplies of these products'. She gave guarantees with respect to the working of the bacon-control scheme which was known to be imminent. And in effect, she promised not to squeeze the Argentinians, the Danes, or the Swedes merely to make more room for the Dominions' foodstuffs.[12]

The Australians later argued that the Anglo-Argentine Agreement was a betrayal of the Ottawa spirit. The Dominions, though informed about these negotiations rather late in the day, were certainly not consulted.[13] But this was not what upset the Australians. Canberra believed – or professed to believe – that the British should be willing to cut back their foreign trade to whatever extent the Dominions required. Hence all these agreements were pernicious, because they limited Britain's freedom to do this, and butter obsessed the Australian Government almost as much as meat did.

These criticisms were ill-founded. The agreements left Britain with plenty of power to freeze or constrict her imports of foreign butter, bacon, and meat. As British consumption could be expected to grow with reviving prosperity, the Dominions could expect a rising vent, and a rising share of the British import market – exactly what the Ottawa Agreements had promised them. Further, at the Dominions' request, Britain had taken considerable trouble to safeguard the most promising development on the Australian agricultural horizon – the trade in chilled beef. Beginning on a very small scale late in 1932, this trade, which depended on new methods of storage, grew rapidly in 1933 and 1934 – far exceeding any reasonable estimate of 'experimental' shipments. More chilled beef also came from South Africa and Southern Rhodesia. J. H. Thomas had known well before 1 May that the shipments would not just be experimental. But he and the Board of Trade had worked hard – and successfully – to devise a form of words which would allow the shipments to continue – at least until the Argentinians might protest, as they did almost immediately. But it was not until late in 1935 that the UK finally admitted what had been obvious for eighteen months – that Australian chilled beef was replacing the Argentine chilled beef which Britain had unilaterally excluded by quota. Neither the negotiation nor the subsequent equivocation were riskless for the UK.[14]

At home, in the Agricultural Marketing Act[15] the Government had laid a logical foundation for these quota schemes.[16] The Act provided that the Government could control any agricultural import if the product in question enjoyed a managed domestic market and if its production was being reorganised.

Of those products regulated under the Act, the most important was bacon. On 9 September 1933 following the report of the 'Lane Fox Commission' on the pig industry, bacon production was reorganised and bacon imports were brought under control. The resulting quotas were later important for trade negotiations – with the Baltic countries and with North America. In 1936, British ministers tried hard to get the Canadian Government to accept a reduction in the Ottawa guarantee. Canadian bacon shipments had never reached 1½ million cwt. per year, but the agreement allowed 2½ million – a figure so large as to embarrass the Government in its negotiations with the Baltic countries, whose literal-minded ministers tended to think that Canada was about to ship the amount it was allowed to ship. In the Anglo-American trade negotiations of 1936–38, the size of the ham quota was a critical matter.

As with bacon, so with other meat, or 'meat proper'. At no time after 1932 was importation free of some quota restraint. Frozen lamb and mutton were restricted by the British Government itself. Frozen and chilled beef were also handled by Whitehall until the end of 1936. Thereafter they were turned over to an International Beef Conference and Empire Beef Council. However, until the outbreak of war the council and conference operated within guidelines which the British Government had laid down.

To create these bodies, the Government had expended an enormous amount of energy and time; negotiations had begun early in 1935, and had involved all the Dominions and Argentina. Their main purposes were to introduce a levy subsidy scheme and to get Britain out of the quota-fixing business. Though import control was to continue, it was to be administered by the supplying countries, who would themselves decide how much to restrict, and how to divide the allowable amount. Subsidies would assist Britain's own stockraisers; 'levies' on imports would finance the subsidies. In such a system, Chamberlain and other ministers hoped, Britain would escape the administrative headaches and the international ill-will which her quota system generated. She might be concerned with the total supply, and so she was represented on the council and conference, but she was not to be concerned about the allocation of import quotas.

In the end the system proved too pure to be workable. Only Australia and Argentina welcomed the scheme with any enthusiasm. New Zealand almost refused to join;

Canada and South Africa did stay outside. Thus Britain had to act as a sort of trustee for these and other 'small suppliers', guaranteeing them a certain total and certain rates of growth. Further, to buy Australian acquiescence she had to prepare elaborate guidelines for the major suppliers. In particular, Britain had to force the Argentinians to acquiesce in a planned reduction of their market share. In these complications, themselves the result of difficult negotiation, we find the explanations for the elaborate guidelines under which the meat conferences operated in 1937–39.

The troubles began late in 1932, when Britain asked Australia and New Zealand to restrict their shipments of mutton and lamb during November and December. The cut was to be 10 per cent. As the Dominions were guaranteed unrestricted entry until the beginning of 1933, when their own voluntary programmes were to take effect, this request caused much unhappiness in Canberra and Wellington.[17] Through 1933, the 'Ottawa programme' was in effect. But in July 1934, Britain would recover her freedom to regulate the Dominions' meat shipments. Negotiations began long before July. At first Whitehall hoped that it would be enough to restrict imports for three months: the British Government hoped that the Dominions would quickly agree to the levy-subsidy plan which is discussed in the next section. As matters did not improve, and as the Dominions and the Argentine proved obdurate, further quarters were added one by one. The cables burned between London and the Antipodes; tempers grew frayed at both ends of the Imperial telegraph line.

Because the quarterly quotas were so hard to fix, they were often established late. Hence they caused great trouble for the Antipodean producers, whose killings and shippings had to be planned months in advance. Nevertheless, the New Zealand Meat Export Control Board seems to have tried to stay within its allotment. In Australia there was no mechanism to control export, and no inclination to devise one.[18] Only in 1934 did the Australians begin to prepare control legislation. Early drafts specifically contained the power to 'regulate shipment of meat' and 'to administer any quota that may be imposed'.[19] The final version[20] contained no such explicit statements – possibly because so many Australian politicians were so strongly opposed to export control. In mid-1934, S. M. Bruce toured Australia to win support for the British Government's programmes of import control. His trip was a failure. With ever-increasing vigour the Australian Government resisted Britain's efforts to plan meat shipments.

It would be fruitless to follow the quarterly bargaining sessions in any detail, elaborately documented though they all are. The scholar who works through the documents must come to one conclusion: it is disastrous to attempt a quantitative control over *anything*. The meat bargainers were obliged to proceed without principles and without quantitative guidelines. On the British side, it was desired to raise prices. How much restriction was needed to achieve a given rise? Nobody knew. What price was desired? Nobody knew that, either. The planners were forced to start from recent supplies, and to provide for constriction if they thought past prices were 'too low'. But if demand was expected to increase – at some unspecified rate – the controllers would allow for 'orderly expansion'. As for assigning quotas to the various national suppliers, they were constrained by many things – commitments to the Dominions and the Argentine; bargaining considerations with respect to the Dominions' own tariff policies; uncontrollable components in certain meat flows. There was no reason for them to favour least-cost producers, since each kind of meat commanded the same price – regardless of production cost or country of origin. Hence world resources could easily have been wasted by the assignment of relatively large quotas to relatively high cost producers. And the suppliers could be equally unprincipled – or could try to be. They all assumed that their own marginal costs were far lower than any relevant British prices. Hence if they could expand their sales they would gain foreign exchange and real national income. Since the various suppliers did not trade among themselves to any extent, they did not fear retaliation from the countries they were attacking in the British market. If Britain should annoy the Danes by giving Canada an especially large bacon quota, it would be the British, not the Canadians, who might suffer from trade retaliation. Perhaps Mackenzie King was right: nothing could more quickly have destroyed the sense of imperial harmony than bilateral bargaining over commodity flows.

An example may show the reader what was going on. On 27 July 1934, J. H. Thomas gave the Dominion representatives in London their meat allowables for the balance of 1934. He explained that, if necessary, the UK would enforce these quotas by Orders under the Agricultural Marketing Act. The representatives urged him that *requests* would be more tactful. Thomas agreed. The same day, telegrams went to the Dominions. These specified the 'desired' Empire shipments, and revealed the percentages by which foreign shipments would be cut back.[21]

The responses were prompt and distressing. Canada immediately contested Britain's right to impose a quota on her live cattle, arguing that, because nothing was said about a quota at Ottawa, free entry was guaranteed.[22] Understandably, the British rejected this contention, and the Canadians, though not withdrawing their protest, settled down to 'forecast' their shipments. Similarly, with much complaint New Zealand and Australia accepted the fact of restriction, and cheerlessly began an unedifying wrangle over quota sizes. But the Australians, fearing that continued acquiescence might prejudice the principle, committing them to regulation, and suspecting that later regulation might be based on these short-run allowables, were increasingly restive. At last, in December 1934, they refused to regulate their shipments of frozen beef during the first quarter of 1935, and the UK was sadly preparing to impose restriction by Order.[23] Responding on 4 January 1935, Australia claimed that such an Order would be 'inconsistent with the spirit and intention of the Ottawa Agreement' – an odd contention, given the fact that the Agreement had specifically reserved Britain's right to impose quantitative restrictions at any time after 1 July 1934. Australia also pointed out that the Order would make it very hard for her to carry out her

Ottawa obligations: Parliament, which was very unruly, might reject the pending tariff-cutting legislation, given the fact that foreign countries were increasingly excluding Australian goods because of the stabilised preferential margins of the Ottawa Agreement.[24] Nevertheless, though filled with irrelevancies, and full of forebodings about the long-term implications of this short-run agreement, the telegram did give sufficient short-term ground to permit the UK to avoid imposing an Order.[25] And so, for the first quarter of 1935, quantitative restriction was again saved – and safe – by 'agreement'.

2. *Butter*

After the byzantine complexity of the meat negotiations, it is a relief to turn to the relatively stable and straightforward world of dairy products. The Ottawa Agreements gave rise to commitments for the whole range of processed milk products – butter, cheese, powdered and condensed milk. Further commitments arose from the trade treaties with Denmark and the other Scandinavian and Baltic countries which Runciman thereafter negotiated in 1933. And the home milk industry was in a condition which demanded, and received, various kinds of government aid. Thus the British Government found itself in roughly the same position with these goods as with beef: it was obliged to reconcile the claims of home producers, the Dominions, and foreign suppliers, in an environment where other import markets were drying up, where productive capacity was rapidly increasing all over the world, and where treaty obligations sharply limited its freedom of manoeuvre. In dairying, however, there were more awkward possibilities of substitution than in ranching: fluid milk could quickly turn into butter or cheese, or vice versa. This fact was of great importance in the various schemes for reviving Britain's own dairy industry. It gave rise to byzantine complexities of its own. Fortunately, as fresh milk did not move in international trade we can ignore most of these matters. Further, we shall ignore dried and canned milk, concentrating solely on butter – the chief concern of policy-makers so far as the

Dominions were concerned. What is said of butter can be said *mutatis mutandis* of cheese.

It was idle, the Ministry of Agriculture thought, to stimulate dairying simply by raising the price of fluid milk. Such a measure would stimulate supply and reduce the quantity demanded, increasing the surplus of milk which would flow into processing – into butter and cheese. During the 1930s Britain imported about 80 per cent of her butter consumption, largely from Denmark and New Zealand. Australian supplies were also significant, and a little came from Canada also. If the Dominion and foreign butter was admitted freely, butter prices would be 'low'. And if British fluid milk prices were supported, British-made butter would be plentiful, driving prices still 'lower'. The Ministry was prolific of schemes which would increase the consumption of fluid milk. This was the decade in which school milk, pasteurisation, tuberculin testing, and various other devices were introduced, mainly to make dairy farmers more prosperous. But there was a continuing temptation to make British farmers still more prosperous by the restriction of butter imports. The more such imports could be constricted, the larger the market for British-made butter – and the higher its price.

When pressed, Ministry spokesmen were inclined to deny that their ingenious schemes were price-raising; they preferred to say that they 'stabilised' the market, and thus, by preventing the shortages which would follow surpluses, kept butter prices lower in the long run. They assumed, without any evidence, that dairy farmers would leave the industry quickly but enter it slowly – an assumption which went clear against the common observation of the period, in which farmers of all descriptions clung to their holdings in bad times. Further, officials ignored the unimportance of domestic production in total supply. However, one can sympathise with the Minister of Agriculture and Fisheries; in pressing for the measures which his constituents demanded, he was obliged to clutch at whatever argumentative straw they might find. And as the decade passed, their clutching grew increasingly desperate.

The Ottawa Agreements guaranteed that Australian and New Zealand butter could enter Britain in unlimited quantity, and without duty, for three years at least. The Agreements also required the British to impose a duty of 15s. per cwt. on foreign butter. Subsequently the British signed agreements with foreign countries which froze this duty until the end of 1936.[26] For Canada the guarantee was five years. For two years after Ottawa, the UK herself showed no public inclination to vary these conditions. However, in 1933 she did make some tentative inquiries into quantitative restriction – at the request of the New Zealand Government. New Zealand dairy farmers were trying to produce their way out of disaster: their exportable output was rising rapidly, just at the time when Danish butter, deflected from Germany by exchange control, was descending on the British market in ever-larger amount. In New Zealand, butter production rose from 99,420 tons in 1928–29 to 165,000 tons in 1935–36. But as the price fell from 183 shillings per cwt. to 66 shillings in 1934, total sterling receipts *fell* from £15.9 million to £12.1 million. Hence the New Zealand request, would the UK please impose quantitative restrictions on foreign butter?

On 19 January 1933 Sir Thomas Wilford, the New Zealand High Commissioner, wrote to J. H. Thomas in the following terms:[27]

'Could I ask you if you would arrange a meeting between yourself, the Right Honourable Major Elliot, the Right Honourable Walter Runciman, and representatives of Australia and New Zealand, in order to discuss Butter and Cheese and their position with relation to Overseas and Home Grown.

The matter is so urgent that I venture to ask you whether it would be possible to have this meeting arranged not later than, say, Monday. I expect it would take about an hour.

Yours faithfully,

T. Wilford, High Commissioner for New Zealand.'

Thomas duly arranged this meeting, which took place on 25 January. Wilford and Bruce attended. Wilford proposed a 25 per cent cut in foreign butter supplies and no reduction in Dominion supplies – in spite of the very large increases in New Zealand shipments. Bruce's attitude was ambiguous, but the three United Kingdom ministers all argued that everyone would have to accept restriction if anyone was to be subject to it.

On 7 February there was a further meeting, this time of officials. The British were embarrassed because they were about to begin trade negotiations with Denmark. Denmark already knew that Britain was about to restrict her bacon shipments; the British doubted their ability to force a restriction of butter as well, but they were certain that if the Dominions were free to increase their shipments the Danes would not swallow any such restriction. Further, as butter and cheese were substitutes in production, it would be necessary to restrict cheese as well. Hence the officials proposed a package: abolition of the Ottawa duty of 15s. per cwt. on foreign butter; Danish supplies to be cut by 20 per cent to 2,000,000 cwt. per year, for three years; other foreign supplies to be cut by 20 per cent; Dominion supplies to be frozen.[28]

The minutes do not make it clear whether this suggestion came from British or Antipodean officials. However, in view of later developments, it presumably came from the Australians or the New Zealanders. On 13 February, Thomas, Runciman and Elliot again met with Wilford and Bruce. Thomas explained that the UK could not accept the officials' proposal: Denmark could not be asked to acquiesce in such a scheme, and the Exchequer could not spare the £3 million in butter duty. Bruce said that he would consider any definite proposal for Dominion restriction, but Wilford 'saw the greatest possible difficulty in any proposals for a definite quantitative restriction on Dominion production'. The problem, he said, was that there was no way to store the additional production which was already in the pipeline. Hence even a freeze at the 1932 level would spell disaster. Thomas urged the Dominions to face facts and restrict production. He then proposed a 20 per cent cut in foreign shipments and a 10 per cent cut in Dominion shipments, together with a reduction in the duty – from 15s. to 10s. This two-for-one cut seems to have occurred to Thomas in the course of the meeting. There is no evidence that it had been discussed beforehand. Indeed, Elliot said he was not sure that the proposed cuts would suffice to restore prices – though he thought they might be enough. Bruce, however, would consider only a freeze at the 1932 level – and then only on a temporary basis.[29] The meeting ended with a request from Thomas – that Wilford and Bruce should get word from their governments by the end of the week.

The officials then met again, and agreed that a 6 per cent/3 per cent restriction would probably be enough, and on 20 February the ministers again met the high commissioners. Bruce had not yet heard from Canberra; Wilford reported that the New Zealand Dairy Board rejected any restriction but that the Government did not necessarily agree with the Board. Both Bruce and Wilford were sent off to cable their governments once more. The next day the New Zealand Finance Minister cabled Neville Chamberlain. Though he said that he hoped all restriction could be avoided, the clear though unstated implication of his cable was that Wellington would restrict if Whitehall told it to.[30] When the ministers met with the high commissioners again on 2 March, Bruce reported that Australia could accept no restriction below 1932 levels, and would demand a 'token cut', perhaps 5 per cent, by Denmark as a condition of her acceptance. Wilford reported a somewhat ambiguous telegram from his Government, which seemed to agree to a 2/1 cut, on condition that the Dominions should accept the restriction. He was sent off to ask his Government exactly what its telegram meant.[31]

The next day, the New Zealand Prime Minister responded in very unsatisfactory terms. He insisted on the 1933 shipments, not 1932, as the basis for the restriction. He explained that by a 2/1 cut he meant 2/1 for the Dominions – not for each Dominion separately. And he said he was not offering a permanent restriction: he would hold back shipments for three months, on the understanding that the retained supplies would be spread throughout the next six months.[32]

When the ministers met the high commissioners once more, on 11 April, Thomas bluntly said that he thought the New Zealand Government's proposal was futile. Bruce agreed, and said that he was prepared to try to get his Government to accept a two-to-three-year restriction on the lines he had suggested on 20 February. Both Bruce and Wilford once more went off to consult with their governments.[33]

Meanwhile, the British Government had begun to negotiate with the Danes. The officials had determined to offer the Danes the 2/1 formula for restriction, without waiting for the Dominions to agree to it. The base period was to be July 1932 to June 1933 – relatively favourable to the Antipodes. In early March, the officials were hopeful that the Danes might accept it.[34] Early in April, Thomas wrote to Wilford and Bruce, explaining that indeed they had done so. But the Danes were to be guaranteed a minimum quota of 2.3 million cwt., and any restriction was to be conditional on the Dominions' acceptance of restriction on the 2/1 basis.[35] In other words, the Danes were prepared to restrict by 12 per cent of 1932–33 – if the Australasians would restrict by 6 per cent.

At this point the UK had no intention of *imposing* restriction on anyone: 'All we are saying is that *if* in their own interest they [Australia and New Zealand] desire restrictions, and *if* restrictions are agreed upon, they must share in them at half the rate imposed on the foreigner.'[36] But the Australasians did not see things that way. In Australia, there was dismay in Parliament and among the dairy farmers. The Government consulted its Dairy Board, and accepted its verdict – no export restrictions.[37] In New Zealand, the Governor General reported, the Government and the dairy farmers 'both fear the unpopularity of initiating some compromise with respect to quota though they feel it is difficult to avoid it'. He suggested that if the UK were to propose a temporary quota, as an experiment, the New Zealand Government might more readily decide, and act. However, the New Zealand Government simply consulted its own Dairy Products Export Control Board. And this Board, like its Australian counterpart, was opposed to any export restriction. Thus by the end of April it seemed that the whole idea of import restriction was dead.[38]

For some time matters remained confused. On 15 May 1933 when Elliot met with the Dominions' high commissioners, Bruce thought that Australia, though still opposed to a universal quota system, might co-operate – in spite of the Dairy Board's verdict. Certainly Bruce himself later campaigned hard for an Australian acceptance of quotas; perhaps in this remark he was anticipating that he would be able to convince his Government and people. Wilford, however, 'could hold out no hope of agreement'.

Asking the Dominions for a standstill in June, July, and August, Elliot told the high commissioners that he was still trying to get foreign agreement to some reduction.[39] However, these efforts, like later discussions between the Dominions and the Europeans, came to nothing. The British themselves were now eager to do something about butter. As Danish and Antipodean butter joined British butter in ever-growing quantities, prices were falling, and Britain's own dairy farmers were unhappy. Thus a butter restriction was no longer just a matter of obliging the Dominions; it was now a matter of obliging Britain's own agriculturists.

Representatives of the National Farmers Union met with the New Zealand delegation to the World Monetary and Economic Conference on 1 August 1933 when they explained the UK position. It was agreed that Mr T. Baxter, the Chairman of the UK Milk Marketing Board, should go to New Zealand and explain matters to New Zealand farmers. When he came back, however, he reported that there was little hope of New Zealand agreeing to reduce her exports of cheese (and presumably butter).[40]

Meanwhile, in New Zealand matters were growing more serious. The dairy farmers' organisations were urging their Government to propose a customs union – free and unrestricted entry for their produce, in exchange for similar privileges for British manufactures. Such a policy, they thought, would also lower their costs, and the prices of their consumer goods. And the opposition Labour Party had begun to demand a guaranteed price plus barter agreements.

Hence, in October 1933, Prime Minister Forbes found it prudent to offer Britain a customs union[41] – free entry to all British goods in exchange for free and unrestricted entry to the British market.

This proposal occasioned anxious discussions in Whitehall, where the Dominions Office consulted the Board of Trade and the Ministry of Agriculture and Food with respect to the answer. The Board of Trade officials saw little merit in the scheme: New Zealand tariffs were already low, Britain already had most of the trade, and presumably the New Zealand Government meant to retain its 'revenue' duties, abolishing only its relatively few 'protective' duties. The agricultural officials were adamant against unrestricted entry. And in the Dominions Office the officials worried about the other Dominions. No similar offer could be made to them, because they could not be trusted to reduce their own tariffs appropriately.[42] Further, the officials suspected, the New Zealand Government probably did not expect the UK to accept their offer: the whole thing probably sprang from internal politicking, not from conviction. Hence after Runciman, Elliot, and Thomas had approved a retort honourable, New Zealand was told that the scheme could not be accepted: it would treat one Dominion differently from the others, and it would be counter to Britain's declared policy of supply-management.[43]

Shortly thereafter the New Zealand Government, pressed by its dairy producers and Labour Party, tried again. On 28 February 1934 it cabled London, saying that it proposed to call a dairy producers' conference and asking whether the UK would furnish them with 'full information regarding proposals for a regulated market'. The British response was vigorous – and according to the New Zealand Governor General it was fully expected. Whitehall reminded New Zealand on 9 March that Dominion opposition had thwarted the quota discussions of 1933. On 13 February 1934 the New Zealand High Commissioner in London had told the Ministry of Agriculture officials that there was no sign of any change in the attitudes of New Zealand dairy farmers, and that 'the matter would have to be left for the time being'.[44] Accordingly, the UK had made other arrangements to subsidise her dairy farmers, and the question of quantitative regulation was no longer a live issue.[45]

This Whitehall response was a little disingenuous. The officials continued to believe that quotas were essential to raise butter prices. But they thought that if the UK were to take the initiative she would embroil herself in tangled negotiations and would probably be asked to give a *quid pro quo* – probably in the form of departure from the Ottawa Agreement. As Australia was far from observing the terms of the Agreement in any case, Whitehall was not prepared to give Canberra any grounds for new objectionable actions. In the meantime, the officials thought, opinion was changing rapidly in the Dominions. Prime Minister Forbes, they knew, had spoken in favour of a quota. For what it was worth, so had the World Economic Conference. On 3 April 1934 the New Zealand High Commissioner asked for the re-opening of quota discussions, explaining that his dairy farmers were now reconciled to the idea of quantitative controls.[46] Later in the month, E. Crutchley reported that the Australian state governments were now agreed in principle to voluntary restriction.[47] And the New Zealand Government cabled its eagerness to reopen the question of quantitative control.[48] S. M. Bruce was visiting Australia with the express purpose of converting his countrymen to the quota principle. During April, Whitehall traced his progress with interest.[49] In New Zealand, Lord Bledisloe had been working hard, and straining the constitutional fabric, to make the locals see the logic of restriction.[50] Hence there must have been hope in the hearts of the officials who drafted a telegram to New Zealand: Britain was sympathetic and would consider any concerted plan which the New Zealanders and other Dominions might want to put forward.[51]

Unfortunately things were not going well at all. It was the Australians whom the New Zealanders distrusted: their cheap and low-grade butter was providing painful competition for the better New Zealand product. Further, Australia's two-price system subsidised butter export, providing unfair competition with New Zealand's dairy produce. Wellington probably did not believe that Canberra would really co-operate. Even if it might agree to a restriction scheme, there was no guarantee that it would enforce the quotas. The whole logic of Australia's 'Patterson Plan', and of her new butter-control law, was to dump excess butter in London, not to control production or export. And the Australians themselves were becoming more definite. While Bruce had extracted some agreement, the commitments were not stable, and Prime Minister Lyons continued to insist that Australia would not regulate butter exports unless she was forced: any initiative must come from the UK.[52] But the British Government had no desire to repeat the wrangles of meat restriction.

And there matters rested for more than two years. Admittedly, in Australasia things were moving slowly in the direction for which the British once had hoped. Early in 1934 the New Zealand Government had appointed a Dairy Industry Commission. Its lengthy report[53] did not recommend quotas as such, but tended to favour them, and urged the New Zealand Government to discuss them with the UK, in the expectation that they might be imposed in 1936.[54] In Australia, the Government had actually established the legal machinery for export control. The Commonwealth Dairy Products Act came into force in May 1934. The Act provided for Commonwealth licensing of interstate butter-shipments, and required the Minister of Commerce to prescribe an export proportion. The Act also provided for the fixing of a domestic butter price. Admittedly, the statute was not designed to limit either production or export. Its intent was to preserve the existing two-price system by which Australia dumped surplus butter in London. The system had originated in 1926 as the voluntary Patterson Plan, which had so stimulated production as to raise the export proportion and reduce the dairy farmer's average return. Thus when the Act was proclaimed, the home consumption price was fixed at 140s. per cwt., as against the London price of 70s. per cwt. But the Act certainly could be used to enforce whatever export quota might be imposed; the

Minister of Commerce would simply choose an appropriate export proportion.[55]

But these developments were now uninteresting to Whitehall, which had chosen the levy-subsidy scheme. In 1934, a white paper announced that it had become government policy. Until levy-subsidies could be introduced, dairy farmers were to be subsidised from the Exchequer, as provided in the 1934 Milk Act.

III. THE LEVY-SUBSIDY IDEA

A levy-subsidy involves a levy on a particular import, whose proceeds are used to subsidise the domestic producer of the same good. The proceeds of the levy, which is of course simply customs duty, are paid into a fund, from which the subsidy is paid. Ideally the total levy will equal the total subsidy.

So far as practical British politics are concerned, levy-subsidies originated with the Conservative Party's vote-winning antics during 1930. Amery urged a form of price guarantee for wheat, Baldwin made it party policy, and Conservative ministers carried the wheat proposals through a reluctant Cabinet during the winter of 1931–32.[56] At that time, there is no sign that anyone envisaged any broader application of the principle. Cabinet ministers and agricultural officials spoke of protection by quota or tariff. The wheat arrangements[57] were thought to be special – a particular concession to the anti-Corn Law sensibilities of the British electorate. The trade treaties of 1932–33 made no provision for any such device; it is by no means clear that the Dominions realised how protectionist the Wheat Act was; British negotiators did not try to retain any powers with respect to the wider use of the device. Nevertheless, by the end of 1933 the Minister of Agriculture and Fisheries was urging his colleagues to extend the levy-subsidy system to new commodities.

It is, as usual, hard to distinguish between the works of a minister and the works of his officials. Nevertheless, it seems fair to say that it was Walter Elliot's enthusiasm, and his eagerness to help British farmers at minimum cost to the Exchequer, which explain the efflorescence of levy-subsidy proposals during the years 1933–34. At critical moments, however, Elliot received weighty help from Neville Chamberlain, and from the economists of the Economic Advisory Council.

On 24 November 1933 Elliot made representations to his Cabinet colleagues with respect to pigmeat, dairy products, and beef.[58] All, he said, were selling at unduly low prices. The Cabinet would have to decide what to do about restricting domestic production and imports. To handle the matter, which was then thought to be a short-term, emergency problem, the Cabinet set up a Produce Markets Supply Committee of nine members – at first Baldwin, Chamberlain, Runciman, Thomas, Elliot himself, and four others.

This Committee soon became a kind of semi-permanent sub-Cabinet which concerned itself with most aspects of food-planning. It met nineteen times between 1 December 1933 and 5 June 1935. With remarkably few references to the full Cabinet it ran the short-term half-yearly and quarterly programme of meat import control, and it also developed the permanent programme which slowly came to seem necessary. Thus in 1933–35 the history of British policy in agricultural trade is largely the history of this Committee. And it was here that the levy-subsidy schemes were first widely aired, elaborated and approved.

The Produce Markets Supply Committee had been invented because Elliot feared an immediate crisis in butter and in beef. Thus it began without any long-run policy for British agriculture. Was British output to rise? If so, by how much? What was to happen to demand? How self-sufficient should Britain aim to become? These problems had plagued J. H. Thomas for more than a year. In 1933 he had asked for a Cabinet directive on the matter, and does not seem to have been wholly satisfied to find the question referred to a committee of the Economic Advisory Council. The Produce Markets Supply Committee itself spent much time discussing long-run matters. By the end of 1934 its members were convinced that the British market for meat was a stable or contracting one. The population would soon be stable or declining. The population seemed to be substituting other meats for beef. Yet domestic production tended to rise, and so did Dominion and South American production. As one reads the accounts of the Committee's proceedings, one gets a growing impression of an irresistible force meeting an immovable object.

There is no suggestion that the Committee members recognised the relation between price and consumption. If pressed they would have admitted that a lower price might somewhat stimulate consumption. But they did not think that a lower price would reduce Empire or foreign production. And in their discussions, price figured only as a production-expanding device: thus they worried about the possibility that a high price might increase production, especially in Britain. But they had no concept of the equilibrating role of price in a market. And even if they had thought in those terms, Walter Elliot would have reminded them that a market-clearing price – at least for British beef – would be far 'too low' for the producers. Elliot indeed was known to think that it was better to support agricultural prices lest low prices put producers out of business and later cause shortage and high prices! If other Committee members did not share his views, they did not say so at its meetings.

On the beef front, Elliot favoured a funded levy-subsidy scheme of the sort already constructed for wheat. The producer at home would receive more than the market price; a small levy would be collected on all imports to pay this levy. Admittedly, the Dominions and Argentina would have to agree to the levy. But the alternative would be fierce quota-cuts. On 1 December 1933 Elliot 'suggested that . . . the Dominions would probably accept some such arrangement because they recognised that our hands would be completely free after June next, and they would prefer any alternative to a large percentage cut in their permitted imports'.[59] If a simple duty were imposed at a sufficient level to make British beef 'payable', there would be large excess profits in the Argentine, where costs were known to be lower. Hence Elliot's preference for the levy-subsidy plan, which would also raise retail prices much less than the simple duty. Imports would still be restricted, but not brought below 1933 levels. Thus 'the fund derived from the levy would be a fixed amount and it would be made clear to the industry that any considerable expansion would bring about a corresponding reduction in payments.'[60]

At first the other ministers were sceptical. Thomas doubted that the Dominions would agree to the levy, and pointed out that they would certainly want to discuss butter and other meats – not just beef. Chamberlain thought that the scheme, which would raise domestic market-prices from 35s. to 45s. per cwt., would produce an avalanche of home-grown beef. Indeed, at this stage Chamberlain was emphatically opposed to the whole scheme. He thought it too permanent a scheme to be a suitable device for a short-term crisis; the only long-run solution, he thought, lay in import restriction combined with production control in the Dominions . . . and, if possible, with some new markets for Dominion beef.[61] The Foreign Office representative doubted that Argentina would agree to the levy. Under the Anglo-Argentine Agreement of 1933 Britain had promised to impose no duty on her meat until the end of 1936. Elliot hoped that Argentina might be led to agree if the UK would renounce its treaty right to reduce chilled beef a further 10 per cent below the Ottawa level. But others were unimpressed.

Thus at this stage, late in 1933, the Committee deadlocked on the levy-subsidy plan with only Elliot favouring it. The ministers resolved instead to deal with the short-run beef problem by imposing punitive cuts on the Irish Free State, which had no Ottawa Agreement, and to ask Canada to impose some export controls. Meanwhile, still unable to agree on any permanent policy, they nevertheless resolved to begin discussing the meat problem with the Dominions.[62] And as preparation:

'there should be prepared a fully reasoned statement of the United Kingdom case for further restriction of meat imports. This statement should put the United Kingdom case as high as possible, and any proposals contained in it should be of a more drastic nature than the proposals which we should ultimately be prepared to accept . . .[63]

By early 1934 the Ministry of Agriculture and Fisheries feared a butter crisis in March and April. Marketing boards, set up under the Agricultural Marketing Act of 1933, would encounter great difficulty if the prices of butter and cheese should continue to fall, because so large a proportion of their throughput went into these manufactures. But the Produce Markets Supply Committee was obliged to report to the Cabinet that it had been unsuccessful in its attempts to arrange voluntary quotas. The Dominions were adamant, and 'all efforts have failed'. Without Dominion agreement, nothing could be done about their butter until August 1935. As we saw above, the Ottawa Agreements had guaranteed free entry for Dominion eggs, poultry, butter, cheese, and other milk products for three years. From August 1935 to August 1937 the United Kingdom was bound to maintain the preferential margin on these Dominion products, though she could impose a duty or quantitative control.[64] And the Anglo-Danish trade agreement had fixed Britain's butter duties until 20 June 1936,[65] while fixing a minimum Danish butter quota. Thus for the time being nothing could be done either via quotas or via duties or levy-subsidies. The Committee did begin to consider some sort of levy-subsidy plan. If a low duty could be levied on butter import, there would be a large sum to pay to UK producers, who supplied only about 10 per cent of UK consumption.[66] But for the time being, something else would be needed.

On 22 February 1934 Elliot announced the Government's milk policy.[67] There would be Exchequer subsidies to the Milk Marketing Boards. These subsidies would have the effect of guaranteeing the prices of manufactured milk until 1 April 1936. If prices were more favourable after that date the Boards would repay the subsidies, which were, therefore, technically advances. The Exchequer would also spend up to £1,250,000 on publicity, school milk, and a campaign for a purer milk supply.

This scheme was intended – and was known to be intended – to bridge the months until a price-improving levy-subsidy scheme could be introduced. Meanwhile, an interdepartmental committee was considering levy-subsidy plans. Among its members was Sir Frederick Leith-Ross, who later emerged as a vigorous champion of levy-subsidies and a fierce enemy of quotas. As the Government's chief economic adviser his weight was considerable. The committee members believed that the Dominions themselves were primarily responsible for the price collapse, because their shipments had increased so monstrously since 1932. They believed that the Dominions would at first like a levy even less than a quota – but

'they may well be in a different frame of mind in the spring when they will be suffering still more severely from the effects on prices of an overloading of the market for which they are largely responsible. If, however, they were induced to agree, reluctantly, to a levy now, they would probably attribute their troubles in the spring to the levy, instead of to their unwillingness hitherto to co-operate in remedial measures, and consequently be less willing to co-operate in the working out of our long range plan for milk . . . from the consumer's point of view, the levy scheme would be a cheaper method of securing a substantial increase in home producers' returns than that of raising the prices of the *total* supply of milk products through quantitative control when so large a proportion of that supply is imported.'

Elliot had earlier[68] favoured levy-subsidy both on domestic dairy production and on imports – but he did not urge the Produce Markets Supply Committee to recommend it to Cabinet. Runciman, however, favoured quantitative regulation if Denmark and the Dominions would agree; he was sure that both would reject the levy.[69] After further examination by Sir Horace Wilson's interdepartmental committee, the levy-subsidy plan was not recommended to Cabinet – killed, it seems, by Treasury opposition.

Between December 1933 and June 1934, several weighty ministers came to think much better of Elliot's levy-subsidy proposal. The reasons are hard to trace, but seem to have been connected with Elliot's demonstration that there was no other politically feasible way to raise prices *sufficiently*. It is also likely that ministers had come to see the scheme as a permanent policy, not as a device for containing a crisis. Thus at the meeting of 13 June, Chamberlain himself strongly favoured it for meat, arguing that the Dominions would prefer it to massive meat restriction. Runciman also favoured it, suggesting that no degree of restriction, even if feasible, was likely to produce the desired increase in fresh-beef prices. Though Elliot himself may have thought the levy-subsidy scheme less desirable in May 1934 than in December 1933;[70] on 13 June he did not oppose it,[71] and on that date the Committee endorsed levy-subsidies in principle.

From that time there was no looking back. After the Committee had accepted the principle, Elliot went off to explore the numerical implications of variant levy-subsidy schemes, combined with various degree of quantitative restriction. As the Committee was unable to agree on the best or most palatable, it decided to ask the Cabinet for permission to approach the Dominions 'on the widest possible basis'.[72] In presenting the matter to the Cabinet, Baldwin emphasised that the Committee was asking for powers to modify the UK's 'powers of quantitative regulation in return for power to raise a levy on overseas imports'. The Cabinet approved the proposals, leaving the Committee free to approach the Dominions – though not, at this stage, Argentina, whose permission would also be required.[73]

The Committee tackled the Dominions on 27 June, when Thomas and Elliot met the high commissioners. Elliot stated that higher meat prices were essential, and pointed out that the Ottawa Agreement and the Anglo-Argentine Agreement precluded duties and made quantitative restriction difficult. He said that he thought foreign supplies must be cut by 15 per cent to produce satisfactory prices. But given the Argentine Agreement, such a cut could be imposed on the Argentine only if Dominion supplies were also cut – by 5 per cent.

This meeting produced a result far beyond the wildest hopes of Thomas and Elliot. Faced with a jeremiad on the subject of quota cuts, the high commissioners themselves stumbled on the idea of a duty. They suggested that the UK should impose a 1d. per lb. duty on foreign meat, and a ½d. duty on Empire meat. Foreign chilled beef could be admitted at 100 per cent of the Ottawa quantity, and foreign frozen meat held to 65 per cent, while Dominion meat could enter at the Ottawa level plus a small agreed increase.[74]

The Committee was understandably jubilant. Though of course the high commissioners had not perceived the subsidy aspect of the matter, they seemed acquiescent in the levy. And Argentina might agree if she were guaranteed 100 per cent of her Ottawa allotment – not the 90 per cent to which, under the Agreement, the UK could unilaterally restrict her.[75] Surely there could be no further obstacles. The Committee went ahead to prepare a scheme for an interim beef subsidy. The £3 million in annual Exchequer advances were to be repaid from the eventual levy proceeds, so that in the end there would be no Exchequer burden. The subsidy would last only until 31 March 1935. To provide ample funds, the levy would be collected on all meat imports.

By 4 July, J. H. Thomas and Walter Elliot had adopted this Dominion proposal. They now thought that a larger cut – as much as 10 per cent – would be needed to achieve satisfactory prices. Any such cut would be 'disastrous' for the Dominions. Accordingly they proposed to the Dominions that Britain should impose a 1d. per pound duty on foreign meat, and a ½d. duty on Empire meat. However, at this stage they wished to combine the scheme with quantitative restriction – the Dominions to keep to the Ottawa-year figures, and the foreigners to the figures set out in the 'agreed Ottawa programme'. If such arrangements could be accepted for a two-year period, His Majesty's Government in the UK would use the time to create a really long-term agricultural policy.[76]

Meanwhile, the time had come when, under the Ottawa Agreements, the UK could impose unilateral cuts on Dominion meat exports. This fact strengthened Whitehall's bargaining power *vis-à-vis* Canberra and Wellington. At least, so

London's officials and ministers believed. A preferential levy would hurt less than any quota cut which could raise beef prices to 'remunerative' levels. Would not the Dominions understand this fact, and agree to the levy-subsidy?

On 11 July the Cabinet considered the levy-subsidy plan. Baldwin reported on the deliberations of the Produce Markets Supply Committee. But since its cheerful meeting of 2 July the Australians had wired that they 'could not contemplate agreement to proposal'.[77] That morning, Thomas had met with the high commissioners, who had refused to accept the proposal of a 1d. levy with 50 per cent preference. Thomas noted that:

'without their consent no duty could be imposed on their produce until . . . August 1937. It would be possible, however, to impose a 10% cut in the amount of the importation from the Dominions. The negotiations with the Argentines had not been unsatisfactory, and it seemed possible that agreement might be reached with them if the attitude of the Dominions were more accommodating.

The Chancellor of the Exchequer thought it possible that later on the Dominions might see that it was in their interest to come to an agreement. They were faced with two alternative possibilities the latter of which . . . the . . . quota, would be much worse for them than the acceptance of the proposed duty. . . .

The Minister of Agriculture and Fisheries pointed out that if the Dominions could not be induced to accept the imposition of a duty it would be necessary to proceed at once with the quota cuts. . . .

The President of the Board of Trade emphasised the importance of this as if the Dominions learned that Treasury advances were being made they would think that their difficulties were at an end.'[78]

After considerable discussion the Cabinet approved the Committee's proposal for an interim Exchequer subsidy to British beef producers. The Cabinet also authorised Elliot to answer a private notice question in terms which mentioned that the Government had been considering drastic quantitative restriction, levy-subsidy plans with unrestricted entry, and combinations of levy-subsidy plans with milder restriction. Believing that the third alternative was the best, not only for beef but for the whole livestock industry, the Government proposed to open negotiations with the Dominions and Argentina. Because of the Ottawa commitments and the Anglo-Argentine Agreement, the UK could not unilaterally impose duties on meat. 'It was not contemplated that the levy would exceed 1d., with a preference for the Dominions.' However, it was contemplated that all meat – not just beef – would pay the levy.[79] Meanwhile, as negotiations would take some time, the Exchequer would pay a temporary subsidy on fat stock of up to 5s. per cwt. live weight. The subsidy would expire on 31 March 1935[80] and the Exchequer would recoup from the proceeds of the eventual levy.

The White Paper was obviously intended as much to influence opinion in the Dominions as to reassure the farmers in the UK. Its gist was cabled to the Dominion governments the day it was issued. Almost immediately there were sharp protests.

From the Dominions some support began to appear. Australia remained unco-operative: 'she could not contemplate agreement to proposal'.[81] Interpreting the Ottawa Agreement to mean 'expanding volume', she would agree neither to quota nor to duty. New Zealand's first response was similar and even more alarmed.[82] But it was also ill-informed. As the Dominions Office pointed out, the new duty would create a fund from which the British producer could be subsidised. Thus he would get a fair price with a degree of restriction much less drastic than the 10 per cent which New Zealand believed the British intended.[83] These comments did not mollify New Zealand, which, if anything, liked a duty even less than a quota;[84] eventually, however, she was willing to discuss a levy as an alternative to drastic restriction. South Africa was eventually prepared to accept the levy, but only if the quantitative restrictions were sufficiently vigorous. And she insisted that in future she would need a vent for 100,000 chilled-beef carcasses a year. Two days later, she raised her terms. She now had no objection to the 11 July proposal so long as the Dominions meat was taxed at half the foreign rate – and so long as she received a chilled-beef quota of not less than 285,000 cwt. per year.[85] Canada expressed no views on the levy proposal, but said the UK had no right to regulate live-cattle shipments.

For some months, nothing happened. The UK officials settled down to regulate imports in the short term;[86] her politicians were working on the details of the levy-subsidy plan, which they hoped to graft on to the duty that the Dominion representatives had themselves proposed. With respect to the long-run solution, some urgency seemed to attach to the end of March 1935: on that date would end Britain's nine-month emergency subsidy for beef farmers. But nothing could be done because the Australians were having a general election. Hence it was not until early 1935 that the long-range plan went forward. In the interim, the Produce Markets Supply Committee reaffirmed its devotion to levy-subsidies for beef – and agreed, at Australia's request, to defer any decision with respect to long-run policies until after Prime Minister Lyons had reached London. He was to come on 21 March. Meanwhile, there were continual discussions with the Dominions representatives. And arrangements were made to extend the emergency subsidy.[87]

On 11 February 1935 the Dominion high commissioners met British ministers to consider a definite proposal.[88] The scheme, which was cabled overseas two days later, involved a duty of 1d. per lb. on all foreign meat, 1s. 2d. per lb. duty on all Empire meat, and no quantitative controls. Thomas suggested self-regulation, but said that Britain would impose no quantitative controls unless, at Dominion request, restriction was substituted for levies. Thus levies were to replace quotas. This idea had originated in the fertile mind of Neville Chamberlain, at a meeting of the Produce Markets Supply Committee on 4 February. Elliot agreed with the Chancellor, chiefly, he said, because such a step would force the producers themselves to regulate supply. Baldwin emphasised the political troubles which quota-setting caused. Runciman urged that unrestricted entry would be very helpful in dealing with the Argentine.

Hence, over the reservations of some lesser lights, the Committee now plumped for the levy-subsidy principle *without any quantitative restriction*.[89] The arrangement was to operate until the expiry of the Anglo-Argentine Agreement, in November 1936.

To this proposal Canada responded very late, and very unhelpfully, concerning herself only with the live-cattle trade. Other Dominions were quicker off the mark. New Zealand refused to countenance a tariff, claiming that such a device would 'terminate the Ottawa Agreement' and might 'react on our own tariff policy'. She was, however, prepared to contemplate universal regulation by quota – though she thought it unlikely that the meat-producing countries could agree on restriction.[90] South Africa would tolerate a duty only if combined with quantitative restriction sufficient to raise prices while allowing her chilled-beef trade to grow. She continued to argue that at Ottawa she had received a specific undertaking with respect to such growth[91] – even though there was no such thing in the Anglo-South African Agreement. The Australians said that they would prefer a duty to a quota for their own meat. However, they pleaded, on grounds of grower poverty, that their frozen beef should escape the levy. And, misled by a confusion in their High Commissioner's report, they misconstrued the proposals with respect to foreign meat: while the British proposed to end all restrictions, the Australians were accepting the duty only because they thought that the UK would retain quotas for foreign meat.[92]

Besides worrying about meat, the Australians and New Zealanders were concerned about butter. Britain's Milk Act provided subsidies until March 1936, while the Dominions could be obliged to pay duties or accept quotas any time after the end of August 1935. Other treaties froze the duties on foreign butter. These expired only at the end of 1936. The Ottawa Agreement guaranteed certain preferential margins for Empire butter. Hence the UK, though eager to introduce a preferential butter levy-subsidy, could impose a duty on *Dominion* butter only by denouncing most of its *foreign* trade agreements.

In the future, a preferential levy-subsidy should be installed – but nothing should be done until January 1937. From 1 March 1936 until 1 January 1937 the Milk Marketing Boards should continue to subsidise dairy farmers, recouping these subsidies after 1 January from the proceeds of the eventual butter levy. So Walter Elliot was arguing in May 1935. If the Dominions had known that the Minister of Agriculture was feeling so kindly towards them, they might have come to London in a more relaxed mood. But the British strategy was to keep them as nervous as possible.[93]

Earlier in the year,[94] Elliot had recommended that there should be no attempt to impose a butter levy-subsidy at least until August 1935, after discussions with the Australians and New Zealanders. As the treaty situation was exactly the same in May as in January, one can explain Elliot's change of mind only by assuming that at the earlier date he or his officials did not understand the documents.

Elliot's memorandum went to an interdepartmental committee of officials. They thought that the Dominions should be told that nothing would be done before March 1936, when the Milk Act payments would cease, but that the UK should reserve its freedom with respect to duties thereafter. The Dominions were not to be told that *foreign* consent would be needed to effect any Dominion butter duty before January 1937. The officials seem to have assumed that Australian and New Zealand officials and ministers could not read the published texts of the treaties. Perhaps they had noticed Walter Elliot's difficulties in this respect.

IV. THE 1935–1936 MEAT TALKS

These short-term wranglings were both the background and the partial explanation for the Government's determination to find another policy – the levy-subsidy. Hoping that the Dominions would quickly agree to this new proposal, the UK was able to convince itself that the quotas of 1934 were temporary: they would soon give way to a levy-subsidy, buttressed, in all likelihood, by supplier regulation. Britain herself could get out of the quota business. But in Australia and New Zealand the politicians and producers were not malleable. Hence the British Government continued to force quarterly quotas down their throats, while it tried to convince them that it meant business. Early in 1935, learning that the Australian and New Zealand leaders would soon come to London, Thomas and Elliot decided to hold their fire, and wait for their arrival.

Prime Minister Lyons was already planning to visit London. Faced with the meat proposals, he advanced his departure date,[95] and brought his Minister for Commercial Treaties, Sir Henry Gullett, and his Attorney General, Robert Menzies. Meanwhile, Earle Page, his Deputy, was deluged with representations from the Australian meat interests. Most of these were pro-duty, but a few preferred a restriction of their sales.[96] The Australian delegation sailed on 19 February, and a New Zealand delegation took ship about the same time. Canada and South Africa, less vitally concerned with the outcome, did not send ministerial representatives; as before, their high commissioners did the job.

While the Antipodean leaders were on the high seas, the British Government published its White Paper on meat policy.[97] It was a logical sequel to the proposals of the preceding July, and did not really go beyond the informal private conversations of early February. But it immediately excited and upset both Australasians and Argentinians. It repeated the earlier argument for a levy-subsidy with moderate restriction, but differed from it in two respects. First, it stated emphatically that the overseas suppliers themselves must regulate their shipments, and that 'the intervention of the UK Government should be limited to the collection of a levy upon imports and the application of the proceeds to the assistance of home industry'. Second, it admitted that, instead of taxing all meat, as had earlier been proposed, it was prepared to discuss a more limited levy – to be imposed only on beef and live cattle.[98]

This mini-concession was a response to New Zealand's telegraphic protests – complaints which were heard at

Whitehall after Forbes and Coates reached Britain. The New Zealanders explained that a mutton and lamb levy would fall on her with especial force, and they intimated that New Zealand would co-operate in a beef scheme only if her lamb and mutton paid no duty. Further, the Board of Trade had discovered formidable administrative difficulties in a levy-subsidy scheme for sheepmeat, and had successfully raised Britain's lamb prices by quotas alone. If sheepmeat was to pay no levy, the beef duty would have to be higher than originally expected. The Dominions quickly revealed that they would insist on a preferential margin of 1d. per lb. To fund the subsidy, therefore, foreign beef would have to pay 1¼d., and Dominion beef ¼d. It would remain to be seen whether either the Australasians or the Argentinians would accept these imposts.[99]

The White Paper ended on an ominous note. Negotiations, it noted, had made little progress. Therefore: 'failing agreement on the payment of a levy on meat imports, His Majesty's Government in the United Kingdom will have no alternative but to take steps to regulate the quantity of imports to whatever extent is necessary to restore livestock prices to a remunerative level.' In effect, the Government was serving notice on the Australian and New Zealand ministers: accept our proposals or we shall do something really nasty to you.

Late in May, the Cabinet authorised the Produce Markets Supply Committee to work out a levy-subsidy plan without further reference to the Cabinet. Import should be controlled through a Meat Board with representatives from the UK, the Dominions, and perhaps Argentina. The levy should give the Dominions a preference but should raise enough to pay the £4 million subsidy. This instruction formed the logical basis for the meat negotiations which soon began.

In March 1935 Whitehall received the Australian meat delegation – Prime Minister Lyons, Robert Menzies, and Sir Henry Gullett. In preparing for the first meeting, the British ministers reminded themselves that though the Australians had come to talk about meat, they themselves also wanted to discuss other aspects of the Ottawa Pact –

especially Australia's performance under Article 10, the 'domestic competitor' clause. Fortunately for the historian, though the two subjects were clearly juxtaposed in the minds of negotiators on both sides, they were sharply separated in the process of negotiation. Hence it is possible to separate them here. However, the reader must remember that to some extent the British must have been trying to buy Australian reasonableness with respect to 'domestic competition' by offering reasonableness on the meat front. And the Australians may have been playing the same game in reverse.

The Anglo-Australian discussions began badly and became rapidly worse. Gullett insisted on Australia's right to expand her share of Britain's meat markets at the foreigner's expense – regardless of the impact on British exports and investment income. He also insisted that Australia must be allowed to switch freely from frozen to chilled beef – a demand which Elliot had privately insisted must be rejected. Lyons argued that Australia was obliged to oppose any quantitative restriction of her exports because her trade surplus was diminishing, and now did not cover her invisible payments. He also insisted on the chilled-beef switch – and freedom from any restriction on shipments of lamb and mutton. He would accept neither an all-levy scheme without a restriction which the UK alone would impose, nor an all-restriction scheme. In other words, probably for political reasons he was most unwilling to be seen to agree to any restriction. If the *British* should *impose* restriction, he could put the blame on London after his return to Australia.

Lyons also claimed that Article I of the Anglo-Argentine Agreement did not preclude the chilled-beef switch he so much desired. Thomas argued that the intent of the Article was clear. He said that the Argentinians would certainly interpret it in that way – and that Britain would not oppose such interpretation. Runciman was willing to admit that it might be all right to raise Australia's shipments of chilled beef so long as her shipments of frozen beef were very sharply cut back. But it was already clear that the Argentinians would almost certainly not accept such a solution: they knew as well as the Australians that there was almost no competition between frozen and chilled beef. The former was low-quality institutional provender, while the latter enjoyed a far wider market.

Lyons then withdrew from the discussions, leaving the pushful Sir Henry Gullett as chief Australian spokesman. The British found Gullett unhelpful. Various proposals were drafted, exchanged, and summarily rejected. At length, on 4 April, S. B. Bruce proposed that they try to draw up a document which could be presented to the Argentinians. This draft was considered at the fifth meeting, on 15 April, and immediately rejected by Gullett. He himself suggested a plan by which Argentine shipments would shrink by 12½ per cent in five years, while no quotas would be imposed on Dominion beef. Duties, he suggested, might be 1d. per pound on chilled beef, ⅜d. on Dominion chilled beef, and ½d. on foreign frozen beef. He also demanded the right to send an extra 200,000 cwt. of frozen lamb and mutton each year for five years. Thus in the fifth year, Australian sheepmeat shipments would have been allowed to rise by more than 50 per cent over 1934. Elliot retorted, 'the scheme is no good, either looked at from the point of view of its duration, or the quantities of meat to be imported, or of the amount of money which the suggested levies would give.'[100]

The staid minutes of these meetings reflect a degree of temper which must surely have been extraordinary. In private, Thomas said that he was determined not to be subjected again to the same kind of pressure which had been used against the UK at the Ottawa Conference. And Runciman thought that the Australians were trading on the British awareness of their own political difficulties at home. As he said, 'they are not meeting us in any way'.[101]

And indeed they were not. On 7 May, Gullett broke off negotiations. In reply, Thomas sent a conciliatory but unyielding memorandum, and a firm letter. This letter seems to have had some effect: on 13 May, the Australians again met the British ministers. But the meeting was not very productive. Thomas explained that he would be willing to open negotiations with the Argentine upon the following terms: a levy with 50 per cent preference and a minimum of ½d. preference; continuation of the 10 per cent cut in Argentine allowables; freedom for the Dominions to switch into chilled meat; preferential treatment for the Dominions if expansion became possible; sharing of restriction between foreigners and Dominions if further restriction became necessary. Immediately, Sir Henry Gullett (who said he was speaking for his Government), rejected this, apparently mainly on the ground that it contemplated a 'standstill' for Argentine beef, and the meeting terminated.[102]

A further meeting occurred on 20 May. No minutes have survived, but it is known that Prime Minister Lyons was present. From later comments it seems that at this meeting Thomas offered basic duties of 1¼d. and ¼d. with comparable duties on frozen beef, a sliding scale of duties in relation to beef prices, and the Meat Council. The details of this proposal were clarified in an exchange of letters between Ramsay MacDonald and Lyons; it was later offered, as the Second Draft, to the full conference of Dominion representatives.[103]

By 15 May, Prime Minister G. W. Forbes and J. G. Coates, his Finance Minister, had arrived from New Zealand. British ministers began to meet in plenary sessions with all the representatives – from Australia, New Zealand, South Africa, Canada, and Southern Rhodesia. It is a measure of the importance with which the Antipodes treated the negotiations that they, and they alone, were represented by prime ministers and members of Cabinet. The others merely sent their high commissioners. In all, six meetings were held, the last occurring on 3 July 1935. In these meetings the Canadians were silent, the South Africans quiescent, the New Zealanders helpful, and the Australians infuriating. Indeed, the negotiations were brought to the edge of breakdown by Sir Henry Gullett's obstructionism.

At the first session, on 21 May, Thomas explained that the UK still stood on the proposals of the March 1935 White Paper. Coates, of New Zealand, immediately accepted Thomas's argument that lamb and mutton must be controlled: 'The Ottawa Agreements . . . had worked like a charm so far as lamb and mutton prices were concerned.'[104] New Zealand would accept regulation so long as quotas were based on the Ottawa year. But Australia would not. It quickly became clear that New Zealand did not trust Australia, whose lamb shipments had increased by 10 per cent while New Zealand's had fallen by 15 per cent. Thus New Zealand's restraint had been responsible for the improvement in prices – while Australia did not even appear willing to restrain output. She was prepared to consider regulation so long as this allowed her to send as much as she wanted.

Forbes was also prepared to accept the regulation of beef. Like Australia, he expected to shift from frozen to chilled beef. But he did not envisage the sort of massive expansion which the Australians clearly had in mind. Gullett was also prepared for regulation, which he much preferred to a levy, but 'restriction must primarily be applied to foreign suppliers'. As for the levy, Coates deplored it as a 'departure from Ottawa principles'. And neither the Australians nor the New Zealanders were able at first to comprehend that the UK was not opposed to regulation – merely to regulation *by the UK*. Her tariff proposals assumed that a single Meat Council would regulate her imports.

Thus the meeting of 30 May made heavy weather of the basic duty scheme – a duty of 1¼d. per lb. on foreign chilled beef, ¼d. on Empire chilled beef, and proportionate duties on frozen beef and other beef products. Only South Africa was unequivocally willing to accept it.[105] This proposal allowed the UK to raise all the duties if British fresh-beef prices should fall below stated levels; it also allowed the UK to impose special duties and/or quotas on the countries whose shipments were causing such awkward price-falls. If UK prices should behave favourably, the duties could be lowered – but the Empire preference would never fall below ½d. per lb.

On 22 May, the question reached the Cabinet, when Thomas made his first report on the negotiations. At that meeting, the Cabinet agreed that the Produce Markets

Supply Committee could work out a scheme, with power to take decisions without further reference to the Cabinet. In so doing, the PMSC was to assume that the Cabinet approved:

1. A levy (providing a preference to the Dominions) on imported meat [sic] sufficient to cover the cost of the subsidy to the home industry (£4 millions). The question of whether some *pro forma* levy should be placed on Dominion meat was left entirely to the Committee. So was the rate of the levy.

2. A control of the beef market through a Meat Control Board, which would have representatives from the United Kingdom, the Dominions, and 'perhaps' the Argentine.

3. Whatever devices were needed to prevent any increased burden on the Exchequer should prices further decline.[106]

Armed with this mandate, on 24 May the Committee began to discuss details. It considered free entry or a ¼d. levy on Dominion beef, and 1d. or 1¼d. on foreign beef. It also discussed the 'excess levy' for overshipments – that is, amounts in excess of the quotas the Meat Conference might fix.[107]

These proposals went to Lyons on 28 May, in a letter which contained only the higher figures for duties, and which stressed the use of extra levies or quantitative restrictions against countries which overshipped. In light of Australia's own performance, this emphasis was understandable.[108]

At this point, the Argentinians were shown the third draft scheme, with its duty of 1¼d. They refused to consider it. Indeed, 'regret was expressed that the UK was so unmindful of her own interests as to countenance the present proposals.'[109] Assuming correctly that the Argentine producers would have to absorb the duty, the Argentine representatives estimated that a 1¼d. levy would reduce producers' returns by 42 per cent. The Argentinians were not prepared to contemplate the economic and political crisis that any such levy would cause. They also thought a 1d. preference excessive.

Sir Horace Wilson suggested to Thomas and Runciman

that the Argentinians might swallow a 1d. levy – though even that represented a 35 per cent cut in producers' returns – but that in the end they might not go beyond ¾d. – the figure eventually agreed and imposed in 1937. Wilson had not, however, discussed alternative rates with the Argentine. And there was no hope that they would accept Sir Henry Gullett's most recent demand – a guaranteed increase in Australia's share of the chilled-beef market.[110]

Explaining the situation to the Dominion representatives that afternoon, Thomas said, 'he did not see how it was in any way possible to get the Argentinians to agree'.[111] He thought it unreasonable for Australia to demand both a sizeable preference and an administratively guaranteed increase in its market share. Surely the preference alone would ensure that the share would rise. But Sir Henry Gullett was unyielding:

'If the supplies were available in Australia, she wanted to be assured that she would in fact obtain her expanding share, although she did not contemplate large increases. It was no use for the Australian delegation to concur in proposals which they could not get through their own Parliament. He pointed out that 200 tariff reductions were before Parliament at the present time, and he doubted whether they would be passed unless they could be assured of an expanding market for meat.[112]

This line of argument, however, did Gullett little good. The British kept saying that the Argentinians would accept neither the third draft nor Gullett's guarantee.

'The United Kingdom Government had come to the end of their ingenuity. . . . If the proposals were to be modified at all they might have to be modified in favour of Argentina. . . . Sir Henry Gullett had urged that over and above reasonable opportunities for an expanding market, Australia should have a dead certainty. There was no dead certainty in life.'

And, doubtless incensed by Gullett's references to prospective tariff cuts, they began to belabour the Australians about the 'domestic competition' clause from Ottawa, on which the British were convinced the Australians were evading their treaty obligations.

Unfortunately they failed to move Sir Henry. As Sir Horace Wilson remarked the next day, 'we are . . . back at the original starting-point of the negotiations'.[113] And Gullett continued to press for more. On 20 June he told Thomas that he would accept no duty on *frozen* beef – the main Australian export, which the British had explicitly planned to tax.[114] (Later, New Zealand also asked for free entry for frozen beef, but Thomas was unable to make this concession.)[115] By this stage the British ministers were very discouraged. Thomas 'thought that little hope remained of any successful issue'. And on 24 June they agreed that it might be necessary to break off negotiations.[116]

Later that day, Thomas and Runciman told Gullett, 'that they really had gone to the extreme limit to meet the Australian point of view, and could go no further'.[117] After chaotic but characteristic debate with respect to the working of a safeguarding clause, it was agreed that the Argentinians should be asked to consider the third draft again, as an agreement for a three-year period, and without any special clause to ensure Australia a rising share. After a further session devoted to drafting details, the delegates delivered the draft to officials for further work, and did not meet again until 3 July – their last plenary session.

On 3 July, the Dominion delegates faced the seventh draft into which the officials had transformed the second and third drafts. After they had suggested various minor changes, Thomas explained that the UK would now proceed to negotiate with the Argentine on the basis of 'the broad general principles' of the draft. He would reconvene the Dominions as soon as there was any response from the Argentine.[118] He had already warned the Dominion representatives that he might have to bribe the Argentine with a lower duty, a larger quota, or both;[119] he now warned them that Argentine politics might preclude any speedy response.

This final meeting also clarified the position with respect to lamb and mutton. Thomas stated that the prospective agreement would relate only to beef. Thus he implied that Coates was right in thinking that during the life of the Ottawa Agreement Britain would impose no levy on lamb or mutton. And he made clear that Britain herself would continue to regulate the lamb and mutton trade; these products would not be turned over to the Meat Council and Conference.

Thus ended the plenary sessions. The Australasians, however, did not immediately go home; they remained for some weeks' wrangling over short-term quotas.

In the actual discussions Australia and New Zealand had set the pace. South Africa had taken little part, and Canada none. Howard Ferguson, the Canadian High Commissioner, chose to refer all questions to Ottawa, and to give Thomas the replies by letter. Canada's main concern was to avoid quantitative regulation of its small but growing live-cattle trade. She also pleaded for exemption from the meat duty, on the ground that her production was high cost. This request Thomas quickly rejected.[120] After 4 July, Gullett and Coates submitted further requests and demands, some of which the UK accepted. The result was a modified basis for discussion – an eighth draft – which was completed on 1 August, and circulated to the Dominions representatives two weeks later.[121]

There followed a long wait while the Argentine Government sat upon the draft and said nothing at all. Months passed. Would the Argentine give up her right of free entry under the 1933 Anglo-Argentine Agreement? Or would she insist that nothing should happen until after the expiry of that Agreement in November 1936? The British, having committed themselves to the principle of the levy-subsidy and to the structure of duties, seem to have thought little about the matter. They waited for the Argentine. And the Dominions used the time to consider the eighth draft more thoroughly, and to report their observations and objections. On 15 August they had agreed to accept it, but only as a basis for further conversations.

The 1935 negotiations had thus settled some things while leaving many issues undecided. The Dominions were not allowed the unregulated entry for which Australia had pressed so hard. For 1936–37, they obtained fixed quotas for mutton and lamb; similarly, the discussions produced quotas for beef and veal shipments during 1936. But there was still no long-run plan, no International Council – and no agreement with respect to any structure of protection. Thus in 1936, with nothing really settled, the Dominion representatives again had to make a meat pilgrimage to London.

Not until April 1936 did the UK Government come to grips with the negotiating tasks it would shortly face. The Australians and New Zealanders were on their way; there was still no word from Buenos Aires. On 3 April, Runciman and Elliot proposed that there should be a Cabinet Committee on Trade and Agriculture. It should concern itself with the general question of protection for home agriculture, and with such specific matters as the extension of the levy-subsidy principle from meat to butter, and the nature of the undertakings to be given to foreign countries.[122] In its three years of life, the Committee did indeed consider many trade questions, including egg-subsidisation and the Anglo-American trade talks. But it was also the main decision-making body with respect to the meat negotiations of 1936, and here we consider only that aspect of its activities.

In the spring of 1936, the Cabinet passed the meat negotiations to this new Committee on Trade and Agriculture, whose membership was much the same as that of the old Produce Markets Supply Committee.[123] At its first meeting, it learnt that Australia was no longer satisfied with the bargain of August 1935. Perhaps because Earle Page of the Australian Country Party had joined the Cabinet and the delegation, the Australians now demanded free entry for their beef – not the ¼d. levy and 1d. preference to which they had agreed in 1935.[124] They, like New Zealand, also wanted free entry for mutton and lamb. Fortunately, the Committee now thought it unnecessary to extend the import-levy to these meats, where quantitative control was satisfactorily sustaining prices. Hence there need be no further discussion about lamb and mutton. But

Argentina was asking for a ½d. levy – clearly consistent with the Australian proposals, and with the financial requirements of the subsidy fund which the levy was to provide.[125] Hence the Committee immediately rejected the Argentine request, and resolved to continue negotiating.

It was fairly clear that the Argentine would not swallow a 1¼d. duty. But if Britain were to recover its freedom *vis-à-vis* the Argentine on 6 November, when the 1933 agreement would expire, she would have to denounce the agreement on 6 May. At the Committee's second meeting this consideration was placed forcibly before it. Should the agreement be denounced? Or should the Argentine be approached again, and asked again to concede a larger preferential margin than ½d? The Committee reminded itself that the levy scheme had originally been changed at the behest of the Dominions, in 1935. A universal levy of 1d. and ½d. on all meat would have produced enough to pay the subsidy. As the Dominions were terrified of levies on lamb and mutton, 1¼d. and ¼d. on beef became necessary to raise enough money while providing the preferential margin that the Dominions wanted. It was decided not to denounce the agreement, and to approach the Argentine once more. But obviously deadlock was at hand.[126]

Since 1934 British beef producers had been subsidised from a fund which was eventually to be replenished from the proceeds of the meat duty, once this could be introduced. Thus the Treasury's financial calculations assumed a levy sufficiently high to pay off these 'advances' and also to pay an aggregate subsidy of £4 million per year. Given the assumed flows of Dominion and Argentine meat imports, these requirements determined the 'necessary' rates of duty. On 4 May, however, Chamberlain told his colleagues that for the sake of agreement with the Argentine on a duty of ¾d. per lb., he was prepared to 'forgive' the arrears of subsidy, and to continue the current subsidy indefinitely, providing it from general revenue – so long as domestic production was not increased. The committee quickly agreed to offer free entry to the Dominions, and ¾d. to the Argentine; the Dominions were to be free to substitute chilled beef for frozen beef, and there would be a meat conference to fix quotas.[127]

Chamberlain's proposal or concession really meant the prospect of agreement, the end of deadlock – and the end, too, of the levy-subsidy plan. He was proposing to keep paying a subsidy of £4 million pounds per year, regardless of the yield from the beef levy. Thereby he cleared the way for the fixing of duties which would satisfy both the Argentinians and the Australians. Argentina would reject 1d. or 1¼d. . . . the amounts necessary to pay the beef subsidy. She could now be offered ¾d., a figure which it was believed she would accept. Australia said that she needed at least ½d. preferential margin to meet the Argentine in Britain. But she really wanted free entry, and a 1d. margin; anyway a ¼d. levy for Australian shipments would yield little revenue. She could now be offered free entry and a margin which, on her own showing, would yield her a definite benefit. If Chamberlain had continued to insist that the levy-revenue must cover the subsidy – even without the arrears – these rates could not have been offered, and eventually enshrined in the Beef and Veal Import Duties Act of 1937.

The levy would have been especially hard on New Zealand. She and Australia were Britain's only considerable suppliers of lamb and mutton, but these two products bulked much larger in her exports, and in her whole economy, than anywhere else. While she did not spell out the terms-of-trade argument, it would obviously have applied in her case. That is, the New Zealand farmer would pay part or all of the British duty. Hence the strong New Zealand preference for the restriction of foreigners and, in her own case, 'regulation' – agreed shipments which did not prevent her from shipping as much as she could produce. Many of the quota arrangements had in fact had exactly this effect.[128]

The Australian position was broadly similar. Lacking alternative outlets for her frozen beef, mutton, and lamb, she too would have had to pay most or all of any duty which the British might impose. Presumably it was because they did not perceive this possibility that the Australian Government initially favoured a duty, rather than quantitative regulation. In the course of the discussions the Australians came to support the New Zealanders perhaps, as Sutch suggests, because the New Zealanders stiffened their resolve, and perhaps Sir Henry Gullett, who was present, had long favoured restriction, while Earle Page, who had long opposed it, was in Australia.[129] Page and his advisers believed that if the British were to impose the particular quotas they proposed, there would immediately be gluts of unsaleable meat, both chilled beef and lamb, in Australia.[130] If he accepted, the scheme would then go to the Argentine and to the other Dominions.

At long last, on 6 July 1936 the Minister of Agriculture and Fisheries was able to tell the House of Commons that a long-term agricultural policy had been devised. It involved free entry for Dominion meat,[131] a duty on foreign meat, a subsidy to domestic fat-stock producers, and quantitative regulation through an Empire Meat Council and an International Meat Conference. Initially allowed to deal with beef alone, and to begin work on 1 January 1937, the council and conference might undertake lamb and mutton regulation after the end of 1937. The idea was to turn over meat regulation to the producer-countries; Britain would protect her own farmers through the subsidy, which would be paid on a stable volume of meat. And the aid would not be of levy-subsidy type: that is, unlike some earlier proposals, the July 1936 version did not propose to pay the subsidy from the proceeds of the meat duty.[132] The rates of duty were to be ¾d. per lb. on foreign chilled beef, ⅔d. per lb. on foreign frozen beef, and comparable *ad valorem* rates on other types.

Elliot's statement was cabled to the Dominions, who already knew that it was hoped Argentina would accept a duty of ¾d. per pound on chilled beef, and proportionate duties on other beef. After further complicated negotiations with South Africa and Canada, and with Argentina itself, the Government was able, very late in 1936, to introduce a Beef and Veal Import Duties Bill. But the expected revenue was far less than the £5 million in Exchequer subsidy to which Chamberlain had at length agreed. Nor was there meant to be any link between revenue and expenditures.

Late in the autumn, the Cabinet had considered the legislation which would give effect to the decisions of the summer. On 28 October they approved the Livestock Industry Bill. This provided for a subsidy of up to £5 million per annum on an unstated quantity of meat. It also provided that the Board of Trade might regulate the import of livestock and meat, when 'desirable in order to secure the stability of the market for livestock and meat in the UK'. Thus the measure, which passed into law in mid-1937, enshrined the divorce between the subsidy and any particular levy; it also provided the legal support for the measures that might be needed if the Meat Conference should fail. And the conference itself was not mentioned.[133] On 2 December, the Cabinet approved a Bill which would provide duties on foreign beef and veal – ¾d. on foreign frozen, ⅔d. on frozen and live, 20 per cent on canned tongue and uncanned offals, boned, and boneless. Sweetbreads were not dutiable; except for tongue, all canned beef and veal and all essences or extracts of beef or veal were dutiable at 10 per cent.[134] This Bill thus enacted the agreed rates of duty. It also signified that the Argentine had won an important point. As the duties were to be levied from mid-December 1936, Argentina had in fact secured free entry for her beef through the entire term of the original Anglo-Argentine Agreement of 1933. It will be remembered that, in 1935, the Dominions and Britain had agreed to ask for an immediate duty on Argentine beef. But the negotiations had taken a year, and statute-drafting nearly six months.

For meat, levy-subsidies were killed on 4 May, when Chamberlain agreed to an indefinite non-funded Exchequer subsidy. For butter and dairy products, however, the device was still government policy. Let us now see how in these other spheres also it was eventually abandoned.

V. BUTTER AND THE DEATH OF LEVY-SUBSIDIES

In the third section of this chapter we noticed that in 1934 the Government publicly committed itself to introduce a levy-subsidy for butter. Meanwhile, there were to be Exchequer subsidies to the Milk Marketing Boards. These were repayable, on the theory that after the levy-subsidy came into existence the Boards would have funds to reimburse the Exchequer.

When the Australians and New Zealanders came to London in 1935, they were almost as worried about butter as about meat. Earlier in the year, they had discussed a voluntary restriction with the Danes. New Zealand and Denmark had agreed on a scale of reduction, but Australia had refused to agree.[135] Hence it is not surprising that in the 1935 discussions the New Zealanders revealed a profound distrust of the Australians, who, they feared, would not maintain quality or honour quotas. Once again they asked if the UK would make some sort of special arrangement with them: 'is it feasible, or is it likely, that in the measurable future it will be feasible for His Majesty's Government in the UK to contemplate a bilateral and reciprocal trade agreement with one Dominion?'[136] The documents do not reveal how the New Zealanders expected the British Government to respond. Certainly they got a dusty answer: only an Imperial conference could properly consider so great a departure from the Spirit of Ottawa.[137]

In fact, the Ottawa Agreements did not really treat all Dominions equally. Canada, for example, enjoyed special privileges with respect to bacon. But in 1935 the British ministers were trying to make the Australians agree that the Australian Tariff Board had not been ruling in accordance with the Ottawa Agreements. And it was Australian butter which the New Zealanders feared. If New Zealand were to receive any special privileges in the British butter market, the Australians were certain to retaliate by refusing to accept the British interpretation of the fair-competition clauses in the Ottawa Agreement. The result might be a painful contraction of British sales in Australia. And New Zealand was not likely to retaliate: her agrarian interests were strong enough to prevent Forbes's coalition government from choosing protectionism, even if Forbes and Coates should want to retaliate. Further, the British decision did New

Zealand no active harm: she continued to enjoy free and unrestricted entry for her butter.

On 19 June, Elliot explained the British position to Gullett and Coates.[138] Ignoring the officials' recommendation, he told them that Britain's treaty obligations precluded any increase in the foreign duty until January 1937. Since the Ottawa Agreements themselves precluded any reduction in the preferential margin, Britain could impose no new butter duties until then. Thus the Dominions were assured of free entry at least until that time. As for quotas, the Ottawa Agreements allowed Britain to impose them unilaterally after August 1935. But, as Thomas explained to Gullett and Coates,[139] she did not intend to do so until March 1936 at the earliest. Even then, he said, there would be quotas only if they could not be avoided. If intervention was required, it would be by duty or levy in the first instance.

It was possible, but inaccurate, for the Australians and New Zealanders to claim some sort of victory over the evil butter duty in 1935. Britain's decision had been taken not because of Dominion representations but because of the treaties she had signed in 1932–33. Elliot's remarks greatly worried Coates – who did not seem to understand that New Zealand was safe from a butter duty until January 1937, not just until March 1936.[140]

In principle, the UK could have introduced a butter *quota* in the summer of 1936. By then, however, other factors were relevant. The levy-subsidy plan was still government policy. But the Cabinet had appointed a Reorganisation Commission to report on the dairy industry. Until this body had reported, nothing could be done about protection, subsidy, or quota. So Malcolm MacDonald told Australia's Earle Page, who in 1936 was presenting the traditional demand: free unrestricted entry for Dominion butter, and a very small quota for Danish.[141] When the Canadian ministers, Dunning and Gardiner, asked MacDonald the same question, they got the same answer.[142] Indeed, when negotiating with the Canadians the British ministers were obliged to insist on retaining their Ottawa right to impose duties or quotas on Canadian butter. And this 'Schedule A Reservation' of

1932 reappeared as Schedule I in the new Anglo-Canadian Trade Agreement of February 1937.

This result was not reached without dispute. Early in August, Runciman pressed Elliot to permit a more definite statement. Noting how distressed the Canadians had been on 28 July, he wrote: 'It is most important that we reassure them as far as possible.' Could they not assure the Canadian ministers that Canada's cheese and manufactured milk were safe until 1 January 1938 – or at least until 1 September 1937? And might it not be possible to assure them that there would be no quotas on cheese and manufactured milk, and only a very low duty on cheese?[143] Elliot, however, refused to consider any such definite commitments; he was prepared to say only that there would be no action against Canadian butter and cheese before 31 July 1937. And MacDonald transmitted Elliot's verdict to Dunning on 6 August.[144]

The Dominions Office tried to prevent the publication of the Milk Reorganisation *Report* until after the Anglo-Canadian Trade Agreement had been signed.[145] But the Ministry of Agriculture and Fisheries was unco-operative, and the *Report* emerged in early December 1936.[146] Fortunately, with respect to trade policy the milk commissioners were noncommittal. They definitely ruled out quotas as devices for aiding producers; they believed that quotas were uncertain in operation, and too painful for consumers, given the fact that, in 1935, 91 per cent of butter consumption and 70 per cent of cheese consumption had been imported. The same arguments applied to an ordinary duty. Hence, for reasons that were by this point conventional, they inclined to favour a levy-subsidy. But they recommended no particular policy of import control.

In fact, quotas were unworkable for legal reasons so far as Australia was concerned. In 1935 Australia's export control legislation was brought before the courts, and in mid-1936 the Privy Council ruled that the butter and dried-fruit laws were unconstitutional in the light of Section 92 of the Constitution.[147]

Meanwhile in New Zealand, the frustration of the dairy farmers had been, at least in part, responsible for the defeat of Forbes's coalition government. Late in 1935, it was replaced by a Labour ministry whose trade programme was known to be radical. And in the late autumn of 1936 the new Finance Minister, Walter Nash, came to London to negotiate a new trade agreement. He was primarily concerned to negotiate a scheme for bilateral balancing and mutual clearing. By conducting all of New Zealand's trade in this way, he hoped to win new markets for her staple exports, especially frozen lamb, mutton, cheese, and butter. Nash was not able to penetrate the British opposition to new bilateral clearing schemes. Thus the conversations soon turned into product-by-product wrangling of a depressingly familiar kind. In the end, these wranglings forced the UK to take certain decisions of principle with respect to the control of dairy products. Hence it is convenient to discuss the entire course of negotiations in the context of butter.

Since the confusions of 1933, the New Zealand Government had taken power to regulate domestic marketing and production of dairy products. And from 1 August 1936 it had made itself the monopoly buyer of all the export butter and cheese in the Dominion. The Reserve Bank was to create the funds to pay New Zealand farmers a guaranteed price, to be fixed at first on recent averages but eventually on 'fairness'.[148] As the Labour Government had reached power in Wellington largely because of this policy, and because of the unpopularity which Forbes and Coates had earned in their handling of the butter problem, this 'nationalisation of butter' was inevitable. But as the British and Nash both realised, it meant that any British butter duty would come directly out of the New Zealand treasury: the Wellington Government would have to pay the duty and export a revenue-maximising quantum of butter.

Soon after taking office, Nash proposed a bilateral balancing agreement: he would offer,

'with minor qualifications, United Kingdom full direct market in New Zealand for British manufactured goods or raw materials equal to the balance of credits from the sales of New Zealand goods in the United Kingdom after making provision for shipping cargoes, other invisible items, debt services, and proportionate redemption of loans due . . . in the United Kingdom.'[149]

When Nash came to London late in 1936, he peddled this proposal with vigour.[150] But the British Government had long since decided that such an arrangement would be contrary to its own policy of freeing trade and discouraging payments plans.[151]

It was hard to make Nash understand the British position. He continued to press for bilateral balancing of Anglo-New Zealand trade long after the British ministers had stated their position. He knew that universal bilateral balancing was impossible, but said that he intended to develop such arrangements with as many countries as possible – for the sake of a 'general expansion of trade'. In effect, New Zealand's Government was now firmly committed to the swapping-of-surpluses approach which Britain's Labour Party had favoured in the late twenties – and which her National Government had refused to consider.

Nash continued to oppose any duty or levy-subsidy on butter. But he did agree to the quantitative control of butter, mutton, and lamb – so long as the controls provided for some growth.[152]

On 10 November, Nash talked with Malcolm MacDonald. It became clear that he wanted New Zealand to have concessions at the expense of other Dominions – or at least, concessions which would not be extended to other Dominions. MacDonald explained that such concessions were politically impossible.[153] On 19 November, when meeting MacDonald, Morrison, and Runciman, Nash explained his bilateral-balancing scheme in some detail. He argued that it would be more sure in its trade-diverting effects than preferential duties or quotas. He was prepared to accept a quota scheme if it allowed for regulated expansion, but he thought the levy-subsidy proposal 'hopeless'. And he was unmoved when Runciman and MacDonald repeated the objections they had already voiced.[154]

Meanwhile, the Board of Trade was at work on the Nash

proposals. Detecting that Nash thought New Zealand had a favourable balance with the UK on current account, they checked to find whether this was indeed the case – and found that New Zealand sold far more to the UK than she bought from the UK. Invisibles were not large enough to absorb this visible surplus; hence, 'As in our view the balance of payments is consistently favourable to New Zealand, it follows that, in any negotiations for a direct balancing agreement, most, if not all, of the concessions must be borne by New Zealand.'[155]

On 19 December, Nash was given a memorandum which presented this conclusion, and which also detailed the other objections to his scheme – difficulties with the Dominions and foreign countries, implications for the price level and for UK agriculture, problems of administrative workability and cost at both ends, and general considerations of UK trade policy.[156] One might expect that this presentation would have put an end to the payments proposal. Certainly the balance-of-payments exercise should have been conclusive. One would like to know how Dr W. B. Sutch, Nash's economics adviser, who was present at these meetings, absorbed such a commentary on his own skill. But whatever Sutch may have thought, Nash would not let the matter drop.

Some British ministers believed that Nash was so strongly committed to this policy because he himself was the author of it. Before answering Nash, Malcolm MacDonald consulted the Trade and Agricultural Committee. He had maintained a solid opposition to Nash's bilateral balancing scheme.[157] Nevertheless, 'it had, however, been found quite impossible to make any impression on Mr Nash . . . a definite deadlock had now been reached.' MacDonald proposed to tell Nash that the UK could not negotiate on these proposals, and that it was better to continue the Ottawa Agreement, subject to variations in detail: 'it was probable that . . . Mr Nash would ultimately acquiesce in our conclusion, just as he had done on the question of the Meat Conference and the expansion of New Zealand exports of mutton and lamb.'

The Committee so resolved,[158] and on 19 February MacDonald wrote to Nash. Bilateral balancing, he said, was wrong in principle, impossible to work fairly or expeditiously in practice, and, if begun with New Zealand, certain to prejudice Britain's trade with other Dominions and with foreign countries.[159]

Thus Nash's gambit was unsuccessful. Ironically, the British forced him to adopt a policy – simple export-restriction – which was probably much more in accordance with his own country's true interests. It certainly raised the national pay-off per unit of input. And it may even have helped New Zealand's foreign currency receipts – no small matter for New Zealand, totally committed as she was after 1935 to domestic reflation and after 1938 to exchange control. But as these side-effects were not understood in New Zealand, the results were hated and feared.

The effect on New Zealand's attitudes can hardly have been good, especially as the New Zealand Government was soon to embark on forced-draft industrialisation behind the barriers of exchange control.[160] It may be argued that the imperatives of New Zealand's reflation were such that she would in any event have been forced to adopt licensing procedures which would have discriminated against finished consumer goods, and in favour of raw materials. To the extent that this was true, Britain lost nothing by her refusal to consider a bilateral balancing arrangement. Further, we know that New Zealand did try to discriminate in favour of Britain – not against her – in operating her licensing system. This is not the action of a vindictive and disappointed trading partner. From the British perspective, the New Zealand attitude must have seemed one of sorrow, not of anger. And the remaining months of peace were too few to test the stability of this Antipodean attitude. Perhaps, if war had not broken out so soon, there would have been time for the South British to visit more ill-effects upon Britain.

After the UK had rejected his plan, Nash pressed the Government for some definite statement about butter policy. Would there be a duty? A quota? Or both? On the answer depended many things – in particular, New Zealand's responsiveness to British proposals for adjusting the Ottawa Agreements.

In April, the Trade and Agriculture Committee discussed the problem exhaustively. The ministers concluded that the UK was already committed not to impose *both* a butter duty *and* a butter quota. But they were unable to decide whether to impose one, the other, or neither. It was necessary to keep a free hand; meanwhile, 'every effort must be made to expedite a decision on the future milk policy of the United Kingdom.'[161] Therefore, the Cabinet set up an Agricultural Policy Committee.

Malcolm MacDonald, the Dominions Secretary, and Oliver Stanley, the President of the Board of Trade, both opposed any change in the existing arrangements of free and unrestricted entry for butter. They said that the Dominions knew who would pay the levy – their own producers, who would get lower prices. Further, the UK could not risk offending the Dominion governments: soon she would need their agreement to the concessions which the United States was demanding. An Anglo-American trade agreement, though of little commercial value, would be of immense political importance. A butter duty would infuriate the Australians, whom the Americans would ask to concede a smaller preferential margin on their dried and canned fruits. It would upset the New Zealanders, who were already inclined towards a new protectionism. Canada would resent any interference with the cheese trade. And Canada was the most difficult nut for the Anglo-American negotiations: she would be asked to give way not only on wheat but on timber. With Chamberlain's agreement, therefore, and over the protests of the Minister of Agriculture, it was agreed that the dairy industry should be aided with price-insurance and direct Exchequer subsidies, not levies or quotas.[162]

After Cabinet approval, the Dominions learned of this decision on 29 July:

'We do not propose any immediate imposition of new or increased duties upon dairy produce. Nor for the moment do we consider it necessary to consider the quantitative regulation of imports (apart from existing voluntary arrangements) . . . but we should like to make it clear that the steps we are now taking are without prejudice to our freedom to take such subsequent action as we may consider necessary within the framework of the agreement' –

that is, the Anglo-Canadian Agreement of 23 February 1937 and in other cases the Ottawa Agreements themselves.[163]

The Cabinet decision was subsequently enshrined in a White Paper.[164] The White Paper continued the repayable advances on manufactured milk to 30 September 1938, released the Milk Boards from any liability for repayment of advances under the 1934 Milk Act and other statutes thereafter which might accrue after 30 September 1937, offered subsidies for five years on the production of better-quality milk, and described the price-insurance scheme. Milk Boards would get Exchequer grants whenever the average prices of imported butter and cheese should fall below 100s. and 56s. per cwt.

To sweeten the pill, the Government explained in the White Paper that it was guaranteeing the dairy farmers a far better deal than they had got in 1934, when actual butter and cheese prices were far lower than the prices at which the Exchequer would now begin to make grants. Nevertheless, the White Paper caused an explosion from the National Farmers Union, who spoke of betrayal. Was the Government not committed publicly to levy-subsidies? Faced with this explosion, and with pressure from its Minister of Agriculture,[165] the Cabinet asked the Agricultural Policy Committee to consider the whole question of levy-subsidies in principle and to report no later than 17 November 1937.[166]

The Committee met on 11 November. Its discussion was long and frank. Oliver Stanley argued strongly against levy-subsidies:

'At the present time levy-subsidies were not a practical alternative. Politically speaking, with butter at its present price, it was out of the question to go to the House of Commons and propose a duty on butter. The conditions in 1934, when prices were low, were very different. From the point of view of one who had to negotiate trade agreements, levy-subsidies provided greater difficulties than any other form of protection. Our foreign and Dominion competitors understood the working of tariffs, and knew that quantitative regulation would sometimes benefit them, as well as ourselves, but they had no use for levy-subsidies. They did not see why they should have to pay a direct subsidy to their British competitor. The only way of inducing them to do so was for us to pay a heavy price in other directions. These considerations applied with great force in the case of New Zealand, where the Government now bought all the butter from their farmers and were responsible for selling it. The levy would come direct out of the New Zealand Treasury . . . a levy-subsidy . . . would remain the most onerous form of agricultural assistance, that is, the one for which we should have to pay the highest price in trade agreements, both foreign and Dominion.'

Sir John Simon agreed, and also noted that the Stamp and Leith-Ross Committees[167] had commended levy-subsidies *for a time of price depression*, and even then not in any absolute way – only as an alternative to quantitative control. Further, 'the idea of assigning revenues derived from particular sources to particular objects could not survive critical examination' – especially at a time when defence outlays were rapidly rising.

Chamberlain spoke strongly in support of Stanley and Simon.

'The protests of the Dominion competition could not be ignored, even if it was possible to ignore those of the foreigner. New Zealand was the head and fount of the difficulties in this connection. Mr Chamberlain thought it impossible for the Government to conceal the fact that they had changed their minds in this department of policy. He himself had once been much attracted to the levy subsidy solution, but he had come to realise that the objections to it were overwhelming . . . The Treasury objections to assigned revenues came home with great force in times like the present . . . Above all there was the conclusive argument from the consumer's point of view . . . it was most important to avoid doing anything which would still further increase the cost of living. The view of the committee appeared to be that, while they felt great sympathy with the farmers, they regarded levy-subsidies as out of the question in present circumstances. If so, a frank announcement to this effect would be necessary.'

Even at this bitter end, William Morrison, the Minister of Agriculture, spoke vehemently in favour of levy-subsidies. But 'the Committee agreed with the Prime Minister'.[168] And on 17 November the full Cabinet confirmed this verdict:[169] 'in present circumstances the principle of applying a levy-subsidy policy in the cases of meat and livestock, bacon, milk, and other dairy products should be definitely abandoned.'

In deciding to impose no levy-subsidies, the President of the Board of Trade reminded the Committee, they should consider the corollary question: should the UK retain *power* to levy dairy duties or to impose dairy quotas?

'Owing to a decision based on considerations of internal policy they did not want to exercise either of these powers, but before making any announcement to that effect he would like to get compensation from the Dominions for any abandonment of this country's rights. In particular, Canada was asking for compensation before agreeing to facilitate trade negotiations with the United States. He suggested that an offer should be made to the Dominions to abandon the right to impose a duty on dairy produce for three years . . . while from the commercial aspect it might also be desirable to abandon the right to apply quantitative regulations he was averse from doing this. He suggested, however, that a more precise indication should be given to the Dominions of the circumstances in which the rights might be operated.'[170]

The Committee agreed with these proposals and so did the Cabinet:[171]

'The occasion of the announcement of the decision in regard to levy-subsidy should be used to put forward (in a way most advantageous to us in our trade negotiations) an offer on our part to abandon the right to levy any duty on the agricultural products in question during the next three years.'

As the Cabinet was relinquishing levy-subsidies not just on dairy products but also on meat, eggs, poultry and bacon, the concession was considerable even if only putative. Given the tense negotiations with the United States, and the recalcitrance of Canada and Australia with respect thereto, it was natural for the Cabinet to try to get whatever mileage it could from its action.

Later the Cabinet agreed on its reservation with respect to quotas: 'the right to impose quantitative regulation of the products concerned if imports were such as to lead to instability in the market for those products in the U.K.' And it agreed about the terms in which enquiring Dominions might be confidentially reassured:

'It is not intended to use the right of quantitative regulation of imports to maintain a high price in this market. The right would only be used to relieve a situation in which the volume of exports coming to the market threatened the stability of the industries concerned in the United Kingdom.'[172]

The next day the Dominions were told what God and Oliver Stanley had wrought. Telegrams confirmed the British decision not to impose a duty on butter, and offered to make a binding commitment at least until 20 August 1940. In wiring Canada, the Dominions Office suggested that this must facilitate revision of the February 1937 trade agreement for the sake of *rapprochement* with the USA. To New Zealand, it suggested that the New Zealand Government might now be able to proceed with the schedules of tariff requests which the UK had submitted earlier in 1937, at the Imperial Conference.[173] Wiring its own high commissioners, the Office pointed out, 'the grant of free entry . . . is not a matter of right, but is a concession in return for which we expect some counter-balancing compensation'.[174]

VI. WHY THE LEVY-SUBSIDY IDEA LASTED SO LONG

With butter, as with meat, it was Exchequer subsidy which

broke the link between farmer prosperity and protectionism, making it possible for the British Government at last to avoid the tangles in which their trading patterns and their trade agreements had enmeshed them. British consumers benefited through lower prices, certainly receiving more in extra 'consumer surplus' than they paid in extra taxation. This retreat from protectionism had been forced on the British Government – largely by the trade agreements of 1932–33. And the escape was never complete. The Wheat Act mechanism continued to subsidise British wheat production out of a flour levy. The food tariffs of 1932 – the legacies of the Import Duties Act and the Ottawa Agreements – were preserved. Meat imports were controlled. Nevertheless, things could have been much worse – and would have been worse if the agreements of 1932–33 had not so narrowly prescribed the initiatives which the UK might take. Indeed, it was these agreements which totally defeated the Government's major innovation with respect to agrarian policy – the 'levy-subsidy' scheme.

As with meat, so with butter, one asks: why did it take the British Government so long to fumble its way towards this logical conclusion? The answer is moderately clear in the documents. Early in the decade, it was emotionally impossible for Neville Chamberlain and other ministers to contemplate a direct subsidy. Further, both Chamberlain and Walter Elliot were predisposed to seek in tariffs the solutions to unprofitability. A levy-subsidy would have had so many advantages, given the small share of British production in British consumption: a small levy would have yielded very large subsidy funds. The reports of the Stamp and Leith-Ross Committees added fuel to this fire. And as it became clear that the Dominions and the foreign governments would not surrender their various rights to free entry, conventionalised duties, and freedom from quotas, the levy-subsidy plan, initially conceived as an emergency device which would cope with the butter deluge of 1934, became a long-run plan and a long-run goal – something to be introduced when treaty obligations should permit. In the interim – from 1934 until 1937 – nothing need be done because nothing could be done. And by 1937 two things had changed. The Government recognised how much the foreigners and the Dominions disliked levy-subsidies. And the Chancellor was much more resigned to semi-permanent subsidisation from general revenue. Admittedly, the milk subsidy schemes of 1937 were still temporary in form. But the beef scheme was not, and after four years of subsidisation, few can have believed that, if needed, the milk subsidies would not become permanent in fact.

It is hard not to laugh at Chamberlain's role in these long proceedings. More than once his insistence on principle had prolonged and complicated matters. The levy-subsidy scheme had been devised partly to assuage his scruples as Chancellor of the Exchequer: since it was WRONG to make subsidies to private producers, and since the national finances were in a parlous state, a new tax must be devised to aid the beef producers. From the exigencies of a self-financing subsidy scheme were devised tariff rates, totally in abstraction from their longer-run effects either on retail prices – which they would have raised – or on resource allocation – which they would have further distorted. When these rates proved a stumbling block to the Dominions and to foreigners, there ensued excruciatingly extended negotiations – negotiations so extended that they could not in the end be allowed to fail. When failure was in sight, Chamberlain removed the stumbling block – a barrier which Elliot had first placed because of Chamberlain's own sensibilities.

Chamberlain knew that British agricultural protectionism raised difficult questions. He had always favoured a food tariff, and had believed since 1930 that it was in livestock and dairy products, not in grain, that British agriculture would find its salvation. But early in 1935, when British wheat and bacon production were already rising rapidly in the shelter of protective devices, he recorded his worries. Someone, he wrote, would have to decide how far to carry home agricultural production. How much could be produced in the UK? Would it be wise to carry production as far as possible? And how were imports to be divided between Empire and foreign suppliers? 'All these want working out, as a basis for action.' And in March 1934 he brought this question *inter alia* before a meeting of Conservative ministers.[175] But to see the problems in protectionism is not to see the particular difficulties which levy-subsidies would create.

Only J. H. Thomas, the Dominions Secretary, had any early premonition of the full troubles which the levy-subsidy would give. Writing to Walter Elliot in mid-1934, he used the same arguments which Oliver Stanley later employed to hammer the nails into the scheme's coffin. In bargaining, he thought, the device would be disastrous, because it clearly revealed that the UK would be taxing overseas producers and spending the proceeds to subsidise their competitors in Britain. A preferential concession would only mitigate the Dominions' opposition, not remove it. And would not the Dominions propose to do the same thing for their own secondary industries? Would not the scheme involve bargaining every bit as acrimonious as the quotas? It would be better, Thomas thought, to levy a simple preferential duty, and pay a separate Exchequer subsidy which was not linked to the resulting revenue.[176]

The Dominions Office was, of course, an ideal vantage point from which to observe an emerging pattern: agricultural protectionism bought more production in Britain, but a large and rising cost in sacrificed imports, and therefore in lost export markets. Thomas was probably especially sensitive to the repercussions on Dominion policy towards Britain's exports of manufactures. In mid-1934, he brought his worries with respect to agricultural protectionism before the Cabinet – only to be told that Ramsay MacDonald had already asked the Committee of Economic Information to report – if possible by October – on the proper co-ordination of trade policy.[177]

The Committee on Economic Information was a sub-committee of the Economic Advisory Council. Set up in 1931, the Council had soon ceased to meet as a single body, functioning instead through its committees. This particular committee prepared regular reports on economic conditions, and irregular reports on particular topics which the Cabinet might refer to it. Though its staff was small, its membership was distinguished – Sir Josiah Stamp, G. D. H. Cole, J. M. Keynes, H. D. Henderson, Sir Frederick Leith-Ross (for some purposes only), and other luminaries.

MacDonald's request passed to the Committee on Economic Information on 19 June 1934. Most members of the Committee then wrote memoranda.[178] Sir Josiah Stamp, the Chairman, also received suggestions from various ministries. In consultation with Stamp and with H. D. Henderson, whose memorandum formed the basis for their work, the two Secretaries, Francis Henning and P. K. Debenham, then drafted a report and circulated it to the Committee members. Several redrafts later, on 23 October 1934, the Committee adopted its report on economic co-ordination – its thirteenth report, and passed it to the Cabinet.[179]

The report presented little hope for the staple industries of the UK. Its authors believed that world demand conditions had permanently turned against them, and that they could not avoid a prolonged shrinkage. But it favoured trade policies which would encourage and develop markets for the 'new goods and new trades' – the products of the electric and gasoline revolutions. It saw little merit in artificial stimulation of British agriculture. The UK's population, it pointed out, would soon stabilise, and eventually decline. Technical progress would reduce the labour-absorbing capacity of agriculture. Hence agricultural expansion would be no solution for unemployment. Further, the overseas countries, having oriented their development on the assumption of a permanently expanding British market, would have trouble enough in adjusting to that market's stability. Agrarian protectionism in the UK would seriously aggravate this problem. Further, if Britain were to protect her agriculture on the continental model, the overseas countries would certainly become more protectionist – thus increasing the problem of industrial transference which Britain would face in any event. Hence there was nothing to be gained from protectionism so far as employment was concerned: 'In these circumstances it seems inevitable that any expansion of home agriculture which one can secure by restricting our imports from these countries will be balanced by at least an equivalent injury in other branches of our economic life.' 'So far as agriculture is concerned, our national objective, in our judgment, should in the main be preservation rather than expansion.'

'It should, we believe, be accepted that the aim of agricultural policy is to raise the incomes of agriculturists rather than to expand the output of agricultural produce. It should further be, and we believe has been, accepted that it is on the whole undesirable to diminish unduly the sterling receipts of the principal agricultural exporting countries. But between policies which equally fulfil these two conditions, it is obviously preferable to choose that which allows the greatest possible volume (as opposed to value) of imports.'

The bacon scheme, by this criterion, is far worse than the wheat scheme.

'Had bacon imports been regulated in the same manner as wheat imports the industrial population would have received the benefits of this large supply without prejudice to the British producers, and the foreign producer would be free from the sense of insecurity, which is induced by the possibility of a progressive reduction in his quota. For the British producer would no longer be, as he is now, insulated from the effects of any increase in his output upon the price of his product.'

These quotations are from the first draft of the report, but they appear with no significant change in the version which was eventually transmitted to the Cabinet – and on 12 December[180] immediately passed to the Produce Markets Supply Committee.

More to the point, however, in light of negotiations: the report contained a strong endorsement of the levy-subsidy principle. Keynes, Leith-Ross, and Henderson were all agreed on this. They had before them a smoothly operating levy-subsidy arrangement – the wheat scheme which since 1932 had levied a small excise on flour and used the proceeds to subsidise British wheat farmers. They also had a dreadful example of quantitative regulation, the bacon scheme. As

Leith-Ross pointed out in his memorandum, this scheme was evil from all angles. Because it raised the return to the foreigner, it increased their sterling earnings, while giving them cause to introduce countervailing quantitative restrictions. It raised the price to the consumer by the full amount necessary to make domestic production payable. A levy, furthermore, would involve a much lower consumer price than the quota system – especially if part of the levy should fall upon the foreigner, as Leith-Ross thought most likely. Summing up, he said, 'I would urge most strongly that the policy should be reconsidered at once as regards *Bacon*, and as regards *Meat* that we should not go further into what I am convinced is a ruinous direction.'[181]

An interdepartmental committee of civil servants under Leith-Ross's chairmanship then examined the Stamp Report. Not surprisingly, it endorsed the economists' conclusions with respect to the levy-subsidy proposal, rubbing in the conclusions even more forcefully.[182]

When the Produce Markets Supply Committee discussed the Stamp and Leith-Ross Reports in December 1934, nobody took much exception to this endorsement.[183] Ministers were more interested in discussing the general recommendations with respect to the size of the agricultural sector. However lightly they may thereafter have taken this part of the committees' advice, subsequent events show how completely the endorsement was internalised.

VII. MEAT AND THE DEATH OF PRODUCER-CONTROL

The meat talks of 1935–36 were as much concerned with quotas as with levy-subsidies. Besides settling their long-range policy, in 1935 the UK ministers were eager to establish the short-term allowables for lamb, mutton and beef.

During July, the British ministers met regularly with the New Zealanders and the Australians to work out the beef quotas for 1935 and the mutton and lamb quotas for 1935–36. These discussions were carried on in the hope that the Argentinians would not insist on their undoubted right to void the 10 per cent cut which Britain had imposed upon their meat shipments. But Argentina in fact did ask the British to release them from the cut, effective 1 August.[184] And the UK responded in an ingenious fashion. Quotas, it said, were now being fixed for a half-yearly period, not quarterly. It remained to be seen whether Australia would in fact send as much chilled beef as she was proposing to send. Until an actual shipment had taken place, there was no ground for the Argentine to increase its own chilled beef shipments. Hence the UK would not release the Argentine from the burden of the 10 per cent cut.[185] This response was, of course, disingenuous to the point of dishonesty: the British knew perfectly well that the main problem was to keep Australia down to quota – not up to estimate. Admittedly, chilled beef had never before been shipped from Australia on any scale. But British officials had every reason to believe that Australia had underestimated her capacity – not overestimated it.

The New Zealanders were unhappy at the thought of a single Meat Council on which they would have to sit with foreigners. Hence they proposed a two-stage procedure – an Empire caucus which would meet first, and then a general council. The British saw no problem in meeting this request, which South Africa also supported. After many emendations in detail, the New Zealand proposal gave rise to the two-tier system of Empire Meat Council and International Meat Conference, a complexity which the British had not originally foreseen.[186]

Meanwhile there was an alarming series of events which the British did not believe were accidental. Though they had not accepted the Australian estimates of their shipments for the balance of 1935, the Australians purported to believe that all was well. They had telegraphed Canberra to that effect, and the cable message had been leaked and published in *The Times*. This leak was disastrous for two reasons – it might lead the Australians to ship more meat than the British ministers were willing to absorb, and it would certainly lead the Argentinians to protest. Under the terms of the Anglo-Argentine Agreement, Britain could impose unilateral cuts on Argentine shipments up to 10 per cent of the Ottawa base year, but only if other imports did not increase to fill the hole thereby created. This cut had been imposed, but in the third quarter Australia proposed to ship so much chilled beef that the terms of the agreement would certainly be broken. Early in July, the Foreign Office informed the Argentine Embassy that if the shipments actually occurred, and if the Argentine should then claim that the British now had no right to impose a cut, Britain would not contest the claim.[187]

Nor did she. Later in 1935, Australian chilled-beef shipments became so large that they could not possibly be called experimental. Britain then removed the 10 per cent cut in the Argentine chilled-beef quota.

In 1936, the basic problem was settled when the Antipodes and the UK were able to agree on a structure of beef duties which Argentina would tolerate. We have already examined this process of bargaining and concession. However, even after 4 May there remained problems about the working of the International Beef Conference and Empire Beef Council – bodies on which Chamberlain's heart was still set. Chamberlain and Malcolm MacDonald, the new Dominions Secretary, both had reservations on the subject of commodity control. The former feared a deluge of home-produced beef, and the latter suspected that the Meat Conference would break down. In 1935, Australia had accepted voluntary quotas and then failed to abide by them. Admittedly, she now had a Meat Board. But was her will any stronger than before? Argentina too was known to fear that she and Australia would fall out. And New Zealand was strongly opposed to the proposed conference. Perhaps there should be a special excess levy on meat in excess of agreed quotas. Certainly there should be guidelines for the conference, at least at first.[188] To keep the Australians happy, the Committee agreed that the conference should not be set totally free, at least at first: Australia could have a guaranteed quota for no more than two years.

Meanwhile, the question of quotas had reached the full Cabinet. On 27 May, the Prime Minister reported that there was a deadlock between Chamberlain and Elliot about the amount of subsidy. This deadlock was holding up the work of the committee, and delaying negotiations with Argentina and the Dominions. A special committee was set up, and on 10 June the Cabinet accepted its recommendations:[189] a £5 million subsidy, with provision for reductions if the price of beef should rise above 44s. 6d. per cwt. The target return was agreed to be 42s. 6d. per cwt. Chamberlain himself accepted these recommendations, thinking them wise and sensible. He must also have rejoiced in the following endorsement of quantitative control:

'We have always contemplated that in the event of a breakdown of the International Meat Conference the U.K. would be free to take whatever measures were necessary to safeguard the situation. We have, however, recognised that it was desirable to avoid making any express provision to this effect. . . .'[190]

'The Minister of Agriculture and Fisheries . . . agreed with this view. Our policy should be to strengthen as much as possible the responsibility of the International Meat Conference, so as not to encourage one party or the other to aim at a breakdown. Any public statement ought to be as guarded as possible.'[191]

Malcolm MacDonald was presumably not so pleased. There was still the strong likelihood that the Dominions would not play the conference game. However, by interchange of letters he eventually clarified the situation – though only after the agreements were duly accepted on all sides.

But there was one more hurdle to be cleared. Australia would not accept the two-year guarantee of her sales which the Committee had authorised on 12 June. She insisted on a three-year guarantee, and on some provision for the growth of her sales at the expense of foreign sales. At this point, for the first time, the Australian trade-diversion policy enters the picture. Malcolm MacDonald, in urging the Committee to compromise with the Australians, drew their attention to this policy. It would, he said, increase British textile exports at the expense of Japanese. But the

Australian Government might be unable to carry the needed tariff adjustments through Parliament unless it could show a British concession on the meat front. 'Mr Menzies had told him (MacDonald) at their last interview that even a very small concession would help Australian Ministers greatly. He, Mr MacDonald, thought that, for the sake of our textile trade, we ought to make such a modification.'[192] After others had suggested that the Argentine would probably give way, and that New Zealand would probably accept whatever was decided, the Committee agreed to offer the Australians the desired concessions.[193]

There followed months of anxious negotiations with the Dominions and the Argentine. Neither South Africa nor Canada wanted any part of the Beef Conference. In July, a British agricultural official suggested that Britain herself should handle the allocations for the 'small suppliers', thus allowing these two Dominions to abstain.[194] New Zealand, however, shortly refused to take part, and had to be talked and threatened into acquiescence: MacDonald and Runciman explained that if New Zealand did not agree, the UK herself would impose quotas, which would be no better than the conference terms.[195] New Zealand then agreed to join, but, like Australia, whose shipments she feared, continued to insist upon the need for a 'guaranteed' starting point.[196] Argentina eventually accepted the duty, and the possibility of a 5 per cent cut in her chilled-beef allowables, but insisted on a guarantee with respect to her shipments of frozen mutton and lamb. Runciman thought their request was justified:

'There is no effective limit to what the Dominions expect in beef, and presumably also in mutton. The issue raised in these discussions goes to the root of the Government's policy and calls in question the principles on which is based the System of Trade Agreements which we have built up laboriously and to which we have committed this country during the past five years. If this system is now to be interrupted rudely in order to satisfy demands made by a section of our supporters in the House of Commons, we shall have to review and restate our attitude to foreign trade, and at the same time surrender much of what by this policy we have already gained.'[197]

When the Cabinet came to discuss the Argentine negotiations, Morrison and Elliot predictably spoke up for the home producer: only by constricting Dominion and foreign sheepmeat could domestic output rise. If this rise is prevented, can deficiency payments long be avoided? And how can the Dominions be made to acquiesce in such a guarantee? Nevertheless, the Cabinet decided to approve the draft agreement while hoping that the relevant clause could be modified or evaded.[198] And in the end, Argentina did accept a new trade agreement which ensured there would be no special cuts in the first year – beyond the 5 per cent cut in her chilled-beef allowables – and no more than specified minimum cuts in the second and third years.[199] At long last, on 3 December, the final quota scheme was ready.[200]

Under the three-year agreement of 1936, the Argentinians were to pay duties on their chilled beef, and also were to restrict sales. However, the restrictions, which were based on 1935 shipments, were not large – no more than 2 per cent in 1937, and no more than 5 per cent in 1939. Frozen beef and pork were to be kept at the 1935 levels; offals and canned beef were to be slightly reduced, and mutton and lamb shipments by 10 per cent in 1938.

But matters did not go well. Because of the disputes between Australia and New Zealand, the Council was unable to agree on mutton and lamb quotas for 1939. Faced with growing home production and extremely unfavourable prices, the UK Government itself imposed quota reductions, which kept the Dominions' shipments well below the 1938 levels. Hence in the case of mutton and lamb, the eventual abdication of British authority was only temporary, and was even more unreal for sheepmeat than for beef.

Thus the final arrangement differed from the 'Eighth Draft' in several respects. It imposed no duty on Dominion producers. It provided for a small reduction in foreign supplies so as to make room for the growth of Dominion supplies. And it made special provision for Canadian live cattle and South African chilled beef. These differences and other minor divergences reflected the second thoughts of the Dominions, the Committee decisions of 24 June, and the outcome of the Argentine negotiations.[201] Thus, for instance, Australian reservations led to the elimination of the 'penalty clause' – a special excess duty on over–quota shipments.[202] Canadian constitutional problems led to a special arrangement for 'small suppliers'. Violent Australian and New Zealand pressure led the UK to guarantee a rising share of Empire meat in her total imports,[203] at least during the transitional period while the Council and Conference were deciding how much to allow each supplier.

From the British viewpoint, this devolution of authority was one of the most attractive aspects of the proposals.[204] Though concerned with total shipments, Britain would no longer have to allocate quotas among suppliers. And the joint impact of tariff and subsidy would help her own producers. But it remained to be seen whether the Conference system was workable, or whether the potential members would work it. New Zealand was strongly opposed,[205] but finally, 'not without misgivings', agreed to join in;[206] their exports were handled by the reservation of an aggregate quota for 'small exporters'.[207]

Indeed, the whole beef scheme nearly came to grief on Canadian opposition. The question of meat was also critical for the early progress of the Anglo-Canadian trade talks of 1936. As the negotiations progressed, meat came to seem ever more critical – especially to Charles Dunning, the Canadian Minister of Finance, who led the Canadian negotiating team.

The reader will remember that the tariff had been the major issue in Canadian federal politics for more than half a century. In 1930, the Liberal Party lost office just after Dunning had brought down a budget which gave larger unilateral preferences to the UK. Its successor, Bennett's Conservative Party, won office largely on a platform of protectionism, and perhaps partly on Bennett's pledge to use the Canadian tariff to 'blast his way into world markets'. In opposition, the Liberal leader, William Lyon Mackenzie

King, violently attacked both the details and the broad sweep of Bennett's tariff arrangements, especially the Ottawa Agreements themselves. In the 1920s King had extended the margin of British preference, but always unilaterally, by action of the Canadian Parliament, without negotiation and without any permanent commitment. But Ottawa had seen bilateral bargaining, and it had bound the participants to various arrangements for periods of up to five years. King, like Philip Snowden, objected to such agreements because they infringed upon the fiscal sovereignty of parliament. And like other Dominion public figures, he feared that the binding of preferential margins would limit Canada's power to exact concessions from foreign countries: she would be able to give less, and so would get less, in such negotiations – especially with the United States, on which King's eyes were constantly fixed. Further, he and Dunning thought that fixed margins permitted cartels to exploit Canadian consumers. Hence it was not surprising that, in the election campaign of 1935, King attacked the Ottawa arrangements, promising to revise them if he should win. Indeed, some Whitehall officials believed that he proposed to denounce the Agreement and begin again.

On winning power in the election of 1935, King hurried to complete the Canadian-American negotiations which Bennett himself had begun. He returned the finance portfolio to Dunning, and established an elderly protectionist, W. D. Euler, in the Department of Trade and Commerce. Dunning was known to be interested in the development of transatlantic trade; Euler, it was feared, was not. And King's Agriculture Minister, James Gardiner, was a vigorous crusader for the Western farming interest, an interest which, having been prostrated by drought and bad prices, was desperately trying to diversify its production out of wheat and into meat and dairy products.

In fact King did not denounce the Ottawa Agreement. After tentative inquiries from the British representatives in Canada, it was proposed that Dunning, Euler, and Gardiner should visit Britain in the summer of 1936, to undertake a revision of the agreement. Officials were also to be present.[208] On 24 June 1936 the Canadian officials arrived and began to discuss points of detail with their British opposite numbers. The Canadians said they had no ministerial instructions, but they knew they were to oppose fixed preferential margins, and they talked of their troubles in third-country negotiations. Discussion centred upon a British schedule of tariff requests, upon the binding of preferential margins in the Canadian tariff, and upon the British policies of agricultural control. Dunning and Euler first met Runciman and MacDonald on 8 July. In their discussions, they said little about the detailed questions of duties and margins; they were much more concerned with the basic anomaly they thought they detected: Britain, while asking for freer entry to the Canadian market, was trying to reduce Canadian entry to the British market . . . especially with respect to meat. And this, as Dunning repeated until his departure in early August, was not good enough.

At Ottawa, Britain had guaranteed Canada free unrestricted entry for up to 2.5 million cwt. of bacon per year. In fact Canadian shipments had always fallen short of that level: in 1934–35 they were just over one million cwt. But the commitment was embarrassing to the British in their negotiations with other countries: by 1936 they were trying to convince the European suppliers to accept the levy-subsidy principle, combined with quotas, but the Europeans did not really believe that the Canadians would in fact never ship the quantity which they were allowed to ship. Hence the 2.5 million cwt. was a problem for the British, who hoped that the Canadians would accept a quota which would fix their bacon shipments at the recent levels, not at 2.5 million cwt. There was no question of a duty; by this time the British had decided to admit Dominion bacon duty-free. But *any* quota control was anathema to King, whose Government lacked power to impose export quotas, and was not prepared to take such power. And a *smaller* quota was doubly anathema: how could he explain such a shrinkage to the prairie and Ontario farmers?

The beef problem was, of course, similar. Britain hoped that Canada would join the Empire Meat Council and

International Meat Conference. But the Government had ideological objections to such bodies. Further, Dunning pointed out, the basis for regulation was to be 1935 – a year when Canada had shipped abnormally few cattle to the UK. Could Canada not be left out of the regulated scheme? How could her farmers be allowed to expand their exports if such controls were introduced? And what of chilled beef? Canada hoped to enter this trade. But the council and conference would preclude this.[209]

All these new problems must have chilled the hearts of the British negotiators, fresh from a two-year tussle with the Australians. Here was Canada repeating the same demands – the right to expand her shipments of beef. As MacDonald explained to Dunning, he could grant no such concessions; the other Dominions would not stand for them. Elliot was prepared to modify the details of the beef arrangement so as to make them more palatable to Canada. Thus 'recent levels' were substituted for 1935 levels so as to allow the Canadian quota to be based upon the larger shipments of 1934. The UK Government agreed to fix a global quota for 'small suppliers', thus allowing the Canadian Government to avoid the administration of a quota scheme. And to provide for some expansion, it was suggested that the conference should definitely reduce foreign shipments by a definite though small amount in its first few years.

By 23 July, the Canadians were prepared to accept the above scheme so long as they were allowed enough expansion. They wanted the right to increase shipments from 50,000 head per year – the recent levels – to 180,000 per year, without encountering any quota controls.[210] They also wanted unrestricted entry for 'store cattle' – those destined for fattening not for immediate slaughter. The British were quite willing to concede the latter demand, but the former was impossible. Though they did not tell the Canadians so, they obviously knew that the Australians and Argentinians would never tolerate any such rate of increase. The result was a deadlock: 'Mr Dunning said that the Canadian Ministers could not accept the proposals at the present moment and could only communicate them to their colleagues as the furthest limit to which the United Kingdom could go.'[211] And on 6 August, when Dunning was handed a memorandum on the cattle proposals, he was no more hopeful:

'He himself did not see any basis of approach to a solution of the problem. The general difficulty remained that the United Kingdom desired greater access to the Canadian market but it was very difficult for the Canadian Government to meet the U.K. to the extent which they would wish if the United Kingdom Government on their side restricted Canada's access to the United Kingdom market. In the case of cattle there had hitherto been no restriction (since 1932) and the principle of restriction was now being introduced . . . the difficulties in the way of agreement were greater on the agricultural side than he had expected when he arrived. . . .'[212]

And so Dunning and his colleagues went home. But negotiations were not broken off. The officials remained until 20 August, discussing the detailed changes in the Canadian tariff. It was expected that there would be further discussions in Canada – either with a British Cabinet Minister or with the British High Commissioner, Sir Francis Floud. Further, though the Canadians had gone away unhappy, they had in fact achieved a good deal. The British had agreed to retain the 2.5 million cwt. of bacon, so long as expansion to that total was steady and not excessively rapid. They had also agreed that the Canadians could have much more flexibility in the fixing of preferential margins. While the British negotiators did wish to retain 'bound margins' on ninety-three tariff items they were prepared to contemplate a marked retrogression from the Ottawa rigidity. And they had agreed to remove the 'tariff board clauses'. These were of little use in any event, and as the Canadians thought they smelt of 'capitulations' the British were quite prepared to see them go.[213] They were also prepared to insert a 'cartel clause', by which the Canadian Government would have the right to unfreeze preferential margins when these margins had been shown to protect some international cartel scheme. Further, the Canadian officials had conceded many, though not all, of the British requests for tariff-cuts. Thus when the officials initialled a tentative draft agreement on 20 August, it was possible for both sides to believe the bargain a good one. However, it remained to be seen what the Canadian Cabinet – and especially Mackenzie King – would do.

At his departure, Dunning doubted that an agreement could be concluded.[214] Though discouraged, however, he was not prepared to give up. He would not commend the agreement to his Cabinet colleagues – or even let them see the draft – until he was satisfied about the form and content of the 'reservation clause' which would allow the British to regulate the Canadian fatstock trade. He had already been obliged to give up on butter and cheese: as the British reconstruction commission on the milk industry had not reported by late August, the British were obliged to insist on their *right* to tax butter and cheese. They could not guarantee free entry, though, as MacDonald had explained to Dunning, nothing could conceivably happen until July 1937 in any event.[215] Anyway, as the Ottawa Agreements already gave the UK power to impose duties or quotas on both products, no point of principle was involved: there would be no agreed retreat from freedom of trade if the Ottawa provision were simply repeated. But for cattle the situation was different, and Dunning obviously expected trouble in Cabinet – especially from his redoubtable but somewhat theoretical Prime Minister. The agreement would certainly annoy King in so far as it retained some rigidity of preferential margins. If it also restricted meat exports too visibly, it would draw a fire both theoretical and electoral.

What could be done? King had gone to Europe to travel and orate in the cause of peace and brotherhood. For the moment he was not thinking of trade. But he would return via London, and so could perhaps be consulted. Back in Ottawa, Dunning was keeping his own counsel; he would not show the draft agreement to his colleagues until he could commend it *in toto*, and this he could not do until a suitable 'reservation formula' had been invented for beef.

Unwilling to see the negotiations fail, in early September he proposed a formula to Sir Francis Floud, with whom he had systematically discussed the problem. Dunning's device was to avoid a quota in the agreement itself while including a clause which would allow either partner to impose quotas on any product in certain circumstances.[216]

In London, an interdepartmental committee rendered Dunning's idea into the following draft:

'It is understood that nothing in this agreement prejudices the right of either country to regulate the imports of any agricultural product from the other country when such regulation applies generally to imports of that product and is deemed necessary for the successful functioning of a scheme regulating supplies of that product on the markets of the importing country. Before introducing any such regulation, the government concerned would consult the other government with a view to avoiding interference with the normal development of trade.'[217]

The committee members believed that this clause would pacify the other Dominions while in fact allowing Canada power to expand her shipments considerably; they expected that most of her exportable surplus would go to the USA under the terms of the 1935 Canadian-American Trade Agreement, and that the 'small country' provisions in the new meat scheme would accommodate whatever relatively small quantities Canada might ship to the UK. Only if Canada proposed to sell abnormally large amounts, or if the Meat Council broke down, would the clause become relevant.

The proposal passed to Floud, who discussed it with Dunning. Still jibbing at certain details, Dunning proposed variations which were explored and rejected via the transatlantic cable.[218] Though still unhappy at the result, at length he agreed that the formula should be offered to King on his passage through London.

King saw the critical words on 20 October. Though non-committal, he showed signs of wanting a quick settlement, and the British thought that all was well. There then occurred an unfortunate confusion. King and O. D. Skelton professed to believe that in offering this perfectly general formula, which had been specifically devised to cope with the Canadians' philosophical objections on the meat question, the British had at first offered to withdraw a particular reservation – the right to impose duties or quotas on the goods which had been listed in Schedule A of the Ottawa Agreements. This list included dairy products, on which the British were not prepared to waive their rights. They tried to explain to King that they had long since clarified this matter with Dunning. But Dunning had not been briefing his Prime Minister, and Skelton appears to have misunderstood a remark of Malcolm MacDonald.

When King sailed for Canada on 31 October, he had still not agreed to the reservation formula; at his departure, he said that he would prefer a specific beef clause, not a general reservation clause. Not until 13 November did he accept a formula which was also acceptable to the British.[219] Thus patient negotiating and endless drafting had removed the last obstacles to the British beef scheme. The Council and Conference could begin to function; with any luck the British civil servants would soon be free of the agonising and continuous disputes over meat allocations.[220] The preliminary work had gone on, in the expectation that Canada would settle eventually; thus the relevant statutes were in draft, and procedural discussions had gone a long way by mid-November. The final Anglo-Canadian Trade Agreement, signed early in 1937, incorporated a formula with which Canada and the UK could jointly live.[221] The clause related only to meat. Under it, Britain promised free entry to Canadian beef and cattle, guaranteed that she would not restrict Canadian shipments below 'recent levels', promised to restrict Canadian beef only if an effective general scheme could not otherwise be worked, and agreed to represent Canadian interests in any international meat conference.

The Beef Council and Conference began to function informally in January 1937, and continued to operate until the outbreak of war. In their early months, Malcolm MacDonald explained the British attitude to the Dominions: the UK would itself regulate beef-import only in response to a Conference decision, a request from a Dominion, or a breakdown in the Conference. Australia, New Zealand, and South Africa recorded their understanding of this position, and assented to it.[222] During 1937 and 1938, the Council and Conference had no trouble agreeing on beef quotas, because British production was falling and British consumption was rising. As the Australian Meat Board happily reported, 'our estimates have always up to the present been accepted by the Conference'.[223] Thus with respect to beef, MacDonald's forebodings had not been justified: the market situation permitted the selling countries to regulate meat shipments with some semblance of amity.

With respect to lamb and mutton, the position was different. It will be remembered that both these meats were eventually excluded from the Conference scheme, because the Australians and New Zealanders wished to negotiate directly with Britain. In 1937 these arrangements continued: foreign shipments were held at 65 per cent of the Ottawa-year shipments, and Antipodean shipments at their 1936 levels.[224] But in the autumn of 1937, largely because of a rising domestic production, British lamb and mutton prices began to fall. Hence quotas were reduced in 1938, in an effort to keep total Dominion shipments at the 1937 level. No duty could be imposed, because of the new Anglo-Argentine Agreement. In any event, the British argued, a duty on foreign sheepmeat would not help British producers because foreign supplies were so small! Accordingly, stiffer regulation was needed.

The British ministers however had always intended to devolve sheepmeat on to the Conference. On 4 October 1938 the Dominions Office proposed to Australia and New Zealand that she turn over mutton and lamb regulation to an international commodity council – perhaps the International Beef Conference and Empire Beef Council.[225] Australia agreed that the Empire Beef Council could become an EMC. New Zealand pointed out that *her* shipments were still well below the Ottawa standard year, 1931–32; it was Australia, whose shipments had risen by almost one-third, who was to blame for the break in lamb prices. Hence she rejected the UK's proposal. As before, she preferred to deal direct with the UK Government – not with a commodity council, whatever its name.[226]

New Zealand's awkward behaviour was discussed at the Cabinet's Agricultural Policy Committee, to whom the Cabinet had referred it, on 14 December. W. E. Morrison, the Minister of Agriculture, asked for an Order, under the 1937 Livestock Industry Act, which would impose quotas on the two Australasian Dominions. What worried him was the low and falling price for domestic sheepmeat; he was not impressed by his colleagues, who argued that there was little relation between the supply of frozen sheepmeat and the price of fresh lamb or mutton. He was also sceptical of the voluntary principle in regulation:

'Since June, 1934 efforts had been made to deal with the problem by the system of input allocation . . . this system had, in fact, served no useful purpose. As the allocations figures had never referred to realities and were never in practice realised . . . New Zealand's unwillingness to accept our proposals was no doubt due in large measure to her distrust of the policy and intentions of the Commonwealth Government (Australia) in this matter'[227]

Swayed by MacDonald's suggestion that New Zealand might be reasonable if she saw that the UK meant business, the committee determined to make an Order if necessary, but to give New Zealand one last chance to see reason. As the Cabinet had authorised the committee to decide the matter without further reference to itself, a telegram could immediately be sent – and was. New Zealand did eventually give in, but most reluctantly.[228]

But matters did not go well. Because of the disputes between Australia and New Zealand, the Council was unable to agree on mutton and lamb quotas for 1939. Faced with growing home production and extremely unfavourable prices, the UK itself imposed quota reductions, which kept the Dominions' shipments well below the 1938 levels.[229] Hence in the case of mutton and lamb, the eventual abdication of British authority was only temporary, and was even more unreal for sheepmeat than for beef.

Chapter 8

OTTAWA AFTERMATH: TARIFF BOARDS, DOMESTIC COMPETITION, AND TRADE DIVERSION, 1932–1939

We have already traced the steps by which the UK delegation convinced itself that it should ask the Dominions and India to make long-term commitments with respect to tariff policy. Certain special duties were to be removed when the Dominions could afford to sacrifice the revenue. But more important, the Dominions were to grant new protection only to plausible industries, and they were to admit British goods on terms which would equalise competitive conditions between British and Dominion producers. That is, British exporters were to be 'domestic competitors' in the Dominion markets. Dominion Tariff Boards were to take tariff-fixing out of politics; British exporters were to have right of audience before these boards.

South Africa refused to countenance these requests. India deferred action on them. But the other three Dominions accepted formularies which satisfied the UK ministers. The results are enshrined in the various Ottawa Agreements. New Zealand, Canada, and Australia promised to protect 'only . . . those industries which are reasonably assured of sound opportunities for success'.[1] New Zealand promised 'to institute an inquiry into the existing protective duties and where necessary to reduce them as speedily as possible to such a level as will place the UK producer in the position of a domestic competitor'.[2] British producers could place their views before this *ad hoc* tribunal.[3] Australia promised to submit all existing protective duties to the Tariff Board, and to ask the Australian parliament to fix duties in accordance with the Board's recommendations; the Australian Government agreed that 'during the currency of this agreement the tariff shall be based upon the principle that protective duties shall not exceed such a level as will give UK producers full opportunity of reasonable competition on the basis of the relative cost of economical and efficient production'. British producers were guaranteed rights of audience before the Tariff Board.[4] Canada promised to set up the Tariff Board for which the Tariff Board Act, 1931, had provided, and to grant British exporters right of audience; she undertook that no duty on British goods should be increased except after a Tariff Board inquiry, and in accordance with its report; she promised to fix duties on the basis of 'full opportunity of reasonable competition on the basis of the relative cost of economical and efficient production'; she agreed that the Tariff Board would undertake inquiries as to duties in the light of this principle on the request of the British Government, and that the Canadian Parliament should be invited to legislate in conformity with the results of any such inquiries.[5]

Because of these commitments, Chamberlain and others were later to argue that the Agreements represented a commitment to gradual tariff reduction. Indeed, given the Dominions' commitment to protectionism, they must have seemed a great achievement. The Dominions, it seemed, had promised to restrain their protectionist tendencies. No nearer approach to Empire Free Trade could be imagined.

Unfortunately, the Articles were full of evasions and vaguenesses. Everything would depend upon the behaviour of the Dominion governments, and upon their tariff tribunals. What was 'reasonable competition'? Which industries were fully established? Which production was 'economical and efficient'? Which industries had 'a reasonable chance of success'?

Better drafting would not have solved the problem. If anyone had pressed for more definite commitments, the Dominion leaders would almost certainly have rejected the Articles, which were tolerable only because of their vagueness. Furthermore, and more fundamentally, on such topics there is no way to avoid vagueness altogether. It is inherently impossible for the participants to make firm and definite commitments.

In this chapter, we trace the British efforts to make the Articles effective, the Dominions' evasions, and the eventual abandonment of principle and practice during 1936–39. We look first at Australia - the Dominion whose trade policies most worried the British Government.

I. AUSTRALIA

On his return from Ottawa, Sir Henry Gullett explained his Government's aims, achievements, and negotiating procedures. Having outlined the pre-conference discussions in Melbourne, he faced the problem of the Australian Government's domestic pledge – not to change *protective* tariffs without reference to the Tariff Board. The Australian Cabinet, he explained, had decided before Ottawa to refer all British requests to the Board whenever a protective tariff was in question. The 'formula', which was offered before Ottawa and made more generous at the conference itself, applied only to the revenue duties. Gullett argued that in accepting Articles 9 to 12 the delegation was completely consistent with the previously-announced tariff policy. Since it was impossible for the Australians to give anything with respect to their protective tariff, the explicit commitment was a necessary *quid pro quo*; it was accepted because the UK had undertaken certain immediate burdens with respect to butter, cheese, meat, and minor foodstuffs.[6]

In the light of this speech, one might have expected the Australian Government manfully to accept its commitments and to act in accordance with them. But it did not do so.

The first and most important problem was the Tariff Board. This body, created in 1921, advised the Australian Government on protective tariffs. Its normal tendency had been to grant whatever protective margin an Australian manufacturer might demand regardless of the basic viability of his industry or firm. These tendencies were understandably strengthened in the depth of the Depression; though the sharp tariff increases of the Scullin Government had not been suggested by the Board, and though the Lyons Government was committed to tariff reduction, the Tariff Board could hardly ignore the employment effects of any tariff cuts. And its membership and staff had changed little since the 1920s. The British authorities hoped that the Australian Government would instruct the Tariff Board to make its rulings on the 'equal competition' basis. They expected that items on which the Tariff Board had already pronounced would be re-referred to the Board, so that protective margins could be re-examined in light of the Ottawa Agreements.

The first shock came early in 1933. When introducing a new tariff structure which embodied the obligatory parts of the Ottawa Agreement, and made certain additional concessions to British goods, the Australian Government argued that the Tariff Board decisions of the preceding three years had been made on criteria which were in line with the Ottawa Agreement. This was the Board's own claim[7] but it was not Britain's understanding. The Commonwealth Government was also laggard in removing some of the customs surcharges, even though it ran a budget surplus in 1932–33. The British naturally suspected that the remaining surcharges had been retained on a selective basis for the sake of protection, not revenue. By mid-June, the British representatives in Australia were convinced that the Agreement was not being carried out in good faith, in spite of the numerous cuts of the spring tariff bill. Part of the trouble, they thought, was the Government's tendency to construe the Agreement very literally. As Bruce was absent in London, and Gullett was ill and out of the Cabinet, there was no one to tell the Australian ministers what the text, and the subsidiary understandings, actually meant. Hence they urged 'a quick formal protest of a general nature, followed by circumstantial representations to Bruce.'[8]

Bruce, the resident Minister in London, was presented with the British objections in an *aide-mémoire* in August. This was a forceful and angry document. It complained of Australian failure to implement many commitments which had been made outside the Agreement itself. These commitments, relating chiefly to Australia's 'deferred' duties and 'bylaw' duties, had been made by Sir Henry Gullett on 22 August 1932; the Australian Government was now refusing to admit them. Further, it was ignoring Tariff Board recommendations, imposing duties without consulting the Tariff Board, and retaining certain temporary duties in a fashion that implied protection in contravention of the Agreement. Finally, it was not answering London's enquiries.[9] Bruce did not refer this document to the Australian Government because he thought that its tone might prejudice the concessions which he knew were to be offered to the UK in the forthcoming Australian budget.[10] Indeed the budget, as announced on 4 October 1933, did contain some useful tariff reductions, and did introduce some new preferences.

However, at the same time the Tariff Board issued its annual report for 1932–33. And its words scared the British considerably. The Board interpreted the Ottawa Agreement to mean that a 'reasonable' duty under Article 10 should yield a price which would compensate for higher Australian costs and provide a 'margin advantage' as well. The British had no quarrel with the compensation, but they regarded this additional margin as unacceptable. According to the Board, the margin was to be 'wide enough to secure Australian manufacturers so much of the market as is represented by goods which can be economically produced in Australia but narrow enough to preclude any inefficiency, uneconomic extension, or undue profit-taking'.

After anxious telegraphic consultation, a formal protest was presented to the Australian Government on 7 November 1933.[11] The protest pointed out that the Tariff Board's interpretation would allow the Australians to exclude UK goods whenever Australian factories could supply the local demand; it would also prevent the UK manufacturer from competing on an equal basis. The Australian Government responded that they did not think Article 10 meant to remove all protection. On this point they were of course in agreement with the British, who accepted the idea of offsetting protection. However, the Australians used this argument to justify their acceptance of the Board's interpretation – in spite of the fact, probably unknown to them, that Bruce himself accepted the British interpretation.[12] On 17 February 1934, Runciman and Thomas asked Bruce to do something about 'the determination of the Australian Tariff Board to exclude the UK from the Benefits of Article X', Runciman reports. 'Apparently Mr Bruce's personal views were the same as ours, but he was careful to say that he would only use his powers of persuasion with his Government and could not commit them to any interpretation of Article X except that which had been officially accepted by Australia on the inspiration and dictum of the Tariff Board.'[13]

The discussions continued through 1934. In their course, the British representatives learned from Prime Minister Lyons that the Tariff Board had in fact recommended numerous tariff-cuts which the Government had not introduced. Its reason was the coming election.[14] On the other hand, the Australian Country Party was pressing hard for tariff cuts. But the discussions did not bring the Australian position nearer to the British. In October, a Whitehall official noted: 'there appears to be only one alternative to a complete deadlock and that is that the Commonwealth Government while not openly receding from their position, should ensure that in practice full effect is given to the provisions of the Article.'[15] But this did not happen. In 1935, Richard Casey, apparently to his surprise, found the British still annoyed about Article 10. And at last, in 1938, when the Australian-British agreement was renegotiated, the British acquiesced in the Australian interpretation.

To an unknown extent the Australian intransigence may have been influenced by the negotiations over meat and butter which began in 1933. The official correspondence contains no hint of any link; we do not find the Australians saying that they would give way on Article 10 if only the British would give them unrestricted access to the British meat and butter markets. Nor is there any sign that the British negotiators linked the two matters. To them, Article 10 had been given in exchange for concessions which were actually in the Ottawa Agreement itself; they seem to have seen no reason to make further concessions as a price for the proper enforcement of the Article. Rather the reverse – in 1935, at least, the British resisted meat and butter concessions because the Australians had not carried out Article 10. Nor did the Australian position become less intransigent when, in 1935–36, they virtually got their own way on the meat and butter fronts. Hence it is hard to see this wrangle as simply a bargaining matter; it seems to have reflected a real difference in interpretation. And this is hardly surprising. Article 10 was very loosely drafted. Indeed, given the nature of the concession it proposed to grant, and the procedure it wished to encourage, it could hardly have been anything else. The idea of a cost-offsetting tariff is inherently ambiguous. Whose costs are measured and at what level of output? After how long? At what exchange rate? Through these gaps the Australian Tariff Board had no difficulty in navigating its protectionist ship.

In 1935, when Lyons, Gullett, and Menzies came to London for the meat talks the UK ministers decided to seize the opportunity and discuss other aspects of the Ottawa Agreement. Though satisfied that Australia had quickly given the contractual margins of preference, they were far from satisfied about Article 10. They wanted to discuss the duty on galvanised iron, and they hoped for the complete removal of primage duty on UK goods. They also intended to press for the restoration of 'bylaw' treatment in certain cases, and for the complete removal of duties. All these things, they thought, Australia had promised to perform in 1932.

Runciman and Gullett first spoke of Article 10, the 'reasonable competition' article, on 28 March. The two men made position speeches but did not really discuss the issue. Gullett was given an *aide-mémoire*, and went away to think about it.[16] On 1 May, he responded in a voluminous and largely irrelevant memorandum which simply rejected the UK's contention. Apparently Britain's overseas representatives were wrong in believing that Gullett wanted to honour his Ottawa commitments.[17] Or perhaps he was overruled by his cabinet colleagues. He now claimed that

'the Australian delegation at Ottawa definitely rejected the "domestic competition" principle. . . . The Australian delegation had believed they were incorporating in the Agreement the pre-election tariff policy enunciated by Mr Lyons before the 1931 election. . . . Had Article 10 intended to establish the principle of placing United Kingdom producers in the position of domestic competitors . . . the Article would have been worded in an entirely different manner. . . . The grant of a marginal advantage is inseparable from any policy of according industry protection by means of a tariff . . . equalising duties can only result in increased costs to consumers.'

The delegation then repeated the Tariff Board argument, with which the British were of course familiar, and went on to claim that Australia's *total* tariff policy suggested they were in fact acting 'on the principle of the grant of reasonably protective duties . . . protective as distinct from prohibitive. . . .'[18]

The Australian contentions, though supported by their own Tariff Board, now look nonsensical. It is not true that a 'protective margin' is needed for effective protection. *Any* tariff provides such protection to some extent; if the Australian tariff were sufficiently high to raise the landed price of British goods above the long-run marginal cost of Australian production, the Australians would eventually have the whole market, and Britain would sell nothing in Australia. This was, perhaps, what the Tariff Board intended. Australian producers were to *raise* their output, and their share of the domestic market. Obviously this increase would be at British expense. As for the increased-consumer-cost proposition, it was not quite nonsense, but it verged upon the dishonest. Let us suppose that in Australian manufacturing there were economies of large-scale production. By giving domestic producers a larger share of the market, the Board would enable the producers to exploit these economies, lowering the domestic *cost of production*. But the price to consumers would not necessarily fall unless the Government were *then* to lower the tariff – that is, once the Australian manufacturers had expanded. The British Government had no reason to expect this would happen, and Australian ministers never claimed that it was their policy. In effect, Australia was asking Britain to acquiesce in indefinite protection at a level higher than Bruce and Gullett had promised, or Britain had expected, at Ottawa. In stating that the Ottawa commitments merely clarified their own election promises, they were being consistent with the stance they had taken at home. But they can hardly have expected the British negotiators to sympathise. From Britain's standpoint, the Australian commitments had been an *additional quid pro quo*, in exchange for which Britain had continued free entry, raised the duties on foreign dairy products, and restricted Argentine meat shipments. If Australia would have done the same things without an agreement, to what end had Britain made any concessions?

Following further discussion, the Australians and the British agreed on the following formula: 'In the understanding of the Commonwealth Government the application to United Kingdom goods of the protective tariff principles embodied in the Agreement should result in the establishment of a competitive as distinct from a prohibitive tariff level.'[19] Runciman and Gullett agreed on this terminology. They also decided that any public statement about the matter should be based on it. The Australians made conciliatory – though partly insincere – noises and semi-commitments about the other British complaints.

In the event, the formula remained secret. The British hoped that the Australians would review the Tariff Board decisions of 1932–35, to make sure that these were consistent with it. This was not done. In July 1936, the Board of Trade reported that these Board recommendations were still in force, even though the Australians had agreed that they breached the Ottawa Agreement.[20]

In 1936, as in earlier years, the Australians were asking the British to allow some narrowing of preferential margins. Wishing to negotiate with foreign countries, Australian ministers complained that the Ottawa Agreement left them with little or nothing to give, because on so many goods the preferential margins were 'bound by formula'.[21] Britain had already given way to some extent, though not to the full extent that the Australians hoped.[22] The Australian request, however, was disingenuous, as the 'problem was entirely of their own making.' As Britain's trade commissioner had reported late in 1932: 'It has been arranged between us [Gullett, Abbott, and Dalton] before leaving Ottawa that we should prepare together a draft of the new tariff to be introduced in the House of Parliament as a schedule to the Ottawa Agreement. In fact this draft was ready for the printers on our arrival in Sydney.' This draft was a three-column tariff. Such a plan would have allowed the Australian Government to concede any foreign government the *intermediate* tariff rates, while safeguarding the Agreement's margin between the intermediate and preferential scales. However, the Australian Cabinet, considering the schedule in Gullet's absence, abolished the intermediate column.[23] It was this action, not the Agreements, which constricted Australia's power to negotiate.

What could be done? Sir Earle Page thought that Britain should bargain on Australia's behalf, seeking concessions for the Dominion in such third countries as Germany. He was told bluntly that for political and economic reasons this was impossible.[24] Since Australia's own performance was so far from the terms of the Agreement, it is hardly surprising that British ministers refused to squander their scarce negotiating powers on her behalf.

By means of a 'trade diversion policy', Australia had enormously compounded her negotiating difficulties. In effect, her 1936 requests were related to the storm which this ill-conceived policy was already bringing down on Canberra's collective head.

The first hint of trade diversion had been dropped in 1934. Prime Minister Lyons then cabled to London that he proposed to open trade negotiations with the United States. He hoped to reduce or end the large passive balance in Australian–American trade. If bilateral negotiations were not possible, he hoped for a tripartite balancing agreement, where Britain would join Australia and the USA. Lyons said:

'If the U.S. is not prepared to accede to our request, His

Majesty's Government in Australia proposed to consider means by which existing export trade from the U.S. to Australia could be repartitioned among other countries as to ensure Australia's export trade against further restriction and to create atmosphere favourable to reopening of markets to meat and butter.'[25]

Lyons was, in other words, linking trade diversion with free and unrestricted entry to the UK market. And he was asking for British help in negotiations with third countries.

British representatives quickly supplied the background to these proposals. As Crutchley wrote,

'the source . . . was an impetuous young assistant secretary in Department of Commerce called Murphy . . . His Minister and the Minister of Customs have passed them without further Departmental advice and the Prime Minister has signed a letter embodying them, apparently quite blindly, and has dispatched it to the U.S. Consul General, asking him to cable summary to Washington immediately. . . . The Cabinet have not considered the matter. I have been shown most confidentially a copy of the letter. The requests are ludicrous. . . .'[26]

In Washington, the British Ambassador believed that the Australians thought the American drought would occasion a food shortage, giving them a market in the United States which might absorb the export surpluses which the British might not indefinitely buy.[27]

In several respects these proposals were obviously grossly unrealistic. First of all, Cordell Hull was known to oppose all bilateral payments agreements. Secondly, the American food problem was known to be one of surplus not shortage. Thirdly, a tripartite payments agreement would almost certainly have defied the negotiating powers of Metternich himself. Nevertheless, the Australians actually persisted with their idea.[28] Returning to London from Australia, Bruce visited Washington and put the scheme to the officials there. His meat, butter and wool requests were politely rejected, but he advised his home government to keep on trying. On reaching London, he told the Board of Trade officials that there was no chance of a trade agreement. And he was right: the Americans finally rejected the proposals in January 1935.[29]

From other evidence we know that Prime Minister Lyons and Sir Earle Page were also hoping to offload their agricultural surpluses in Europe. Though these had never taken any significant quality of Australian primary products, the Australians blamed them for the collapse in butter prices, and for the failure of meat prices to rise conveniently. We do not know precisely why Australia was so interested in the securing of bilateral balances. Admittedly her overall payments position was far from strong. Probably, too, she was exposed to pressure from foreign countries with which she ran trading surpluses. There is some evidence to suggest that some public figures believed bilateral balancing would open new vents for Australian produce.

Whatever the reasoning, however, it is really extraordinary that the Australian Government should have thought it could enrol the British Government to fight for an Australian bilateral-balancing scheme. Admittedly, the UK had entered into some payments agreements, most noticeably with Argentina and with several continental countries. But both Runciman and Chamberlain were known to dislike them; they, and other ministers, accepted such schemes only when compelled to do so. And it is hard to see why the Australian Government could have thought that the British would dissipate their own limited bargaining power mainly to negotiate entry for Australian primary products–especially as the Australian Government itself was not granting UK goods the Australian opportunities to which Whitehall believed the Ottawa Agreement entitled them. No wonder Lyons received a dusty answer from London. Britain, he was told, would be glad to help with third-country negotiations, but probably could not exert much pressure without sacrificing her own trading interests. As for quotas, the Australians were welcome to invent whatever schemes they liked, so long as they safeguarded the British position under the Ottawa Agreement. The telegram also reminded Lyons that as yet his Government had not answered Whitehall's repeated queries about the operation of Article 10.[30]

Early in 1936, Sir Henry Gullett again raised with the American Consul-General the question of an American–Australian trade agreement. Again he was rebuffed.[31] As the payments position and the bilateral imbalances still worried him, and as meat restriction and butter restriction were still very much on the Imperial horizon, he began to germinate a scheme. Australia should restrict total imports so as to rebuild her sterling balances. If a Labour government should come to power and find small sterling balances, it would default, thus destroying confidence and breaking up the British Empire. More Australian demand should be met from Australian production, and more importation should come from Australia's good customers. There should be a bounty and quota scheme for motor engines and chassis, so that Australia could become more self-sufficient in motor cars, thus saving foreign exchange and hurting the Americans, who refused to buy Australian primary products and who sold to Australia far more than they bought from Australia.

Thus Gullett explained matters to Sir Geoffrey Whiskard in late April 1936, before the Australian Cabinet had considered the trade diversion scheme. It is reasonably clear that the push came from Gullett himself, and that he or his staff were responsible for such characteristic devices as the bounty quota scheme for cars.[32]

A few weeks later, after the scheme had been announced, Whiskard provided London with a more circumstantial account, which differs in detail but not in outline from his earlier report.[33] According to him the Australian Government began by worrying about imports from Japan. This concern led them to consider the attractions of more home manufacturing. So as not to seem to trangress Articles 10 to 12 of the Ottawa Agreement, they wanted to give the UK some uncovenanted benefits. They also hoped thereby to expand the sales of Australian meat and dairy products at the expense of Argentina and Denmark. There was, Whiskard said, no doubt about Australia's desire to influence the London meat negotiations. But she also intended to use the licensing system to bargain with foreign countries. And she genuinely hoped to attract more British direct investment.[34] If the details seemed incoherent, Whitehall should remember that 'the policy has been conceived and brought to birth with no external assistance or pre-natal advice of any kind, in a period of 10 weeks . . . the administration of the powers which they have conferred on themselves is likely to be guided largely, if not entirely, by opportunism.'

The trade diversion policy was a wondrous mixture of protectionism and bilateral balancing. Its methods were to be tariff manipulation, import licensing, and bounties. Its aims were to reduce imports of motor cars, to build up sterling balances, and to cut imports from Japan, the United States, and Canada. Incidental benefits were to be extended to Britain. The UK High Commissioner first gave warning of the policy on 23 March 1936; on 16 May, he was able to make a reasonably full report; on 18 May Prime Minister Lyons cabled Baldwin[35] with respect to it; on 22 May the scheme was publicly announced in Australia. The Australian Government had not conferred with the British: 'they had thought it best to reach decision without prior consultation with United Kingdom as they feared United Kingdom Government might be embarrassed if it were suspected that they had in any way been parties to decision'.[36] They might also have worried about British reactions: though in the short run the scheme would certainly help British textiles *vis-à-vis* Japanese, in the longer run it would certainly harm British motor exports to Australia. And it was small consolation to be told that Australia earnestly desired to include a British subsidiary plant in its set of Australian motor industries.

Shortly thereafter, Sir Geoffrey Whiskard reported further on the political situation which had followed the announcement of trade diversion. As the policy discriminated so forcibly against Japan and Canada,[37] it was raising criticism in rural areas. By early June, the Japanese were already threatening to cut their Australian purchases, if the Australians did not withdraw their quota proposals.

Lyons and Gullett were terrified lest the policy should damage their electoral chances in the primary producing districts. Hence, Whiskard suggested, they felt they *must* press for an extra share in Britain's meat market.[38] In other words, the trade diversion policy, initially conceived in part as a device for manipulating the British, had generated political pressures which were forcing the Australian negotiators to demand more than before.

It is not hard to assess the net effect of these Australian developments. The trade diversion policy did give the British some reason for gratitude – while creating a need to press the Australians in certain respects.[39] Knowing the Australian political situation, the British thought that they could be sure of getting the benefits of trade diversion only by conceding more than they really wanted to concede. Wishing to strengthen their hands for future bargaining, and to express gratitude for the benefits which the trade diversion policy would actually confer, in the meat talks they conceded more than they would otherwise have given – though as much at Argentine expense as at British.

Trade diversion, however, was not obviously to Britain's advantage. There was a real risk that the new motor arrangements would soon exclude British cars from the Australian market. The Australian Government hoped that British interests would establish an assembly plant, and make their own engines and chassis. But British interests doubted if they could sell enough cars to justify the expense. Meanwhile, Australia was unco-operative with respect to the duty on British body panels – a critical matter, since the existing Australian firms were unwilling or unable to produce such panels to British designs.

Further, on 'domestic competition' matters were still unsatisfactory. In 1937, the Australians were still arguing that they could not afford to remove the remaining primage duties, which at Ottawa they had promised to shed as soon as possible.[40] Further, the Australian Government would not force tariff measures through its Parliament. Accordingly, in 1936–37 the inevitable finally happened: the Australian Tariff Board recommended lower duties on British cement and sanitary earthenware, but the Australian Parliament refused to sanction the reductions. The British authorities believed that Australia had deliberately contrived – not for the first time – to breach the Ottawa Agreement.

The Agreement expired on 20 August 1937. However, it could run on, subject to six months' notice of denunciation from either side. The British authorities did not want to renegotiate an Anglo-Australian agreement; by 1937 their principal concern was the American trade talks. However, late in the year the Australian Government announced that it wanted a new trade treaty. Accordingly, in mid-1938, Earle Page and Robert Menzies arrived in London.

Page and his advisers were still daydreaming. The population of Australia must continue to grow. But new productive capacity demanded new markets – in Asia and in Continental Europe, and perhaps in the United States. 'In 1932 we excluded the foreigner from Empire markets; today we want to persuade him not to exclude us from his markets.'[41] Britain must be asked to restrict foreign foodstuffs still more severely, but she might not do so; anyway, the Empire could not supply sufficient markets to absorb Australia's population growth. There might be something to be said for putting most of the Ottawa preferential system into the pot, so as to win a settlement with Europe – so long as Australia could retain certain 'essential preferences' –for her meat, sugar, wine, dried fruits, and canned fruits. There should be no quotas on Australian goods, and no new duties 'as far as possible'. As for Australia's own duties, the Ottawa 'formula method' should be replaced by a schedule, with specified margins. 'This is important from the point of view of bargaining with foreign countries.' Finally, Australia must refuse to limit her tariff-fixing power, as Articles 9 to 12 had attempted.[42] In other words, 'domestic competition' must go.

The whole thing made the British rather unhappy. The Board of Trade chronicled Britain's disappointment over Australian performance with respect to the Tariff Board. The officials concluded, rather tentatively, that on balance the 1932 Agreement had 'probably' been of value. Oliver

Stanley, the new President of the Board of Trade, was even more forthright. The Anglo-Australian agreement, he wrote, was the least satisfactory of all the Ottawa pacts. British manufacturers continually criticised the tariff behaviour of the Australian Government. Hence, the House of Commons would not quietly tolerate any large concession by the UK. Australia was proposing to revise the Agreement because *her* manufacturers so strongly opposed the Tariff Board clauses. But these had been her main Ottawa concession. Hence she could not be absolved from them. In any event, there could be no new Anglo-Australian agreement until after the Anglo-American-Canadian discussions had ended.[43]

The Anglo-Australian talks began on 19 May, and ended late in June. Page and Menzies must have found Oliver Stanley a sterner foe than Walter Runciman. Menzies pressed Britain to introduce a *general* quantitative restriction, giving Australia a growing share of the British market for all primary products; all Australia wanted, he said, 'was a further share at the expense of the foreigner'. British ministers and officials, however, rejected any such idea. Stanley pointed out that the logical conclusion would be a closed Empire economy – which, he disingenuously remarked, nobody would want. He told the Australians that they were really asking Britain to denounce many trade agreements, while, at the same time, withdrawing their preferences and making their Tariff Board a purely advisory body. He was prepared to let the Australians replace the formula with a definite list of specified preferential margins – but only if they offered enough concessions. Menzies, playing an old Australian card, mentioned Australia's difficulties in setting tariff maxima: because the courts fixed money wages rates, an 'appropriate tariff' could easily become 'too low'. But Stanley repeated that Britain must ask for a *quid pro quo*. Further, he continued, no preferential *margin* would be effective if the preferential *duty* were to become prohibitive. 'What would prevent an unfettered Commonwealth Government from offering unlimited protection to any industry that was prepared to set up in it?' To this the Australians had no answer.

The British then explored the problems with respect to cement and sanitary earthenware – the two products on which the Australian Parliament had rejected Tariff Board recommendations. The Australians argued that in their Parliament the whips had *never* been used to pass tariff measures; hence when the Agreement said their Government would 'invite parliament' to legislate, it meant exactly that. Stanley, who does not seem to have known this, immediately decided that the disputed Articles – 9 to 12 – were 'no good to the United Kingdom'. Only a schedule of maximum rates would do. He was prepared to accept a sliding scale so as to cover Arbitration Court wage awards. But the list would be a long one and would have to include protective duties as well as revenue duties. The Australians must have wondered just what Pandora's Box they had opened. They temporised. Refusing to commit themselves to the principle of maximum rates, they asked for a list. They would take it away and brood over it.

The list was subsequently produced. Page pronounced it terrifying and impossible. Menzies agreed. If the UK wanted to reduce and consolidate 'duties on protective items of real importance', there was no point in proceeding. Stanley insisted that protective duties must be included. He reminded Menzies and Page that it was they who had initiated the discussion, and they who wanted to revise the Tariff Board articles.

'The views expressed by Australian Ministers regarding these articles had led the United Kingdom Government to realise the necessity, on their side, for rewording the Articles to ensure that they bore the meaning which the United Kingdom had previously attributed to them. The proposals for a schedule of maximum duties had only been put forward by the United Kingdom as a possible way out of the impasse over the Tariff Board articles.'

He went farther: if Australia would not concede maximum duties but insisted on absolving herself from carrying out Tariff Board rulings, and on revising the Articles, 'the United Kingdom would have to insist on corresponding changes with regard to Australia's right to free entry'. Not unexpectedly, Page 'deprecated Mr Stanley's attitude'. And the result was deadlock.[44]

In the end, the Australians decided that the existing agreement was the best available in the circumstances. They proposed that the 1932 Agreement should continue for the time being. After some friction, in which Menzies repeated his principled rejection of maximum duties, a joint statement was concocted, released, and subsequently printed.[45] Australia agreed to consider the possibility of conventionalising duties on British goods; Britain agreed not to press her objections to the interpretation that the Tariff Board now placed upon Article 10 – the reasonable competition clause; 'Australian ministers have undertaken to make every effort to ensure that Tariff Board recommendations under Article Eleven are made effective'. That is, the Australians would try to ensure that Parliament would legislate in line with Tariff Board recommendations, while Britain agreed not to insist on a strict interpretation of the rules which should govern the Board's decisions. Meanwhile, the 1932 Agreement should remain in force.

On his return to Australia, Page told the House of Representatives that Britain had accepted the Tariff Board interpretation of Article 10. That is, he said, Britain would not object if the tariff should give a margin 'of a genuinely protective kind'; further, if Australia should fail to lower a tariff as recommended by the Tariff Board under Article 11, Britain would not hold Australia in breach of the Ottawa Agreement.[46]

Unfortunately, this was not what Britain thought it had said. As Sir Eric Machtig wrote,

'it cannot, of course, be accepted here that Sir Earle Page was justified in announcing . . . that it had been agreed that the Australian tariff should be fixed in such a way as to provide a further margin "of a genuinely protective kind" . . . while we are prepared to accept the 1935 interpretation (i.e. that the Commonwealth should establish a competitive as distinct from a prohibitive tariff level), we are not prepared to go back still further to the interpretation adopted by the Tariff Board between 1932 and 1935.'[47]

In the autumn, the British Government consulted the Law Officers of the Crown with respect to the interpretation of Article 11. And shortly thereafter, a Board of Trade official wrote:

'I think that the Commonwealth Ministers in the end understood that if further cases like that of sanitary earthenware were to happen the chances were that the Ottawa Agreement would be denounced. If Sir Earle Page has made it more difficult for him to secure Parliamentary approval for Tariff Board Reports that is his funeral, and I do not think there is anything we can do to help him.'

What mattered, he concluded, was the *effect* given to Article 11.[48]

To historical common sense, as distinct from legal interpretation, the record of the thirties suggests that Australia was consistently in breach of her Ottawa obligations from 1932 until 1939 at least. This fact helps to explain the increasingly rigid posture from which British ministers surveyed Australian demands and hectorings on the meat and butter fronts. Why should Britain destroy her livestock industry merely to placate a Dominion which showed no sign of honouring her treaty obligations?

On the other hand, however great their departure from the strict canons of the Agreement, the Australians did lower their tariffs on British goods, both absolutely and relative to tariffs on foreign goods. Corden reports that by 1939–40 'the average British preferential rate was only 8% above the pre-depression average of 1928, while the average General tariff was 54% higher'.[49] Australia was still more protectionist than before 1929, but towards British goods her tariffs had become relatively less protectionist. Perhaps this fact, vaguely perceived in Whitehall, explains Britain's failure to denounce the Agreement. Certainly Ottawa itself, and Britain's subsequent pressure, must claim much credit for this evolution in Australian tariff structure.

II. NEW ZEALAND

After Australia, New Zealand's story is quickly told. The smaller Dominion went ahead in 1933 to hold the tariff enquiry which Articles 8 and 9 had enjoined. She invited British producers to provide information about 'factory costs' and other necessary information. The Tariff Commission reported in March 1934. Most of the recommendations were adopted on 11 July. But within six weeks, manufacturers were complaining to the Ministry of Customs, and they were successful in getting higher rates on some British goods. Their representations affected thirty-six items, of which the UK had sold New Zealand £226,000. But initial action had affected 141 items, in which Anglo-New Zealand trade was £2,050,000. Thus the UK had little reason to complain, especially in light of the fact that New Zealand tariffs were already very low.[50]

Matters looked different late in 1935, when a Labour Government came to power at Wellington. Its members wanted more self-sufficiency in manufactures. The idea was to organise rationalised industry in efficient units, and if necessary to use import-licensing and an enforced control of production.

When Walter Nash came to London for trade talks late in 1936, British ministers and officials were very nervous about these plans. Nash did not want to continue the Ottawa Agreement in any form, but British officials would tolerate only minor modifications. In particular, they wished to retain the 'reasonable competition' articles, and to add, 'Imports from the United Kingdom shall not be restricted by embargoes'. But Nash was inclined to resist, arguing that New Zealand producers would need high tariffs to protect their small local market. He would not accept any general prohibition of embargoes, but he would agree not to embargo specific goods. Malcolm MacDonald proceeded to ask for fixed tariffs on 130 items, reductions on another 40, and new or increased preferences on another 35. But Nash, demanding British guarantees with respect to butter, still would give no assurances with respect to import prohibitions or restrictions.

He asked the British to list all the goods in which they had a substantial interest. By 15 May, the Board of Trade had asked for guaranteed free entry in 186 cases, a reduced preferential duty in another 64, a guarantee of the present preferential duty on 76 items, and certain increased or new margins of preference, chiefly to deal with Japanese competition.

In June, Nash told Morrison and Oliver Stanley that there had been no discussion of the British requests, because, given Britain's inability to settle her own butter policy, there was little chance of an agreement. MacDonald explained that the Government hoped to make an announcement before the end of July. Would New Zealand like to wait until then? Nash said he would consider the matter. But on 3 July he sailed for home, having made no agreement and given no commitment.

Late in 1938, following a severe crisis, the New Zealand Government did indeed adopt foreign-exchange control. Almost immediately, the British Government noticed there was a risk. If the licensing provisions were to favour goods which New Zealand could produce herself, how could Britain be sure of the reasonable competitive entry to which the Ottawa Agreement entitled her? The New Zealand ministers promised to do all they could to prevent discrimination; however, they noted, their controls were bound to favour raw materials, at the expense of finished goods.[51]

Shortly thereafter, Walter Nash came back to London for new talks on trade and finance. British ministers took the opportunity to discuss licensing. The results were not unsatisfactory for Britain, though they did seem to derogate from the Ottawa principles. Nash said that his Government did not want to prevent 'reasonable competition' through licensing, but he noted that in some industries he would have to prevent imports in order to attain sufficient scale. He promised Britain that he would not use licensing to foster uneconomic industries, and that 'in cases where it is proposed to grant a limited number of licenses to manufacture particular kinds of goods, the New Zealand Government would give United Kingdom interests the opportunity to put forward, should they so desire, proposals for undertaking such manufacture'.[52]

III. CANADA

After Ottawa, the British Government must have expected more trouble from Canada's Prime Minister Bennett than from any other Empire leader. His tactics had nearly wrecked the conference, and, more alarming, his manners were deplorable. Further, he quickly gave cause for alarm: with respect to cotton textiles he introduced duties which did not accord with the Agreement. Finally, he seemed reluctant to constitute his new Tariff Board.

However, by the middle of the autumn, Sir William Clark was reporting that Bennett really did want to make the Agreement work. And his later performance does suggest that he took it seriously. When he visited London in December 1932, he explained that he had had trouble in setting up an absolutely impartial Tariff Board – one whose membership would inspire confidence. He explained that he could not go ahead and abolish the exchange dumping duty and the provisions for par valuation of British goods, because 'the depreciation had practically wiped out . . . protection' for Canadian manufactures. That is, sterling's foreign exchange value had fallen relative to the Canadian dollar's. However, he said, he would announce the Board early in the New Year.[53] Later he decided that it would begin its work on 1 May 1933.

During 1933, the UK found Bennett co-operative with respect to most tariff requests. Several additional concessions were thus extracted, and Canada gradually removed the more obnoxious aspects of her exchange dumping and valuation rules. In February, Britain began to submit lists of items for Tariff Board review. However, later in the year British officials voiced some complaints about the Board's rulings and its procedures – especially its slowness. Further, there were troubles over coal, steel plates, and doubled cotton yarn. In May, Sir William Clark wrote that with respect to steel plates and cotton yarn the principal advantages conferred by the Ottawa Agreements had been removed by administrative action.[54]

Because broad steel plate was now made in Canada, it automatically became subject to anti-dumping duty. British representatives argued that, though strictly required under the Canadian Customs Act, and not violating the letter of the Ottawa Agreement or discussion thereon, the action was contrary to the Ottawa spirit. It had been understood, they claimed, that the UK would have security above the 66-inch width for five years. By 14 December, Bennett had accepted the British argument, and in April 1934 he introduced legislation to exempt British steel plates from the relevant customs provisions where more than 66 inches wide. This exemption allowed the British Steel Export Association to continue the practice which had caused the trouble – selling these widths in Canada for less than the British home-market price.[55]

As for coal, a similar difficulty had arisen. Coal did not figure in the Ottawa Agreements, but the Canadians understood they were to continue their prohibitions on Soviet coal. British dumping, however, was another matter. Early in 1933, Canada began to ask for British help in controlling Anglo-Canadian coal shipments. Britain denied that she was dumping, or spoiling the Canadian market, insisted that American coal was the problem, and urged an agreement between Nova Scotia and South Wales coal interests. However, Canadian officials discovered that South Wales was pricing export coal lower than home-market coal. Therefore, Canadian law required an anti-dumping duty, and this was imposed on 29 May. Three days later, Sir William Clark reported:

'Yesterday afternoon I saw the Prime Minister. He rather staggered me by saying at the start that unintentionally he had misled me on the telephone about the dumping duty on coal three days before, when he had implied that it was imposed by decision taken in Order in Council though at a meeting from which he was absent. He now found, he said, that it was a result of purely departmental action following usual course prescribed by Statute in cases where after inquiry home prices are proved to exceed export prices. I made no attempt to disguise my astonishment . . . his statement may be true and anything is possible in administrative system of Ottawa, but circumstances are suspicious to say the least. In Nova Scotia a General Election is imminent, and position of present provincial Conservative Government is insecure . . . and one cannot forget that the present Finance Minister in Ottawa was himself formerly Conservative Premier of Nova Scotia.'[56]

About coal nothing could be done: in terms of Canadian law, British exporters *were* dumping in Canada, and the Anglo-Canadian Agreement said nothing about the stuff. Doubled cotton yarn was another matter. Here, the Canadian customs officials took from standard reference manuals a description which had the effect of increasing the duty on British yarn exports. After British expostulation Canada accepted Lancashire's contentions, and the matter was soon tidied away.[57]

As for the Canadian Tariff Board, it was proceeding on its leisurely way. Late in 1934, Dominions Office officials recorded that they had no reason to be discontented with it. Reminding their superiors that the Board inquired only on British requests, they noted that it had lowered two preferential duties and raised one, but that it had probably prevented various increases. In June 1934, the Canadian Supreme Court trimmed the Board's powers, but the inquiry function had emerged unscathed.[58]

Thus Bennett had come to smell sweet in Whitehall's nostrils. His actions in 1935 did nothing to render him sour. In January, he dined with Britain's acting High Commissioner, and asked him to consult the records and suggest any concessions which Canada might make the UK in the forthcoming budget. He wanted, he said, to get the British position straight before opening his American discussions. The Board of Trade produced a long list[59] and Bennett did modify some tariff items in line with it.

Bennett's concessions, like many of his other actions during

1935, may reflect the coming of an election. Mackenzie King and the Liberals had long opposed the 1932 Agreements. They found the Tariff Board clauses capitulatory. And, for the sake of trade negotiations with other countries, they wanted more power to narrow the preferential margins.[60] Indeed, King made it clear that if elected he would seek a new Anglo-Canadian trade agreement. Soon after he returned to power late in 1935, he completed the Canadian-American trade negotiations which Bennett had begun. Though not a breach of the Ottawa Agreement, Canadian concessions did damage the British competitive position. At least, so Whitehall thought, and so the High Commissioner urged. He found King sympathetic, but unwilling to restore preferential margins entirely; he would wait until the Anglo-Canadian talks were well under way.[61]

In an earlier chapter we saw that Dunning and Euler came to London from Canada in July 1936. Perhaps to their surprise, they found that nobody wanted to retain the Tariff Board clauses, reasonable competition, and other paraphernalia of the old Agreement. Articles 10 to 15 had in fact yielded little, though they had on the whole been honestly administered; it would be better simply to fix maximum duties. Accordingly, in the new Agreement the old clauses were swept away; Canada simply promised that she would impose no new protective duties, and would raise no existing ones, except after an inquiry 'at which United Kingdom producers shall enjoy full rights of audience'.[62] As Canada did not want to retain Article 21, the 'Russia clause' of the 1932 agreement, it too vanished without trace or trouble. On the question of maximum duties, however, the new negotiation almost foundered.

Dunning wanted the power to cut intermediate tariff rates and preferential margins whenever necessary to frustrate cartels, which worried him and other Liberals. Runciman proposed sliding duties, so that if intermediate rates were reduced preferential rates would also fall. He did not ask for fixed preferential margins, except where British goods now paid no duty. The result, he thought, would help the Canadians in their other trade talks. Dunning responded that nothing could be decided in London; he would take a list of proposals to Canada, where the Cabinet could consider the matter.[63] A week later, Canadian officials proposed a 'cartel clause', whereby in proven cases the Canadian Government could reduce its intermediate tariff rate and so defeat cartels. British officials did not disagree; an appropriate clause found its way into the final Agreement.[64] Thereafter, the ministers talked mostly about British food-import policy. However, at their last meeting, after explaining that he understood the value of fixed margins to the UK, Dunning asked that Britain should 'not make his position difficult by asking for too much. One of the chief criticisms of the 1932 agreement made by the Canadian Prime Minister had been the fixing of the margins of preference'.[65] The officials continued to meet, and on 20 August a draft Agreement was initialled. Dunning then went off to Ottawa.

For four months little occurred. In Ottawa, Dunning and Floud were working on the terminology of the food clauses.[66] When he visited London on 16–30 October, King himself appears to have discussed only food. So far as Whitehall could discover, King and his Cabinet had considered neither the general question of maximum duties and fixed margins, nor the particular tariff arrangements which the officials had devised during the summer.

Indeed, the Canadian Cabinet first saw the draft Agreement on 17 November. Six days later they began to examine the concessions which Britain was requesting. There is reason to believe that King himself, and some of his ministers, feared Britain was asking too much and offering too little, especially on the agricultural front. The Cabinet was especially nervous about the woollen and shoe duties. Prominent ministers came from constituencies which produced both shoes and woollens.

King was suspicious of Dunning. He believed that his Finance Minister was a secretive and devious person who was unduly favourable to the UK. On 2 December, partly because he did not trust Dunning, he formed a Cabinet subcommittee to cary on the negotiations. On 15 December, the subcommittee was disrupted by a furious and completely unexpected row. King had just noticed that for ninety-three goods the draft trade agreement retained fixed preferential margins. He insisted that the new agreement must fix no margins. And he took control of the negotiations. With the assistance of his officials he drafted an *aide-mémoire* which he gave to Sir Francis Floud on 17 December.

The next morning Floud cabled London in some dismay. He reported that King was jibbing at the remaining ninety-three margins, and that he proposed slightly higher duties on a few items. In exchange he was offering concessions which Floud thought trivial and frivolous. He wanted the power to reduce margins, after consultation. And he asked for a quick reply, so that he could announce an agreement on Christmas Eve.[67]

In Whitehall irritated mandarins wrote minutes: the Canadians had taken four months, but expected Britain to approve such modifications in four days; the suggestions involved 'major alterations in principle'; nothing could be decided until the new requests had been fully scrutinised.[68]

King, however, was as adamant as his nature permitted: on 4 January he cabled at length, reiterating his objection to fixed preferential margins, and regretting that 'it is not possible for us to conclude an agreement in the terms of the draft submitted'.[69]

Dunning, however, told Floud that if Britain would give way on a few specific tariff-items, Canada would accept the British demands with respect to guaranteed margins, dairy products, cattle, and beef.[70]

After Dunning's message reached London, British officials and ministers speedily acted in accordance with it. The officials hastily drafted a suitable cable; Runciman and Morrison approved it; Malcolm MacDonald sent it on 9 January.[71]

MacDonald accepted much of King's *aide-mémoire*. Britain would accept the detailed modifications in schedules. She would change the preamble to meet Canada's requests. But she could do nothing about the Schedule A reservation with respect to dairy products. And she would insist upon the ninety-three margins – while retaining the article of the draft agreement which already allowed for modification of such margins after consultation.[72]

On 11 January, the Canadian Cabinet considered its response. They agreed to give way on all points except the apple and zinc duties. King regretted that the UK had not met the Canadian proposals completely, but he admitted that the positions were much closer together,[73] and he accepted the British view with respect to fixed preferential margins.[74]

Why did King brew up such a storm and then so quickly calm the troubled waters? Professor Donald Forster, who has examined the King Diaries, believes that King never expected Britain to accept his ultimatum of 17 December. After 4 January, Forster suggests, King was in a position to attain his *real* goals – a better text for the preamble, and better terms for woollens, boots and shoes. But Forster finds no real explanation for King's brainstorm of 15 December. Had he only just noticed the fixed margins of the agreement? Did he suddenly come to distrust Dunning more acutely? Or did he really believe that he could frighten the British into withdrawing the 'Schedule A reservation'? Or had he only just noticed that the draft contained some of the 'fixed margins' which he had so disliked in the original Ottawa Agreement, and ever after?[75]

When the Canadian Parliament reassembled on 14 January it was told that an agreement had been reached. Drafting proceeded, and the final document was signed on 23 February. The Canadian Government did conventionalise the preferential rates on a long list of items. It did agree not to reduce preferential margins on another list of goods, and to maintain specified margins on a third list.[76] Though shorter than the British had wanted, all three lists were much longer than the Canadians had demanded. And there were no escape clauses such as King had requested in mid-December.

The Agreement, in fact, represented a considerable triumph for the UK. Having abandoned their faith in 'reasonable competition' and tariff boards, the British negotiators now wanted fixed rates and fixed margins; to a considerable extent they got both.

In the Australian negotiations, as we saw, the British were more concerned with maximum rates than with stable margins. In dealing with Canada, fixed margins mattered more than stable maximum rates, though both were wanted. The difference seems to reflect British assessment of the governments with which they were dealing. For fifteen years, British officials had been observing Australian protectionism; by 1938 they must have been convinced that the Tariff Board and the Government would raise preferential *rates* as high as necessary to protect Australian producers. Stable *margins*, therefore, were not much good, because the preferential rate itself could and would be prohibitive. The Canadian situation was different. Mackenzie King led a party which was explicitly committed to tariff reduction and freer trade. In the late 1920s, and in 1930, he had acted unilaterally to lower the preferential tariffs and to widen the preferential margins. He had just won an election campaign in which he had loudly sounded both notes. Early in 1936, at budget time, he had taken some steps in the right direction – though only after London had made strong representations. Charles Dunning, his Minister of Finance, was visibly committed to tariff reduction. However, American firms competed vigorously in the Canadian market. To fix the *margins* was to give British firms some security in this competition. It was especially important to get this protection because King was likely to give away the preferential margins in his trade dealings with third countries.

IV. FIXED RATES, FIXED MARGINS, AND THE PREFERENTIAL SYSTEM

In conclusion we leave the negotiations themselves and turn to a purer analysis. Exactly what did Britain stand to gain from preferential tariff rates and margins? In Britain's own market, preferences often gave little; wherever Empire production exceeded Empire consumption, competition was bound to erase the preferential margin on Empire sales to Britain. Might the same be true of Dominion preferential tariffs?

The Dominions bought manufactures from the UK. They could or did buy similar goods from foreign countries, and they might produce the same items at home. These manufactures were of two basic types – homogeneous and differentiated. Among the former goods were chemicals, coal, sheet glass, textiles, iron shapes, and other intermediate products which Dominion producers bought for further fabrication. Among the latter goods – the differentiated ones – were all consumer durables and some semi-durables – motor cars, electrical equipment, clothing, china, and such things.

First consider homogeneous goods. Since each Dominion was a 'small buyer' of such manufacture, no Dominion's purchase was likely to affect price in the supplying country. In other words, each Dominion was a 'price taker'. With free trade, Britain's competitive position would depend on her costs, foreign costs, transport changes, and the exchange rate. Low transport costs might offset relatively high production costs, or might accentuate a production-cost disadvantage. If British and foreign imports pay the same duty, the situation is unchanged so far as external competition is concerned, but domestic production is stimulated. The higher the duty, the lower total sales in the Dominion, and the larger the proportion of domestic production in total sales. The ruling price in the Dominion will be the supply price of the lowest-cost external supplier country – Britain or foreign. If Britain is the lowest-cost supplier she will have *all* the import market; if she is not, she will sell *nothing*.

However, if the Dominion instals a preferential tariff, the margin can be so set as to make Britain the effectual lowest-cost supplier. That is, the margin offsets whatever disadvantages Britain may suffer – from high domestic production costs, an overvalued exchange rate, or high transport costs. In principle, transport improvements or subsidies could have the same effect; so could devaluation. If the margin is just enough to offset Britain's competitive disadvantage, Britain will supply all the imports, and foreigners will now sell nothing. If the margin is more than sufficient, the price in the Dominion will fall. Dominion consumers will buy more, but Dominion producers will sell less, and British sales will rise for three reasons: the preferential tariff cut has simultaneously raised the total quantity demanded, reduced local sales, and diverted all import trade from foreign to British factories.

In this situation, the important thing is to get the preferential *rate* as low as possible. Once the rate is low enough to admit British trade at all, *margins* do not matter; it is British price plus preferential rate that fixes the Dominion price, and foreign goods are excluded by the mere fact that preferential rates are so low. Further, 'reasonable competition' is hard to define. Once the preferential rate is low enough for British goods to replace foreign goods, any further cuts will trench upon Dominion production. If the Dominion long-run supply curve is horizontal and sufficiently high relative to the British, one can easily cut the preferential rate so severely as to eliminate the Dominion industry altogether. In the thirties, no Dominion government could do such a thing. Ideally, therefore, the preferential rate should be low enough to exclude foreign goods, but high enough to equate the local long-run supply price with the British supply price plus the tariff. If the tariff fixers do their sums right, British and Dominion firms will compete equally in the Dominion market, and we cannot say how much each *country* will sell. But if the Dominion industry is an increasing-cost or a decreasing-cost industry, it is *impossible* to fix any such equalising tariff. And even if the industry is constant-cost, if the tariff fixers get their sums wrong there will be a constant tendency for Dominion production to displace British exports, or vice versa.

In short, for homogeneous goods tariff cuts were worth fighting for; preferential *margins* were uninteresting; 'reasonable competition' was largely meaningless in principle, and wholly incalculable in practice.

Now consider differentiated goods. Whenever the product was differentiated in the user's minds the Dominion market could in principle contain domestic production, British imports, and foreign imports, at any tariff structure.

However, each country's sales would depend on the ruling prices, inside the Dominion, for domestic production and for the goods of the other external suppliers. A low rate on British goods meant a low delivered price for British goods, and smaller sales both for foreigners and for domestic producers – whatever the preferential margin might be. On the other hand, given the preferential rate, a wider margin meant larger sales for British and domestic goods. In other words, British sales were sensitive both to the preferential rate and to the preferential margin; it made sense for British negotiators to worry about *both*.

For homogeneous products, it is hard or impossible to *attain* 'reasonable competition' through tariff-tinkering. For differentiated products, we cannot even *define* reasonable competition. We can certainly detect a prohibitive tariff. But suppose the preferential rate is low enough to admit *some* British goods. That is, suppose some consumers are willing to buy some British goods at the local price which the preferential tariff allows. Is competition 'reasonable'? Dominion producers, unions, and governments may answer, 'Yes': local production, employment, and sales are at reasonable levels. But British producers, unions, and government may answer, 'No': British sales are too small relative to local sales. Unless the two governments can agree about the division of the local market, they cannot possibly decide whether competition is or is not 'reasonable'.

Chapter 9

CONCLUSION

I. THE DOMINANT OBJECTIVES

In the preceding chapters I have tried to examine the issues of Imperial economic policy which actually did preoccupy the top levels of British government and administration during the interwar years. The Indian question[1] and the Imperial-preference debates of the twenties[2] have been omitted, chiefly because I have recently explored them in another place. It should now be clear that we cannot understand Imperial economic diplomacy during this period if we approach it with exploitation in mind. British politicians were not trying to exploit anybody; they were preoccupied with the Dominions, where they lacked the political power to impose policies, and to a much lesser extent with India, where in economic policy-making they systematically abstained from using what political power they still possessed. They worried very little about the Dependent Empire, which interested them in the twenties as a locus for a little employment-generating government expenditure, and in the thirties as a budgetary problem. We can best understand the Imperial economic policies of our period if we think about sterling, debt service, the budget, and unemployment.

To a small extent, British governments tried to manage the Empire's economic affairs to improve sterling's position – the exchange rate, the reserves, or both. We see this most clearly in the commodity management schemes of the twenties and thirties, especially the tin and rubber plans. Sterling also mattered for the quota and levy-subsidy plans which we explored in Chapter 7.

To a larger extent, governments tried to ensure that overseas borrowers would be able to pay their debts. The creditors were usually in the UK. In the twenties the Treasury, and some ministers, worried about Australia's development borrowings. In the thirties, everybody recognised that Argentina, Australia, and New Zealand must be allowed to earn 'enough' sterling – enough, that is, to pay interest on their past borrowings.

In connection with the Empire, monetary policies did raise their head, but not very far, and, especially at the Ottawa Conference, not far enough. There is some sign that the authorities were intermittently interested in the emergence of the Sterling Area, and in the management of intra-Imperial exchange rates, at least now and then. The evidence is hard to summarise, and the developments are not well documented. We do know that in 1920–23 there was a good deal of concern in the Treasury, and overseas, about the floating of Empire currencies *vis-à-vis* sterling. In 1923, the Imperial Economic Conference resolved that the Dominions should keep foreign-exchange reserves in London, and should use these reserves to stabilise intra-Imperial exchange rates. Nothing seems to have been done, and the suggestion became otiose when Britain returned to gold in 1925. However, the return itself was considered, at least casually, in relation to Empire questions. Sir Otto Neimeyer believed that a gold standard would be in the Empire's interest, because so many Empire countries produced gold. Some officials may have feared that if Britain did not return to gold, the Empire countries would remove their foreign exchange reserves from London. And it was certainly hoped that a gold standard would scotch the sillier plans for an Empire paper money which Amery and other enthusiasts had been proposing in 1920–22.

To a much greater extent, however, politicians and officials brooded about the UK budget. Would Empire settlement loans congest the new issue market, raising the rate of interest on British Government loans? Could the Exchequer afford £5 million per year for settlement? Five million pounds in butter and meat subsidies? How much revenue could safely be sacrificed through the preferential taxation of Empire products? How much subsidy would bankrupt colonies require?

In earlier chapters of this book I described the disputes of the twenties as a battle between development-minded visionaries and orthodox free-traders. I also suggested that the meat and butter disputes of the thirties arose from the Ottawa Agreements and from a British desire for agricultural protection after Ottawa. But we could also blame the budget for such troubles. In the twenties, the visionaries wanted to spend money. In the thirties, protectionists wanted to help British agriculture without spending money. Indeed, they hoped for an increase in revenue from new food taxes. Such budgetary ideas were always present, and always important.

Nevertheless, however large the budget loomed, unemployment loomed larger. The protectionist measures of the thirties obviously aimed at job creation and job protection. But so did the Imperial initiatives of the 1920s.

Overseas settlement was adopted to reduce unemployment by exporting people. This statement is true in small part of the soldier settlement plans, and the documents show that it was the major explanation for the introduction of the Empire Settlement Bill. The evidence suggests that Amery would have got nowhere with Empire settlement if Britain had not faced serious unemployment. First was the cyclical slump of 1920–22 and then the structural problem of 1927–29. Amery himself would have wanted to people the Empire in any event. And he was careful to deny that his settlement plans were meant to export the unemployed themselves. Indeed, under the Act there was very little movement of the really destitute, and much emigration of women and children. However, Empire settlement was part of a long-range unemployment programme. By peopling the Empire it would create new export markets for Britain. And in the short run it took some people off the labour market, while creating overseas development that would quickly raise Britain's exports.

In Africa the development planning of the twenties did

not involve settlement. Few went to South Africa, Kenya, or Rhodesia under the Empire Settlement Act. The British Government did little to encourage white migration to Africa. Nevertheless, it did nothing to impede such movement as the Kenya and Rhodesia authorities were able to contrive. And its African development initiatives were all taken to fight British unemployment by quickly raising British capital-goods exports. This was true of the 'financial co-operation' plan of 1923, the guaranteed loans to East Africa, and the Colonial Development Act of 1929. Every one of these measures was urged, and adopted, as a way to help British exports while also helping the colonies. Even the cotton development plans had some relation to unemployment. If cotton prices could be kept down, more cottons would be sold, and so there would be more employment in Britain's mill towns.

Imperial preference itself was an anti-unemployment device, at least to a large extent, even in the twenties. Yet the preference problem was linked with the debt-service problem because preferences had implications for budgetary balance overseas. Tariff reformers hoped that preferences would raise the volume and value of Empire trade. Empire governments, heavily dependent on customs revenues, would then be able to service their overseas debts more readily. If domestic producers were more prosperous, they might also be able to impose more direct taxation. In the Dominions and India, buoyant revenues helped the UK. London loans would be promptly serviced, and governments would be able to keep their rates of tariff relatively low. In the Dependent Empire, buoyant revenues would obviate London subsidies, and would probably encourage development spending. For the Empire as a whole, therefore, prosperous governments were good for Britain both as exporter and as creditor, even though Britain herself derived no budgetary revenue from the Empire. On the other hand, because so many Empire governments were so dependent on customs revenues, they could not be expected to remove all duties from British goods. Indeed, because Whitehall worried about colonial budgets it could not demand the preferential concessions which it might otherwise have exacted. We know at Ottawa the British delegates worried about this matter. We may therefore suspect that the worry was chronic. And we should also recall that the overseas governments must have balanced concessions to Britain against increases on foreign goods. A cut in preferential rates meant a loss of revenue which must often have caused an increase in general or intermediate tariff rates. To foreign governments such increases could often look contrived, deliberate, and actively hostile. Yet one suspects that in many instances they were simply the result of an inflexible and unimaginative tax system which depended far too heavily upon customs revenues.

Economists of my generation, and of younger generations, are inclined to ignore a large part of the controversy over economic policy which actually raged in interwar Britain. Most of us see the period almost entirely in terms of Britain's return to gold, and the overvaluation of sterling, followed by the collapse of the international gold standard and the international economy after 1931. Some of us know a little about reparations and war debts. Though economic historians know more, they too have concentrated upon monetary history, and upon the discussions it generated at the time. Other considerations enter in, but only vaguely. It is remembered that Britain was 'free trade' until 1932, and 'protectionist' thereafter.[3] It is recalled that Britain did not apply Keynsian medicine to the Depression of the thirties. Of course the bones of this 'skeleton view' were really present, and very important to the economic policy-making of the period. But a great deal more was under way as well. Which aspects of policy-making were most important to contemporary governments? Suppose we judge by the time and effort which politicians and departments spent on the various topics. Certainly the Cabinet spent more time worrying about Imperial economic policy than about any other aspect of economic affairs. The 'Imperial questions', therefore, deserve some place in the economic historiography of the period.

II. THE EXPLOITATION HYPOTHESIS

If we cannot understand Imperial economic diplomacy in terms of exploitation, can we none the less say something about the phenomenon of exploitation within the interwar Empire? Because I began to study the Empire with this question in mind, I should like to conclude this investigation by presenting my tentative conclusions with respect to it. The findings must be preliminary. Before anyone can reach finality, we must know much more about the policy-making process in each of the colonies and protectorates. Nevertheless, if only for purposes of clarification, it may be useful to offer this final section.

We must first ask ourselves what 'exploitation' means. Many definitions are in circulation, but few are useful to the economist, or to the serious student of society, either because they cannot be used for observation or because they define a universal phenomenon as exploitation. Both troubles arise with the Marxian definition, by which capitalists exploit by definition, and therefore profits are always exploitative. Neo-Marxist analysis of imperialism is doubly unhelpful. It is not very informative to be told that because there was capitalism in the British Empire, and because many of the capitalists lived in the British Isles, the Empire was exploited by Britain. Nor is it helpful to be told that because most of the capitalists were white while in certain areas their employees were usually black, the Empire involved the automatic exploitation of blacks by whites. I propose to use a definition which is more relevant for research. Exploitation may be said to exist when markets are so arranged that buyers pay more than they would otherwise have to, or that sellers get less than they would otherwise get. In the context of Empire, therefore, exploitation means the use of political power, or the power of the white imperialist, to force unjust prices on the local population. It also means the support of a local white administration by non-white taxpayers.

Next we must ask ourselves how to relate exploitation to the British economy. Even though alien white rule may be thought unjust, wrong, prejudiced, or simply unimaginative, it does not follow that the white rulers are necessarily exploiting their non-white subjects, either in intention or in fact. And it certainly does not follow that because the white parts of an empire are more prosperous or more advanced than the coloured parts, the prosperity of the former rests on the exploitation of the latter.

It is with respect to dependent Africa that a catalogue of interwar British sins might most sensibly be compiled. But these African economies were very small relative to the British, and not very involved with British production or trade. Exploitation in Kenya coffee farming or Rhodesian labour supply might have been terribly important for Kenya or Rhodesia, but terribly unimportant for Britain, because it cannot significantly have affected the terms on which Britain sold outputs or bought inputs.

To India the same argument applies. Throughout the interwar period India supplied about 5 per cent of Britain's imports, and bought about 10 per cent of her exports. Imports represented about 1 per cent of British national expenditure. Even if all these goods had been extorted from the Indians without payment, their loss could have hardly affected the British standard of living. In fact, of course, these goods were bought and paid for, partly by prior export of capital to India and partly by current British exports to India and elsewhere. It might be argued that the prices of these goods were somehow unfair – that the Indians would have got more or paid less if there had been no British Raj. The nature of this contention is such that it cannot be completely refuted. However, it does not look plausible in light of the evidence. British firms and foreign firms bought and sold Indian goods on exactly the same terms. Indian capital was not excluded from the export industries, and was vigorously active in jute, cotton, and tea-planting. Nor did Britain's tariff policy hurt India. In the twenties, India gave no tariff concessions to British goods. In the thirties, her concessions were few and small. And from 1919 to 1929, and 1932 to the outbreak of war, Indian tea entered Britain at a preferentially low rate whose effect, though presumably small, was to make the duty much less painful for India. In so far as India granted tariff concessions at the Ottawa Conference, these were the result of a bargaining process by which Britain also made concessions which have since proved of immense value to the Indian textile and iron industries.

In the Dependent Empire, preferential tariffs could be imposed by the UK. So could quotas, to exclude, for instance, Japanese textiles. But it is easy to exaggerate the pay-off to Britain from the preferential system. And it is even easier to exaggerate the extent to which Britain's gain was her colonies' loss. Since the British economy was under-employed throughout our period, she would gain sales, output, and income if she could divert trade from foreign factories to British. But this gain was at her colonies' expense only in so far as the diversion was effected by a price-raising device. Further, the preferential system was by no means universal. To protect their entrepôt trades, Hong Kong and Singapore levied no tariffs of any significance. In the Africa of the new Imperialism, international agreements had long prevented a preferential tariff system. Furthermore, mandatory powers were not allowed to impose preferential or discriminatory tariffs. Thus British and foreign goods paid the same low rates of duty throughout Uganda, Kenya, Tanganyika, Nyasaland, part of Northern Rhodesia, Cameroon, Nigeria, Togo, the Gold Coast, Palestine, and Iraq. Only in the remainder of Northern Rhodesia, Gambia, Sierra Leone, and British Somaliland did British goods receive any concessions. To these African areas must be added the West Indies, Ceylon after 1932, and the rather uninteresting dependencies of the South Pacific. But the total area is very much less than the area of the Dependent Empire; and its total trade was not great.

The real preferences were administrative and informal, not fiscal. For example, colonial governments ordered most of their imported material through the Crown Agents in London. The Agents maintained lists of firms who were invited to tender for colonial orders, or to fill an order without tender. Foreign firms appeared on these lists only when British firms could not supply, or could do so only at a heavy cost disadvantage. This practice must have given British firms some special advantage in the colonial market. However, the advantage was limited. The colonies were not obliged to deal through the Crown Agents, and the Agents must have known that if the colonies could save appreciable sums through other purchasing agents they would do so. In view of the fiscal predicament of most African colonies during the interwar period, one suspects that the Agents could not have done much by way of administrative preference. Very careful research would be needed to show whether, and if so to what extent, the colonies paid more than they needed to pay for their imports on government account. The matter is especially important because railways and other public works were almost entirely governmental. Thus the overseas orders for investment goods passed largely through the Crown Agents.

The cartel arrangements of the period could have had some exploitative effect. Some British firms made higher profits and charged higher prices because the cartels assigned the Empire to them. Presumably the dependent territories would not have been thus assigned if the Empire had not existed. But after all, the natives were not very important buyers of heavy chemicals, sophisticated dyestuffs, explosives, or primary iron and steel. What they lost they lost indirectly, through the higher taxes which were needed to cover the larger import bill which the cartels imposed on colonial governments.

In none of these cases does the value of the preference equal the total sale, nor does exploitation equal British receipts or profits. Figure 3 (page 431) is meant to illustrate some of the possibilities. In both panels we have the demand in a single colony for a single importable. It is assumed that, at least for the time being, the colony does not produce the good. Transport costs are assumed to be zero. In Panel A, it is assumed that Britain is a constant-cost producer of the good in question, but that at existing exchange rates Britain can deliver the good to the colony only at a price in excess of the world price. If a general tariff is levied at the rate *ji*, and a preferential tariff at the rate *de*, British sales will rise

Figure 3 *Costs and prices*

Panel A

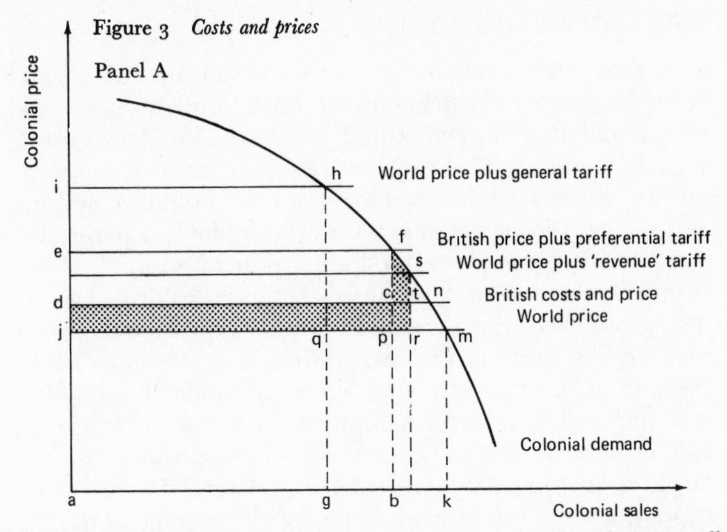

Here the preferential tariff raises British sales from zero to *ab*, and removes all foreign sales. Britain's revenue is *abcd*, but this equals costs, and so no extra producers' surplus is earned. Colonial tariff revenue is *dcfe*. Colonial sales go up from *ag* to *ab*, and colonial buyers gain consumer surplus in the amount *efhi*.

Panel B

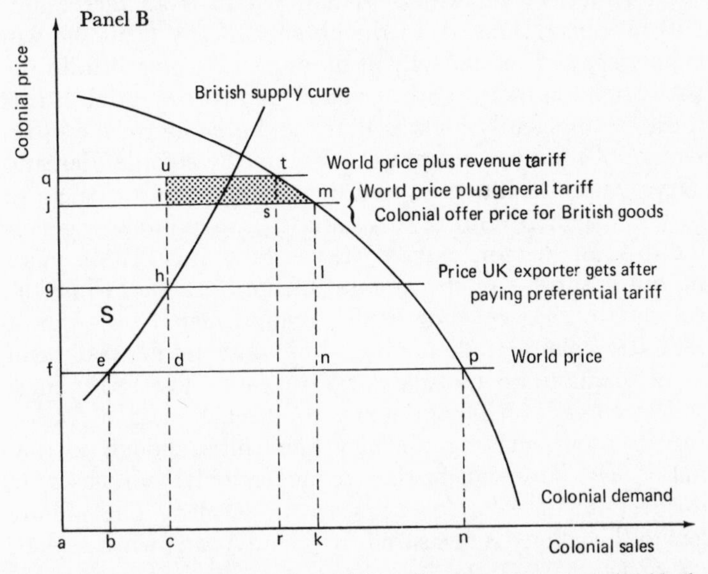

The preferential concession raises British sales from *ab* to *ac*, and adds the area *S*=*fehg* to British producers' surplus, while reducing foreigners' sales from *bk* to *ck*. Colonial tax revenue is *dnmi* from the general tariff on foreign goods plus *ghij* from the preferential tariff on British goods.

from zero to *ab*, while foreign sales will fall from *ak* to zero. If British goods paid the common tariff, foreign sales would be *ag*, and British sales would be zero. Thus by granting a preferential tariff the colony *gains* an area of consumer surplus equal to *efhi*.[4] Britain gains no producer surplus, and the gain in her sales is not at the colony's expense. But if the tariff *ji* is imposed for the purpose of granting a preferential rebate so as to produce a market for British goods, the colony *loses* the consumer surplus represented by the area *pmf*. If *some* tariff was needed in any event to raise revenue, in the amount *dcfe*, but if the preferential system was imposed by British power, the net loss of consumer surplus is the difference between *rms* – the loss from a 'revenue tariff' *rs* and *pmf* – the loss from a preferential tariff which raises the same revenue while giving the market to the UK. To this must be added the area *jpcd* – the excess cost of buying *ab* from the UK. In this last case, therefore, the welfare loss is measured by the shaded area *jrsfcd*.

In Panel B, it is assumed that Britain is an increasing-cost producer. That is, in the absence of any tariff she will supply *ab*, and foreigners will supply *bn*. To give Britain the the whole market, both general and preferential tariffs must be sufficiently high so that *j* and *g* lie above the intersection of the British supply curve and the colonial demand curve. Suppose, however, that the actual duties are as shown in the Panel. Britain sells *ac*, and British producers get *ag* for this. In Britain, extra costs are *bche*, and Britain gains producer surplus in the amount of the area *fehg*, while the colony sacrifices revenue in the amount *fdhg*. Now suppose that the colony is then obliged to raise its general tariff so as to maintain its total tariff revenue. That is, it must collect enough on foreign goods to offset the loss of *fdhg* on British goods, making the new tariff high enough so that *istu* = *fdhg*. This will further reduce colonial purchases, to the level *ar*, and foreign sales, to the level *cr*. The welfare loss to the colony is measured by the area *imtu*, which equals *smt*+*fdhg*.

We could explore other possibilities. But there is little point in doing so. The message should now be clear: the measure of 'welfare loss' is so complicated that in the real world we cannot hope to undertake it; British gains have little or nothing to do with the gains or losses of the colonies; British gains are as hard to estimate as are colonial losses. If we were to pursue the gains from government purchasing policies and from cartels, similar puzzles would arise. Fortunately, the relevant trade flows are so small relative to British output and exports that we are justified in ignoring the calculations, on the ground that, however they might come out, they would reveal gains which were small relative to British output, employment, or living standards.

For interwar Britain the most obvious exploitative device would certainly have been a tariff on Empire foods. Such a tariff would presumably have been shifted backward to the producers in the short run, lowering suppliers' receipts by most or all of the tariff. This possibility was clearly recognised by British ministers during the period 1932–37. They knew that the butter duties of 1932, and the meat duties of 1937, were shifted on to Danish and Argentine producers. But to a quite remarkable extent the British Government preserved the principle of free entry for Empire foods – even when, after 1932, her own farmers were under heavy pressure. Admittedly it was Australasian opposition, not Whitehall reluctance, which prevented the imposition of duties on Empire meat and butter during 1934–37. Admittedly, too, the tea duty was re-imposed as a revenue measure in 1932, only three years after its abolition. But the tea duties of 1919–29 and 1932–39 contained preferential concessions which mitigated their price-reducing effect. So did the old sugar-related duties on dried and canned fruits. So did the wine and spirits duties. And throughout the prewar years the sugar duties included preferential provisions which certainly *raised* the receipts of the West Indies and Mauritius, not to mention Australia.

So much for outputs. What of inputs? Did Britain force capital funds and labour upon her dependencies, thus extracting revenue for British nationals? Obviously she did so in so far as British personnel staffed colonial administrations. But the colonial and Indian establishments were so small relative to British population that it is hard to take this category seriously. Indeed, some would argue that whatever the short-term gains might have been, these arrangements imposed severe long-term losses, by drawing off imaginative and energetic young people which the British economy could ill spare. Obviously, too, she did so in so far as British farmers and miners settled in Africa. In the aggregate, too, this item can be ignored, because net migration to Africa was so very small. However, the gross migration involved the working out of the visionary development strategy in an African context. And from this elaboration developed an exploitation more serious than we would think if we simply considered the new migration of capital and labour.

Figure 4 is an application of visionary ideas in a backward area. I do not suggest that anyone in London had a really

Figure 4. *Sociogram of colonial development*

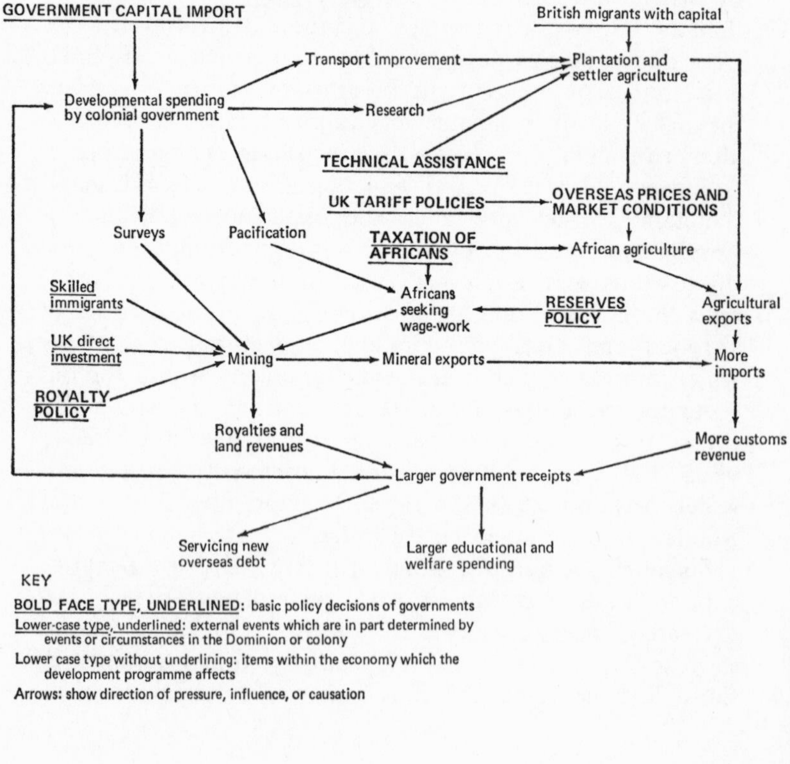

KEY

BOLD FACE TYPE, UNDERLINED: basic policy decisions of governments

Lower-case type, underlined: external events which are in part determined by events or circumstances in the Dominion or colony

Lower case type without underlining: items within the economy which the development programme affects

Arrows: show direction of pressure, influence, or causation

articulate or coherent strategy for productive arrangements within the overseas Empire. Yet the vacuum was not complete. In the Colonial Office, in the overseas colonial services, and in many politicians' minds, there were certain assumptions about economic development which served, in effect, as a policy. These assumptions made it natural for London to acquiesce in overseas arrangements which made the whites the managers and skilled workers, and left the blacks to fill the unskilled jobs, Of course one had to avoid forced labour. It was morally objectionable, inefficient, and all too visible to informed opinion. One must also try to ensure that black workers would be reasonably fed, housed, and cared for. But one could not develop a backward economy without introducing overseas men and overseas capital.

In intent the vision is not exploitative, and in practice it need not be. If the blacks work for wages, they become monetised and 'civilised'. Gradually, the colonial government is able to spend more on African welfare and education, as development expands its tax base. African society changes, but slowly, and as it were voluntarily, because nobody is compelling the African to seek wage work. But things are not that simple. If a civil servant believes he knows how to develop a backward economy, he is not likely to oppose the processes by which local inhabitants are converted into wage-labourers on farms, plantations, and in mines. In particular he may use the tax system and the land-reserve system to encourage the blacks to seek wage work. And he will see no reason to protest when mineral rights are exploited on terms which yield little or no government revenue.

The colonial governments had a two-fold developmental role. Government was to provide the infra-structure, chiefly by creating a transport system. For this purpose it would borrow abroad, in London. The transport improvements would create the exports from which the government can service the new debt. It was also to assist the development of primary production. African agriculture might be commercialised, as in Uganda and Ghana. The quality of its output might be improved through research, grading, and marketing schemes. White farmers might be welcomed, as in Kenya and the Rhodesias. And, most important in some areas, mining was to be encouraged.

For white agriculture and mining, native labour was needed. No one envisaged a white African proletariat. Given the vague idea that wage work would help civilise the African, the authorities were not thinking of exploitation when they encouraged the growth of an African one.

In principle, the Colonial Office and colonial administrations might have borrowed too much for development purposes. In fact, if anything, they borrowed too little. Administrative controls were against them. And they were trapped in an unfortunate tradition of fiscal rectitude. For decades, the Colonial Office and the City had assessed colonial borrowings in simple terms. Were the loans to be used for 'remunerative' purposes? If not, were the general prospects sufficiently good to justify the loan? Such tests, deeply rooted in fiscal habit both in Britain and overseas, assumed that each unit of government should be self-financing. Throughout the interwar period, the Treasury and Whitehall were strong and successful in defence of these traditions.

But there was more to British capital than loan finance. To some extent the British exchequer lent its support to the colonies during the twenties and thirties. There were exchequer guarantees, advances, and gifts. There were also the Colonial Stock Acts, which were believed to lower the supply price of capital to colonies by at least one percentage point. At ruling interest rates, such a reduction would save a colony from one-fifth to one-third of the annual interest it would otherwise have to pay. Further, in the thirties the UK provided small amounts of development finance under the Colonial Development Act of 1929. If we concentrated only on colonial borrowing, therefore, we would not find much exploitation. But the twenties and thirties saw a great deal of direct investment, and in most directions it became much more important than ever before. To the rubber, tea, gold, and diamond mines of the prewar years were added oil, copper, lead, zinc, and especially in the thirties an enormously expanded involvement in gold mining. In this new and growing direct investment how much exploitation can we trace?

Feinstein[5] reports that in 1938 Britain received £229 million from her overseas investments. But only a fraction of this flow came from oil, diamonds, gold, and copper. And only a fraction of the mineral earnings came from the Dependent Empire properly defined – that is, excluding the Union of South Africa. From Sir Robert Kindersley's data[6] we learn that in 1930 only 17 per cent of British overseas investments were in Malaya, Egypt, the Middle East, South Africa, and other colonies. And only £70 million, or 2.1 per cent of the total, was in mines, of which 71 per cent was in South Africa. Kindersley reports that in 1930 mines yielded 8.6 per cent on their nominal capitals, and oils yielded 12.4 per cent while the average yield on all overseas placements was 5.6 per cent. By the end of 1938 the nominal equity capital of mines had risen to £197 million, of oil companies to £131 million, and of rubber plantations to £81 million. Thus the new lending of the thirties, combined with default and repayment of some old placements, had raised such investments to 11 per cent of Britain's total long-term foreign assets. By 1938 it was producing £54.3 million in dividends. But this was only 24 per cent of Feinstein's estimate of gross foreign investment income, and only 1.1 per cent of 1938 GNP. Further, we should remember that not all these dividends represented the yield from exploitation as we have defined it. Let us suppose that for these moderately risky enterprises the supply price of capital funds was 6 per cent. Then excess dividends on these three sectors were only £24.5 million – an insignificant fraction of 1938 GNP.

Admittedly, Kindersley's figures understate total profits, because they report only dividends. But it is hard to see how British firms could have been retaining sufficient profits to change the qualitative impression which these figures give. Gold mining, of course, was immensely profitable in the thirties. But it was in the Union, not in the Dependent Empire. For much of the interwar period rubber was in a bad way. And through the thirties Empire copper and oil production was not large enough to generate any great flow of earnings for retention.

The above accounting is not meant to excuse the fact that land and natural resources had been appropriated from native peoples and made over to British firms for inadequate payment or for no payment at all. It is not meant as an apologia for wage rates and recruitment arrangements in the mines of British dependent Africa. It certainly does not claim that individuals never gained from these unfortunate arrangements. Large gains were made from stock-exchange operations. Sizeable dividends were paid. Some good jobs were created in the London head-office operations on which the relevant firms spent £1.2 million in 1938.[7] And a few thousand British migrants presumably did better overseas than they would have done at home. The accounting merely shows that even in the late thirties, when it had been rapidly expanding, direct investment in the Dependent Empire cannot have been making much of a contribution to British economic well-being in the aggregate.

It might nevertheless be argued that the development of the Dependent Empire in the interwar period had, as the visionaries hoped, stimulated employment and output at home in Britain. Any such stimulus would necessarily be linked with overseas investment of a developmental kind. Unfortunately there are no relevant investment statistics for the Dependent Empire. From Kindersley we learn the nominal value of company and public securities in South Africa, Rhodesia, and other parts of the Dependent Empire. By the end of 1938 British buyers had taken up £440.7 million in such securities. But this figure certainly overstates the autonomous stimulus which Britain might have derived from the development of the Dependent Empire during the interwar period. First of all, it includes British claims on South Africa. Second, some debt and many company securities in the 1938 total had been issued before 1914. Thirdly, overseas investment had a high domestic content, because it involved so much construction. Fourthly, Britain was not the only country to supply the Dependent Empire with capital goods and consumer goods. Finally, some nominal capitalisation did not represent real investment. On the other hand, Kindersley's figures do not include any of the self-financed investment within the Dependent Empire. Let us suppose that the import content was 50 per cent, that Britain supplied 80 per cent of the relevant imports, and that the other complications offset one another. Our autonomous stimulus is then 40 per cent of £440.7 million, or £176.3 million. This figure looks small beside Britain's gross investment of £9,895 million, and net investment of £3,575 million, during the period 1920–38. Any plausible numbers would produce an answer of similar insignificance. In short, the development of the Dependent Empire cannot have had a large impact on British output and employment between 1918 and 1939.

An imperial power might be expected to discourage industrial development in its dependencies. What did Britain's governments think of Empire industrialisation? Did they try to impede it?

In the late twenties, civil servants and politicians were much concerned about 'excessive' protection, especially in Australia. By 1932 they also worried about Canada in the same terms. Amery did not question the Dominions' right to industrialise, and to protect their infant industries. But British officials, especially in the Treasury, tended to assume that Dominion production was high-cost production, and that Dominion politicians would probably impose 'too many' tariffs. Hence, in 1928–32, there was much discussion of Imperial 'rationalisation'. By dividing product lines, British and Dominion manufacturers could share the Dominion markets; Britain could retain some of her export trade, and the Dominions would be spared the excessive costs of really misconceived industrialisation, because they would not try to produce everything. There was even some suggestion that British industry could provide technical assistance![8]

Nothing much came of all this.[9] Before the Ottawa Conference, Anglo-Canadian ironmasters devised a plan for sharing the Canadian steel market. But mill-owners failed to devise a similar plan for cottons. Later in the thirties, arrangements were made to share the South African steel market. Australian politicians suggested similar arrangements for chemicals, electrical equipment, and even motor cars.[10] And that seems to have been that. The cartel arrangements of the period may, of course, have had similar effects, without any active encouragement from Whitehall.

As for India, Britain acquiesced in India's policy of selective protection, partly because the system was planned by a non-political Tariff Board. Indian industrialisation came before Cabinet only when the cotton and iron duties were in question. And the industrialisation of colonies was largely ignored, perhaps because no one thought it would occur.

Nevertheless, after the Ottawa Conference British manufacturers did become aware of home-market competition from Singapore and Hong Kong. The Import Duties Act had imposed tariffs on Japanese goods but not on colonial manufactures; the rubber restriction scheme had raised the supply price of rubber to British, European, and American manufacturers but not in Malaya itself. Hence there was a noticeable expansion in the production and export of tyres and rubber footwear. To this was soon added an export trade in flashlights and other simple manufactures.

What should be done? Early in 1934, an interdepartmental committee of officials considered the matter. Its members were drawn from the Colonial Office, the Dominions Office, and the Board of Trade. Its recommendations[11] went to the Cabinet on 6 June 1934, where they occasioned a dispute between Sir Philip Cunliffe-Lister and Neville Chamberlain. The former argued that though colonial manufactures might sometimes hurt British trade, there was no point in discouraging colonial industrialisation. If Britain were not to allow factories in her colonies, other countries would make room in their colonies, and Britain would gain nothing. On the other hand, there was no point in actively encouraging the creation of new factories in the colonies and mandates. It was convenient for them to concentrate on primary production; for the near future it was likely that they would do so. Meanwhile, Britain should place no duties or quotas on colonial produce. Chamberlain, following Treasury briefs, argued that it was absurd to consider the Dependent Empire as a whole; one must have separate policies for Asia, Africa, and the West Indies. The Cabinet took no decision, and the matter lapsed until, early in 1936, the Colonial Secretary asked the Chancellor to help formulate a general policy.

This Colonial Office initiative met strong opposition in the Treasury, where the officials stonewalled until November. But as there were great difficulties in designing a suitable interdepartmental committee, even after the Treasury gave in nothing was done until 26 February 1937, when a committee began to 'consider and report how far it is desirable to frame and pursue a policy either to encourage or to discourage the establishment of industrial enterprises in the Colonial Empire'.

The committee met three times. Its chairman was the Financial Secretary to the Treasury, Colonel J. Colville. Its members were drawn from all the relevant departments and from the Bank of England. The Colonial Office prepared a series of briefs, tracing the projects which had worried it – false teeth in Cyprus, soap in the West Indies, brewing on the Gold Coast, textiles in East Africa, and so on. In fact the projects were not at all numerous. But they were important in principle because they all involved some sort of fiscal concession – an increase in tariffs, an abstention from a countervailing excise, or free entry for some critical raw material. In every instance the Colonial Office and the local administrators had acquiesced in the relevant concession. Thus the *de facto* policy had been one of encouragement. Should this continue?

After the third meeting, the Colonial Office representative prepared a draft report. He argued that in fact there were only limited opportunities for industrial development overseas, except in Hong Kong and Malaya, where in fact no local protection had been given. As for policy, he wrote, it would be inappropriate to discourage 'natural' growth in colonial industry, and colonial goods of all sorts should continue to pay no tariff at British ports. But to equalise competitive conditions it would be a good idea to control overseas labour conditions more closely. Further, there would often be local circumstances which would justify the colonial authorities in giving aid. Also, in many colonies it would be politically impossible for the Colonial Secretary to impose any policy, because so many colonial councils had substantial unofficial memberships. Wherever possible, however, London should examine any request for special assistance. Local governors and councils should not act on their own authorities. Because infant industries were unlikely to attain independence, the infant industry argument should not be accepted as a justification for protection. Hence only 'special considerations' could justify the granting of special assistance. In the absence of such considerations, excises should countervail all tariffs.[12]

Certainly nothing went to the Cabinet. The Treasury did not much like the draft report. It had hoped for an even stronger denunciation of uncountervailed duties and unsound industrial development. Treasury officials also argued along traditional lines, that Britain could rightly claim to control colonial tariff policy because Britain bore the full cost of colonial defence. But we may reasonably assume that the draft report was *de facto* Colonial Office policy until the outbreak of war. Further, the committee's discussions reveal that, though nothing much had been done to speed the industrialisation of the Dependent Empire, the Office had done nothing to thwart it, and did not want to do so. The Empire of 1937 was not the Empire of 1775.

Certainly Britain's tariff system did nothing to discourage overseas industrialisation. In 1918, and for the entire interwar period, Britain levied remarkably few duties on colonial goods. Her tariff system discriminated against poorer countries only in so far as she taxed tobacco, sugar, coffee, and tea. Presumably these duties were shifted backwards to the producers, at least in part. But it was precisely these duties on which preferential concessions were granted in 1919. Further, throughout the interwar period Britain maintained free entry for all Empire products – primary and manufactured – which had enjoyed this status in 1919.

Much attention went to commodity management, especially in the thirties. Here we must pause to refute a preconception. Nobody was trying to manage commodity flows so as to increase Britain's political power. Nor was the Empire to blame for Hitler's problems with raw materials. After 1933 Germany was massively reflating her economy while maintaining a set of unrealistic exchange rates. These policies, not the British Empire, disrupted the German balance of payments.

In 1920 we find the British authorities worried about cotton. With the reserves of wartime stabilisation schemes they established the Empire Cotton Growing Corporation, which was to spend developmentally. At various times in the twenties the Cabinet authorised further guarantees for the Gezira cotton project, a Sudanese scheme which dated from before the war.

In 1922 Britain devised the Stevenson Plan for rubber. This output control scheme, which lasted until 1928, was meant to raise rubber prices and thereby to increase the Empire's dollar earnings. In the early thirties, Britain accepted Holland's initiative, and co-operated to establish new international agreements for rubber and for tin. She co-operated eagerly with all the attempts of the thirties to devise an international sugar agreement, primarily with an eye on the West Indies, but also with a glance at her own protected and subsidised sugar beet farmers. By tariff adjustments at the Ottawa Conference she tried to strengthen the positions of Empire copper and zinc producers in international cartels. Most important of all, as we have seen, at Ottawa and afterwards she involved herself in unending negotiations for the planning of world trade in butter and meat.

All these plans had mixed motives. By reviving sugar, tin, and rubber prices, the UK Government could reduce the budgetary burden of subsidising her colonial governments, while helping the shareholders in plantation companies. By properly managing the trade in meat, butter, and wheat, she could conciliate the Dominions, Argentina, and Denmark. By so doing she could retain old concessions, on tariffs and on exchange. Perhaps she could win new concessions.

And she could protect and subsidise her own farmers. If Australia and New Zealand could be made prosperous, they could more readily service their old debts to British residents. If rubber prices were relatively high, Britain's dollar earnings were expected to be relatively large.

These schemes were costly to British consumers and users of the controlled products. They benefited British shareholders. Other Europeans also gained because the British were not the only owners or creditors of such enterprises. But native peasant producers gained too, most obviously in the rubber plans, even though the control formulae did not properly recognise their full productive powers. Roughly speaking, we could say that these plans involved an exploitation of British and foreign users by British, foreign, and colonial capitalist and peasant producers.

Exploitation, or something like it, does appear in connection with colonial currency boards. In so far as these kept excessive sterling reserves, often 100 per cent of their note issues, they were lending to the UK. Especially in the thirties, their citizens would surely have been better served if reserves had been smaller and imports and government spending had been larger. However, nobody yet knows whether anybody planned things this way. Certainly the Cabinet never considered this aspect of the Sterling Area. When Currency boards were being set up, Treasury discussion centred on other matters. Perhaps by the late thirties, Whitehall officials had become more perceptive. At any event, no one had yet shown how much these 'forced loans' may have strengthened the British payments position. During the Second Great War, and afterwards, such arrangements were of course immensely valuable to the UK. Before 1939 things must have been very different. Since Britain eschewed exchange control and made only limited use of quotas and preferential tariffs, there was no presumption that she would retain the foreign exchange which her colonies might earn in their trade with foreign countries. If currency boards had held smaller sterling reserves, the UK would certainly have lost some gold or foreign exchange. We can be sure that the loss of reserves would be smaller than the reduction in sterling balances. Beyond this statement we can only guess how large the loss might have been.

If the interwar British governments and civil servants had been development-minded in any modern sense, we should have expected them to consider such matters as the Sterling Area in relation to development. We have seen that they did have ideas about development. But they were not development-minded, and they did nothing which we would call economic planning. Latter-day development theorists and administrators naturally often regret that the British did not equip the Empire with the capital goods and economic structures which their diverse theories and goals require. Unfortunately, hobby horses are as common among development economists as among politicians. We have no reason to think that the Empire's successor states would have been better served, at the time or later, merely because today's economist or official wishes that things had been different in the twenties and thirties.

It is easy to imagine colonial policies, with or without development planning, which would have protected native peoples against the more unpleasant aspects of interwar economic development. It is harder to imagine how such policies could have been carried out. And to explain such exploitation as took place it is both wrong and unnecessary to invoke Marx, Hobson, or Lenin. Marx himself is relevant only in so far as he reminds us that the whites had capital funds and guns, while the blacks had neither. Hobson and Lenin are both wrong in so far as they link exploitation with a general crisis of British capitalism. The relevant capital flows did not arise from any such crisis. They were sucked out by the rich prospects in gold, oil, and other minerals. Many of the settlers, especially in Kenya and Rhodesia, were anything but capitalistic. Lenin is wrong in so far as he links the rising British standard of living with the exploitation of the colonials. However large the surplus thus extracted may have been, it cannot conceivably have been large relative to the interwar rise in British consumption. Trade and payments data are enough to tell us this. Further, many of the exploiters stayed in Africa and ate up their share of the surplus, which thus did not affect living standards in Britain. Finally, in so far as a surplus was transferred to Britain it went into very few hands – those which held African mining shares. Thus it is impossible to believe that the British working man was somehow bribed with a surplus which the colonies produced. Development planning bribed the British workman only in so far as it created new jobs and lowered food prices. The preferential system bribed him only in so far as it raised his real earnings. We have seen that neither effect can have been large enough to have much impact, and that some relevant effects were obtained at the expense of other developed countries. It was technical change and home investment which was raising British living standards during the interwar period. In the thirties, as in 1870–1900, cheap food gave invaluable help. For ordinary people in Britain things would have been much the same if the Dependent Empire had never existed.

Notes

CHAPTER 1

1. W. K. Hancock *Survey of British Commonwealth Affairs, Vol. II: Problems of Economic Policy* (Oxford University Press, London 1942).
2. For a more detailed account see Hancock, op. cit., or Ian M. Drummond *British Economic Policy and the Empire 1919–1939* (Allen & Unwin, London 1972), chs. 2–4, where documentation may be found.
3. University of Sheffield, W. A. S. Hewins Papers, diary entries for 1923. Unlike some diary entries for earlier years, Hewins's 1923 diaries do not appear to have been edited or transcribed before his death.
4. Drummond, op. cit., ch. 2.

CHAPTER 2

1. CO 532/96, 7 February 1917.
2. CO 532/106, 16 July 1917: minute by A. Lambert.
3. CO 532/128, 19 October 1918.
4. CO 532/104, 17 February 1917: memorandum by Professor Chapman.
5. CO 532/114, 12 March 1918: draft memorandum from Walter Long to War Cabinet.
6. CO 532/104, 17 February 1917: minute.
7. CO 532/84, MO, 1 May 1916: letter from Haggard to Lord D'Abernon, 6 May 1916. Minuting this letter, T. C. Macnaghten noted, 'the government in the United Kingdom have not decided whether they want land offered to their ex-soldiers'.
8. CO 532/88, MO, 23 February 1916: Board of Agriculture and Fisheries to Colonial Office, 8 May 1916.
9. CO 532/89, MO, 11 August 1916: letter, Reconstruction Committee to Colonial Office, 11 August 1916.
10. CO 532/89, MO, 5 August 1916: minute by T. C. Macnaghten.
11. CO 532/89, MO, 29 May 1916: Law to Crawford, 25 July 1916.
12. Commonwealth of Australia, House of Representatives, *Miscellaneous Papers 1913 to 1917–19*, 'Report of the ... Premiers' Conference ... May 1916', p. 116.
13. ibid., vi.
14. ibid., pp. 77–9.
15. CO 532/89, MO, 5 August 1916: dispatch from Secretary of State for the Colonies to Governors General, 21 September 1916.
16. CO 532/85: dispatch, Governor General of New Zealand to Secretary of State for the Colonies, 26 September 1916.

17. CO 532/85: dispatch, Governor of South Australia to Colonial Secretary, 10 November 1916.
18. CO 532/85: dispatches, Governor of Western Australia to Colonial Secretary, 22 November 1916. It is amusing and distressing to note that the Western Australians were already proposing the group settlement and the dairy farming which were to go so badly awry after 1922.
19. CO 532/89: telegram, Colonial Secretary to Governor General of Australia, 19 December 1916 (from Board of Agriculture, 5 August 1916).
20. CO 532/85: dispatches, Governor General of Canada to Colonial Secretary, 30 December 1916.
21. Commonwealth of Australia, House of Representatives, *Miscellaneous Papers 1913 to 1917–19*, 'Report of Premiers' Conference (with Minister of Lands), January 1917 (adjourned from December 1916)', p. 68.
22. ibid., pp. 58–9. Admittedly the policy of equal treatment did not long survive the peace. (See Australia *Parliamentary Papers 1923 and 1923–4*, vol. II, 'Conference of Commonwealth and State Ministers (no. 38 of 1923 (2d session))', 424.) But the States did continue to receive British soldiers on the land, and did assist them to some extent.
23. CO 532/96, 7 February 1917.
24. Cd. 8672, 1917–18. Advance copies reached the Colonial Office in July 1917.
25. Cd. 8462, ch. VIII.
26. CO 532/106, 16 July 1917: minute by E. J. Harding.
27. CAB 23/40, Imperial War Cabinet 11, 24 April 1917, and 12, 26 April 1917.
28. CO 532/102: from Board of Trade, 18 July 1917.
29. CO 532/114, 13 May 1918.
30. CO 532/114, 30 April 1918: minute by T. C. Macnaghten.
31. Emigration Bill.
32. CO 532/115, 16 May 1918.
33. CO 532/117, 19 October 1918: minute by Harding.
34. CO 532/117, October 1918.
35. CO 532/117, 16 October 1918; CO 532/117, 19 October 1918.
36. CO 532/90, from Colonial Office, 23 November 1918. The three-man committee was transformed within a week into a much larger body of officials and non-officials.
37. CO 532/118, 23 November 1918.
38. CO 532/118, 23 November 1918: letter, H. Lambert to four departments, 27 November 1918.
39. CO 532/118, 20 December 1918: letter, H. Lambert to Secretary of Government Emigration Committee, 20 December 1918.
40. CO 532/145, 26 March 1919. See also Cmd. 933 and 745, CO 708/7A.
41. CO 532/146, 10 February 1919: memorandum on emigration policy.
42. CO 532/150, 20 October 1919: minutes of 8th meeting, Government Emigration Committee, 4 February 1919.
43. CAB 23/9, p. 132: Cabinet conclusions of 31 March 1919.
44. 114 HC Deb 5s 1919, col. 1857–8.
45. CO 532/137, 3 July 1919: H. Lambert to Treasury, 3 July 1919.
46. CO 532/151, 18 December 1919.
47. CO 532/150, 20 October 1919: minutes of 28th meeting, Overseas Settlement Committee, 19 August 1919.
48. ibid., minutes of 27th meeting, 24 July 1919.

49. CO 532/150, 20 October 1919: minutes of meetings of High Commissioners and Agents General.
50. CAB 24/75, pp. 192–204: memorandum by Secretary of State for the Colonies and revised Draft of Emigration Bill. In February, the Office believed that the Prime Minister had approved of the Bill going ahead. This was not the case. See CO 532/135, 18 February 1919: minute by Sir E. Harding.
51. CAB 24/75, 367–76: shorthand notes of a Conference of Ministers . . . on Unemployment and the State of Trade, 25 February 1919.
52. CAB 24/75, GT 6846, 20 February 1919.
53. CO 532/168, 6 January 1920: minutes of 47th meeting, Overseas Settlement Committee.
54. CO 532/167, 12 June 1920: memorandum by Lord Milner for circulation to Cabinet.
55. CAB 23/22, 27 July 1920.
56. CO 532/167, 16 October 1920.
57. By this time it had become common to distinguish between 'Empire settlement' and 'emigration'. The latter label applied only when the migrants left the Empire. On the negotiations with the Treasury, see CO 532/167, 28 February 1920. The OSC asked £25,000 for female exportation, £12,500 for the export of children, and £5,000 for the Society for the Overseas Settlement of British Women. Only the £5,000 was provided.
58. Cmd. 573, 1920: report covering year ended 31 December 1919.
59. CO 532/158, 7 July 1920: minute by L. S. Amery, 24 September 1920.
60. CO 532/168, 6 January 1920: minutes of 66th meeting, Overseas Settlement Committee, 9 November 1920.
61. CO 532/158, 15 October 1920.
62. CO 532/167, 11 November 1920.
63. CO 532/167: telegrams from the Secretary of State for the Colonies to the Governors General of Australia and New Zealand and to the Governors of the Australian States. South Africa, Newfoundland, and Canada received simple statements of the new policy, without the above injunction.
64. CO 532/168, 6 January 1920: memorandum on a Colonial Office conference, 10 November 1920.
65. CAB 23/22, 48(20), 13 August 1920.
66. CO 532/168, 6 January 1920: minutes of the 59th meeting, Overseas Settlement Committee, 21 September 1920.
67. CAB 27/114/1: conclusions of Cabinet Committee on Unemployment, 6th meeting, 15 October 1920.
68. CAB 23/23, 6 December 1920.
69. CO 532/158, 21 December 1920: telegram from Secretary of State for the Colonies to Dominion Governors-General, sent 21 December 1920.
70. Borden *Memoirs*, II, pp. 1037–8: from Borden's farewell address to the Canadian Conservative Caucus, 30 June 1920.
71. W. A. S. Hewins *Apologia of an Imperialist* (Constable, London 1929), vol. II, pp. 168–70.
72. T 161/110/S.8787: memorandum of a discussion between Chamberlain Amery, and Milner, 27 January 1921; memorandum by Chamberlain to G. Upcott, 19 February 1921.
73. *ibid.*, letter, Upcott to Amery on Chamberlain's instructions, 15 February 1921; memorandum, Upcott to Chamberlain, 24 May 1921.
74. The conference consisted of Milner, Amery, Senator E. D. Millen (Aus-

tralia's Minister of Repatriation), Sir George Perley (Canada's High Commissioner), and Sir James Allen (New Zealand's High Commissioner).

75. CO 418/205: telegram, Colonial Secretary to Governors General of Canada, Australia, and New Zealand, 28 February 1921.

76. For details, revised proposals, and elaborate debates, see Commonwealth of Australia, House of Representatives, *Miscellaneous Papers 1913 to 1917–19*, p. 515: 'Report of . . . Premiers' Conference (with Minister of Lands), January 1917 (adjourned from December 1916)', pp. 575–630.

77. Australia *Parliamentary Papers*, Session 1917–18–19, vol. IV, pp. 51 ff.: Report of the Resolutions, Proceedings, and Debates of the Conference of Commonwealth and State Ministers, Melbourne' (no. 142 of 1919). For the 1916 Premiers' Conference see ibid., Session 1914–15–16–17, vol. V., p. 1235 ff.: 'Report . . . of the Conference of Representatives of Commonwealth and State Governments . . . in Respect of the Settlement of Returned Soldiers on the Land, etc., Melbourne, 17–19 February 1916' (no. 299 of 1916).

78. T 161/110/S.8787: letter, G. Headlam to Masterson Smith, 8 December 1921; CO 418/205: Colonial Office minute on telegram, Governor General of Australia to Colonial Office, 24 November 1921.

79. CO 418/215, from Treasury: Treasury to Colonial Office, 17 May 1921.

80. CO 532/178, 11 February 1921.

81. CO 532/179: telegram, Colonial Office to Governors General of Canada, Australia, New Zealand, and South Africa, 18 March 1921. The proceedings of the Conference are in Colonial Office Confidential Print Dominions No. 77, 1921.

82. See Chapter 3, section V, 'The Treasury and Empire Settlement and Development', for documentation.

83. CAB 24/123, CP 2943, 6 May 1921.

84. CAB 23/26, 16 June 1921.

85. CO 536/198, from miscellaneous offices, 13 July 1921: minutes of Committee of Imperial Conference on Empire Settlement and Migration, 28 June 1921.

86. ibid., from miscellaneous offices, 18 July 1921.

87. Cmd. 1474, Appendix V.

88. T 161/110/S.8787: memorandum by Upcott, 24 May 1921. See also a similar memorandum by Sir G. Barstow.

89. T 161/110/S.8787: minute, Sir Robert Horne, 16 August 1921.

90. CO 532/200, from miscellaneous offices, 28 October 1921: memorandum, by T. C. Macnaghten, 28 October 1921; letter, Macnaghten to Harding, 28 October 1921; minute by Harding on above.

91. CO 532/201, from miscellaneous offices, 12 November 1921: minute by Edward Harding, 24 November 1921. Sir Henry Lambert concurred: 'I do not think that Mr Harding's criticisms are overstated'.

92. The £1 million, the £200,000 and also £40,000 for Western Australian land-settlement and some minor grants to voluntary bodies.

93. CO 532/201, from miscellaneous offices, 12 November 1921: letter, Colonial Office to Treasury, 21 December 1921, transmitting the OSO estimate.

94. CO 532/191, from Treasury, 10 December 1921: letter, Treasury to Colonial Office, 10 October 1921.

95. CO 532/223, from Treasury, 21 January 1922: minute, T. C. Macnaghten.

96. CO 418/205: telegram, Governor General of Australia to Colonial Office,

24 November 1921. In response to a Colonial Office inquiry, Hughes later made it clear that he wanted half the interest for five years only. See telegram, Governor General of Australia to Colonial Office, 19 December 1921.
97. ibid., Amery's minute on above telegram.
98. The preceding two paragraphs are based upon conversation with Mr Fitzhardinge, Prime Minister Hughes's biographer.
99. CAB 27/114/1: minutes of Cabinet committee on unemployment, 31st meeting, 29 September 1921, and 38th meeting, 13 October 1921. On 7 October the Cabinet had been told that the Committee was not overlooking migration as a solution for unemployment. CAB 23/27, 7 October 1921.
100. CAB 27/120, CU 279, 13 October 1921.
101. CO 532/199, from miscellaneous offices, 27 September 1921, for text of the letter.
102. CO 532/190, from Board of Trade, 29 November 1921: letter, Board of Trade to Colonial Office.
103. CO 532/200, from miscellaneous offices, 20 October 1921: letters, Ministry of Labour and Ministry of Health to Colonial Office, 12 and 20 October 1921.
104. T 161/110/S.8787. Several papers in this file bear upon the decision.
105. CAB 24/131, CP 3582, 23 December 1921. Amery's supporting memorandum (CP 3582A) is in similar terms, but also emphasises that emigration would strengthen Britain's best overseas markets.
106. CAB 24/133, CP 3778.
107. CO 532/203, from miscellaneous offices, 15 December 1921: memorandum of a conference of CO and OSO officials and Amery held at the Admiralty, 7 December 1921.
108. CO 532/255, from miscellaneous offices, 16 February 1922. Amery's already-circulated Cabinet Paper (CP 3582, 12 December 1921) had indeed mentioned Hughes's telegram, but had not mentioned the reservations in Treasury or Colonial Office with respect to it.
109. CAB 23/29, 24 February 1922, 6 March 1922. The Committee consisted of Churchill, Amery, Horne, Mond, and the Secretary of State for India.
110. CAB 27/174: Treasury memorandum.
111. CAB 27/174: memorandum by Macnaghten and Amery, 10 March 1922.
112. CAB 27/174: report and proceedings of the Cabinet Overseas Settlement Committee.
113. CAB 23/30, pp. 35–6: conclusions of Cabinet Committee of Home Affairs, 4 April 1922.
114. 12 and 13 Geo. 5, ch. 13.
115. CO 118/218: telegram, Prime Minister of Australia to Colonial Secretary, 24 March 1922, and Colonial Secretary to Prime Minister, 3 April 1922. Sir John Mitchell was Prime Minister of Western Australia.
116. ibid., telegram, Prime Minister of Australia to Colonial Secretary, 6 April 1922.
117. 153 HC Deb 5s (1922), cols. 575–91, 627–30.
118. ibid., 655.

CHAPTER 3

1. CO 418/218. The telegram went on 9 June 1922 – considerably before any official despatch or cable.
2. Public Archives of Canada, W. L. M. King Papers: letter, Amery to King, 1 May 1922.

3. King Papers: letter, King to Amery, 29 May 1922.
4. CO 532/211, despatches, 4 December 1922. The New Zealand response is in CO 532/209, despatches, 31 August 1922.
5. Australia, *Parliamentary Debates*, XCIX, 6 July 1922, pp. 187–9.
6. CO 418/218: minutes on telegram, Prime Minister of Australia to Colonial Office, 22 June 1922.
7. CO 532/213, 31 May 1922: report on a Conference between officials, representatives of the Overseas Settlement Committee, and Amery, 18 May 1922, on the principles to govern schemes submitted under the Overseas Settlement Bill. The Treasury agreed to accept two kinds of contribution to land settlement schemes – the £300 advance to individual settlers which had first been proposed in 1921, and 'larger schemes of block settlement and development' where the UK Government would grant from one-third to one-half of the interest for the first five years. The Treasury representatives urged that any agreements 'should not be so worded as to suggest that His Majesty's Government [in the UK] were accepting responsibility for part interest of a loan raised by an Overseas Government'.
8. CAB 24/137, CP 4062, 22 June 1922.
9. CAB 27/123, CU 432, 29 June 1922.
10. CAB 23/30, 23 July 1922.
11. CAB 24/138, CP 4129, 28 July 1922; CAB 23/30, 24 July 1922.
12. CAB 27/179. TP 5,14,43.
13. CAB 23/30, 12 August 1922.
14. King Papers: Amery to King, 19 September 1922.
15. CAB 24/161, CP 372(24).
16. CO 532/267, from Scottish Office, 31 July 1923.
17. CAB 24/158, CP 35(23).
18. CO 532/214, from Colonial Office, 25 November 1922: minute by Sir Gilbert Grindle.
19. CO 532/267, from Scottish Office, 31 July 1923: memorandum by T. C. Macnaghten.
20. CAB 24/161, CP 372(24): memorandum by Albert Buckley, chairman of Overseas Settlement Committee.
21. CAB 23/45, 14 February 1923.
22. T. Jones *Whitehall Diary* (Oxford University Press, London 1969), pp. 237–8: entry for 28 May 1923.
23. CAB 24/160, CP 261(23): a memorandum circulated to the Dominions prior to the conference.
24. King Papers: letter, W. L. M. King to P. C. Larkin, 12 May 1923: vol. 80, file 626: memorandum by King on conversation with Sir William Clark, 15 November 1928.
25. King Papers, vol. 80, file 623: memorandum for Charles Stewart by F. C. Blair on the Empire Settlement Act, 20 August 1923.
26. King Papers, vol. 80, file 605: memorandum for the Imperial Conference, 1923. The document is unsigned, but can safely be attributed to Skelton.
27. King Papers: letter, P. C. Larkin to King, 8 December 1923.
28. Cmd. 2009.
29. 'Net balance outward' figures from Overseas Settlement Committee, *Reports*.
30. 182 HC Debs 5s 1924–25, 1590.
31. CAB 24/167, CP 307(24): CAB 23/48, 21 May 1924.
32. King Papers: letter, J. A. Robb to W. L. M. King, 18 October 1923, covering memorandum by J. Bogue Smart, Superintendent of Juvenile

Immigration. The memorandum proposed great expansion of such migration, and offered a detailed scheme for adolescents. Robb, the Minister of Immigration, said, 'I rather like the general outline. I believe that this sort of immigration would lay the foundation for splendid citizenship . . . better than encouraging adult immigration.'

33. King Papers: letter, A. E. Ames to W. L. M. King, 20 October 1926: 'I believe . . . that there are . . . classes – including boys just finishing school and older people having some familiarity with farm work, or at least with horses, who might be got if they are sought out. . . .' Ames was a Methodist bond-dealer and a strong supporter of the Liberal party machine.

34. That is, no children under 14.

35. Later in the decade, agreements were made with New Brunswick, Nova Scotia, the Canadian Pacific Railway, and the Hudson's Bay Company. These agreements, and a small Federal project, settled 690 families. By early 1932, 611 remained.

36. See Hewins *Apologia*, II, pp. 302–6. On 3 November 1925, Hewins outlined his suggestions for economic policy at Baldwin's request. *Inter alia* he wrote: 'Empire settlement and trade expansion within the Empire are mutually dependent. Empire settlement has been disappointing in its results, so far as the numbers of emigrants are concerned. We cannot expect much by the way of relief from this policy, unless the Dominions and Colonies enjoy greater facilities in Great Britain for marketing their produce, and nothing would more speedily promote that end than a generous preference in our markets.' For Amery's manoeuvrings, especially with respect to the agenda for the 1926 Imperial Conference, see DO 117/16: minute, Amery to Harding, 31 May 1926.

37. King Papers: letter, Amery to King, 21 September 1926.

38. University of New Brunswick, Harriet Irving Library, R. B. Bennett Papers, pp. 109, 196–232. Skelton himself may not have drafted the memorandum, but it passed to Bennett via a committee which he chaired.

39. University of Cambridge Library, Stanley Baldwin Papers, vol. 94, file 30: letters, Amery to Baldwin, 11 April 1927, and accompanying memorandum.

40. Baldwin Papers, vol. 97, p. 3: letter, Lord Willingdon to Baldwin, 30 January 1928.

41. Baldwin Papers, vol. 12: letter, Baldwin to Sir John Cadman, 31 December 1927.

42. Members were Sir Warren Fisher, Sir John Cadman, and Sir David Shakleton. The report was transmitted to Cabinet on 29 June. See CAB 24/196, CP 206(28); it was published in July as Cmd. 3156.

43. CAB 24/195, CP 198(28).

44. CAB 24/195, CP 198(28).

45. See CAB 27/374, UP(M)(28) 2nd concls., 17 July 1928 and UP(M)(28)3. This idea was revived with respect to the Peace River District of British Columbia early in 1929. See Baldwin Papers, vol. 12: memorandum, Worthington Evans for Baldwin, 18 February 1929. Baldwin was sufficiently interested to discuss the idea with Amery and Churchill.

46. The idea of a big 'colony' was in more general circulation at this time. Cunliffe-Lister favoured it. Sir John Gilmour thought Britain should buy a province in Canada; Neville Chamberlain wanted 'communal emigration . . . to a national state in Canada'. See Jones *Whitehall Diary*, II (Macmillan, London 1946), p. 140, and K. Feiling *The Life of Neville Chamberlain*, p. 162.

47. A Canadian parliamentary select committee on migration had recommended that for the present there should be no more land settlement schemes.

This conclusion was laid before the British cabinet subcommittee, but they seem to have ignored it. For prairie disenchantment, see King Papers: letters, Sir Henry Thornton to King, 29 June 1928 and King to Sir Henry Thornton, 5 July 1928; Robert Forke to King, 30 October 1928.

48. CAB 27/374, UP(28)3.

49. CAB 27/374, UP(M)(28) 1st concls., 11 July 1928.

50. King Papers: letter, Amery to King, 14 June 1928.

51. CAB 27/374, UP(28) 3rd concls., 23 July 1928.

52. CAB 23/58, 23 July 1928; CAB 24/196, CP 245(28). On the general question of Canada's willingness to accept non-agricultural migrants, see H. Blair Neatby *William Lyon MacKenzie King: the Lonely Heights* (University of Toronto Press ,Toronto 1963), pp. 240–1.

53. T 161/295/S.34376/01: notes of a conference held in Ottawa between Canadian Ministers, officials, and Lord Lovat, 17, 18 and 20 August 1928; statement by G. Plant to the Overseas Settlement Committee, 16 October 1928, on the fruits of Lovat's tour. Throughout this file there is very hostile Treasury minuting. The officials did not accept Lovat's 'estimates' of the numbers of settlers Canada could absorb. For the Canadian reaction to the Land Bond scheme, see King Papers: letter, Robert Forke to King, 30 October 1928; cable, Forke to King 1928 n.d.; letter, Lord Lovat to King, 3 September 1928 (in secondary series, vol. 80, file 625).

54. CAB 27/380, MC(28) 2nd minutes, 30 November 1928. The eventual arrangements were very informal. All loan-assisted migrants were to be approved by Canada's director of European Emigration in London, and the British Ministry of Labour was to vouch for them. See CAB 27/380, MC(28) 10, 20 December 1928. The UK was also expected to exercise reasonable discretion with respect to the number and type of migrants to whom it loaned the £10 fare. The Canadian Government insisted that there be no public announcement of the loan plan.

55. See CAB 27/380, MC(28) 2nd minutes, 30 November 1928. For his proposal, see MC(28)6, 27 November 1928. In Canada, deputy ministers are the equivalents of permanent secretaries in the UK.

56. CAB 27/380, MC(28)8, 7 December 1928; MC(28)3.

57. CAB 27/380, MC(28)13, 23 January 1929: letter, Amery to Samuel, 23 January 1929.

58. CAB 27/380, MC(28)5, 14 November 1928. See also CAB 27/375:UPS(28) 1st cons., November 1928, and CAB 24/198, CP 336(38).

59. Statistics from Overseas Settlement Committee, *Reports*. The totals are 'net balances outwards'.

60. Jones *Whitehall Diary*, II, pp. 132 ff.; King Papers: letter, Bickersteth to King, 13 July 1928.

61. King Papers: letter, King to Bickersteth, 13 July 1928.

62. King Papers: letter, Bickersteth to King, 15 July 1928.

63. King Papers, vol. 80, file 625: memorandum of conversations with Sir William Clark, 15 and 17 November 1928. King was right to suspect that the renewed burst of migration talk in November 1928 was directly related to the coming British election. See CAB 24/198, CP 325(28), CP 334(28); CAB 23/59, 7 November 1928; CAB 27/375.

64. See F. Shann, 'Group Settlement of Migrants in Western Australia', *Economic Record*, I, Nov. 1925, pp. 73–93, and Gordon Taylor, 'The Development of Group Settlement in Western Australia', *Economic Record*, VI, May 1930, pp. 28–43.

65. T 161/231/S.23957/2: letter, Macnaghten to Headlam, 4 June 1924.
66. T 161/231/S.23957/1: letter, Bankes Amery to Cuthbertson, 30 April 1924; memorandum, Cuthbertson, April 1924, on meeting with OSO and marginal notes by Niemeyer.
67. T 161/231/S.23957/1: letter, Lunn to Wilson, 5 May 1924.
68. T 161/231/S.23957/1: letter, Thomas to Snowden, 12 May 1924. See also CAB 24/167, CP 302, 307(24).
69. ibid., letter, Snowden to Thomas, 15 May 1924.
70. CAB 23/48, 21 May 1924.
71. T 161/231/S.23957/2: memorandum, Niemeyer to Headlam, 9 September 1924.
72. T 161/231/S.23957/2: letter, Macnaghten to Treasury, 3 December 1924.
73. T 161/231/S.23957/2: letter, H. Fass to Macnaghten, 2 March 1925. Bruce was demanding that the UK should pay interest on loans which would settle Australians, not Britons, on Australian farms.
74. T 161/231/S.23957/3: minute, H. Fass, 16 March 1925.
75. ibid., minute, R. S. Meiklejohn, 17 March 1925.
76. ibid., letter, G. Barstow to Overseas Settlement Office, 18 March 1925.
77. National Library of Australia, Sir George Pearce Papers, MS 23, Ser. 15, 'Minutes of a Conference', 3 November 1927 *et seq.*
78. CAB 24/167, CP 307(24).
79. ibid.
80. Development and Migration Commission, *Third Report* (Australia *Parliamentary Papers* 1929–30–31, vol. II) (no. 149 of 1929–31), pp. 1319–20.
81. ibid., pp. 1304–5.
82. British Economic Mission, *Report* (Australia *Parliamentary Papers* 1929–30–31, vol. V) (no. 6 of 1929), pp. 1231 ff., submitted 7 January 1929.
83. Development and Migration Commission, *Second Report* (Australia *Parliamentary Papers* 1929–30–31, vol. II), pp. 1541–3, 1583.
84. ibid., pp. 1320–1.
85. Development and Migration Commission, *Third Report*, pp. 1326–7. These numbers reflect downward revisions of costs during 1929–30; already, by the end of 1928, a larger total had been authorised.
86. For what follows I am heavily indebted to Kathleen Jupp, 'Factors affecting the Structure of the Australian Population, with special Reference to the Period 1921–33', unpublished M.A. thesis, Australian National University. I must also thank Professor Appleyard of the University of Western Australia, for directing me to this thesis.
87. ibid., p. 76.
88. See New Zealand *Parliamentary Debates*, vol. 183, p. 286, and vol. 191, p. 643.
89. See New Zealand Department of Immigration, *Reports*, 1920–21 to 1932–33.
90. I owe this point to Sir Keith Hancock.
91. T 176/11: memorandum by R. Hawtrey, 6 January 1922. See also T 161/111/S.8787/01: memorandum by Sir G. Barstow, 19 January 1922. Barstow saw no advantage and much cost in transferring an industrial population and converting them into agriculturalists. He saw no reason to believe that 'state intervention will be more successful in this than it has been in other fields of activity'. The true remedy for unemployment, he thought, was 'to get our industries going again by reduction of working costs and of Government expenditure and the millions a year which it is proposed to spend on emigration will do their part in retarding the revival of trade'.

92. T 161/231/S.23957/1: memorandum by Niemeyer for Snowden, 12 May 1924: 'I am personally sceptical about the whole policy of Empire Settlement'. T 160/184/F.6984/3: memorandum, Niemeyer for Churchill, 28 May 1926; T 161/231/S.23957/1: memorandum, Cuthbertson, 1 April 1924, on a meeting to discuss the £34 million agreement: 'The whole policy may be wrong, it is largely ineffective, and migration will develop without it when circumstances are more favourable'; T 161/297/S.34609/1: memorandum, Sir Richard Hopkins for Snowden, 27 June 1929.
93. T 161/292/S.33978: memorandum by A. Waterfield for Phillips and Hopkins, 7 January 1929: 'Mr. Amery's letter of 26 November [urging a block grant of £500,000 p.a. for colonial development] is really only a rehash of all the worst features of projects which have been fully discussed during the past five years'.
94. T 176/20: letter, Niemeyer to Montague Norman, 13 December 1926.
95. T 161/231/S.23957/2.
96. T 161/111/S.8787/01: unsigned and undated memorandum, apparently late 1921.
97. T 161/297/S.34608: memorandum by L. Cuthbertson, 2 March 1929. Amery had accused the Treasury of delaying the execution of the policy enunciated in the East African and Palestine Guaranteed Loans Act. For more on Treasury distrust of the CO and DO, see T 161/291/S.33978: memorandum, A. Waterfield to Phillips, 7 January 1929, and memorandum, F. Phillips to Hopkins, 8 January 1929. On the tendency to put the Dominions up to things, see T 160/184/F.6984/3: memorandum, Niemeyer for Churchill, 28 May 1926.
98. This point greatly worried Austen Chamberlain; indeed, it seems to have been responsible for his rejection of the Millen scheme, and it was used against the Hughes request of November 1921. See T 161/111/S.8787/01: memorandum by Sir G. Barstow, 19 January 1922: as for the Hughes proposals, 'the objections to this from a Parliamentary and constitutional point of view are so great as hardly to need stating at length'. Barstow's memorandum was later circulated to the Cabinet under the name of Sir Robert Horne, who was then Chancellor of the Exchequer. On the relation between a contribution to interest and a guarantee of a Dominion loan, see T 161/111/S.8787/02: memorandum, R. S. Meiklejohn to Hilton Young, and proceedings of a conference between Treasury and Overseas Settlement officials, 18 May 1922. Niemeyer believed that the Hughes proposal involved a part-guarantee of Australian credit. See T 161/111/S.8787/01: memorandum by Niemeyer, 15 March 1922. This memorandum was prepared at the request of another Treasury official, who wanted a destructive memorandum because he was convinced that the Treasury must condemn the Hughes idea. See ibid., memorandum, Headlam to Niemeyer, 15 March 1922.
99. T 160/184/F.6984/1: memorandum, Niemeyer, 20 June 1923; T 160/184/F.6984/3: marginal notes on memorandum by Amery, 19 May 1926.
100. T 161/233/S.23957/103/3: memorandum, A. Waterfield to G. Upcott, late 1929. For Niemeyer's earlier distrust, see T 161/231/S/23957/2: memorandum, Niemeyer to Headlam, 9 September 1924, and T 160/184/F.6984/3: memorandum, Neimeyer to Churchill, 28 May 1926.
101. On funding, see T 160/184/F.6984/3: memorandum, Niemeyer to Churchill, 28 May 1926; on the Colonial Stock Act, see T 160/184/F.6984/3: marginal notations on memorandum by Amery, 19 May 1926; on the cost of credit to British users, see T 161/291/S.33978: memorandum, Hopkins to

Churchill, 23 February 1929, and T 160/184/F.6984/2: memorandum by Phillips, 2 February 1926. On the general strategy, and the relation of Empire development to it, see T 160/184/F.6984/1: memorandum, Viemeyer to Chamberlain, autumn 1923, and T 176/11: undated memorandum, Neimeyer, apparently early 1923.

102. On the relation between the gold standard and the stabilisation of exchange rates within the Empire, see various materials in T 160/550/F.7219/1. See in particular a memorandum by J. Phillips, 22 April 1926. On the interest of the gold-producing Dominions in a return to gold, see T 176/5, pt. 1, pp. 208–213: memorandum, Niemeyer for Snowden, March 1924. Niemeyer was of course confused in arguing that a gold standard at prewar parity would necessarily help the gold-producing Dominions.

103. See in particular T 176/17, pt. 1: letter, Norman to Niemeyer, 11 May 1925, and other materials in this file.

104. T 161/474/S.23957/014: minute by A. Waterfield, 27 September 1930.

105. ibid, minute by F. Skevington, 6 March 1931.

106. CAB 32/76, IEC(20) 107: also CAB 24/215, CP 343(30).

107. CAB 24/215, CP 329(30), 1 October 1930. The subcommittee consisted of Viscount Astor, Professor Carr-Saunders, G. D. H. Cole, L. Ellis, and Christopher Turnor.

108. CAB 24/224, CP 297(31), 27 November 1931. Published as Cmd. 4075.

109. CAB 23/65, 15 October 1930.

110. CAB 32/82, EE(30)60: report of committee on overseas settlement of Imperial Conference, 1930. For Lunn's and Maloney's comments, see CAB 32/98, proceedings of committee, EE(S)(30) 2 and 3.

111. Though white labour produced export sugar in Australia, production and marketing were so tightly controlled in the twenties and thirties that the Act cannot have significantly affected either.

112. Meat marketing was not controlled until the mid-thirties, but butter export was subsidised from 1926; by 1929 there had long been subsidy and two-price systems for canned and dried fruits.

113. The following four paragraphs paraphrase material in my *British Economic Policy and the Empire, 1919–1939*, ch. 2.

CHAPTER 4

1. DO 35/90/4011/48: telegram, Australian Government to Dominions Office, 7 May 1930.

2. Cables relating to the agenda are in DO 114/31.

3. For the first report of the interdepartmental committee on the conference, see DO 35/90/4011/13, 12 February 1930.

4. DO 3/21, file 4011: telegram, Australian Government to Dominions Office, 16 July 1930.

5. See W. M. Corden *The Theory of Protection* (Clarendon Press, Oxford 1971), pp. 13 ff.

6. CAB 24/213, CP 234(30), 5 July 1930.

7. CAB 32/84, EE(B)(30)18. See also EE(B)(30)26.

8. CAB 24/213, CP 244(30), 15 July 1930. John Simon was chairman of the committee. In the disputes of December 1931, Ramsay MacDonald re-circulated this report – without apparent effect.

9. CAB 24/213, CP 250(30), 17 July 1930.

10. See Philip Snowden *Autobiography* (London, 1936), II, p. 884.

11. CAB 24/214, CP 272(30), 25 July 1930.
12. CAB 24/214, CP 298(30).
13. CAB 24/214, CP 287(30), 6 August 1930, embracing IEC(30)45 and IEC (30)61.
14. CAB 24/214, CP 298(30).
15. CAB 24/215, CP 305(30), 11 September 1930.
16. CAB 24/215, CP 307(30), 15 September 1930.
17. CAB 23/165, 17 September 1930.
18. CAB 24/215, CP 313(30), 23 September 1930.
19. CAB 32/80, 2nd plenary session, 8 October 1930. See also Cmd. 3717, 3718.
20. For the Cabinet decision, CAB 23/65, 9 October 1930. For the officials' view, DO 35/233/8691/5: Note prepared by Board of Trade on Bennett's 10 per cent offer, November 1930.
21. Robert Skidelsky (*Politicians and the Slump* (Macmillan, London 1967), p. 244) gives a misleading impression of Bennett's offer, which he describes as a 'ten per cent preferential Empire tariff'. What Bennett proposed was that all Dominions should raise their tariff rates on *foreign* goods by 10 per cent of their present levels. British exports would pay the same rate as before. Thus if British pots had paid 25 per cent and foreign pots 30 per cent at the Canadian border, the Bennett proposal would raise the foreign rate to 33 per cent while leaving the preferential rate at 25 per cent. Further, there were to be 'exceptions' which Bennett did not spell out. No sane British Government would have imposed new food taxes to earn such a concession.
22. CAB 32/79, minutes of meeting of prime ministers and heads of delegations, 13 October 1930.
23. CAB 24/216, CP 366(30); Bennett Papers, 102,841–44; memorandum; H. H. Stevens to R. B. Bennett, 17 October 1930.
24. DO 35/196/8079/45: despatch, Sir William Clark to Dominions Office, 29 May 1930. See also DO 35/196/8079/48: despatch, Sir William Clark to Dominions Office, 15 August 1930.
25. On the malfunctioning of the Pools in 1929–30 see various items in DO 35/196/8079.
26. Public Archives of Canada, H. H. Stevens Papers, vol. 12, file 4: letter, Stevens to Bennett, 17 October 1930, and attached memorandum by D. C. MacGibbon. The letter is in the Bennett Papers (102,841–44) but without the memorandum. However, even if Bennett never saw MacGibbon's typescript he must have encountered its arguments when his advisers briefed him. Bennett Papers, 102,262; 102,265; 192,255.
27. idem.
28. Bennett Papers, 102,760–807: 'State Bulk Purchase of Agricultural and Other Commodities'. Data in ibid., 102, 162, allow us to attribute this anonymous document to Swanson.
29. CAB 32/90, p. 50.
30. CAB 32/90, E (1930), 2nd Concls.: Stenographic Notes of Plenary Sessions, pp. 23, 45, 57. For an elaboration of the New Zealand government's position, see *New Zealand Parliamentary Debates*, vol. 228, p. 545, 21 July 1931, where Prime Minister Forbes explained that quotas and bulk purchase were not practicable, and that they would be useless for New Zealand, which already exported almost all her butter to the UK. The Labour opposition thought differently, and criticised Forbes for wrongly representing New Zealand attitudes at the London Conference.

31. Commonwealth Archives Office, CP 103/3/6: letter, Scullin to P. J. Maloney (Minister for Markets), 28 June 1930.
32. Commonwealth Archives Office, CP 103/3/12: memorandum prepared in Department for Markets.
33. idem.
34. idem.
35. Commonwealth Archives Office, CP 103/3/6, letters F. McDougall to Prime Minister Scullin, 4 June and 19 June 1930. Both marked 'personal and confidential'. Snowden believed (*Autobiography*, II, p. 781) that if Thomas had not been restrained by the declared policy of the Labour Party he would have conceded the Dominions' demands for new food taxes and wider preferential arrangements.
36. CAB 32/90, E (1930) 2nd Concls.: Stenographic Notes of Plenary Sessions, pp. 23, 45, CAB 32/79, minutes of meeting of prime ministers and heads of delegations, 13 October 1930.
37. Snowden, *Autobiography*, p. 869. For an account of the meeting at which it was decided to investigate quotas and bulk purchase, see CAB 32/79, minutes of meeting of prime ministers and heads of delegations, 13 October 1930. The Cabinet had agreed on 9 October to refer the questions of import boards, price stabilisation, and bulk purchase to a committee of the conference. See CAB 23/65, 9 October 1930.
38. CAB 32/99, EE(Q)(30), 1A, 2, 3.
39. CAB 24/216, CP 352(30), 24 October 30. The scheme involved percentage-of-output quotas to be applied to milling in the UK. Millers would be required to use 55 per cent Empire and British wheat. Imports of wheat flour would be mixed with Empire flour so as to obtain the same composition. Further, Britain would be required to import at least 335,000 tons of Dominion wheat flour per year. Both the percentage and the flour imports had been smaller in 1924–29. The President later explained (CP 364(30), 27 October 1930) that there was no proposal to guarantee a price to the Dominion exporters and no expectation that the UK would pay more for her wheat. Also, he thought, the arrangements would not 'seriously' affect trade relations with the Argentine.
40. CAB 24/216, CP 366(30), 27 October 1930.
41. CAB 23/65, Cabinet 64(30), 28 October 1930.
42. CAB 32/99, EE(30)62, Revise.
43. CAB 23/65, 11 November 1930.
44. CAB 32/79, PM(30)23: minutes of meeting of prime ministers and heads of delegations, 11 November 1930.
45. CAB 32/79, PM(30)24, 12 November 1930, and PM(30)26.
46. CAB 32/79, PM(30)9, 16 October 1930.
47. idem. In the Quota Committee of the Conference, the Australians and the Irish continued to press for 'voluntary preferences': that is, British import boards ought to pay higher prices for Dominion produce. See CAB 32/99, EE(Q)(30) 4th conclusions, 21 October 1930.
48. 245 HC Debs 5s 1930–31, cols. 1547–8, 1550–1, 1558, 1961–3.
49. See CAB 24/220, CP 69(31), 14 March 1931.
50. idem.
51. CAB 23/166, 18 March 1931.
52. CAB 23/65, 10 December 1930.
53. CAB 24/221, CP 107(31), 2 May 1931.
54. CAB 24/224, CP 288(31), 23 November 1931. On 2 December, the Cabinet

endorsed these recommendations, which were originally formulated to guide Thomas in his tour of Empire capitals. This tour never took place.

55. Baldwin Papers, vol. 31, pp. 44–8: letters, Amery to Baldwin, 25 February 1930 and 4 July 1930. Amery thought that both quota and price guarantee could be extended to cover Dominion wheat.

56. CAB 23/69, 11 and 15 November 1931. The announcement was made in the House on 26 November.

57. CAB 23/69, 2 December 1931; CAB 23/70, 20 January 1932, 27 January 1932, 17 February 1932. Gilmour's proposals in their final form are in CAB 24/227, CP 22(32).

58. 262 HC Deb 5s, 1931–2, cols. 959–74.

59. In addition to the 10 per cent tariff on foreign flour.

60. Wheat Act, 1932, 22–23 Geo 5, c. 24; royal assent 12 May 1932.

61. For Australian reaction see DO 35/240/8831H/35: note of a conversation between J. H. Thomas and F. L. MacDougall; 7 April 1932, DO 35/240/8831H/77, reporting a conversation between MacDougall and Walter Runciman, 27 May 1932. For the attitude of the Canadian grain trade, see CAB 32/105/0 (B) (32)147. The Calgary and Winnipeg grain exchange members opposed the quota because they thought it would raise neither sales nor prices in the UK, would disrupt the course of trade, and would leave a large surplus for extra-Imperial sale in any event.

62. See Bennett Papers, 110,744 (also in Stevens Papers, vol. 13, file 6): letter, Stevens to Bennett, 29 July 1932: 'It will be recalled that an indication was given by the British that a quota might be given on wheat and a quota on flour . . . I would strongly advise that Canada resist any quota on flour, as, with a 10% preference, there is an opportunity for Canada to greatly increase its export to the British market.'

63. Bennett Papers, 115,704: telegram, Bennett (in London) to Perley (in Ottawa), 23 November 1931.

64. Bennett Papers, 98,432–3: letter, Amery to Bennett, 7 July 1932: 'I am a little afraid that our delegates will be disposed to begin by trotting out the wheat quota which nobody here really wants and which is only a survival from a previous stage in the evolution of party politics here. I think our delegates themselves will really be glad to be able to come to say that after fully examining the quota we had come to the conclusion that a duty on foreign wheat was really simpler and more widely acceptable. The same I think really applies to all forms of meat. . . .'

65. Bennett Papers, 109,487,109–677.

66. Bennett Papers, 108,792–3. The paper may have been written by Bennett's brother-in-law and confidant, W. Herridge, but it passed through the committee of officials which was preparing Canada's case.

67. Roland Wilson (then an economics lecturer at the University of Tasmania) in *The Australian Quarterly*, 14 March 1932, p. 12.

68. Commonwealth Archives Office, CP 272/3: memorandum, June 1932.

69. Bennett Papers, 115,252: telegram, Prime Minister of Australia to Prime Minister of Canada, 18 May 1932.

70. Bennett Papers, 111,921–5, 112,116: letters, Bennett to the various wheat pools, 9 May 1932.

71. DO 35/211/8324/29.

72. DO 35/211/8324/45.

73. DO 35/238/8831G/8: letter, G. Whiskard to Sir W. Clark, 16 March

1932; circulated to high commissioners in Australia and South Africa. Clark was Britain's high commissioner in Canada.
74. DO 35/211/8324/69: minute by G. Whiskard, 22 March 1932.
75. See CAB 32/104, O(B)(32)18. The Committee recommended a global quota for all Dominion wheat, and doubted the Dominions would benefit. Its members thought that restriction or prohibition of Russian wheat, as urged by Australia, would prejudice the UK's milling and poultry industries.
76. DO 35/211/8324/89: minute by G. Whiskard, 30 June 1932. For the meetings see DO 35/212/8834/82, 83, 86.
77. DO 35/239/8831G/157: telegram, Sir William Clark to Dominions Office, 11 July 1932. See also CAB 32/105, O(B)(32)137.
78. CAB 32/101, O(UK)(32) 17th meeting, 27 July 1932. Plan A of OC(73).
79. CAB 32/101, O(UK)(32) 27th meeting, 3 August 1932.

CHAPTER 5

1. Julian Amery *The Life of Joseph Chamberlain* (Macmillan, London 1969), vol. 6, ch. CXXI.
2. Feiling *Chamberlain*; K. Middlemas and J. Barnes *Baldwin* (Weidenfeld and Nicolson, London 1969), ch. 25; R. Kottman *Reciprocity and the North Atlantic Triangle 1932–1938* (Cornell University Press, Ithaca 1968), ch. I.
3. For a convenient summary of proceedings at the several conferences, see Ollivier *The Colonial and Imperial Conferences*. For the 1923 meeting see Hancock *Survey*, ii, pt. 1, p. 135 ff.
4. For the Dominions Office case against bargaining for mutual preferential concessions see DO 35/194/8039/28: a brief prepared for J. H. Thomas, the Dominions Secretary, in July 1930.
5. On the Conference, see Drummond *British Economic Policy*, pp. 67–9, and the references therein. The link to the Ottawa Conference is summarised in DO 35/237/8831/222. A stenographic summary of the London discussions is in CAB 32/79. The public proceedings are in Ollivier *Colonial and Imperial Conferences*, and in Cond. 3718 of 1930. See also Hancock *Survey*, ii, pt. 1, pp. 212–14.
6. First meeting, 26 November 1930. Membership: Snowden, Thomas, Addison, Graham, Shaw, Trevelyan, and Alexander.
7. For discussion as to dates and postponement, see DO 114/36, various telegrams 21 January 1931 to 6 June 1931. See also DO 3/34, register of file 8831. The principal problem was Australia, who could send no delegation till 1932. And within 1932, South Africa could send a delegation only from August to November. Canada, too, may have been delaying in the belief that a more malleable Tory ministry would soon replace MacDonald and Snowden. See Kottman *Reciprocity and the North Atlantic Triangle*.
8. DO 35/243/8835: Minutes of Cabinet Committee on Proposed Economic Conference at Ottawa, 5th meeting, 22 April 1931. See also CAB 24/221, CP 107(31).
9. Harriet Irving Library, University of New Brunswick, R. B. Bennett Papers, 109,389–10.
10. DO 3/34, file 8831, item 35: telegram, UK representative in South Africa to Dominions Office, 1 May 1931.
11. Bennett Papers, 113,907: letter, H. H. Stevens to R. B. Bennett, 22 June 1932, reporting the views of G. R. Stevens: 'Mr. Havenga has decided that if British preference is unobtainable on the items of wool, maize, and meat, the

remaining preferences are of little or no value to South Africa . . . Mr. Havenga has expressed his regret that Great Britain extended the temporary preferences to South Africa . . . little or nothing can be expected from the South African delegation at Ottawa.'

12. Stevens Papers, vol. 12, file 3, file 4: Public Archives of Canada.

13. Bennett Papers, 112,745: telegram, Prime Minister of New Zealand to Prime Minister of Canada, 7 March 1931.

14. Bennett Papers, 111,570: letter, R. B. Bennett to Sir Arthur Duckham, 25 January 1932. Duckham had suggested that the Conference should meet in London, not in Ottawa.

15. CAB 23/69, 2 December 1931, approving first report of Ottawa Preparatory Committee, in CAB 24/224, CP 288(31) of 23 November 1931.

16. See University of Newcastle Upon Tyne, Lord Runciman Papers, Box 3, File 'Cabinet Colleagues', letters, Runciman to MacDonald and vice versa, 21 December 1931 and 28 December 1931. See also Snowden *Autobiography*, II, p. 1004 and Feiling *Chamberlain*, p. 195.

17. See materials in T 172/1768: an undated and unsigned memorandum that seems to be Chamberlain's own work; and a memorandum by R. V. N. Hopkins, 15 December 1931, later circulated to Cabinet by Chamberlain as BT(31)5. See also an undated memorandum by Chamberlain, which appears to date from December 1931. On 19 September, he had written in his diary 'there is only one way of redressing it [the deficit] and it is by a tariff. I should like the Prime Minister . . . to go to the country on a programme of the full tariff and a free hand' (Feiling *Chamberlain*, p. 195).

18. CAB 24/224, 25 September 1931. The Council foresaw a deficit of £71 to £101 million in 1931, largely because invisible income had dropped so sharply.

19. T 172/1768: memorandum by Chamberlain, undated but apparently December 1931.

20. ibid., memorandum by R. V. N. Hopkins, 15 December 1931.

21. T 172/1768, undated and unsigned memorandum.

22. See R. A. Mundell *International Economics* (Macmillan, New York 1968), pp. 246–7.

23. T 172/1768: letter, Cunliffe-Lister to Chamberlain, 18 January 1932.

24. For the Cabinet Committee Report, see CAB 24/227, CP 25(32), 19 January 1932. The Committee expected a current-account deficit of £150 million for 1932. Samuel and Snowden dissented from its recommendations: see CAB 24/227, CP 31(32).

25. CAB 24/227, p. 293.

26. idem.

27. CAB 24/227, CP 21(32).

28. CAB 24/225, CP 324(31), 15 December 1931.

29. For the discussion in Cabinet, see CAB 23/70, 21 and 22 January 1932. For Cabinet's 'agreement to disagree' publicly with respect to import duties, see *inter alia* Snowden *Autobiography*, II, pp. 1004 ff.

30. CAB 24/227, CP 49(32), 28 January 1932. In this form the Bill also exempted wheat but not wheat flour or meat from the 10 per cent duty on all Empire goods except colonial goods, but it could be withdrawn.

31. Bennett Papers, 113,568–575: memorandum by Perley and Dupre on 'Meeting of British Commonwealth Representatives on 3 February 1932 at Hotel Beau Rivage'. At the end of the meeting, Thomas explained privately to Perley that there had been tremendous pressure from Ottawa for a change in

the original policy – a general tariff with eventually, after the Conference, free or preferential entry for the Dominions.

32. Snowden, of course, dissented, regarding any preference as perverse in respect both of revenue and of protectiveness. See CAB 24/227. CP 31(32), 18 January 1932.

33. 261 HC Deb 5s 1931–32, 287–91.

34. T 172/1768: letter, Sir Philip Cunliffe-Lister to Chamberlain, 15 January 1932.

35. ibid., letter, Cunliffe-Lister to Chamberlain, 27 January 1932.

36. T 172/1768: memorandum attached to letter, Cunliffe-Lister to Chamberlain, 15 January 1932.

37. T 172/1768: letter, E. R. Forbes to Sir Richard Hopkins, 17 December 1931.

38. As late as 27 January 1932, Chamberlain wanted to specify those colonial products which would enter duty-free. Cunliffe-Lister argued, however, that the result would involve constant negotiations with the Colonies, and constant debates in the House, because so many new colonial products were likely to emerge in the coming years. T 172/1768: letter, Cunliffe-Lister to Chamberlain, 27 January 1932.

39. DO 35/238/8831G/8: letter, Sir Geoffrey Whiskard to Sir William Clark, 10 March 1932.

40. DO 114/36: telegram, Dominions Office to overseas governments, 10 December 1931.

41. DO 35/237/8831/86: minute, Sir Edward Harding, 27 January 1932.

42. DO 35/238/8831G/4: telegram, Dominions Office to United Kingdom trade commissioners and representatives in Canada, New Zealand, and South Africa, 16 February 1932. In fact, the Australians wanted to examine Britain's requests both in London and in Australia.

43. DO 114/42, pp. 112–14: telegram, Dominions Office to Canadian, Australian, New Zealand, and South African governments, 9 May 1932. Reproduced in part in Drummond *British Economic Policy*, p. 189.

44. DO 35/243/8847/16.

45. DO 35/245/9808/10, 14. If a country had left the gold standard the South African Finance Minister could arbitrarily fix an exchange rate for valuation purposes.

46. Public Archives of Canada, H. H. Stevens Papers, vol. 12, file 3: memorandum, H. H. Stevens to R. B. Bennett, 22 May 1931, reporting cables from G. R. Stevens, Canadian Trade Commissioner in South Africa.

47. DO 35/238/8831E/65A.

48. Bennett Papers, 113,907–8: memorandum, H. H. Stevens to R. B. Bennett, 22 June 1932.

49. DO 35/238/8831E/67.

50. DO 35/241/8831J/10.

51. DO 35/241/8831J/12.

52. DO 35/241/8831J/19: telegram, New Zealand Government to Dominions Office, 19 May 1932.

53. DO 35/240/3831H/70: minute of visit by representative of New Zealand High Commission to Dominions Office, 25 May 1932.

54. DO 35/241/8831J/47: despatch, United Kingdom Trade Commissioner in Wellington to Department of Overseas Trade, 30 May 1932.

55. DO 35/241/8831J/48: despatch, United Kingdom Trade Commissioner in Wellington to Department of Overseas Trade, 4 June 1932.
56. DO 35/241/8831J/43, 45.
57. DO 35/241/8831J/50.
58. Bennett Papers, 111,570: letter, R. B. Bennett to Sir Arthur Duckham, 25 January 1932.
59. DO 35/195/8039/75: despatch, Sir William Clark to Dominions Office, 12 December 1930.
60. Stevens Papers: letters, H. H. Stevens to Sir George Perley, 14 November 1931: 'Mr McKinnon is one of the very few men in the Government Service who are qualified to deal with tariff matters in the preparation of trade agreements. . . .'
61. Bennett Papers, 112,913 ff.
62. DO 35/238/8831G/3: letter, Sir William Clark to Sir Geoffrey Whiskard, 21 January 1932, reporting a conversation between Britain's Senior Trade Commissioner and the CMA staff.
63. Bennett Papers, 112,913–113,405.
64. For Bennett's acid comments to the CMA Manager, see Bennett Papers, 113,405: letter, R. B. Bennett to J. K. Walsh, 11 July 1932.
65. DO 35/237/8831/87: despatch, Dominions Office to Sir William Clark, 14 January 1932.
66. DO 35/238/8831G/13.
67. Bennett Papers, 113,576–609: memorandum of Cabinet meeting, 20 February 1932.
68. DO 35/239/8831G/48: letter, Frederick Field to Department of Overseas Trade, 7 March 1932.
69. Bennett Papers, 111,940 ff.
70. Bennett Papers, 113,615: letter, Sir William Clark to R. B. Bennett, 26 March 1932.
71. DO 35/239/8831G/113: letter, Sir William Clark to Sir E. Harding, 11 May 1932.
72. DO 35/239/8831G/141: despatch, Sir William Clark to Dominions Office, 15 June 1932.
73. DO 35/239/8831G/147.
74. DO 35/239/8831G/157: despatch, Sir William Clark to Dominions Office, 29 June 1932.
75. DO 35/239/8831G/170: despatch, Sir William Clark to Dominions Office, 30 June 1932.
76. DO 35/239/8831G/172: telegram, Sir William Clark to Dominions Office, 11 July 1932.
77. DO 35/239/8831G/148: letter, Sir William Clark to Sir Geoffrey Whiskard, 15 June 1932. For the complete and permanent failure of the cottons talks, see DO 35/239/8831G/162. The preliminary discussions with Canadian officials are in DO 35/239/8831G/48: letter, Frederick Field to Department of Overseas Trade, 7 March 1932.
78. DO 35/188/8002/100: despatch, W. C. Hankinson to Dominions Office, 18 February 1932.
79. DO 35/236/8831/79.
80. DO 35/240/8831H/10: despatch, Sir Robert Dalton to Department of Overseas Trade, 27 January 1932.
81. DO 35/240/8831H/26: despatch, Sir Robert Dalton to Department of Overseas Trade, 7 February 1932.

82. DO 35/240/8831H/90: despatch, W. C. Hankinson to Dominions Office, 17 May 1932.
83. Deputy Controller General of the Australian Customs Department.
84. DO 35/240/8831H/89: despatch, Sir Robert Dalton to Department of Overseas Trade, 17 May 1932.
85. DO 35/240/8831H/99: despatch, W. C. Hankinson to Dominions Office, 1 June 1932.
86. Dalton was much less sure it would do so. See DO 35/240/8831H/63: minutes by R. Wiseman on a despatch of Sir Robert Dalton, 9 June 1932.
87. DO 35/240/8831H/99: despatch, W. C. Hankinson to Dominions Office, 1 June 1932.
88. The formula was:
12½ per cent preference when British goods pay 0 per cent to 14 per cent
15 per cent preference when British goods pay 15 per cent to 19 per cent
17½ per cent preference when British goods pay 20 per cent to 29 per cent
20 per cent preference when British goods pay 30 per cent or more
The sub-formula was:
15 per cent preference when British goods pay 0 per cent to 19 per cent
20 per cent preference when British goods pay 20 per cent or more.
89. DO 35/240/8831H/37: Board of Trade Note, 25 June 1932. One-half by value.
90. Bennett Papers 113,640–641: memorandum on Australian plans as reported by Australian Trade Commissioner 4 May 1932; 113,712–713: telegram, J. A. Lyons to R. B. Bennett, 18 May 1932.
91. Commonwealth Archives Office, Canberra: CP 272/3: memorandum on meat, March 1932.
92. ibid., memorandum on dairy products, February 1932. On butter the *ad valorem* rate works out at 11.2 per cent – only slightly higher than the existing duty.
93. ibid., various memoranda.
94. DO 35/240/8831H/35: note of a conversation, 7 April 1932.
95. DO 35/188/8002/112: note of a meeting, 13 April 1932.
96. DO 35/240/8831H/61: letter, F. L. McDougall to Sir Horace Wilson, 9 June 1932.
97. DO 35/254/9105/18: memorandum, F. L. McDougall, 30 June 1932.
98. DO 35/8831H/91: memorandum, F. L. McDougall, 21 June 1932.
99. Bennett Papers, 114,750: letter, R. E. Powell to R. B. Bennett, 16 July 1932.
100. Bennett Papers, 114,728–30: letters, R. B. Bennett to J. J. Warren and vice versa, 21 and 23 June 1932.
101. Bennett Papers, 114,703–707: letter, President of International Nickel Company to R. B. Bennett, 24 May 1932.
102. DO 35/239/8831G/117, May 1932.
103. Bennett Papers, 114,732–4. The American duty was 72 per cent of the world price – so high as to exclude foreign copper from the American market entirely. See A. Skelton, 'Copper', in W. Y. Elliott *et al. International Control in the Non-Ferrous Metals* (Macmillan, New York 1937), for data on the breakdown of the copper cartel following the entry of lowest Canadian and Rhodesian producers.
104. Bennett Papers, 114,746: letter, J. J. Warren to Sir George, May, no date.
105. Bennett Papers, 114,748–9: letter, J. J. Warren to R. B. Bennett, 12 July 1932.

106. Bennett Papers, 114,744: letter, R. B. Bennett to J. J. Warren, 2 July 1932.
107. CAB 32/79, 6th meeting, 9 October 1930, p. 21. See above, Ch. 4, pp. 159–62.
108. ibid., p. 22.
109. ibid., 7th meeting, 13 October 1930, p. 26.
110. ibid., 25th meeting, 12 November 1930, p. 104.
111. For some indication of the level of information then current in Canadian government circles with respect to Soviet affairs, see Bennett Papers, 108,493–541. In this officials' memorandum, prepared by the Government's General Economic Committee as prepared for the Ottawa Conference, the USSR is discussed as a *market* without any mention of the Soviet Five-Year Plan.
112. Public Archives of Canada, H. H. Stevens Papers, vol. 12, file 3.
113. For the lobbying and manoeuvring which led up to the ban, see DO 35/202/8165/109: despatch, Sir William Clark to Dominions Office, 2 March 1931.
114. Order in Council, PC 463.
115. Bennett Papers, 180,513.
116. ibid., 108,004; 108,519; 108,527.
117. ibid., 114,031–114,038.
118. DO 114/42: letter, Ferguson to J. H. Thomas, 9 January 1932.
119. DO 114/42: letters, Ferguson to Thomas, 16 January and 5 February 1932; letter, Thomas to Ferguson, 20 January 1932.
120. DO 35/239/8831G/157: despatch, Sir William Clark to Dominions Office, 29 June 1932. Clark's emphasis.
121. DO 114/42: telegrams, Canadian Government to Dominions Office, 3 July and 30 May 1932; telegram, Dominions Office to Canadian Government, 24 May 1932.
122. DO 35/240/8831H/77.
123. Bennett Papers, 115,252: telegram, Prime Minister of Australia to R. B. Bennett, 18 May 1932.
124. For the material on the wheat and timber trades which flowed through the Dominions Office in London, see DO 3/33, file 8917, covering the period 13 March 1931 to 23 August 1932.
125. CAB 24/230, CP 169(32).
126. CAB 23/71 (1 June, 8 July 1932(2)); CAB 23/72, 4 and 27 August 1932.
127. The substance of this section first appeared in my 'Empire Trade and Russian Trade: Economic Diplomacy in the Nineteen-Thirties', *Canadian Journal of Economics*, 5: 35–47 (February 1972).
128. DO 114/42: telegram, Sir William Clark to Dominions Office, 19 March 1932.
129. DO 114/42: telegram, Sir William Clark to Dominions Office, 12 March 1932.
130. DO 114/42: telegram, Sir William Clark to Dominions Office, 19 March 1932.
131. DO 114/42: telegram, Sir William Clark to Dominions Office, 19 May 1932.
132. DO 114/42: telegrams, Sir William Clark to Dominions Office, 12 and 19 March 1932.
133. DO 35/235/8831G/36: telegram, Sir William Clark to Dominions Office, 26 March 1932.
134. Bennett Papers, 112,760.

135. DO 114/42: telegram, Canadian Government to Dominions Office, 24 May 1932.
136. DO 114/32: telegram, Dominions Office to Canadian Government, 30 May 1932.
137. CAB 32/79, p. 110.
138. DO 35/236/8831/72: memorandum of informal meeting between Walter Runciman and officials from the Board of Trade and the Dominions Office, 23 December 1931.
139. T 172/1738: letter, J. H. Thomas to Neville Chamberlain, 4 January 1932.
140. T 172/1738: letter, J. H. Thomas to Neville Chamberlain, 3 March 1932. Thomas wrote plaintively, 'Are you yet in a position to say anything further regarding the question of monetary policy (including silver) at the Ottawa Conference, about which I wrote you on January 4? . . . The Ottawa Cabinet Committee ought to discuss this matter fairly soon. You have no doubt read the Press reports of the debate in the House of Commons of Canada on Empire Currency.' The next day, Chamberlain answered, 'I hope to be in a position to let you have something about monetary policy and the Ottawa Conference fairly soon now.'
141. T 172/1768: memorandum, R. H. Hawtrey for Neville Chamberlain, 18 January 1932.
142. T 175/64: three memoranda, Sir Richard Hopkins, 1932.
143. T 172/1768: memorandum, Sir Richard Hopkins, 15 December 1931. In the same file is an undated and unsigned memorandum which adds further reasons. If sterling simply floated downwards, other countries would not peg their currencies to it. There would be risk of a capital flight. The burden of war debts would become intolerable, as Britain was owed sterling but owed dollars. Financial business would leave London, and such as remained would yield less in terms of foreign currency.
144. Bennett Papers, 115,190: letter, L. S. Amery to R. B. Bennett, 25 January 1932.
145. DO 114/42: telegram, Sir William Clark to Dominions Office, 12 March 1932.
146. T 172/1738: letter, D. Ferguson (Treasury) to C. G. L. Syers (Dominions Office), 16 March 1932.
147. T 160/550/F.7219/1; DO 114/42: telegram, Thomas to Clark, 23 March 1932.
148. T 160/550/F.7219/1: letter, Sir William Clark to Sir Ernest Harding, 13 April 1932.
149. T 160/550/F.7219/1: telegram, Government of India to Secretary of State for India, 16 April 1932.
150. T 160/550/F.7219/1: memorandum, unsigned, 29 April 1932.
151. Bennett Papers, 105,686. The Lausanne Conference, in fact, was concerned only with the winding up of reparations.
152. DO 114/42: telegram, Canadian Government to Dominions Office, 24 May 1932.
153. Bennett Papers, 105,689: telegram, New Zealand Government to Canadian Government, no date.
154. DO 114/42: telegram, Dominions Office to Canadian Government, 30 May 1932. See also Bennett Papers, 105,897–900.
155. Bennett Papers, 105,875–6.

156. T 172/1738: undated and unsigned Treasury memorandum, with pencil note thereon.

157. This account omits the pre-Conference negotiations with Southern Rhodesia, Newfoundland, and India. The first two countries were not very important, and the last has left little trace in the documents. Though the Irish Free State sent a delegation to Ottawa, there were no Anglo-Irish trade talks.

158. On 25 May, the American Secretary of State had explained to Ramsay MacDonald that if the British wanted to call an 'Economic and Monetary Conference' the Americans 'were inclined to think it would be useful'. On 30 May, Sir John Simon explained to the American Ambassador that the conference could not meet for some months because British ministers would be so occupied at Geneva, Lausanne, and Ottawa. After an American announcement, Whitehall informed the Dominions on 1 June. See T 160/486/F.13017/1, and DO 35/266/9223/2.

CHAPTER 6

1. The text of this cable appears as Appendix I to this chapter (page 290).
2. CAB 32/103, O(UK)(32)49.
3. CAB 32/103, O(UK)(32)54, 16 August 1932. Full text.
4. CAB 32/102, O(UK)(32), 50th meeting, 14 August 1932.
5. CAB 32/103, O(UK)(32)25, 7 August 1932.
6. CAB 32/101, 30th and 32nd meetings, 4 August 1932. See also Kottman, *Reciprocity and the North Atlantic Triangle*, pp. 27–8.
7. See below, Section III.
8. Anglo-Canadian Agreement, Article 16.
9. CAB 32/104, O(B)(32)17, 20 April 1932.
10. Bennett Papers, 114,168–72: memorandum, 'Conference Position, August 1st'.
11. For Skelton's views, see Bennett Papers, 114,370–377.
12. H. H. Stevens. See Bennett Papers, 102,841–44: memorandum, Stevens to Bennett, 17 October 1930.
13. Cmd. 4335.
14. DO 35/232/8671/66, July 1933. For Canadian comment, see Bennett Papers, 115,704.
15. CAB 32/101, O(UK)(32), 21st meeting, 29 July 1932; statement printed in Cmd. 4175, pp. 166–72.
16. CAB 24/232, CP 277(32), 3 August 1932.
17. Cmd. 4175, *Imperial Economic Conference at Ottawa: Appendices to the Summary of Proceedings*, pp. 166–72.
18. See the letter by Geoffrey Lloyd cited in Middlemas and Barnes *Baldwin*, p. 679.
19. Cmd. 4175, pp. 68 ff.
20. See CAB 32/105, O(B)(32)141.
21. CAB 32/101, 9th meeting, 21 July 1932, and 11th meeting, 22 July 1932.
22. Kottman, op. cit., pp. 21–5.
23. ibid., p. 24.
24. See Chapter 5, section III.4.
25. See Appendix II (page 296).
26. CAB 32/101, 13th meeting, Appendix. See also CAB 32/105, O(B)(32)-133,135,137.

27. For examples, see CAB 32/101, 18th meeting, 27 July 1932.
28. G.N.P. at market prices from London and Cambridge Economic Service, *Key Statistics*.
29. Feiling *Chamberlain*, p. 212, citing Chamberlain's diary entry for 23 July 1932. See also Middlemas and Barnes, op. cit., p. 676.
30. Baldwin expressed the same pessimism later. See CAB 32/101, O(UK)(32), 18th meeting, 27 July 1932.
31. CAB 32/101, O(UK)(32), 14th meeting, 25 July 1932. On shipboard there had been talks with India, South Africa, and Rhodesia, but these had been informal and exploratory only.
32. CAB 32/103, O(UK)(32)7, 26 July 1932.
33. See Cmd. 4175.
34. CAB 32/101, O(UK)(32), 24th meeting, 1 August 1932.
35. For an account of its concoction over a weekend, see Kottman, op. cit., p. 27. For Bennett's comments on its basis in the domestic competition principle, see CAB 32/101, O(UK)(32), 31st meeting, 4 August 1932.
36. CAB 32/101, 30th and 32nd meetings, 4 August 1932. See also Kottman, op. cit., pp. 27–8.
37. CAB 32/101, O(UK)(32) 43rd meeting, 9 August 1932; 40th meeting, 8 August 1932. See also Feiling, op. cit., for diary entry of 9 August.
38. CAB 32/101, O(UK)(32), 36th meeting, 5 August 1932. For Bennett's insistence that there was no need, in view of his Tariff Board statute, to embed the principle of domestic competition in the trade agreement, see O(UK)(32), 30th meeting, 4 August 1932, and O(UK)(32), 44th meeting, 10 August 1932.
39. CAB 32/102, O(UK)(32), 60th meeting, 17 August 1932.
40. idem. 'After careful consideration he [Mr Baldwin] had come to the conclusion that it was the duty of the United Kingdom delegation to endeavour to obtain the best agreement with Canada that was possible in the circumstances.'
41. CAB 32/102, O(UK)(32), 66th meeting, 18 August 1932.
42. Articles 10 to 15.
43. See Kottman, op. cit., p. 32; see also CAB 32/105, O(B)(32)159 for the schedule the United Kingdom proposed after 4 August.
44. For one minister's recollections of the resulting difficulties see Stevens Papers, vol. 163, 10th and 11th interviews. For a contemporary Canadian comment on the Cabinet divisions, see *Canadian Forum*, April 1933, p. 243.
45. See Bennett Papers, 110,985: letter, H. H. Stevens to R. B. Bennett, 28 July 1932: 'I am informed that a duty on canned salmon will be opposed by strong influences within the Government emanating from the Private Secretary to the Prime Minister, Mr Ramsay MacDonald, who is closely associated with the Scottish Co-op, who are, I understand, the source of the objection.' See also Bennett Papers, 110,863: letter, H. H. Stevens to R. B. Bennett, 3 August 1932: 'The British adviser in fish, like the lumber adviser, is personally and vitally interested in maintaining the Japanese Fish trust and their interest in Great Britain.'
46. See Stevens Papers, vol. 163, 10th and 11th interviews.
47. See Bennett Papers, 115,575–604: anonymous official memorandum written before the conference, but after the British and Canadian cotton magnates had failed to agree.
48. See Bennett Papers, 115,283 and 115,287 for Bennett's correspondence with a Canadian textile magnate.

49. For excerpts from the advice tendered to Bennett, see Drummond, *British Economic Policy*, op. cit., pp. 200–4. Most of the surviving memoranda in the Bennett Papers were probably written by W. D. Herridge, Bennett's confidant. Some may come from Dr O. D. Skelton, the Canadian undersecretary of state for external affairs.
50. CAB 32/103, O(UK)(32)29A, 5 August 1932.
51. Bennett Papers, 114,804: letter, H. B. McKinnon to R. B. Bennett, with long accompanying memorandum, n.d. See also 115,329–31: 'it is difficult to see in the above any major diversion to her [UK] of tonnage, in the near future. . . .'
52. Bennett Papers, 114,083: 'Notes re Tariff Items Listed in Schedule Attached to Sir H. Wilson's Letter', n.d., anon.
53. Kottman, op. cit., p. 30. For Bennett's manipulations, see CAB 32/102, O(UK)(32), 54th, 55th, 60th, 61st meetings, 15, 16, 17, 19, 23 August.
54. Kottman, op. cit., p. 31: Middlemas and Barnes, op.. cit., p. 680.
55. Feiling, op. cit., pp. 214–15.
56. The cable might have come to rest in the papers of the delegation, in the Prime Minister's semi-official (PREMIER) files, or in the Dominions Office. It is not to be found in any of those places.
57. Article 17 in Anglo-Canadian Agreement.
58. CAB 32/102, O(UK)(32), 74th meeting, 19 August 1932.
59. PREMIER 1/112: telegram, J. H. Thomas to Ramsay MacDonald via Dominions Office, 19 August 1932.
60. Reported in J. H. Thomas's picturesque language, in Middlemas and Barnes, op. cit., p. 683, who do not report the cause of the late-night fight.
61. Article 9, Anglo-Canadian Agreement.
62. CAB 32/101, O(UK)(32), 31st and 37th conclusions.
63. Anglo-Australian Agreement, Articles 9 to 13.
64. CAB 32/101, O(UK)(32), 9th meeting, 21 July 1932.
65. CAB 32/101, O(UK)(32), 25th meeting, 2 August 1932, and Appendix.
66. CAB 32/101, O(UK)(32), 27th meeting, 3 August 1932; 37th meeting, 5 August 1932.
67. Anglo-Australian Agreement, Article 8.
68. Article 9.
69. See National Library of Australia, J. H. N. Cook Papers, MS601/IV, for Hume Cook's Ottawa diary.
70. CAB 32/101, O(UK)(32), 34th conclusions. For Havenga's proposal see CAB 32/101, O(UK)(32) 23.
71. CAB 32/101, O(UK)(32), 37th conclusions, 7 August 1932.
72. CAB 32/102, O(UK)(32), 52nd conclusions, 15 August 1932.
73. CAB 32/105, O(B)(32)160, 9 August 1932.
74. CAB 32/105, O(B)(32)150, 4 August 1932.
75. See Schedule E of Anglo-South African Agreement.
76. Anglo-New Zealand Agreement, Articles 7–9. See CAB 32/101, O(UK)(32), 31st and 37th conclusions, 4 and 7 August 1932.
77. CAB 32/101, O(UK)(32), 25th meeting, 2 August 1932.
78. CAB 32/101, O(UK)(32), 31st meeting, 4 August 1932.
79. Anglo-New Zealand Agreement, Articles 6, 10.
80. CAB 32/101, O(UK)(32) 23rd meeting, 30 July 1932. The arrangements are in CAB 32/105, O(UK)(32)8.
81. CAB 32/101, O(UK)(32), 20th meeting, 3 August 1932 and 35(B)th meeting, 9 August 1932.

82. Anglo-Indian Agreement, Article 12 and Schedule G.
83. Anglo-Indian Agreement, Article 1 and exchange of correspondence, 22 September 1932 (See United Kingdom *State Papers*, 1937, pp. 224–5).
84. Anglo-Indian Agreement, Article 10 and Schedule F.
85. For the Committee's view, see CAB 32/108, IEC(32)/193(CD)(2). For the Minister's request, see Bennett Papers, 110,769–70; letter, Ryckman to Bennett, 15 August 1932. For the correspondence, see CAB 32/103; Appendix, 'Summary of Conclusions and Copies of Trade Agreement'.
86. Article 16 of Canadian Agreement.
87. This may have been perceived in Australia. Prime Minister Lyons thought he could not waive primage on goods which already bore a protective tariff – even when the Tariff Board had already recommended such a step. See Commonwealth Archives Office, CP 272/3: telegram, Lyons to Bruce, 10 August 1932.
88. Article 14 of Australian Agreement; Article 11 of New Zealand Agreement; Article 16 of Canadian Agreement.
89. Canadian Agreement, Article 17.
90. In CAB 32/104, O(B)(32)136.
91. CAB 32/101, O(UK)(32), 7th meeting, 18 July 1932.
92. See Middlemas and Barnes, *Baldwin*, p. 674.
93. CAB 32/101, O(UK)(32), 21st meeting, 29 July 1932.
94. CAB 32/101, O(UK)(32), 24th meeting, 2 August 1932.
95. Middlemas and Barnes, op. cit., p. 681: letter, Coates to Baldwin, 8 August 1932.
96. CAB 32/101, O(UK)(32), 27th meeting, 3 August 1932.
97. CAB 32/101, O(UK)(32), 36th meeting, 5 August 1932. A quota duty involved a higher duty upon foreign shipments which exceeded a stated quota.
98. CAB 32/101, O(UK)(32), 32nd meeting, 5 August 1932.
99. CAB 32/101, O(UK)(32), 31st meeting, 4 August 1932.
100. CAB 32/101, O(UK)(32), 36th meeting, 5 August 1932.
101. CAB 32/103, O(UK)(32)10, 29 July 1932.
102. CAB 32/101, O(UK)(32), 45th meeting.
103. CAB 32/101, O(UK)(32), 31(A) meeting, 9 August 1932.
104. CAB 32/101, O(UK)(32), 49th meeting, 12 August 1932.
105. See Middlemas and Barnes, op. cit., p. 682, for an account that purports to be based on such an interview. The account is misleading in that it suggests Baldwin himself invented the quota scheme, that Bruce worked it out, and that Chamberlain had never seen it before Bruce produced it. According to Middlemas and Barnes, 'Chamberlain agreed to try and persuade the British Government to accept the quota scheme'. In fact, as was shown above, Chamberlain himself invented the quota plan, and the details had long since been worked out by British civil servants. Kottman (*Reciprocity*) does not mention the meat crisis.
106. CAB 32/102, 54th meeting, 16 August 1932.
107. CAB 32/102, 57th meeting, 16 August 1932, and 60th meeting.
108. CAB 23/103, O(UK)(32)49.
109. PREMIER 1/112: 'The Australian and New Zealand negotiations and a duty on meat', expanding O(UK)(32), 54th conclusions, minute 4, for the Prime Minister. See also Middlemas and Barnes, op. cit., pp. 682–3, for background.
110. idem.

111. Middlemas and Barnes, op. cit., p. 683, reporting the telephone call but not its result.
112. On telephone tapping, see Thomas's comment in CAB 32/102, O(UK)(32), 66th meeting, 18 August 1932.
113. CAB 32/102, 57th meeting, 16 August 1932.
114. CAB 32/103, O(UK)(32)54.
115. See Kottman, op. cit., p. 31, and note 32, with references cited therein.
116. See Kottman, op. cit., p. 29, citing letter, Robert Manion to Bennett, 16 August 1932, from the Bennett Papers.
117. Especially Middlemas and Barnes, op. cit., pp. 681–4; see also Feiling *Chamberlain*, pp. 211–15; I. MacLeod *Chamberlain* (Muller, London 1961), pp. 159–62;
118. CAB 32/102, O(UK)(32), 66th meeting, 18 August 1932.
119. CAB 32/102, O(UK)(32), 67th meeting, 18 August 1932.
120. CAB 32/102, O(UK)(32), 68th meeting, 18 August 1932.
121. CAB 32/102, O(UK)(32), 70th meeting, 19 August 1932.
122. For the last-minute crises which arose with respect to the allocation of the Dominions' lamb quotas, see Middlemas and Barnes, op. cit., p. 683.
123. Most of these provisions are in the Ottawa Agreements themselves or in Schedules thereto; a few, however, such as the South African commitment, were informal undertakings.
124. If the plan is the one which is to be found in the Austen Chamberlain Papers (University of Birmingham Library, AC 49/1/3), it hardly deserves the label of 'detailed' which it receives from Feiling (op. cit., p. 181).
125. Sir John Gilmour, the Minister of Agriculture and Fisheries, was remarkably silent throughout the conference. Presumably he enjoyed the many parties and excursions.
126. See Kottman, op. cit., p. 26.
127. Plan A of OC(31)73.
128. CAB 32/101, O(UK)(32), 27th meeting, 3 August 1932.
129. CAB 32/102, O(UK)(32), 47th meeting, 12 August 1932.
130. CAB 32/102, O(UK)(32), 48th meeting, 12 August 1932.
131. CAB 32/102, O(UK)(32), 49th conclusions, 12 August 1932.
132. CAB 32/103, O(UK)(32)49, 12 August 1932.
133. CAB 32/102, O(UK)(32), 67th meeting, 18 August 1932.
134. CAB 32/102, O(UK)(32), 69th meeting, 18 August 1932; 70th, 72nd, and 74th meetings, 19 August 1932.
135. See Article 4 of the Anglo-Canadian Agreement, which also covers copper.
136. For fruit requests, CAB 32,103, O(UK)(32)4, 28 July 1932; for butter, CAB 32/103, O(UK)(32)2, 25 July 1932.
137. CAB 32/101, O(UK)(32), 25th meeting, 2 August 1932, and Appendix.
138. Schedule A in all agreements.
139. CAB 32/101, O(UK)(32), 4th meeting, 15 July 1932.
140. CAB 32/102, O(UK)(32), 46th meeting, 10 August 1932.
141. On the Canadian government requests, see CAB 31/105, O(B)(32)166, 11 August 1932. For Rhokana's representations to the UK Government, see the record of Sir Philip Cunliffe-Lister's conversation with Sir Auckland Geddes, DO 35/239/8331G/117, May 1932. For Canada's reluctant acceptance of the existing tariff structure, see Bennett Papers, 110,847–8: letter, J. J. Weir to Sir Horace Wilson, 13 August 1932: 'of course half a loaf is better than no bread, and we are necessarily obliged to accept this rather than nothing' so far as lead and zinc are concerned. For details about the continuous attempts to

cartelise copper, lead, and zinc in the interwar period, see A. Skelton, 'Copper' and 'Lead and Zinc' in W. Y. Elliott *et al. Control in the Non-Ferrous Metals* (New York 1937). There had, for example, been cartels in copper since 1918, but they had not succeeded in controlling production or energy. Hence the unplanned and inconvenient expansion of low-cost copper production in Rhodesia.
142. See above, Chapter 5, Section IV.
143. Bennett Papers, 108,004–108,519; 108,527.
144. Bennett Papers, 114,031–114,038.
145. The 'Tariff Committee'.
146. Bennett Papers, 112,892: memorandum, H. H. Stevens to Bennett, 30 July 1932.
147. *Canadian Forum*, 12 (September 1932), 443.
148. Bennett Papers, 112,850–1: memorandum, H. R. Macmillan to Bennett, n.d.
149. See Bennett Papers, 115,404.
150. Bennett Papers, 115,389.
151. For the Canadian request, see Bennett Papers, 115,380.
152. CAB 32/103, O(B)(32)162,163, 10 August 1932, and CAB 32/102 O(UK)(32), 47th and 48th meetings, 12 and 13 August 1932.
153. CAB 32/101, 54th and 55th meetings.
154. CAB 32/101, 11th and 13th meetings.
155. CAB 32/105, O(B)(32)143.
156. CAB 32/101, 26th meeting.
157. CAB 32/101, 33rd meeting.
158. CAB 32/101, 46th meeting.
159. CAB 32/101, 49th meeting. Kottman (op. cit., p. 26) is incorrect in believing that Bennett had abandoned all hope of an embargo by the end of July.
160. Bennett Papers, 115,371–2.
161. In the Ottawa Agreements Act (22–3 Geo. V, 1932, ch. 53, s. 5) the UK took the necessary powers.
162. Article 21 stated that 'if either Government is satisfied that any preferences hereby granted in respect of any particular class of commodities are likely to be frustrated in whole or in part by reason of the creation or maintenance directly or indirectly of prices for such classes of commodities through state action on the part of any foreign country, that Government hereby declares that it will exercise the powers it now has or will hereafter take to prohibit the entry from such foreign country directly or indirectly for such time as may be necessary to make effective and to maintain the preference hereby granted to it'.
163. Bennett Papers, 115,405–7 contain congratulations from lumbermen's associations. For subsequent Anglo-Canadian disputes about Article 21, see Drummond, 'Empire Trade and Russian Trade', op. cit., pp. 42–7.
164. Cmd. 4174, pp. 9–10.
165. Bennett Papers, 115,243–4.
166. Cahan, indeed, argued that Canada could not even stabilise *vis-à-vis* sterling until preferential concessions ensured their sterling earnings. See CAB 32/114, 1EC(32)/145(CD)(4), 18 August 1932.
167. Bennett's advisers had produced a memorandum on 'Monetary Reconstruction' which urged that as many Empire countries as possible should stabilise *vis-à-vis* a floating pound, and that Canada should consider devaluation. See Bennett Papers, 112,587–112,592.

168. CAB 32/103, O(UK)(32)8: Sir Horace Wilson a memorandum on the Anglo-Indian negotiations.
169. CAB 32/103, O(UK)(32)25, 7 August 1932.
170. DO 35/278/9279A/26B, 8 November 1932: Dalton's final estimate of the agreement's impact claimed that UK exports would rise by £1.8 million on the 1931–32 trading volume, or by £4 million when Australian imports were £100 million. The earlier offer he had valued at £0.5 million and £1.25 million.
171. Thus allowing for a rather high marginal propensity to import.
172. The German case is ambiguous because, though pretending to maintain the gold parity, Germany rapidly developed a system of multiple exchange rates.
173. This section draws upon and develops material which first appeared in my *British Economic Policy and the Empire 1919–1939*, pp. 100–4.
174. Cmd. 4175, pp. 31–2.

CHAPTER 7

1. Ottawa Agreements Act (22–3 Geo. V, ch. 53, 1931–32), s. 7.
2. Agricultural Marketing Act (24–5 Geo. V, ch. 1, 1933–34), s. I,1.
3. On the preceding six paragraphs see DO 35/266/9223F/1: letter, J. A. Barlow to E. H. Marsh, 28 February 1933; ibid., letter, Sir Frederick Leith-Ross to E. H. Marsh, 28 February 1933; DO 35/266/9223F/3: notes of a meeting, 1 May 1933; DO 35/266/9223F/2; minute, Sir E. J. Harding, 1 May 1933; DO 35/266/9223F/3,4,7: notes of meetings, 1 and 4 May 1933, 1 June 1933; CAB 29/143: ME(BC)(33), 3rd meeting, 22 June 1933; CAB 29/144: ME(BC)(PS)(33), 1st, 2nd, and 3rd meetings, 2, 17, and 26 July 1933.
4. Cmd. 4357: 'Statement by the Chancellor of the Exchequer at the Monetary and Economic Conference on 14 June 1933'.
5. Anglo-Australian Agreement, Article 6 and Schedule H.
6. DO 35/258/9105/2/10: memorandum by W. Bankes Amery, 14 March 1930.
7. 269 HC Deb 5s 1931–2, cols. 39–41.
8. DO 35/255/9105/81; DO 114/50, pp. 175–8: letters between Runciman, Bruce, and Wilford, 19–21 February 1933. Runciman also arranged that an Imperial meat committee would meet in advance of the World Economic Conference.
9. See Runciman's comments, CAB 23/75, Cabinet 18(33), 15 May 1933.
10. For the later troubles over 'experimental' shipments see *inter alia* DO 35/260/9105/6/90,92,100.
11. Cmd. 4310, 4492, and 4494: Anglo-Argentine Convention relating to Trade and Commerce, 1 May 1933, and Supplementary convention, 26 September 1933. As both conventions were ratified on 7 November 1933 they would last until 7 November 1936. Thereafter they could continue unless denounced. This provision had been added at the earnest behest of the Dominion high commissioners. On 12 April 1933, Thomas had told Bruce and Wilford of the proposed guarantees. He was surprised and alarmed to learn that large chilled-beef shipments were soon to be expected from the Antipodes. See DO 35/295/9307/20: letters, J. H. Thomas to S. B. Bruce and Sir T. Wilford, 11 April 1933, and DO 35/295/9307/21, letter, S. B. Bruce to J. H. Thomas, 12 April 1933.
12. For the agreements with Denmark, Sweden, and Norway, see Cmd. 4424, Cmd. 4421, and Cmd. 4323. All the agreements ran for three years from their several dates of ratification – in mid-1933. Denmark and Sweden were promised minimum butter quotas – 2,300,000 cwt. and 185,000 cwt. Denmark

also got a minimum bacon quota – 62 per cent of all foreign shipments. Norway was promised that, because she had shipped so little bacon, ham, butter, and cheese in recent years, the UK would try to ensure that Norwegian shipments would remain unregulated even if quotas were introduced. She gave guarantees with respect to the working of the bacon-control scheme which was known to be imminent.

13. DO 114/50, pp. 178–9: letters, J. H. Thomas to S. B. Bruce and Sir T. Wilford, 11 April 1933.

14. For correspondence on the 'experimental shipments', see DO 114/50, pp. 180–2: letter, S. B. Bruce to J. H. Thomas, 12 April 1933, and letters, J. H. Thomas to S. B. Bruce and Sir T. Wilford, 25 April 1933.

15. I 23–24 Geo. 5, 1933, c. 31.

16. The Livestock Industry Act, 1937, made independent and supplementary provision for livestock and meat (1 Edw. 2, 1 Geo.6, 1937, ch. 50).

17. DO 35/314/9503/6.

18. W. B. Sutch *The Quest for Security in New Zealand 1840–1966* (Oxford University Press, Wellington 1966), pp. 62–4.

19. National Library of Australia, Page Papers, MS 1633/67 and /69.

20. No. 52 of 1935.

21. DO 114/55: telegrams from Dominions Office to various governments, 27 July 1934.

22. DO 114/55, pp. 112–13: letter, G. P. Vanier to Sir E. Harding, 7 August 1934.

23. DO 114/55, pp. 129–31: telegram, Australian Government to Dominions Office, 10 December 1934; Dominions Office to Australian Government, 18 December 1934.

24. DO 114/61, pp. 66–8: telegram, Australian Government to Dominions Office, 4 January 1935.

25. DO 114/61, p. 70: telegram, Dominions Office to Australian Government, 10 January 1935.

26. DO 114/61: letters, J. H. Thomas to Sir H. Gullett and J. G. Coates, 9 July 1935.

27. DO 35/288/9291/2: letter, Sir T. Wilford to J. H. Thomas, 19 January 1933.

28. DO 35/288/9291/2: note of discussion of United Kingdom, Australian, and New Zealand officials, 7 February 1933. See also DO 35/288/9291/5.

29. DO 35/288/9291/5: note of meeting of UK and Dominion ministers, 13 February 1933.

30. DO 35/289/9291/8: telegram, J. G. Coates to Chancellor of the Exchequer, 21 February 1933.

31. DO 35/289/9291/10: minute of meeting of UK ministers and high commissioners, 2 March 1933.

32. DO 35/289/9291/11: telegram, Forbes to New Zealand High Commissioner in London, 3 March 1933.

33. DO 35/289/9291/13: note of ministers' meeting with high commissioners, 6 March 1933.

34. DO 35/289/9291/13: letter, T. Quentin-Hill to G. Whiskard, 8 March 1933.

35. DO 35/289/9291/30: letters, J. H. Thomas to S. B. Bruce and Sir Thomas Wilford, 11 April 1933.

36. DO 114/50, p. 86: telegram, Under-Secretary of State for Dominions to UK Representative in Australia, 16 March 1933.

37. DO 114/50, p. 86: telegram, Crutchley to Under-Secretary, 24 April 1933.
38. DO 35/289/9291/49: minute by W. Bankes Amery, 2 May 1933.
39. DO 35/317/9513/2.
40. DO 35/289/9291/81, 12 August 1933; /103, 9 November 1933.
41. Telegram, New Zealand Government to Dominions Office, 25 October 1933; printed in DO 114/50, p. 189 and in Cmd. 4557, 'Dairy Produce: telegraphic correspondence between His Majesty's Government in the United Kingdom and His Majesty's Government in New Zealand with regard to Quantitative Regulation', April 1934.
42. DO 35/317/9513/14.
43. Published in Cmd. 4557: telegram, Dominions Office to New Zealand Government, 22 December 1933. The Governor General, Lord Bledisloe, later explained (DO 35/318/915/126: telegram, Lord Bledisloe to Dominions Office, 23 June 1934) that the proposal had been urged by the Dairy Produce Export Board and the New Zealand Farmers' Union. The Government dared not endorse it, because the manufacturers so strongly opposed it, but it could not refuse to transmit the request. The ministers, he said, fully expected to get the response they got.
44. DO 35/290/9291/143: minute of meeting between Sir James Parr and Walter Elliot, 14 February 1934: 'Sir J. Parr said that there were no signs of any change of attitude of New Zealand farmers towards proposals for quotas on dairy produce. . . . He thought . . . that the question of quantitative regulation would have to be left until there was some change of attitude on the part of the New Zealand producer.'
45. Cmd. 4557: telegram, New Zealand Government to Dominions Office, 28 February 1934, and telegram, Dominions Office to New Zealand Government, 9 March 1934. See also W. B. Sutch *Recent Economic Changes in New Zealand* (1936), pp. 90–6, for contemporary comment by a participant on the New Zealand end.
46. DO 35/318/9513/46: letter, Sir James Parr to J. H. Thomas, 3 April 1934.
47. DO 35/318/9513/52: telegram, United Kingdom representative in Australia to Dominions Office, 21 April 1934.
48. DO 35/318/9513/53: telegram, New Zealand Government to Dominions Office, 23 April 1934.
49. DO 35/318/9513/74.
50. Baldwin Papers, vol. 98, pp. 252 ff.: letter, Lord Bledisloe to Ramsay MacDonald, 16 April 1934. Also Baldwin Papers, vol. 97, p. 123: letter, Lord Bledisloe to Baldwin, 21 May 1934: 'The lack of any very clear (ultimate) objective in Britain's trade policy . . . has so severely agitated the minds and deflected the policy of industrial and political leaders in this Dominion. Moreover the undiscriminating nature of the quota plan . . . the suddenness of the decision to subsidise the British dairy farmer was a little unfortunate.' Bledisloe goes on to say that the Dominions Office telegram, announcing temporary Exchequer subsidies to milk boards, arrived just at the moment when New Zealand's Prime Minister, in response to Bledisloe's urgings, was publicly explaining the need to acquiesce in the quota.
51. DO 35/318/9513/58: telegram, Dominions Office to New Zealand Government, 4 May 1934.
52. DO 35/318/9513/72, 79, 88: minute, 18 June 1934, by M. Flett, records Lyons' final position and notes the nervousness of the State politicians.
53. New Zealand Dairy Industry Commission, *Report* (New Zealand Parliamentary Paper H. 30 of 1934).

54. No. 58 of 1933.
55. For comment on the Statute and its background, see DO 35/291/9291/345.
56. See for Cabinet action CAB 23/69, 11 and 15 November 1931; 2 December 1931; CAB 23/70, 20 and 27 January 1932, 17 February 1932. Gilmour's proposals in their final form are in CAB 24/227, CP 22(32).
57. Wheat Act, 22–23 Geo.5, c.24, 1932. Millers and flour importers were to collect a levy on their entire throughput, sufficient to guarantee a price of 10s. per cwt. for domestic wheat, on annual 'anticipated supply' of up to 27 million cwt.
58. Lamb and mutton were not a problem in 1933; prices were satisfactory partly because of the 'Ottawa' restriction on foreign shipments, and partly because New Zealand had reluctantly acquiesced in the British requests for the regulation of Dominion shipments. Having in her meat export control board the necessary administrative apparatus, she actively tried to stay within the allowables. Australia, however, had no such machinery, and the evidence is that her governments neither estimated shipments responsibly nor tried to control the volumes shipped. However, for the time being it was not necessary to worry about new controls for lamb and mutton.
59. CAB 27/560, PMS (33) 1st Meeting. See also PMS(33) 4th Meeting where Thomas argued that the Dominions would be more likely to accept the levy if they were guaranteed free entry for quantities up to the level of 'Ottawa year plus 10'.
60. CAB 27/560, PMS(33), 2nd Meeting.
61. CAB 27/560, PMS(33), 2nd Meeting.
62. CAB 27/560, PMS(33), 6th Meeting, 27 March 1934.
63. idem.
64. Schedule A of the Anglo-Canadian and Anglo-Australian Agreements.
65. Article 2 of Anglo-Danish Trade Agreement, ratified 20 June 1933.
66. CAB 27/560, PMS(33), 5th meeting, 16 February 1934. The Report to Cabinet was CP 47(34).
67. Cmd. 4519: 'Milk Policy: Statement by the Minister of Agriculture and Fisheries in the House of Commons on Thursday, February 22, 1934'.
68. CAB 27/560, PMS(33), 7 December 1933. This scheme had involved a universal levy without preferences and without any quantitative control.
69. CAB 27/560, PMS(33)7, 15 December 1933.
70. CAB 27/560, PMS(33)11, 30 May 1934.
71. CAB 27/560, PMS(33), 7th meeting, 13 June 1934; see also PMS(33) 11,12,13.
72. CAB 27/560, PMS(33), 8th meeting, 18 June 1934. Runciman's proposals are in PMS(33)15.
73. CAB 23/80, pp. 203–4: Cabinet 25(34)6, 19 June 1934.
74. DO 114/55: notes of a meeting, 27 June 1934.
75. CAB 27/560, PMS(33), 9th meeting, 2 July 1934.
76. DO 114/55, p. 99: memorandum, 5 July 1934. For a summary of responses see CAB 27/560, PMS(33)24.
77. DO 114/55, p. 120: telegram, Australian Government to Australian High Commissioner in the United Kingdom, 10 July 1934.
78. CAB 23/80, 28(24)7, 11 July 1934, pp. 287–90.
79. Cmd. 4651: 'The Livestock Situation'.
80. Later, as negotiations dragged on, the subsidy was extended – to June 1935, September 1935, and June 1936 – always with protestations about its

temporary character, and always with a promise that the grants would be recouped from the levy. See Cmd. 4807 and Cmd. 4941.
81. DO 114/55, p. 120: telegram, Australian Government to Australian High Commissioners, 10 July 1934.
82. DO 114/55, pp. 131–2: telegram, New Zealand Government to Dominions Office, 9 July 1934.
83. DO 114/55, p. 133: telegram, Dominions Office to New Zealand Government, 10 July 1934.
84. DO 114/55, pp. 134–5: telegram, New Zealand Government to Dominions Office, 11 July 1934.
85. DO 114/55, p. 146: telegram, Union Government to Dominions Office, 20 August 1934; DO 35/255/9105/209: telegram, Prime Minister of the Union to South African High Commissioner, 13 July 1934.
86. New Zealand was virtually forced to accept the 'voluntary' programme, and Australia was recalcitrant, while Canada was equivocating. See DO 35/255/9105/237,257: letters, Thomas to Bruce, 25 September 1934 and 22 October 1934; minute by Bankes Amery, 20 September 1934.
87. CAB 23/81, 23 January 1935. On Lyons' visit, CAB 27/560, PMS(33), 14th meeting, 17 January 1935.
88. Later published, somewhat amplified with respect to self-regulation of the producing countries, in Cmd. 4828. For meeting, see CAB 27/567, TS/R/16(8), 11 February 1935.
89. CAB 27/560, PMS(33), 16th meeting, 4 February 1933.
90. DO 114/61, pp. 64,86: letter, G. H. Ferguson to J. H. Thomas, 28 June 1935; telegram, New Zealand Government to Dominions Office, 23 February 1935.
91. DO 114/61, p. 101: telegram, Union Government to Dominions Office, 14 March 1935.
92. CAB 23/81, 22 May 1935.
93. DO 35/291/9291/355: memorandum by Walter Elliot, 10 May 1935.
94. CAB 27/560, PMS(33)29, 11 January 1935.
95. DO 114/61, p. 71: telegram, Australian Government to Dominions Office, 18 February 1935; p. 73: telegram, Under-Secretary of State for Dominions Affairs to United Kingdom Representative in Australia, 21 February 1935. See also National Library of Australia, Sir Earle Page Papers, MS 1633/71.
96. Page Papers, MS 1633/71.
97. Cmd. 4828: 'Imports of Meat into the United Kingdom'.
98. The New Zealanders had been complaining that they would be hit especially hard if sheepmeat were taxed. In November 1934, Bruce had urged that it be admitted duty-free. He argued that the Antipodes might accept a levy or quota on beef if they could keep free entry for mutton and lamb. See DO 35/246/9105/318.
99. On the Board of Trade position, see DO 35/256/9105/447: memorandum by A. Kilroy, 20 June 1936.
100. CAB 32/124, EDA(A)(35), 5th meeting, 15 April 1935.
101. CAB 32/124, EDA(35), 2nd meeting.
102. CAB 32/124, EDA(35)25: notes of a meeting, 13 May 1935.
103. CAB 32/124, EDA(35)29 and 31: letters between J. A. Lyons and Ramsay MacDonald, 21 May 1935 and 28 May 1935.
104. CAB 32/136, ED(D)(35), 1st meeting.
105. CAB 32/136, ED(D)(35), 1st and 2nd meetings: ED(D)(35)2.
106. CAB 23/81, Cabinet 28(35)5, 22 May 1935, p. 431.

107. CAB 27/560, PMS(33), 18th meeting.
108. CAB 27/560, PMS(33)42.
109. CAB 32/136, ED(D)(UK)(35), 1st meeting, 19 June 1935. For the text of the Argentine response see ED(D)(35)4.
110. CAB 23/136, ED(D)(35)3: letter, Sir Henry Gullett to Sir Horace Wilson, 14 June 1935.
111. CAB 23/136, ED(D)(35), 3rd meeting, 19 June 1935.
112. idem.
113. CAB 32/136, ED(D)(35)7, 20 June 1935, commenting on letter, Sir Henry Gullett to J. H. Thomas, 20 June 1935 (in ED(D)(35)6).
114. CAB 32/136, ED(D)(35)9, letter, Gullett to J. H. Thomas, 20 June 1935.
115. CAB 32/136, ED(D)(35)16, letter, J. G. Coates to J. H. Thomas, 4 July 1935, and J. H. Thomas to J. G. Coates, 12 July 1935.
116. CAB 32/136, ED(D)(UK)(35), 2nd meeting.
117. CAB 32/136, ED(D)(35), 4th meeting, 24 June 1935.
118. CAB 32/136, ED(D)(35), 6th meeting, 3 July 1935.
119. CAB 32/136, ED(D)(35)16, letter, J. H. Thomas to Dominion representatives, 2 July 1935.
120. CAB 32/136, ED(D)(35)10, letters, Howard Ferguson to J. H. Thomas, 28 June 1935.
121. CAB 32/136, (ED)(D)(35)19.
122. CAB 24/261, CP 104(36).
123. Established in pursuance of Cabinet 28(36) 12. First meeting, 9 April 1936. Members: Chamberlain, Hailsham, M. MacDonald, Runciman, Elliot, and representatives of the Scottish Office, the Foreign Office, and the Department of Overseas Trade.
124. CAB 27/619, TAC(36), 1st meeting.
125. CAB 27/619, TAC(36), 2nd meeting, 27 April 1936.
126. CAB 27/619, TAC(36), 3rd meeting, 4 May 1936. Runciman was especially certain that Argentina would never accept a beef duty of $1\frac{1}{4}$d.
127. idem.
128. For a contemporary New Zealand comment which does not make the terms-of-trade point, see W. B. Sutch *Recent Economic Changes*, p. 79.
129. See a draft speech in the Page Papers (MS 1633/71), in which Page threatened the British with dire penalties if they introduce restriction. Australia, he says, will immediately recast the Australian economy in the interest of self-sufficiency, declare a moratorium on all past debts to British persons, and attempt by every means to get foreign markets. On Australian Cabinet attitudes see DO 25/278/9279/68: dispatch by G. Crutchley to Dominions Office, 12 December 1934: Gullett's 'is the only voice in the Cabinet which is being raised in favour of compliance with British views about the restriction of meat imports'. Page, Crutchley reported, was violently hostile to British meat policy, and White, the Minister of Customs, was protectionist.
130. See Page Papers, MS 1633/71, for undated and unsigned memoranda on the subject.
131. Because with a free duty of $\frac{3}{4}$d., an Empire duty of $\frac{1}{4}$d. would not have been worth the cost of collection even if the Australians had agreed to it. See CAB 27/619, TAC(36), 9th meeting, 17 December 1936.
132. See Cmd. 4828.
133. CAB 23/86, 60(36)10, 28 October 1936, p. 26; Livestock Industry Act, 1 Ed. 8 and 1 Geo. 6, 1937, c. 50.

134. CAB 23/86, Cabinet 69(36)10, 2 December 1936, pp. 206–7; Beef and Veal Customs Duties Act, 1 Edw. 8 and 1 Geo. 6, 1937, c. 8.
135. DO/35/291/9291/363: minute by W. Bankes Amery, 5 August 1935. At the end of August the Danes suggested that the talks should be reopened. See DO 35/291/9291/377: letter, Danish Government to Australian and New Zealand Governments (transmitted via United Kingdom Foreign Office), 31 August 1935. There had been earlier conversations in July and November 1934.
136. DO 114/61, p. 127: letter, J. G. Coates to Stanley Baldwin, 19 July 1935.
137. DO 114/61, p. 128: letter, Stanley Baldwin to J. G. Coates, 19 July 1935.
138. CAB 32/126, ED(D)(35)18: notes of Mr Elliot's discussion with Sir Henry Gullett and Mr Coates, 19 June 1935.
139. ibid., letter, J. H. Thomas to Sir Henry Gullett and J. G. Coates, 19 July 1935.
140. DO 35/291/9291/370: note of discussion between Elliot and Coates, 19 July 1935.
141. DO 114/71, pp. 54–60: letter, Earle Page to Malcolm MacDonald, 15 July 1936. This letter also contains Page's demand with respect to mutton, lamb, dried fruit, canned goods, sugar, and other primary products. For MacDonald's unyielding comments, see DO 35/259/9105/3/194: notes of a meeting between MacDonald and Page, 26 June 1936.
142. DO 35/259/9105/5/41: notes of a meeting between MacDonald, Elliot, Gardiner, Dunning, and Vincent Massey, 28 July 1936.
143. DO 35/291/9291/408: letter, Runciman to Elliot, 1 August 1936. Runciman also expressed surprise that Elliot had spoken of a quota on Canadian oats; he pointed out that the Trade and Agriculture Committee had never discussed the matter, and that it would be impossible for the United Kingdom to contemplate such a quota when she was about to guarantee free entry to the highly competitive Argentine maize.
144. DO 35/291/9291/408: memorandum, 6 August 1936; DO 35/291/9291/409: note of meeting with Dunning, 6 August 1936.
145. DO 35/292/9291/418: minute by W. Bankes Amery, 9 December 1936.
146. Milk Reorganisation Commission, *Report*, Ministry of Agriculture and Fisheries Agricultural Series no. 44, 1936. See pp. 161–9 for the Commission's comments on quotas and duties.
147. See DO 35/288/9289/31: despatch, E. Crutchley to Dominions Office, 2 July 1935; and DO 35/291/9291/410: despatch, U.K. High Commissioner in Australia to Dominions Office, 27 July 1936.
148. See W. B. Sutch *Recent Economic Changes*, p. 120, and Sutch *The Quest for Security*, pp. 172–207.
149. DO 114/71, p. 182: telegram, New Zealand Government to Dominions Office, 22 October 1936.
150. See DO 35/274/9263/22; see also Sutch for comment on the relation between the proposal and the meat and butter negotiations.
151. DO 114/71, pp. 181–2: telegram, Dominions Office to Governor General of New Zealand, 18 December 1936. This cable was in response to an early and informal inquiry.
152. In this he was at least consistent: the New Zealand Government itself would soon impose a quota on British footwear. See DO 114/77, p. 141: telegram, New Zealand Government to Dominions Office, 24 November 1936.
153. DO 35/274/9263/27.
154. DO 35/274/9263/33.

155. DO 35/274/9263/27: Board of Trade memorandum, 7 December 1936.
156. DO 35/274/9263/43.
157. For reasons see CAB 27/619, TAC(36)34.
158. CAB 27/619, TAC(36), 10th meeting, 2 February 1937.
159. DO 114/77, pp. 81–3: letter, Malcolm MacDonald to W. Nash, 19 February 1937.
160. Nash was given a schedule of the articles on which the UK wanted revision of the Ottawa terms – conventionalisation, reduction, free entry, and/or preference. As the committee of officials notes, 'Mr Nash has indicated that, as part of a policy of developing secondary industry in New Zealand, the New Zealand Government may find it necessary to place a complete embargo on imports of particular products, and he has agreed that this would not apply to goods included in conventionalisation schedules. Consequently it has been necessary to include in our schedules all goods in which we have a substantial interest. So far, there has been no detailed discussion of the schedules, and we have no idea how far Mr Nash is prepared to go to meet us.' Agreement appeared possible only if some concessions were made on meat and/or butter. (CAB 27/620, TAC (36)38.) It is hardly surprising that the New Zealand Government brooded long over this schedule after Nash's return to Wellington. See below.
161. CAB 27/360, TAC(36), 11th meeting, 12 April 1937. The members of the committee could not agree whether Nash would rather have a quota or a duty, but they did suspect he thought a duty more likely, and they remarked that he knew the New Zealand treasury would pay whatever duty might be imposed. In conversation Nash had made this point to Morrison.
162. CAB 27/632, AP(37), 1st meeting, 13 July 1937, and 2nd meeting, 19 July 1937: CAB 23/88, Cabinet 32(37). Malcolm MacDonald was Dominions Secretary, Oliver Stanley was President of the Board of Trade, and Morrison was Minister for Agriculture and Fisheries. Runciman had already argued that there was little point in imperilling trade relations with New Zealand by insisting on the right to impose quotas – when in fact the weapon was most unlikely to be used. See CAB 27/620, TAC(36)39.
163. DO 114/77, p. 21: telegrams, Dominions Office to Dominions Governments, 29 July 1937.
164. CAB 23/88, Cabinet 32(37)10; Cmd. 5533: 'Milk Policy'.
165. CP 268(37).
166. CAB 23/90, 10 November 1937.
167. See below.
168. CAB 27/632, AP(37), 4th meeting, 11 November 1937. The committee was considering and in effect endorsed CP 268(37), the work of an interdepartmental committee of officials.
169. CAB 23/90, 17 November 1937.
170. CAB 27/632, AP(37), 4th meeting.
171. CAB 23/90, Cabinet 42(37) 8.
172. CAB 23/90, 24 November 1937.
173. DO 114/77, p. 21: telegrams, Dominions Office to various Dominion Governments, 25 November 1937.
174. DO 114/77, p. 24: telegrams, Dominions Office to High Commissioners, 25 November 1937.
175. Feiling *Chamberlain*, pp. 229–30 (Diary, 17 February 1934), and p. 238. On protection, tariffs, and livestock see p. 182 (Diary, 6 December 1930).
176. DO 35/317/9513/93: letter, J. H. Thomas to Walter Elliot, 13 June 1934.

At the same time, Thomas recorded his suspicion (CAB 27/560, PMS(33)12, June 1934) that it would be counterproductive to expand agriculture very much.
177. CAB 24/250, CP 199(34), 20 July 1934.
178. See CAB 58/19 EAC(EI)74 to 79, for memoranda by G. D. H. Cole, H. D. Henderson, J. M. Keynes, Sir F. Leith-Ross, Sir Alfred Lewis, and Sir Arthur Salter.
179. First draft, CAB 58/19, EAC(EI)87; final report CAB 58/20, EAC(EI)104.
180. CAB 23/80, Cabinet 46(34)10, 12 December 1934.
181. CAB 58/19, EAC(EI)78 and 78A, 6 July 1934. Also CP 284(34).
182. CP 272(34).
183. CAB 27/560, PMS(33), 12th meeting, 17 December 1934, and 14th meeting, 11 January 1935.
184. CAB 32/136, ED(D)(35), 13 to 16.
185. CAB 32/136, ED(D)(35)17, 20 July 1935.
186. For the first version see CAB 32/136, ED(D)(35)3: '3rd Draft of Proposals'.
187. ED(D)(35)11, 3 July 1935. For discussion of the leak itself, which occurred in *The Times* of 21 June, see ED(D)(35), 4th meeting, 24 June 1935.
188. CAB 27/619, TAC(36), 4th meeting, 21 May 1936, and 5th meeting, 12 June 1936.
189. For the report, see CAB 24/263: CP 152(36). For the P.B.T.'s comments, see CP 158(36).
190. From CP 158(36).
191. CAB 23/84, Cabinet 41(36), 10 June 1936.
192. CAB 27/619, TAC(36), 6th meeting, 24 June 1936.
193. For the details of the agreed offer, see CAB 27/619, TAC(36)20.
194. DO 35/257/9105/466: 12th meeting of official committee, 20 July 1936. The suggestion came from A. W. Street.
195. DO 35/258/9105/1/95: notes of a meeting between Walter Nash and British ministers, 13 November 1936.
196. DO 32/258/9105/1/100; DO 35/258/9105/1/106: letter, Nash to MacDonald, 23 December 1936. Nash agreed that if she was guaranteed her 1934 levels of shipment she would join the beef conference. But he said that he found it 'disappointing' that the UK would not increase its imports of beef and other meat, in view of the defective British diet.
197. CAB 24/265, CP 281(36), 23 October 1936.
198. CAB 23–85, 27 October 1936.
199. CAB 23/86, 25 November 1936.
200. DO 35/257/9105/492.
201. DO 114/71, pp. 137–9: 'Memorandum', 4 August 1936.
202. DO 114/71, p. 140: letter, Earle Page to Malcolm MacDonald, 14 April 1936.
203. DO 114/71, pp. 144–5: letter S. B. Bruce to Malcolm MacDonald, 16 June 1936; telegram, Australian Government to Dominions Office, 17 June 1936.
204. DO 114/71, p. 153: letter, Malcolm MacDonald to Sir James Parr, 11 July 1936.
205. DO 114/71, p. 154: letter, R. M. Campbell to G. Machtig, 30 July 1936.
206. DO 114/71, pp. 156–7: letter, W. Nash to Malcolm MacDonald, 23 December 1936.
207. DO 35/316/9503/223, 224.
208. DO 35/271/9259/1/14 to 54.

209. For Gardiner's views on this, see DO 35/272/9259/1B/21: minutes of meeting of 21 July 1936.
210. DO 35/273/9259/1B/25: meeting of 24 July 1936.
211. DO 35/274/9259/1B/27: minutes of meeting of 28 July 1936.
212. DO 35/273/9259/1B/38: minutes of meeting of 6 August 1936, the final meeting between Canadian and United Kingdom ministers.
213. The obnoxious clauses had vanished from the draft agreement by 5 August. DO 35/271/9259/1/74.
214. DO 35/273/9279/1B/27: minutes of meeting of 28 July 1936.
215. DO 35/273/9279/1B/38: meeting of 6 August 1936.
216. DO 35/271/9259/1/89, 29 September 1936.
217. DO 35/271/9259/1/89: minute by E. G. Machtig, 5 October 1936.
218. See DO 35/272/9259/93.
219. DO 35/272/9259/1/109: telegram, Sir Francis Floud to Dominions Office, 13 November 1936.
220. By this time further difficulties had arisen to plague the Anglo-Canadian negotiations as a whole. But these problems are not recounted here, as they do not relate to meat.
221. Trade Agreement between the United Kingdom and Canada, 23 February 1937, Clause 5.
222. DO 114/77, pp. 70–6: letters, Malcolm MacDonald to C. T. Tewater, 28 January 1937, Walter Nash, 24 May 1937, and S. B. Bruce, 25 June 1937; letters to Malcolm MacDonald from C. T. Tewater, 28 January 1937, Walter Nash, 24 May 1937, and S. B. Bruce, 25 June 1937.
223. Australian Meat Board, *3rd Annual Report*, 1937–38. Statement refers to period ending 31 August 1938.
224. DO 114/77, pp. 77–9.
225. DO 114/84: telegrams, Dominions Office to Australia and New Zealand Governments, 4 October 1938.
226. DO 114/84: telegrams, New Zealand Government to Dominions Office, 9 November 1938 and 14 December 1938.
227. CAB 27/632, AP(37), 7th meeting, 14 December 1938. See also CAB 24/281, CP 286(38).
228. DO 114/84: telegram, New Zealand Government to Dominions Office, 20 September 1938.
229. DO 114/96: Sir Thomas Inskip to J. S. Duncan and W. K. Jordan, 15 February 1939. For 1939, the Dominions' quotas were to be 3 per cent lower than for 1938, while the foreign quota was cut 10 per cent.

CHAPTER 8

1. New Zealand Agreement, Article 7, Canadian Agreement, Article 10, Australian Agreement, Article 9.
2. New Zealand Agreement, Article 8; the Article continues: 'the protection afforded to the New Zealand producer shall be on a level which will give the United Kingdom producer full opportunity of reasonable competition on the basis of the relative cost of economical and efficient production'.
3. New Zealand Agreement, Article 9.
4. Australian Agreement, Articles 10, 11, 12, 13. Article 10 included the proviso that 'special consideration may be given in the case of industries not fully established'.
5. Canadian Agreement, Articles 11 to 15. Article 11 included a proviso, like

that in Australia's Article 10, relating to industries which were not yet fully established.

6. National Library of Australia, Page Papers, MS 1633/252/5.

7. DO 114/50, pp. 41 ff.

8. DO 114/50, p. 53: telegram, E. T. Crutchley to Dominions Office, 17 June 1933. The Commonwealth was admitted to have carried out its undertakings under Schedule F and Articles 14 (a) and (b) of the Agreement.

9. DO 114/50, pp. 62–3.

10. DO 114/50, p. 72: letter, S. M. Bruce to J. H. Thomas, 9 October 1933.

11. DO 114/50, pp. 81–2.

12. DO 114/50: telegram, E. T. Crutchley to Dominions Office, 23 December 1933, pp. 81–2; letter, J. A. Lyons to E. T. Crutchley, 7 December 1933; note of interview with Mr Bruce, 23 October 1933, p. 74.

13. DO 114/55, p. 4: 'Note by Walter Runciman of a Meeting between Mr. Bruce, Mr. Runciman, and Mr. Thomas, 15 February 1934.'

14. DO 114/55, p. 7: telegram, Crutchley to Dominions Office, 30 May 1934.

15. DO 114/55, pp. 11–12: Dominions Office to Crutchley, 22 October 1934.

16. CAB 32/124, EDA(35)14.

17. DO 35/278/9279/68: despatch, E. T. Crutchley to Dominions Office, 12 December 1934.

18. CAB 32/124, EDA(35)19: memorandum dated 17 April 1935.

19. CAB 32/124, EDA(35)33: memorandum, 2 August 1935, accompanying letters, Runciman to Gullett, 2 August 1935, and Gullett to Runciman, 2 August 1935.

20. DO 35/273/9265/5/3: memorandum by Board of Trade, July 1936.

21. See DO 35/273/9261/1/9: note of meeting, 31 July 1936. On Gullett's earlier negotiations with Germany and Japan, see DO 35/278/9269/61: message from Malcolm MacDonald in Australia, 19 December 1934, and DO 35/278/9279/66: correspondence between HMG Representative in Australia and Dominions Office regarding the Gullett-MacDonald conversations of November 1934.

22. DO 114/55, pp. 14–21: on 7 May 1934, Australia had requested British consent for some reduction of preferential margins to facilitate concessions to Italy and Belgium.

23. DO 35/278/9279/26A: despatches and enclosures from R. M. Dalton, Senior Trade Commissioner in Australia, 31 October 1932. Even at Ottawa, Britain had agreed to most of the Australian requests for reduction in preferential margins, when these requests were linked to third-country bargaining. See DO 35/278/9279/26A: dispatch from R. M. Dalton, 25 October 1932.

24. DO 35/273/9265/1/7,9; DO 35/273/9261/1/9.

25. DO 35/313/9469C/1: telegram, Lyons to Dominions Office, 5 June 1934.

26. DO 35/313/9469C/2: telegram, Crutchley to Dominions Office, 7 June 1934.

27. DO 35/313/9469C/13: despatch, Sir R. Lindsay to Foreign Office, 5 September 1934.

28. On the genesis of the scheme, and its passage through the Australian governmental machine, see DO 35/313/9469C/2: telegram, E. Crutchley to Dominions Office, 7 June 1934, and DO 35/313/9469C/10: letter, E. Crutchley to E. Machtig, 12 June 1934.

29. DO 35/313/9249C/11: minute of meeting, 28 July 1934; and DO 35/313/9249C/35: memorandum by W. Hankinson, 4 November 1936.

30. DO 35/313/9249C/7: telegram, Dominions Office to Prime Minister Lyons, 16 July 1934.
31. DO 35/313/9469C/35: memorandum by W. Hankinson, 4 November 1936.
32. See Sir Geoffrey Whiskard's memorandum on a conversation with Gullett in DO 35/313/9469C/24, 27 April 1936.
33. DO 114/71. pp. 19 ff.: dispatch, Sir Geoffrey Whiskard to Dominions Office, 3 June 1936.
34. DO 35/278/9279/112: telegram, UK High Commissioner in Aust. to DO, 16 May 1936. On the background in Australian thinking see National Library of Australia, Page Papers, MS 1633/294, MS 1633/762/2–7.
35. PREMIER 1/202: telegram, Prime Minister of Australia to Prime Minister of the UK, 18 May 1936.
36. DO 114/71, p. 11: telegram, United Kingdom High Commissioner in Australia to Dominions Office, 16 May 1936; see also telegram of 23 March 1936. In a letter to Baldwin on 18 May, Lyons claimed that the restrictions on foreign goods had been imposed because of repeated requests from the UK (DO 35/278/9279/112). With respect to Japanese textiles, it was true, Britain had made several requests.
37. Canada was hit because the Australians wanted to hit the Americans, who had refused to enter into trade negotiations. Because motor cars could reach Australia from either country, one could neither punish the Americans nor change the locus of motor-car manufacturing without hitting Canada as well.
38. DO 114/71, p. 146: telegram, United Kingdom High Commissioner in Australia to Dominions Office, 18 June 1936.
39. DO 35/278/9279/112: telegram, United Kingdom High Commissioner in Australia to Dominions Office, 16 May 1936; DO 35/278/9279/160: despatch, United Kingdom High Commissioner in Australia to Dominions Office, 15 June 1936.
40. DO 114/77, pp. 127–8: letter, Australian Government to United Kingdom High Commissioner in Australia, 2 September 1937.
41. Page Papers, MS 1633/737/11.
42. Page Papers, MS 1633/737/3: 'Trade Negotiations 1938: Guiding principles'. No indication of authorship. Attached memorandum seems to come from Australian Department of External Affairs.
43. T 161/840/S.40927/03/5: memoranda, Board of Trade, 27 April 1938, and President of Board of Trade, n.d.
44. For the preceding three paragraphs see T 161/841/S.40927/03/6: transcripts of Anglo-Australian trade talks.
45. CAB 24/277, CP 162(38); CAB 23/94, 13 July and 20 July 1938; Cmd. 5805: 'Memorandum of Conclusions'.
46. Page Papers, MS 1633/232/4.
47. DO 114/96: letter, Sir E. Machtig to Sir Geoffrey Whiskard, 3 April 1939.
48. DO 114/84: minute; the Duke of Devonshire, regarding the law officers' reference in October 1938; letter, T. Jenkins to E. Machtig, 2 December 1938.
49. W. M. Corden, 'The Tariff', in Alex Hunter (ed.) *The Economics of Australian Industry* (Melbourne University Press, 1963), pp. 187–8, reporting Carmody's findings on tariff levels.
50. DO 114/50, pp. 191–3; DO 35/274/9263/26: memorandum by Board of Trade, 7 November 1936. See also W. B. Sutch *Recent Economic Changes*, p. 130.
51. On the preceding three paragraphs see T 160/965/F.14687/3,4,5: NZ

Minutes (UK) 12/36, 9 February 1937; 14/36, 15 February 1937; NZ 10/36; NZ 12/36, 9 June 1937; DO 114/96, p. 13: telegrams, Dominions Office to New Zealand Government, 15 March 1939, and vice versa, 29 March 1939.
52. Cmd. 6059: 'Memorandum, signed in London, on the 12th July 1939'.
53. DO 35/314/9503/15.
54. DO 114/50, p. 122: telegram, Sir George Clark to Dominions Office, 29 May 1933.
55. DO 114/50, pp. 213–15; DO 114/55, pp. 191–2.
56. DO 114/50: telegram, Sir William Clark to Dominions Office, 2 June 1933.
57. DO 114/50, p. 144: telegram, Sir William Clark to Dominions Office, 31 October 1933.
58. DO 35/274/9277A/348: memorandum prepared in Dominions Office, 20 September 1934; DO 35/274/9277A/343: minutes, 16 June 1934.
59. DO 35/274/9277A/376: telegram, acting United Kingdom High Commissioner in Canada to Dominions Office, 17 January 1935.
60. Article 9 and Schedule E fixed a list of maximum duties, while allowing the Canadian Government to lower them 'so long as the margin of British preference . . . is preserved'.
61. DO 114/71, p. 74: despatch, Sir Francis Floud to Dominions Office, 13 March 1936.
62. Trade Agreement, 23 February 1937, Article 6.
63. DO 35/272/9259/1B/22: minutes of ministerial conversations, 23 July 1936.
64. Article 10.
65. DO 35/273/9259/1B/38: minutes of ministerial conversations, 6 August 1936.
66. See above.
67. DO 35/273/9259/1/125: telegram, Sir Francis Floud to Dominions Office, 18 December 1936.
68. DO 35/273/9259/1/127: telegram, Dominions Office to Sir Francis Floud, 22 December 1936; minutes by Eric Machtig, 19 December 1936.
69. T 160/681/F.14601/3: telegram, Sir Francis Floud to Dominions Office, 5 January 1937, reporting King's letter of 4 January 1937.
70. DO 35/755/0.51/8: telegram, Sir Francis Floud to Dominions Office, 5 January 1937.
71. DO 35/755/0.51/8: memorandum, W. C. Hankinson, 9 January 1937.
72. King Papers: telegram, Malcolm MacDonald to W. L. M. King, 9 January 1937.
73. DO 35/755/0.51/18: telegram, Sir Francis Floud to Dominions Office, 12 January 1937.
74. T 161/840/S.40927/03/4: telegram, Sir Francis Floud to Dominions Office, 13 January 1937.
75. These comments are based upon conversations with Professor D. F. Forster, Provost of the University of Toronto.
76. Agreement, Articles 6, 7, 8.

CHAPTER 9

1. For details, see Drummond *British Economic Policy*, ch. 4.
2. ibid., ch. 2.
3. Often with rather misleading emphasis. See David Landes *The Unbound Prometheus* (Cambridge University Press, 1969), pp. 359–60.
4. However, if the loss of revenue must be balanced by some other tax increase,

the net gain from the introduction of the preference is *efhi* minus the loss of consumer surplus which this other tax occasions.

5. C. H. Feinstein *National Income, Expenditure, and Output of the United Kingdom* (Cambridge University Press, 1972), tables 1 to 5.

6. R. H. Kindersley, 'British Overseas Investments, 1938', *Economic Journal* 69: pp. 678–95.

7. idem.

8. Ramsay MacDonald first wanted to establish an Economic Advisory Council to undertake rationalisation studies. See T. Jones *Whitehall Diary* (ed. Keith Middlemas) vol. II, p. 220. In 1929, Australia received a mission of British industrialists, who discussed the question with Australian manufacturers; Prime Minister Bruce also seems to have favoured it. See Public Record Office, D.O. 35/205/8202/1, 22 January 1930. During 1930, the Australian Prime Minister's office explored the question, consulting with an academic economist, Professor Giblin. See Commonwealth Archives Office, Canberra, CP 103/3/6: letter, L. Giblin to G. Lightfoot, 15 August 1930. In 1931, Canada welcomed a group of British industrialists from the Federation of British Industry, who were 'busily engaged in spreading the gospel of "complementary production"'; in Britain they approached pottery, non-ferrous metals, and cold rolled brass industries, among others. DO 35/244/8885/5: dispatch, Sir William Clark to Dominions Office, 14 May 1931; letter, Sir Edward Harding to Sir William Clark, 23 June 1931. Before the Ottawa Conference, Prime Minister Bennett received a memorandum which urged the advantages of rationalisation through cartelisation. R. B. Bennett Papers, 106,749–758: anonymous memorandum on Cartels and Empire Trade, 26 May 1932. In 1936, the South Africans proposed a division of the internal iron and steel market by which the British Iron and Steel Federation would receive that part of the market which the South African State steel works could not supply. See DO 35/224/8453/26: memorandum of meeting between UK officials and the South African Commissioner of Customs, 2 January 1936. In the staff work for the 1930 Imperial Conference and the 1932 Ottawa Conference the Dominions Office, partly following the lead of J. H. Thomas, gave great attention to the question. See CAB 32/104, O(B)(32)1: 'On Imperial Industrial Co-operation'; the meetings with industrialists recorded in DO 35/242/8831M/1/7: meetings of 17 June 1932. The officials' reservations are expressed in CAB 32/104, O(B)(32)20: 'it must be recognised that until the integration of industry both here and in the Dominions has gone much further than it has at present – and not every industry is by nature suited to large-scale organisation – the working out of the policy of industrial co-operation by agreements between representatives of industries must be confined to a comparatively limited field'. Late in 1931, the Cabinet committee on the Ottawa conference endorsed the principle of industrial co-operation. See CAB 24/224, CP 288(31), 23 November 1931.

9. This did not surprise senior Dominions Office officials. Early in 1932, it had been agreed to print and circulate the Imperial Economic Committee's report on the subject, partly in the hope that Canada would act to put it on the Ottawa agenda. DO 35/264/9175/1. But in June Sir Horace Wilson was writing, 'I am a little anxious that if we on our side press the question of industrial co-operation too hard we may find the Dominions inclined to restrict their tariff concessions to cases in which co-operation between industries in this country and their opposite numbers in the Dominions takes place.' DO 35/264/9175/10: letter, H. Wilson to E. J. Harding, 3 June 1932. The Dominions Office staff wrote minutes and drafts to the effect that 'industrial co-operation'

was possible only when the firms in the relevant industry were 'fully rationalised'.

10. DO 35/264/9175/7: notes submitted by Australian officials on Imperial Industrial Co-operation, 26 May 1936.

11. CAB 24/249, CP 145(34), 31 May 1934.

12. For the Committee's adventures and for Treasury reaction thereto, see T 160/763/F.13811/1,2.

INDEX